The Music between Us

The Music between Us

IS MUSIC A UNIVERSAL LANGUAGE?

Kathleen Marie Higgins

The University of Chicago Press CHICAGO & LONDON

KATHLEEN MARIE HIGGINS is professor of philosophy at the
University of Texas at Austin. She is the author of *The Music of Our Lives*
and *Nietzsche's "Zarathustra."*

The University of Chicago Press, Chicago 60637
The University of Chicago Press, Ltd., London
© 2012 by The University of Chicago
All rights reserved. Published 2012.
Printed in the United States of America

21 20 19 18 17 16 15 14 13 12   1 2 3 4 5

ISBN-13: 978-0-226-33328-1 (cloth)
ISBN-10: 0-226-33328-0 (cloth)

Library of Congress Cataloging-in-Publication Data
Higgins, Kathleen Marie.
    The music between us : is music a universal language? / Kathleen
Marie Higgins.
        p.   cm.
    Includes bibliographical references and index.
    ISBN-13: 978-0-226-33328-1 (hardcover : alkaline paper)
    ISBN-10: 0-226-33328-0 (hardcover : alkaline paper)   1. Communication
in music.   2. Music—Social aspects.   3. Music and language.   4. Intercultural communication in the performing arts.   5. Music—Philosophy
and aesthetics.   I. Title.
ML3916.H54   2012
781'.1—dc23
                                                           2011033761

♾ This paper meets the requirements of ANSI/NISO Z39.48–1992
(Permanence of Paper).

For Bob, with love and gratitude

CONTENTS

ACKNOWLEDGMENTS

I am indebted to many people whose support, music-making, and ideas about music have helped me to write this book. In particular, my father, Eugene Higgins, acquainted me with many kinds of music and encouraged my musical studies. My grandfather, Otto Merz, also encouraged my interest in music by getting me to sing in public; and my grandmother, Margaret Higgins, let my family have her piano so that I could take lessons. My entire immediate family accommodated my absurdly early morning practice sessions. Besides my father, I am grateful to my mother, Kathryn Higgins, and my siblings, Tim Higgins, Colleen Cook, Jeanine Felten, Maureen Daily, and Jim Higgins, for their tolerance as well as their ongoing support. For moral support, I also want to thank Jenene Allison, Sheila Asher, Douglas Buhrer, Sarah Canright, Paula Fulks, Clancy Martin, David Sherman, and Garret Sokoloff.

I learned about music from many teachers, especially James Evans, Marjorie Ounsworth, Marion Peterson, LeRoy Pogemiller, and John Swanay, who first acquainted me with non-Western music. Steven Feld and Stephen Slawek graciously permitted me to audit their ethnomusicology classes, and both have been generous in sharing their ideas about music with me.

I wish to thank many individuals whose ideas and advice have helped me in connection with this book. I am particularly indebted to Stephen Davies, who read a draft in its entirety and gave me extensive comments. He has also been an invaluable interlocutor and supporter of this project. Others whose insights and suggestions have assisted me in writing this book include Roger Ames, Nicholas Asher, James Averill, Martha Nussbaum, Kimasi Browne, Eric Charry, Ya-Hui Cheng, Julia Ching, Meribeth Clark, Amber Clifford-

Napoleone, Kathleen Costello, Steven Feld, Marilyn Fischer, Danielle Fosler-Lussier, Nico Frijda, Gavin Garcia, Luis-Manuel Garcia, Peter J. García, Jay Garfield, Ron Grant, Jeremy Grimshaw, Anthony Kwame Harrison, Mary Ellen Junda, Patrik Juslin, Max Katz, Jennifer Kyker, Petri Laukka, Jerrold Levinson, George Lewis, Justin London, Heather MacLachlan, James Makubuya, Jeffrey Malpas, Eva Kit-Wah Man, Daniel Margolies, Lisa Margulis, Richard C. McKim, Rebecca Moore, Ali Colleen Neff, Charles Nussbaum, W. Gerrod Parrott, Aniruddh Patel, Stephen Phillips, Thomas Porcello, Sarah Quick, Jesus Ramos-Kittrell, Daniel Reed, Jenefer Robinson, Joel Rudinow, Sandra Salstrom, David Samuels, Klaus Scherer, Walter Sinnott-Armstrong, Stephen Slawek, Mark Slobin, K. Denea Steward Shaheed, Susan Pratt Walton, Wolfgang Welsch, Mina Yang, Marcel Zentner, and Su Zheng. Others with whom I have discussed music to my profit include Philip Alperson, Elliott Antokoletz, Ed Baklini, John Benoit, Frances Berenson, Neil Blumofe, Mary Bodine, Timothy Brace, Christopher Brooks, Lee B. Brown, Donna Buchanan, J. Byron Butts, Victor Caston, Jeffrey Cook, Peter Czipott, William Day, James P. Davis, Peter Derksen, Dionisio Escobedo, Wanda Farah, Aaron Fox, Gabriela Lena Frank, Cynthia Freeland, Roger Gathmann, Mary Gilbert, Lydia Goehr, Stan Godlovitch, Dana Gooley, Ron Grant, Roger Graybill, Douglass Green, Lars Gustafsson, Garry Hagberg, Karsten Harries, Eileen Heaney, Timothy P. Higgins, Elizabeth Hornbuckle, Gregg Horowitz, Jay Hullett, Jo Ellen Jacobs, Jennifer Judkins, Michael Kelly, Kevin Kissinger, Peter Kivy, Robert Kraut, Michael Krausz, Jerrold Levinson, Eric Lewis, Renee Lorraine, Louis Mackey, Janice MacRae, Alejandro Madrid, Bernd Magnus, Joel Mann, Joseph Margolis, Lisa McCormick, Christopher Middleton, Denise Milstein, Alexander Nehamas, Jonathan A. Neufield, Martha Nussbaum, Nicholas Partridge, Lynne Peterson, John Fischer, Diana Raffman, David Ring, Fred Rush, Richard Schacht, Janet McCrackery, Anita Silvers, Julietta Shuey, Garret Sokoloff, Andy Solomon, Carrie Solomon, Jon Solomon, Rachel Solomon, Francis Sparshott, Michael Tanner, Laurence Thomas, Alan Tormey, Leo Treitler, Jorge Valadez, Bruce Vermazen, Kendall Walton, Sanford Weimer, Paul Woodruff, Julian Young, and Marl Young.

I want to thank my editor, Elizabeth Branch Dyson, for her consistent support and encouragement in getting this book into print. I have received institutional support during the writing of this book from the Canberra School of Music and the Philosophy Department of the Australian National University as well as from the Liberal Arts College Research Fellowship Program and the Faculty Research Assignment Program of the University of Texas at Austin. I also wish to express my appreciation to the National Endowment for the Hu-

manities and the Society for Ethnomusicology for the opportunity to participate in the Ethnomusicology and Global Culture Institute held at Wesleyan
University in the summer of 2011.

Finally, I want to express my great debt to Robert C. Solomon. Bob, my
husband, discussed innumerable aspects of this book with me throughout the
writing process, and he also provided me with comments on a full draft. He
supported me in this project and all others until his death in January of 2007.
I dedicate this book to him.

CHAPTER 1

Other People's Music

Music itself [is] the supreme mystery of the science of man, a mystery that all the various disciplines come up against and which holds the key to their progress.

CLAUDE LÉVI-STRAUSS, *The Raw and the Cooked*

A few years ago I visited Hong Kong as a member of an evaluation committee for a university humanities program. At one juncture, the committee was taken to a courtyard where students in the program had set up an exhibit and were available to discuss it. In the same courtyard, some music students had set up a stage with an assortment of African drums, occasionally trying them out. We visited for a while with the humanities students and then gathered in preparation to leave. One of the music students called out, "Professors can drum, too!" To my surprise, the professor in charge of us said, "Well, we do have about five minutes." So we each grabbed a drum. A student musician demonstrated some alternative ways to strike the drums, and we began drumming, our strong beats more or less in tandem, while our music student host drummed counterrhythms. We were refreshed and jovial when we boarded the van that was to take us to our next appointment a few minutes later. There we encountered one of the local members of our committee, who had briefly gone to her office to attend to some business. "Did you hear all that noise?" she asked. "That was us," one of our group replied. She laughed and said, "No, I mean the drumming." "That was *us*," the same person repeated, and all of us erstwhile drummers burst out laughing.

This scene—academics from Asia, Europe, and North America exhilarated by African drums and rhythms—illustrates one of the central themes of this book: people from around the globe can be brought together by one another's music. Occasions like this, in which people from various cultures enjoy music, bring to mind the adage that music is a universal language. But this saying has lost its currency, however much music seems to communicate.

My purpose in this book is to reassess this idea. Although I will suggest that the notion of music as a language is of limited usefulness, I aim to rehabilitate the notion that music is a significant means of cross-cultural communication. Music, I will contend, is an important part of what makes us human as well as a vehicle for recognizing—and directly experiencing—our common humanity. By enabling us to feel our interconnection as human beings, music can help to make us more humane. But for this impact to affect our cross-cultural interactions, we need to broaden our musical horizons to encompass music beyond our own culture.

HOW UNIVERSAL IS THE UNIVERSAL LANGUAGE?

Once upon a time, music was said to be a universal language. Verbal languages varied from place to place, so the reasoning went, and speakers of different languages could not usually understand each other; but music moved people across linguistic boundaries. Germans who spoke no Italian could still understand Italian music. In fact, they could do more than understand it. They could embrace it as speaking of their own inner life. They might not understand the words someone sang, but they could feel the emotion expressed. Friedrich Nietzsche acknowledges music's independent emotional power when he remarks,

> With just a little more impertinence, Rossini would have had everyone sing nothing but la-la-la-la—and that would have made good, rational sense. Confronted with the characters in an opera, we are not supposed to take their word for it, but the sound![1]

Over time the idea that music could speak to everyone became a piece of common wisdom. Henry Wadsworth Longfellow is credited with the line, "Music is the universal language of mankind"; but others—including Arthur Schopenhauer, Charles Batteux, Eduard Hanslick, and E. T. A. Hoffmann—made the same point in similar words. The idea retains currency among musicians, particularly those whose music gets classified as "world music." Mandawuy Yunupingu, spokesman and founder of the Aborigine group Yothu Yindi claims, "Music is a universal language without prejudice." Peter Gabriel asserts, "Music is the universal language. There is nothing more powerful, more moving."[2] I could cite many other musicians saying more or less the same thing.

Nevertheless, the maxim is less commonplace than it once was, and skeptics are convinced that they have grounds for their doubts. Not that Germans have ceased to understand Italian music and vice versa. But as Europeans began to encounter music from Asia, they realized that not all music resembled that of their own societies. In fact, some of it seemed unintelligible. What should they make of these strange sounds from distant lands?

European theorists in the nineteenth century commonly held that other people's music was less advanced than that of Europe. Music everywhere aimed at the same basic organization, even if some nations had yet to attain it. The explanation that some nations lagged behind in musical development served to account for various features of so-called primitive music. Such music was considered redundant, too simplistic, too raucous, or just plain out of tune. Charles Darwin's characterization of the music of "savage" peoples is fairly typical:

> But we must not judge of the tastes of distinct species by a uniform standard; nor must we judge by the standard of man's taste. Even with man, we should remember what discordant noises, the beating of tom-toms and the shrill notes of reeds, please the ears of savages. Sir S. Baker remarks, that "as the stomach of the Arab prefers the raw meat and reeking liver taken hot from the animal, so does his ear prefer his equally coarse and discordant music to all other."[3]

A common nineteenth-century view was that "primitive" music had emerged from societies that had embarked, but gone only some way, on the journey toward tonal music, with all its potential for intricate structure and drama. The tonal system of music, a European discovery, was the apex of musical progress. At least implicitly, it was posited as a universal goal.[4]

Some proponents of the theory of musical progress were at least interested in why some foreign music sounded alien and not just undeveloped. John Pyke Hullah in England recognized that music from other cultures was often organized on different principles than those underlying Western tonality. "How can there be music acceptable to one comparatively civilized people and altogether unacceptable, unintelligible even to another? The answer is to be found in the different nature of their musical system." Yet he continues:

> It is difficult enough for an ear trained in the nineteenth century to reconcile itself to the various modes used in the fifteenth and sixteenth centuries. But to reconcile itself to another *system* seems impossible. Happily it is not in the least necessary. The European system, though the exigencies of practice prevent its being absolutely true, is nearer the truth than any other.[5]

Through the twentieth century, the view that one could reasonably restrict one's gaze to Western music remained commonplace. As recently as 1977, a graduate student in music at an Ivy League university told me that while other societies of course had music, "there is only one culture in which music became an art." In 1986 Judith Becker challenged the alleged superiority of Western music in print, suggesting that the position was still seriously held.[6] A view only slightly less extreme continues to have adherents today, even among the most thoughtful and musically knowledgeable.

Roger Scruton, for example, is well aware that the music of the world operates according to multifarious structural principles. Indeed, he draws attention to structural diversity even within modern Western music. Yet he betrays no qualms about restricting his attention to Western music, and he argues that tonal music as it became formulated in the West is the optimal employment of musical resources.[7] In his impressive book *The Aesthetics of Music*, he contends that the superiority of Western musical culture is demonstrated by its discovery of tonality and its development of multivoiced counterpoint. "The distinction between melody and bass is known in many cultures; so too is the distinction between melody and harmony," he acknowledges. "But how many cultures pay this kind of detailed attention to the inner voice, and attempt to compose harmonies from independent melodic lines?"[8] "Our tradition," he concludes, "could fairly claim to be the richest and most fertile that has yet existed."[9]

Scruton elsewhere comments, "The suspicion of tonality, like Marx's suspicion of private property . . . should be seen for what it is: an act of rebellion against the only way we have of making sense of things."[10] Charles Rosen rightly criticizes this remark:

> The claim that Western tonality is the only way music can make sense ignores the different ways other civilizations have organized their music. Scruton, however, wants to have nothing to do with non-tonal Oriental systems. "For three hundred years," he writes, "Japan remained cut off from Western art music, locked in its grisly imitations of the Chinese court orchestras, dutifully producing sounds as cacophonous to local ears as the croaking of jackdaws." Scruton obviously is not interested in being politically correct, but it is curious that he doesn't know that when the Japanese first heard Western tonal music in the late sixteenth century (when the Jesuits came to Japan), they were horrified at the unpleasant noise it made. . . . At any rate, he . . . at least admits that experts can make sense of non-tonal music, though even experts cannot understand it from experience but only because they are able to decode it.[11]

The Western atonal music that Scruton acknowledges (but interprets as implicitly tonal or meaningless) is only one type of music that has been organized on other bases besides tonality. Scruton fails to grant that tonality is only one of the bases on which music can be valued—or that Western tonal music can sound just as alien to those accustomed to their societies' nontonal music as atonal music sounds to him. This is brought home by James Garson's anecdotal report of taking Pandit Nikhil Banerjee to a concert in which Mstislav Rostropovich performed Bach's Cello Suites. When Garson asked afterward how he had liked the concert, Banerjee remarked, "He played out of tune the entire time; he didn't develop any of the themes; and it sounded almost like the music was written out in advance."[12] In a similar vein, musicologist Curt Sachs (1881–1959) described the distinguished Albanian folk musician who attended a performance of Beethoven's Ninth Symphony and commented, "Fine—but very, very plain." Sachs attributed this judgment to the Albanian's expectation of more variegated rhythm than one gets in Beethoven's evenly metered music.[13]

One might also point to musical cultures that attend much more than the West to the way in which particular tones are articulated in performance. Japanese music exploits the range of possibilities for attacks and releases of individual tones.[14] So does much Chinese music, in particular that involving the qin (or ch'in, pronounced "chin"), an unfretted lute, which is so sensitive that ambient air currents can produce sounds. Even the grain of one's fingerprints encountering the strings can be heard. To play the qin well the performer must learn a vast number of nuances of touch.[15] In his paeans to the achievements of Western music, Scruton does not acknowledge that other cultures have often had different musical aims, and that their achievements should be judged accordingly.

The view that non-Western music has not achieved the artistic distinction of Western music has declined over time, in part because of more extensive Western encounters with music from outside Europe. At the beginning of the twenty-first century, when "world music" is a marketing category for the recording industry, it is difficult for us to remember how recently the West gained its exposure to the rest of the world's music. Certainly, there was some awareness of non-Western music during the so-called Age of Discovery, when European navigators explored the globe in search of knowledge and riches. Sir Francis Drake, for example, describes in his captain's log his first encounter with Javanese music in 1580. "Raia Donan coming aboard us . . . presented our Generall with his country musick, which though it were of a very strange kind, yet the sound was pleasant and delightfull."[16] Drake's report, however, had no immediate consequence on European musical experience, or on Western musical theory. Non-European music was relegated by Western culture to the status of exotica, where it remained until the dawn of the twentieth century.

At the 1889 Paris World's Fair, the Exposition Universelle, for which the Eiffel Tower was built, Claude Debussy and Paul Dukas (composer of *The Sorcerer's Apprentice*) attended the concerts of the Javanese gamelan and the musical theater from Cochin, China, presented in the Palais du Trocadéro.[17] The tuning of the Javanese instruments was affected by the long sea voyage, and it is not clear how much the sounds Debussy and Dukas heard actually resembled music heard in Java.[18] Nevertheless, Debussy was so inspired by this exposure to Javanese music that it motivated a new direction in his compositions, the use of a whole-tone scale of six steps. For Debussy, Javanese music was more than a mere novelty. Clearly under the sway of the noble savage myth, he wrote in 1913,

> There were, and there still are, despite the evils of civilization, some delightful native peoples for whom music is as natural as breathing. Their conservatoire is the eternal rhythm of the sea, the wind among the leaves and the thousand sounds of nature which they understand without consulting an arbitrary treatise. Their traditions reside in old songs, combined with dances, built up throughout the centuries. Yet Javanese music is based on a type of counterpoint by comparison with which that of Palestrina is child's play. And if we listen without European prejudice to the charm of their percussion we must confess that our percussion is like primitive noises at a county fair.[19]

The romantic view of the "natives" and their music notwithstanding, what strikes me as most interesting in this comment is that Debussy was taking the achievements of Javanese music seriously. The highly developed rhythms and counterpoint not only struck him as remarkable, they also suggested new possibilities for Europeans to explore.

Most of Debussy's contemporaries among European composers were not as interested as he in the nature of non-Western music on its own terms. But his experiments with musical resources derived from non-Western music exposed his listeners to sounds outside the purview of what they had taken to be music heretofore. If music was the universal language, accordingly, it was a language of which they were to some degree ignorant.

Early twentieth-century composition led some listeners to question the universality of music on other grounds. Experimental forms, such as dodecaphonic music and serial music, were constructed on the basis of different principles from the familiar tonal framework. The formal structures involved in such music were universal in the sense that they did not hail from any particular tradition; but they were far from universal in the sense of being understood by all who heard them. Many Westerners who encountered such music had difficulty understanding it, and they were thus led to doubt their ability to make sense even of some of the music produced in their own societies, let alone music from foreign lands.

Probably the most important development for precipitating widespread awareness of other cultures' music was the development and widespread dissemination of recording technology. Recordings documenting the diversity of music provided definitive evidence that the world's music is not all constructed in the same way. The tape recorder, in particular, enabled ethnographers to preserve the sonic impressions of non-Western music and to play it at great distances from its original production. Listeners no longer needed to go to the source, or have the source come to them, in order to hear music vastly different from that of their own culture. Eventually, some elements of non-Western music became not only available but also popular for certain Western audiences. George Harrison's introduction of a sitar into the Beatles' and his own solo works and Paul Simon's collaboration with the South African group Ladysmith Black Mambazo on his *Graceland* album are only two of the better known cases of this development becoming mainstream in the West.[20] Certainly, the appropriation of features of non-Western music by Western musicians does not establish that cross-cultural communication has been accomplished. Whether such musical borrowing replicates the long-term tendency of Westerners to exploit non-Western resources for their own benefit is worth pondering. My point here is that recordings have enabled individuals in far-flung nations to be aware of one another's music as well as to be influenced and to incorporate features of it into their own musical productions.

Recordings also decontextualized music, removing it from its original context (if only the studio in which it has been engineered) and potentially resituating it in diverse cultural settings, where it might be interpreted in various ways. This, as we shall see, complicates any effort to assess or even to track music's role in cross-cultural communication. Recordings combined with international travel, musical broadcasting, and the Internet have resulted in musical diasporas and transnational exchanges that call into question the very idea of distinct musical cultures. It would be hard to find many places in the world in which music has been culturally insular. We all enjoy hybridized music to a greater or lesser extent. One of my primary aims in this book is to defend the value of being open to exploring music from across the globe—however foreign or startling it initially sounds. The widespread diffusion of music of various cultural origins indicates that many people throughout the world have found such openness rewarding and supports my point that the boundaries dividing cultural groups are musically porous.

While we should not overly reify the notion of a musical culture, particularly in light of the fast pace of current transnational musical transfers, I will continue to make reference to "Western" and "non-Western" music in this book. The reason is that I am interested in how music permeates cultural barriers, and I am defending the importance of taking philosophical account of a wider swath of music than the (traditional) Western music on which Western philosophers typically focus. It is convenient to continue to refer to the music developed outside the Western world as "non-Western" in contrast. I want to consider the extent to which music that is quite unfamiliar can nevertheless become accessible to those who lack the background that would be presupposed in its originating context. For Westerners, this is likely to be especially evident in the cases of "traditional" non-Western music that is minimally (or not at all) influenced by Western musical tendencies.

Another reason for referring to non-Western cultures is that in accounting for the reasons that some foreign music can be jarring, I make use of the notion of internalized templates that individuals employ to orient themselves in music. Making reference to "Western," and "non-Western" music (as well as music from cultures that are more precisely specified) is a means of indicating the distinct sets of expectations that members of various societies have learned from their cultural environments, though these may be evolving. My ultimate aim is to suggest that such divergences, even when they are extensive, are not absolute barriers dividing musical cultures.

NON-WESTERN MUSIC AND WESTERN PHILOSOPHY

Although the West in general has been slow to pay much attention to non-Western music, contemporary audiences have grown enthusiastic, at least in principle, to music from elsewhere. The burgeoning popularity of what is marketed as "world music" testifies to the fact that a significant Western audience has become interested in what the rest of the world has to offer. Even if most academic music departments in the West continue to concentrate on Western music of the classical tradition, programs and departments of ethnomusicology are flourishing.[21] In psychology a growing number of studies dealing with music make efforts to test hypotheses cross-culturally, and even more acknowledge the importance of such work. Musicologist David Huron expresses a view that has become increasingly widespread when he remarks, "It may be that all of the important lessons regarding music can be found in Western music. But who would be so presumptuous as to assume this to be the case before we investigate the matter thoroughly?"[22]

In contemporary scholarship Western philosophy is the outlier in its approach to non-Western music. On the whole, the field ignores it. Even within the philosophy of music, those indicating more than passing interest in non-Western music are few.[23] Peter Kivy, for example, while admirably considering the many ways that the stylistic characteristics of one's native musical culture affects one's ability to hear expressiveness in music, still concludes, "it must suffice for our purposes to acknowledge that breaking the culture barrier is at least very difficult, and conclusions relying on such perilous doings, perilous themselves."[24]

My response is that we need not to be so cautious. To the obvious counter that our knowledge of unfamiliar foreign music is necessarily too limited to guide philosophical investigation, I counter that we should not restrict our focus to music about which we have become expert. To do so is to distort the nature of much of actual musical experience.[25] Aspects of musical experience that have been undertheorized philosophically include the situation of encountering unfamiliar music and the processes through which we broaden our musical horizons. Indeed, as we will consider, we have reason to believe that the process of gaining an orientation in previously unfamiliar music is much more rapid than we might imagine prima facie.

Failure to attend to the full gamut of music is a loss for philosophy. Philosophy of mind, for example, is impoverished if music is not taken into account. Broad acknowledgment of the importance of music would challenge the adequacy of philosophical models that see the structure of language as the structure of thought. Unless music and language parallel each other in every respect, we should be open to the possibility that music illuminates features of thought that language does not. At the same time, greater philosophical attention to the ways that language resembles music (as opposed to the other way around) might result in a reconsideration of linguistic communication, particularly regarding the importance of pragmatics in the generation of meaning. Too often music is modeled on conceptions of language in which syntax and semantics are taken as primary, with the consequence that "music" is understood principally in terms of structures apart from context. We should include in our purview music from societies and musical subcultures in which conformity to a score notating pitches and rhythms is not a standard basis for judging the acceptability of performances. Recognition of the fact that "music" is not restricted to sonic phenomena that accord with Western structural principles and conventions is important for understanding music's place in human life and thought.

In philosophy of music, more specifically, attention to the full range of music, including that from outside the West, is imperative if the subfield is to deal adequately with its subject matter. Among the particular topics that would be better addressed if the full range of music were considered are (1) the nature and extent of musical universality, (2) the ways in which music and emotion are connected, (3) the political and propagandistic roles of music, and (4) the ethical impact of music. In this book I will make some preliminary forays into discussion of the first three of these topic areas in light of an inclusive notion of music that is not limited to music of the West.[26]

INVESTIGATIONS OF MUSICAL UNIVERSALITY

My focus in this book will not be non-Western music as such. Instead my topic is the notion of musical universality. I will be concerned with both its extent and its limitations, and the potential it may offer for stimulating a sense of our affinity as human beings. I will begin by considering ubiquitous features of human music and the extent to which they facilitate cross-cultural affiliation and understanding.

In chapter 2 I address the extent to which musical universality, in the sense of music's ubiquity, might extend not only to all human beings but to some species of animals as well. Despite current scholarly caution regarding the term *universality*, I will go on in the next two chapters to draw attention to apparently universal features of perceiving, structuring, and appreciating music. Although such universals only take us so far in making sense of extremely foreign music, they offer a means of access that enables us to take pleasure in such music from early in our exposure to it. They also ground the possibility of our coming to understand music more fully as our acquaintance with it grows.

Chapters 3 and 4 focus on universals and near-universals that appear to operate in the human experience of music and the extent to which these enable cross-cultural musical understanding. Although they ensure that music from anywhere on the globe will be addressed to faculties that we share with others in our species, they also enable the development of schemata that can interfere with comprehension of foreign music. I will conclude that while the universals of music cannot ensure cross-cultural communication of all, or even most, dimensions of musical meaning, they are grounds on which such communication can be initiated.

The language model that has traditionally been used to summarize music's universal character is my concern in chapter 5. In this chapter I suggest that the linguistic model obscures powers of music that are disanalogous to those of language, as well as the ways in which language relies more on "musical" characteristics than is commonly recognized. Regarding the idea that music is a kind of language, I suggest that we stand to gain by considering the metaphor in reverse.[27] Given the similarities between music and language, we have as much warrant for considering language a music as the other way around. If my arguments strike some readers as overemphasizing certain features of language to the deficit of others, this will only reinforce my points that the two are not exact parallels and that pushing the comparison results in an imbalanced and overly narrow understanding.

Chapter 6 considers a basis for musical communication that draws on sensory associations. Synesthesia (broadly understood) is a ubiquitous feature of musical response. However, although some associations that are grounded on synesthetic analogies refer to common features of human experience, many are more culturally specific, as are the interpretations that are given to them. The result is that some aspects of musical experience that draw on its synesthetic character can interfere with cross-cultural musical intelligibility, although others can assist it.

The emotional aspects of musical experience, by contrast, involve considerable cross-cultural convergence, even though cultures play significant roles in shaping both the arousal and the recognition of emotion in music. I consider music and emotion in chapters 7 and 8. Some of music's emotional impact draws on features of musical experience (such as physiological responses to music) and participation that are not limited by cultural membership.

Certain recent debates within anglophone philosophy of music implicitly raise questions that touch on universality. Among the issues are: (1) the nature of the relationship between music and emotions, and (2) whether the notion of a hypothetical persona that undergoes emotional experience is a useful heuristic in making sense of music's expressive character. I suggest that the various standard accounts of the music-emotion connection deal with different degrees of identification with the music that are available to listeners. Accordingly, they should be seen as complementary rather than as competitors. I also contend that the notion of a persona can be useful for tracking musical expression, so long as we adopt a suitably minimal definition. The use of such a thin definition, somewhat surprisingly, primes us for empathizing broadly with the wide variety of people who are also emotionally related to the music.

Chapter 8 considers an underappreciated aspect of music's connection with emotion. I hold that a component of music's emotional character is its role in establishing and reinforcing feelings of security, including a sense of ontological security, or secure being in the world. While some of the features of musical experience that link it to feelings of security are culturally specific (its connection to societal membership and associations, as well as deep familiarity with musical patterns), some are transcultural, depending in large part on the nature of musical perception.

I conclude with some reflections on music as a potential means for healing discord among subgroups of humanity. I acknowledge, as I must, that some of the very features of musical experience that facilitate bonding can be utilized for rallying one faction against another. However, while music clearly has the ability to reinforce sectarian divisions, the same mechanisms used for this purpose can also be directed toward more broadly humanizing ends. What I try to show in this book is that it is not naive to think that music can enable intensely shared affinity among participants who are to a large extent foreign to each other. In many ways—perceptually, affectively, and associationally— music can forge and further a sense of connection with other members of our species. What remains is for us to make use of music toward these ends.

I am hardly the first to defend the value of cross-cultural musical experience for promoting a sense of common humanity across cultural divides. Daniel Barenboim articulately defended such a message in his 2006 Reith Lectures.[28] My efforts to show that music's universal dimensions provide grounds for facilitating our engagement with foreign music provide support for Barenboim's claim. Our shared musicality is a real ground for developing a sense of human commonality across cultural boundaries, while the range of music we might encounter encourages appreciation of cultural diversity. In contemporary circumstances, in which listening is not restricted to specific contexts, music affords opportunities to experience human connectedness in a manner that transcends sectarianism. Such opportunities are needed in the contemporary world. Music has a role to play in healing exacerbated and contentious divisions, even if it is a mistake to consider it either possible or entirely desirable to eliminate divisions in the social world. We would do well to make more of music's potential to help us recognize our human kinship, however varied our cultures.

POTENTIAL OBJECTIONS TO MY APPROACH

Before proceeding I should counter some potential objections to my discussion of musical universality. One of these is the complaint that I am endorsing an unwarranted essentialism in appealing to human nature and human characteristics. I recognize that essentialist analyses often amount to privileging one's own outlook as the truth, applicable to everyone. But although appeals to human nature have gone out of fashion, partially in response to recognizing this danger, I think that it remains worthwhile to draw attention to those traits and relations among them that are characteristic of members of our species. My claim is that musicality—a disposition to make and enjoy music—is among these. If we imagine what generalizations extraterrestrial anthropologists might make about our species, one striking characteristic of human beings that I would expect them to note would be the human tendency to make and enjoy music.

I do not deny that cultures shape the way music is made and impress specific perceptual schemes on their members. My conviction that such differences are important will become increasingly apparent. But I am convinced that even the most adamant cultural constructivist presupposes certain capacities, both physical and psychological, that typify human beings. I will not try to articulate a complete definition of human nature. Indeed, I am among those who suspect that such efforts usually do project the tendencies of one's own society onto all people everywhere. Nor will I weigh in on the question of whether music has evolved as an evolutionary adaptation, a spandrel, or something else. Nevertheless, I think that some notion of typical human traits is indispensable to many of our efforts in philosophy, which is concerned with big questions that are recurrently encountered in human life. One can, I believe, make use of some notion of what is typically human while nonetheless recognizing that one may be overgeneralizing from one's own experience and being prepared to revise one's views should this become evident. I will attempt to maintain such a stance.

A related objection is that I too easily accept psychologists' and linguists' claims about universal features of perception. Admittedly, this is a problem in that, at best, claims about musical universals have been supported by inductive evidence, and many studies have not endeavored to demonstrate the cross-cultural validity of their claims. At most these studies offer provisional grounds for accepting certain descriptions of musical perception as holding universally, and I acknowledge this up front. Empirical evidence is always falsifiable, and it is possible that some of the evidence I appeal to will be falsified by future research.[29] This demonstrates the importance of further empirical research that pays greater attention to cross-cultural similarities and differences.

To minimize the impact of the problem of overly hasty induction here, I will indicate noteworthy exceptions to generalized claims about universals. I will also use the available empirical evidence to suggest a general profile of human music (which is considerably more restricted than the range of sonic possibilities within our auditory frequency range would suggest) and to indicate perceptual grounds that underlie the experience (or "illusion") of animation in music.[30] Even if certain alleged universals come to be rejected, others are likely to be confirmed, and this is sufficient to support my case. I would be extremely surprised if the science of auditory perception at its current stage has been wrong in all its generalizations.

A third potential objection to my approach is to challenge it on the grounds that it does not take the deaf into account. My response is that, far from being counterexamples, the deaf provide evidence for my position that musicality is a basic human trait. The deaf engage with and enjoy music, not sonically, but tactilely.[31] The fact that this segment of the population, which is unable to access music through the sensory modality that most of us rely on, nevertheless experiences music through another sensory mode suggests how basic interaction with music is to virtually all members of our species. The exceptions are extremely atypical, examples being those who lose such basic cognitive capacities as appreciation of sensory pattern or capacity to track temporal sequence, such as some of the patients neurologist Oliver Sacks describes.[32]

Another possible objection is that my focus on listeners' experience distorts what music is. Philosophers often discuss music and its meaning from the standpoint of listeners, discussing the perspective of performers secondarily, if much at all. Psychologists, too, most often focus on listeners in their musical studies, presumably because the pool of listening subjects (at least in the West) is larger than that of those who would identify themselves as performers and because listening is more easily monitored in lab conditions than the activities involved in performance. Anthropologists and anthropologically oriented ethnomusicologists, however, tend to see this emphasis on listening as perverse and a reflection of one of the quirks of Western musical culture. In many societies, everyone is an active music-maker.[33] Some individuals may be particularly good at making music, but musical performance is not the province of experts.

Given that my audience is likely to be comprised primarily of Westerners, I cannot assume that most of my readers will consider themselves musical performers, desirable as such a state of affairs might be.[34] Nevertheless, I concede the importance of the anthropological/ethnomusicological point that music-making is essentially important for understanding music, and that "music" is more commonly understood in reference to this than to listening. I will finesse this point by referring at times to musical participants, taking listeners to be among them. Some empirical justification for considering listeners to be active participants comes from neuroscientific evidence of similar brain activation patterns in listeners and performers, notably in regions implicated in motor activity.[35] My taking both music-making and music partaking as modes of musical participation reflects the complexity of modern musical life even among those who are the most musically active. It encompasses the mutually enlivening roles that musicians and audience perform for each other in the context of live performance, and it acknowledges that music-makers are responsive to other music-makers, a possibility that depends upon listening. Finally, to consider listening a form of musical participation is to recognize that musical listening is not a purely passive form of consumption but is itself a mode of active engagement, mentally, physically, and emotionally.[36]

A fifth possible objection is that I am reifying cultures when I refer to them as sources of musical meaning and interpretation. Although I am emphasizing the importance of culture in shaping musical activity and experience, I do not understand *culture* as a well-bounded concept. In a world in which we can easily encounter one another's music, musical cultures are not isolated. Instead, they are influenced by one another. We should acknowledge the considerable extent to which the world's music includes much that is hybridized, reflecting the increase of musical encounters and collaborations among members of different societies. I see these hybridizations as a reflection of music's potential to facilitate cross-cultural encounter and communication of an unusually cooperative sort. If philosophy of music is to reflect the range of musical experience, including its emotional and ethical dimensions, such developments must be recognized. Even restricting our view to musical experience within the West, multicultural musical collaborations and transnational influences should be considered as a growing part of the musical terrain.

A sixth objection is that my analysis is overly focused on the individual experiencing music and insufficiently concerned with music as a social practice. Indeed, I will be discussing individuals' responses to music and drawing on psychological experiments that study the responses of individual subjects. I do not mean to imply, however, that the values implicit in music are essentially matters of the intrapsychical processing of musical structures. Music has value to people by virtue of the way it is made and used. Cultures can and do contribute layers of meaning to musical patterns, as well as templates for making sense of musical structures. Even the structural characteristics of music express modes of valuing that extend beyond the context of music, and cultural values shape these. Cultural ideals for human interaction, as we shall see, are among the extramusical meanings implicit in music. While nonmembers of a culture may recognize these, the full emotional force of their musical reinforcement may be available only to members or long-term residents. Cultures also elaborate associations and symbolisms that are inextricably linked to music for its members.

No one experiences music outside of some cultural context; even infants in utero appear to be gaining acquaintance with the musical culture they will soon encounter more fully.[37] Those immersed in a culture will inevitably have a different and fuller perspective on that culture's music than those who are not, although people can gradually become more assimilated to a foreign culture. Perfect transparency of musical communication is not available cross-culturally (nor even, perhaps, from one individual to another). What is available is real encounter through music among those whose backgrounds are significantly different and who express themselves musically in ways that may initially seem inaccessible to one another. Such encounter, I will argue, can be a step toward recognizing mutual humanity in an emotionally powerful way.

CHAPTER 2

Musical Animals

When birds do sing, hey ding a ding, ding,
Sweet lovers love the spring.

SHAKESPEARE, *As You Like It*

The most important musical universal of all . . .
[is] the possibility that man is a musical animal.

JOHN BLACKING, *"Can Musical Universals Be Heard?"*

Our body grows no wings and cannot fly,
Yet it is innate in our race
That our feelings surge in us and long
When over us, lost in the azure space
The lark trills out her glorious song.

GOETHE, *Faust*

THE MUSICAL ANIMAL

Aristotle characterized human beings as essentially rational animals—but suppose he had described us as musical animals instead. How would we Westerners think of ourselves? Had the musicality of humanity been taken as central, would mind/body dualism ever have been considered plausible? Would philosophers ever have argued that thought necessarily involves language?

Although Aristotle did not define the human being as musical, he had no doubts about music's importance in human life. "Music," he maintains, "should be studied, not for the sake of one, but of many benefits, that is to say, with a view to (1) education, (2) purgation . . . music may also serve (3) for intellectual enjoyment, for relaxation and for recreation after exertion."[1] Even if music is not central to Aristotle's theory of human nature, he claims that we "naturally" enjoy it. "The pleasure given by music is natural," he contends, "and therefore adapted to all ages and characters."[2]

Why didn't Aristotle define human beings as essentially musical? In his definitions he sought to differentiate the class of objects covered by the term in question from all other objects. Thus in defining the human being, he designates the conjunction of traits that characterize human beings uniquely. Music does not indicate what is unique to human beings, for other animals also enjoy music. In the *Politics* Aristotle advises, "Let the young practise even such music as we have prescribed, only until they are able to feel delight in noble melodies and rhythms, and not merely in that common part of music in which every slave or child and even some animals find pleasure."[3] It is not obvious what "the common part of music" is, but probably he had in mind simple rhythms and melodies, by contrast with those that are "noble" and more difficult to appreciate.

How musical are other species? Aristotle does not elaborate, but his inclusion of some animals among the musical raises the question of how universal music might be. Do the bounds of musical universality extend beyond the human species? Should we restrict our attention to humanity just because the proponents of the universal language idea do not include animals in this putative universality?

The idea of extending the universality of music to animals might seem perverse, and I do not intend to suggest that all nonhuman animals have anything akin to human music. Even for those who do, "animal music" bears some notable dissimilarities to that of human beings. The human potential to get into sync with an external beat does not appear to be shared with any other animals.[4] Human beings also display a unique level of complexity in organizing musical structures—coordinating voices, developing themes, elaborating large-scale musical forms, and so on.

I have two reasons for suggesting that some animals' sounds might be music, however. The first is that *we* can hear the sounds as music, and when we do, this puts into relief certain expectations we have about what music offers us. In particular, we hear music as a manifestation of vitality, and part of our enjoyment is empathy with its liveliness. Just as we recognize the life and energy of other human beings when we listen to music, we recognize kindred life and energy of birds and other creatures through the sounds they produce. The delight we take in birdsong, for example, is continuous with our pleasure in human music, for it is similarly grounded in a recognition that we are part of the same living world.

My second reason for discussing animal vocalizations here is that many people strenuously object to calling them music. The insistence that music be restricted to human beings indicates an implicit acknowledgment that music is an important characteristic of the human species and that it marks those who are kindred to us. Whether or not we consciously formulate the notion of "sounding human," I suspect this is a regulative idea for most of us. Before getting into the arguments for and against the idea of animal music, however, I should offer an operating definition of music, since the plausibility of animal music depends in part on what *music* is taken to mean.

What is music? The answer to this question is not straightforward. Is music essentially sound? Some philosophers deny this, arguing that sounded music is only the external embodiment of "real" music, which consists of abstract, ideal entities.[5] Such musical Platonism is not a popular position, but other philosophers, too, want to emphasize that physical sound waves are not themselves music.[6] *Music* as we understand it depends on a mind that interprets what is heard in a particular way, recognizing patterns, relating them to one another. Even if we can imagine a sound being made by a tree falling in a forest when no one is around, we cannot imagine music without a mind perceiving or imagining it. Even if we make the attempt, we ourselves are imagining the unperceived music. Music is phenomenal, existing not "objectively," but for a mind. I will take this point for granted.

Nevertheless, I will define music in terms of sound. We formulate definitions for purposes of picking out instances that fall into a certain category, and uncontroversial cases that we would include as falling into the category *music* importantly involve sound, even if they also involve an interpreting mind. This holds even if the sound is only imagined; we can *imagine* music, but when we do, we imagine it sounding.

To return to the problem of defining *music*, must a definition include every instance of music and exclude every noninstance? Such precision would seem to be a desideratum for a definition. But if music is an "open concept," as Lydia Goehr contends, it is not clear that any proposed definition will succeed in establishing the precise scope of the term.[7] The open concept argument is that *music*, like *art* in general, is a concept that evolves as innovations occur, extending the scope of what the term is understood to mean. This being so, we should not expect to find a fixed definition, even for the Western music to which Goehr restricts her discussions.

I will use the term *music* broadly. I will roughly employ John Blacking's characterization that music is "humanly organized sound,"[8] adding, "and sounds produced by other species that we can hear as organized" because I am open to the idea that some animals' sonic productions might warrant application of the term.[9] I will use this broad definition despite the fact that this does not clearly exclude many noninstances of sound that do not seem to be music (such as sonic signals at road crossings) nor clearly include some arguable instances (the "music" that John Cage urges us to seek in environmental sound).[10] I will count as "musicality" the various sensitivities and capabilities required for performance and appreciation of uncontroversial cases of music—capacities to recognize and respond to melodic shape, rhythm, timbral differences, and such. Human beings are musical insofar as such sensitivities are part of our standard operating equipment. Evidence that they are is found in the pervasive human enjoyment in sound (including language) manipulated and structured by members of our species.

The use of such a broad definition of music will undoubtedly be unsatisfactory to some.[11] I think my usage is justified, given the diversity of music across history and cultures.[12] John Cage's *4′33″*, a "piece" of music in which a performer sits at a piano for four minutes and thirty-three seconds, makes sense as music to at least some members of the society in which he presented it; but it is far from clear that most listeners, even in Cage's own milieu, would accept this as music (or even a "work," for that matter).[13] And yet *4′33″* is considered noteworthy in music history.

The relativity of what people understand as music is important for my purposes, for a listener who does not recognize what is going on in another culture's music may not acknowledge that it is music. I recall playing a tape of some percussive Nigerian music in my office one day, only to have a colleague from a nearby office come to ask me what that "noise" was. In many homes in the United States and, I assume, much of the industrialized world, parents of teenage children are annoyed by the "racket" their children choose to listen to. In these cases, music sufficiently different from what a person understands as paradigm does not sound to that person like music.

One might argue that these cases confuse honorific and classificatory definitions. The older person who hears the CDs beloved of the younger generation as something other than music implicitly defines *music* honorifically, insisting that the particular case does not attain a certain threshold level of merit, based on what that person counts as paradigm. What we are attempting here is a classificatory definition of music, which does not appeal to standards of merit but simply distinguishes what fits into a category and what does not, an example being the definition of a bachelor as an unmarried adult male.

Even in classificatory definitions, however, it is not always easy to keep honorific efforts at bay. A fellow philosopher once acknowledged to me that he was bemused to think that the Japanese actually enjoy the various "pings" and "boings" he hears in their music.[14] He had no problem classifying it as music, but he was implicitly questioning whether such Japanese performances were music in an honorific sense.[15] Less generously, the colleague mentioned earlier used the music/noise dichotomy, seemingly a distinction between classificatory categories, to assert an evaluative judgment. In principle, one might have a nonjudgmental understanding of *noise* and apply the term on a strictly classificatory basis. However, when is *noise* regarded in contrast to *music* not implicitly pejorative?

To recognize that a definition covers a particular case will depend on one's perceptual habits. In a particular case of foreign music, an uninitiated listener might not recognize it as organized if it deviates too much from learned perceptual expectations. A case in point is Steven Feld's account of Christian missionaries who reported that the Kaluli of Papua New Guinea were an extremely unmusical people, a conclusion they drew from the fact that the Kaluli seemed unable to sing in unison. Feld points out that the Kaluli ideal for singing is diametrically opposed to unison singing. The Kaluli value "layering, juxtaposing, arching, 'lifting-up-over,' and densifying."[16] No doubt the Kaluli wondered why the Christian missionaries were adamant about singing so unmusically. In any case, one will only hear as "musical" sound that exhibits an order one can recognize.

Slippage between classificatory and honorific definitions also occurs because the criteria used in applying one are likely to overlap significantly with those used in applying the other. One's honorific definition of *music* may well use amount of consonance as a criterion, for example, but so might a classificatory definition. This example illustrates the role that musical background can play in one's sense of the term. In fact, consonance can be defined in various ways (in terms of how an interval has been generated, whether the interval seems to call for further movement, the ratio of frequency of vibrations for the tones that compose it, and such, as well as some decision about where to draw the line between consonance and dissonance).

I suspect that implicitly normative features always infiltrate classificatory definitions to some extent, in that what one counts as paradigmatic depends on one's experiences. The implicit normativity of seemingly descriptive definitions and concepts holds as much for my own use of categories as it does for anyone else's. Indeed, my desire to tinker with Blacking's definition so as to create room for animal music indicates my evaluation of some animal sonic productions and my willingness to adjust my classificatory definition accordingly. Perhaps the main value of the distinction between classificatory and honorific definitions of music is its helping to indicate points of slippage between descriptive and evaluative usage.

How useful, finally, is it to construe *music* as an open concept? It is useful in much the way that terms for medical conditions are. Both are meant to cover a plethora of diverse cases and are accordingly imprecise. One can, of course, stipulate certain absolute criteria for a disease or for music and refuse to count anything that fails to satisfy all of the criteria. But to follow this course is to be excessively pedantic. A seasoned doctor recognizes a disease on the basis of a general profile, even if not all the associated symptoms are observable. I urge that we use the term *music*, similarly, on the basis of general profile. The added complication in the musical case is that other cultures' sonic productions may startle the uninitiated listener, presumably more than a case of flu in which a common symptom is not evident would surprise a family doctor.

The challenge one is offered by unfamiliar, foreign-sounding music is reason to use a broad definition of *music*. "Humanly organized sound" is a description that will cover other cultures' sonic productions quite easily, even when they deviate significantly from one's paradigm. I am assuming that Blacking intends his definition to capture cases in which the sound is deliberately organized, and does not intend those cases in which intentional human activities result in sonic patterns as a by-product.[17] To say this, however, is not to deny that music, in many if not most cultures, plays functional roles. In my view, sound does not have to be appreciated for its own sake (or at least not exclusively for this reason) to be deliberately organized sound.[18]

I anticipate that some in the fields of anthropology and ethnomusicology, among others, would challenge my claim that the term *music* is broad enough to encompass the deliberate productions of organized sounds across the world for another reason. The notion of *music*, they might argue, is inherently ethnocentric, for it presupposes instances of Western music and musical practices as the standard for judgment. This is particularly the case when one takes a relatively narrow subset of Western music—such as "classical" music (understood as upper-class Western music of the sixteenth through nineteenth centuries)—as paradigm. With such a paradigm, one is more likely to acknowledge a sonic production as music the more it conforms to the expectations based on that subset. The anthropologist and ethnomusicologist would also likely object to my focusing so much on the listener's point of view, as I noted in chapter 1.

I agree that the Western paradigm is ethnocentric, and that focus on the listener is a Western tendency. I think my focus here on listeners recognizing music in sonic signals is justified in that the ability to perceive something as musical would seem to be essential to music-making Admittedly, we should not lose sight of the fact that the predominance of music consumption over music-making in the lives of most Westerners is a departure from the practices of much of humanity. The value of a broad definition such as Blacking's is that it accommodates a huge range of possible sound patterns and practices while acknowledging some common features among various cultures' practices. The very existence of the field of ethnomusicology presupposes some broad conception of *music* that is applicable across cultural boundaries. Different cultures' music may exhibit deep differences, but this does not render different cultures' music completely incomparable.

ANIMAL MUSIC

Despite defending the centrality of music to human nature, I am quite content to extend the term to sounds made by whales, songbirds, and gibbons, and a variety of other animals. I am keen to do so, in fact, because to recognize continuities between human and animal sonic productions is to acknowledge biological bases for music that figure in our own species' experience and enjoyment of music. Hence, I add to Blacking's definition: "and sounds produced by other species that we can hear as organized." Not only do many animals' sonic productions resemble human music in certain respects; I think we are also able to empathize with animal music much as we identify with human music.

Music, broadly understood, is one of the specialties of our species. This claim is no more vitiated by instances of nonhuman music than the claim that the human being is the tool-making animal is undercut by examples of other mammals and birds using tools.[19] Our accomplishments are exemplars for both kinds of activities. Still, I think it is reasonable to describe other animals who use tools as "toolmakers," even if their tools are not as sophisticated as many of ours, and to call some animal sounds "music" even if there are some important differences between their "music" and ours. Perhaps the most noteworthy such difference is our recombination of meaningful sonic elements into structures from which new meanings emerge, which is not characteristic of animal vocalizations.[20]

I grant that animals may use music for a more limited set of functions than we do. We, after all, employ music and musical parameters to an astonishing degree in conducting our lives (as we shall consider). However, given our lack of access to the perspective of these animals, I remain agnostic about the extent to which some animals organize their experience in comparably musical ways. My purposes in making the comparison between human and animal music are to raise the possibility that musicality runs deep in our biological inheritance and to draw attention to the fact that many of us implicitly assume that musicality is a broadly human trait.

As for whether we can hear the sonic productions of some other animals as music, it seems clear to me that we often do. Classical Persian musicians take the song of the nightingale as a model for music-making. In the eighteenth century, Immanuel Kant similarly compared bird song to human music, suggesting that bird song has more freedom and therefore offers more to our taste than the singing of human beings.[21] Charles Hartshorne has emphasized the beauty he finds in the singing of birds.[22] Steven Feld points out that among the Kaluli, "improvised human duets with birds, cicadas, or other forest sounds are not uncommon everyday events."[23] Another people in New Guinea have a symbiotic musical relationship with the drone beetle. They put beetles in their mouths and use their bodies as resonators for the beetles' sounds.[24] Whale song has been recorded and marketed for seemingly "musical" pleasure; it has also been incorporated into human music.[25] Trevor Wishart includes the whinny of a horse and a baby crying into his *Vox 5*.[26] The howls of wolves may seem more potentially threatening than musical to many people, but I suspect that people often entertain these howls empathetically. (Presumably this is the point of the moniker "Howlin' Wolf.")

In fact, we often hear "music" across a larger swath of the world than the animal kingdom. We tend to associate movement with sentience, and sometimes even the sound of machine motion gives the impression of intentional behavior. We speak of humming motors. The Kaluli sing duets with inanimate natural phenomena such as waterfalls as well as animate nature.[27] Composer Paul Lansky has incorporated the sounds of dishware in the kitchen, along with recognizable physiological sounds, into his music.[28] Musical instruments themselves amount to inanimate materials that have been given voice.

Creationism in Music

In Western history, music was sometimes characterized as a human invention, not to contrast it with animal sounds, but as part of what might be termed the *creationist debate over music*. This long-standing dispute concerned the question of whether or not music was part of humanity's original endowment from God. This issue was given impetus by the suspicion with which some religious thinkers regarded music. If God directly gave music to human beings, the reasoning went, it is above reproach. If music is a human creation, on the other hand, it may be sinful or conducive to sin.

The view that music was of divine origin had many defenders, including Clement of Alexandria in the second century; Francisco de Salinas, Gaspar Stoquerus, and Zarlino in the Renaissance; and a number of baroque thinkers.[29] Many held that vocal music was given to human beings in Paradise while instrumental music was a later, human invention, of more questionable pedigree, although this differential assessment was not universal.[30]

The naturalistic view that human beings invented all music was defended as early as Lucretius, who described the origin of human music in the attempt to imitate chirping birds.[31] The later development of scientific thought in the West also gave impetus to the naturalistic understanding of the origin of music.[32] The relevant sense of naturalism did not, however, preclude interpreting music as a gift from God. Geoffrey Miller points out that natural theologians, among them William Paley, "considered birdsong to have no possible function for the animals themselves, but rather to signal the creator's benevolence to human worshippers through miracles of beauty. . . . The idea that birdsong would be of any use to birds was quite alien before around 1800."[33]

Charles Darwin's theory of the evolution of music, like his evolutionary theory more generally, presents human beings as closer to the animals than they had previously thought. He contends that animal sounds evolved primarily for reproductive purposes. Female birds are attracted by the song of the males of their species. Similarly, human music evolved to facilitate mating. "The impassioned orator, bard, or musician, when with his varied tones and cadences he excites the strongest emotions in his hearers, little suspects that he uses the same means by which his half-human ancestors long ago aroused each other's ardent passions, during their courtship and rivalry."[34]

Animal Musicality

One might consider whether more recent efforts to dismiss the notion of animal music are motivated by an effort to reassert humanity's claim to distinction in the face of evolutionary theory. I find rather fascinating the marked species pride vis-à-vis music that is evident in the wildly speculative remarks that some thinkers have enlisted in their cases for music's uniquely human character. Occasionally, the purpose in denying that animals have music is to emphasize our common nature as human beings. This seems to have been Louis Armstrong's point when he said, "All music is folk music, I ain't never heard no horse sing a song."[35] More often, however, the aim seems to be a defense of human superiority, often by means of loaded criteria for music and musicality. For example, Graham Gordon asserts, "the cry of a bird has no melody and is in no key," and he describes this as an "important and incontestable fact."[36]

But this statement is not uncontestable. Peter J. B. Slater points out that some birds sing in near perfect scales (e.g., musician wren, *Cyphorhinus aradus*).[37] Darwin cites with approval a report that gibbons sing in halftones and across the range of an octave.[38] He also points out that his son, Francis, "attentively listened in the Zoological Gardens to *H. leuciscus* whilst singing a cadence of three notes, in true musical intervals and with a clear musical tone."

Darwin does not stop there; he reports that "certain rodents utter musical sounds." He cites Rev. S. Lockwood reporting on the singing of an American species of mouse, the *Hesperomys cognatus*. Lockwood notated the mouse's two main songs and described several of their musical characteristics, such as the use of distinct semitones. According to Lockwood, the mouse "had no ear for time, yet she would keep to the key of B (two flats) and strictly in a major key. . . . Her soft clear voice falls an octave with all the precision possible; then at the wind up, it rises again into a very quick trill on C sharp and D."[39]

One common contention among those who deny music among animals is that music is a consequence of intelligent design, where intelligence is defined in such a way that animals lack it. For example, Graham Gordon insists that human intentionality is essential for sound to be music.

> Natural sounds are not musical. . . . The only thing in nature which may be said to be truly musical is the human voice when it sings, and, of course, singing is itself *making* music, an intentional activity in which human beings uniquely engage.[40]

Such reasoning ignores evidence that many nonhuman species are clearly intentional in their sonic productions.[41] According to Carol Whaling, songbirds must memorize their songs and then practice what they learn. The young bird's first effort to repeat a song that has been memorized is usually imperfect, and a practice period is necessary for it to fine-tune its performance.[42] Björn Merker claims that learning may be involved in chimpanzee vocalizing as well. He mentions "a report of instances in which individual chimpanzees take over the distinctive pant-hoot pattern of a fellow group member after the latter's disappearance or death."[43]

If intentionality is the criterion that makes an acoustic production *music*, many nonhuman sounds surely count as well, as Robin Maconie asserts. He defines music as "any acoustic activity intended to influence the behavior of others," and he acknowledges that this is to treat "the roar of a lion, squeal of a dolphin, or chirping of a bird as the same kind of activity in principle as a concerto or symphony."[44] Such sociable intentionality is certainly displayed by vervet monkeys, who make distinct alarm calls for different kinds of predators, inciting distinct avoidance strategies in those who hear these responses.[45] Male gorillas sometimes join together in vocalizing, starting and stopping independently, but joining together in chest beating at a climax.[46] Chimpanzees sometimes drum on trees with their hands and feet while vocalizing.[47] Darwin points out that during courtship, "the males of various birds practise . . . what may be called instrumental music." He cites quill rattling, wing scraping, buzzing, striking wings together, using beaks to strike tree branches, quivering wings to make a whirring sound, as well as a combination of vocal and instrumental effects achieved by the male hoopoe (*Upupa epops*). He reports, "during the breeding season this bird, as Mr. Swinhoe observed, first draws in air, and then taps the end of its beak perpendicularly down against a stone or the trunk of a tree, 'when the breath being forced down the tubular bill produces the correct sound.'"[48] Intentionality is difficult to deny in such instances.

Another argument for restricting music to human beings is that animals lack the capacities for musical experience. Roger Scruton takes this line:

> But surely, although animals may perceive the redness of a flower, the loudness of a sound, the bitterness of a leaf, they do not hear the sadness of a melody. To hear such a quality you need not only sensory capacities, but also intellect, imagination, perhaps even self-consciousness.[49]

Colin Radford also doubts that nonhuman animals have the mental wherewithal to respond musically. Along these lines, he claims that animals are even less musical than the least musical human beings. "There are some human beings who scarcely respond to music in any way, except perhaps to tap their feet to the simplest and most insistent of rhythms. Animals are seemingly incapable even of that."[50] This argument implicitly requires that music provoke more than a sympathetic response to regular rhythm.

If the point is to establish that nonhuman animals are unmusical, Radford is wise to be so specific in itemizing their limitations. Even Eduard Hanslick, champion of music's intellectual appeal, acknowledged animal responses to music, albeit in a sarcastic passage. "The call of the trumpet fills the horse with courage and eagerness for battle; the fiddle inspires the bear to attempt ballet steps; the delicate spider and the ponderous elephant are set in motion by hearing the beloved sounds."[51] Hanslick's point is that the alleged moral effects of music are nothing people should be proud of, since they occur in beasts as well. Gordon L. Shaw cites a report from a woman on the island of Islay in Scotland: seals would swim up to her boat and stick their heads out of the water when she played the violin, with more seals appearing the longer she played.[52] Scientific studies have shown that dogs and rhesus monkeys are able to recognize a link between a tone and its octave.[53] Many Islamic thinkers of the medieval age also reported that animals were emotionally affected by music. Al-Kindi asserts that flutes and horns delighted dolphins and whales. Al-Farabi and Ibn Sina claim that vocal music had such an impact on camels.[54]

I can report a number of occasions when my own dogs reacted in a marked, I would say enthusiastic, manner when I wore jingling jewelry that produced a regular rhythm as I walked, though admittedly they did not tap their feet. Although this is a mere anecdote, it suggests that Radford is wrong to claim that animals are incapable of responding to pronounced rhythms. The specific response of tapping one's foot or deliberately marking any external rhythm does seem to be a particularly human skill, but this need not be construed as the decisive capacity involved in musical response. My dogs in fact responded to other musical features besides the regular jingling of my jewelry. The timbre of a siren would set them to howling, as would the timbre of my husband's saxophone. Perhaps Aristotle observed similar reactions of dogs to musical instruments and rhythms. Apparently Darwin did. He reports observing a dog that was "always whining, when one note on a concertina, which was out of tune, was played."[55]

Darwin contends that because noise is the result of "several aerial 'simple vibrations' of various periods, each of which intermits so frequently that its separate existence cannot be perceived," only the lack of continuity and harmony among these vibrations distinguishes noise from musical tones. Accordingly, "an ear to be capable of discriminating noises—and their high importance of this power to all animals is admitted by every one—must be sensitive to musical notes." Darwin amasses considerable evidence that nonhuman animals are responsive to musical tones.

Crustaceans are provided with auditory hairs of different lengths, which have been seen to vibrate when the proper musical notes are struck . . . similar observations have been made on the hairs of the antennae of gnats. It has been positively asserted by good observers that spiders are attracted by music. It is also well known that some dogs howl when hearing particular tones. Seals apparently appreciate music, and their fondness for it "was well known to the ancients, and is often taken advantage of by the hunters at the present day."[56]

Why should we count foot tapping as a (limited) musical response but not these other reactions?

No doubt, we do have an unusual range of options in vocalizing because of the human descended larynx, which gives considerable control over the details of our vocal expression.[57] But if complexity of musical structure is taken as the criterion for music, it is unclear that human beings have techniques that are completely unavailable to animals. François-Bernard Mâche indicates a wide range of techniques used in human music that also appear in some animals' vocal productions. He points out that the musical rhythms common to a large sweep of Alexander the Great's erstwhile empire involve "an irregular number of basic units, very often grouped by three and by two." The same rhythmic tendencies characterize the vocalizations of some animal species, such as the red-billed hornbill and the red-legged partridge. Devices such as accelerando, crescendo, and climbing pitch are used by some species (such as the blue-headed dove and the chestnut-headed pygmy rail), and "sometimes, a song is rhythmically organized as a whole. This means that the bird may have an overview of a very long duration."[58]

Mâche also denies that we are unique in using musical scales as framework, claiming that "many animals use precise and stable sets of pitches in their signals." He goes on to cite several songbird examples, including a bird from Kenya (the scaly-breasted illadopsis [*Illadopsis albipectus*]) that makes variations in articulation, repeating a staccato pattern in legato. The tones in some songbirds' music also indicate a hierarchy, and gibbons and some birds make use of transposition.

Moreover, the sonic productions of certain nonhuman creatures offer evidence of an aesthetic sense, a genuine pleasure in song as such. Peter Slater observes the role that birdsong plays in sexual selection is hardly incompatible with "aesthetics or the enjoyment of song."[59] I would go further. If female birds do select mates on the basis of musical ability, they are revealing an aesthetic preference.[60] This was Darwin's view:

That [musical tones] . . . do give pleasure of some kind to animals, we may infer from their being produced during the season of courtship by many insects, spiders, fishes, amphibians, and birds; for unless females were able to appreciate such sounds and were excited or charmed by them, the persevering efforts of the males, and the complex structures often possessed by them alone, would be useless; and this is impossible to believe.[61]

One could, perhaps, argue against animal music that animal music is merely functional, while human music is appreciated aesthetically, for itself. This argument is a nonstarter, however. In the first place, it supposes that functional and aesthetic character are mutually exclusive, which is false. Charles Hartshorne contends that songbirds enjoy their singing, even if it also protects their territory.[62] The argument that the functionality of animal sounds is incompatible with those sounds being music would also ignore the fact that human music performs a wide variety of functions. Music serves vital educational purposes in virtually every culture; it is well suited to preserving and transmitting knowledge because it is a powerful mnemonic.[63] For the same reason, it has been used in the preservation of cultural history and foundational texts (such as the Homeric poems and the Vedas).[64] The Australian Aboriginals use the contours of the song to map routes across the country, and the ancient Hawaiians stored navigational and astronomical information in their songs.[65] Music also facilitates cooperation in common activities, work songs being an obvious example. It can be used to manipulate the pace of various activities (shopping, dining, and working); Muzak and other environmental music systems are used precisely for this purpose. Music also promotes a sense of interpersonal solidarity, which has made it a useful tool for rallying support among political leaders and politicians. Many societies also use music for healing. This includes the Western world, where many people use it for emotional regulation, and the field of music therapy is burgeoning.[66]

Donald Hodges proposes another basis for differentiating human music from the "music" of other animals: "the degree of human involvement in such behaviors as language, social organizations, rituals, and music."[67] While it is not clear what "involvement" means, perhaps Hodges is suggesting that music is elaborated in connection with the other human practices he lists: language, social organization, and ritual. The links between human music and these practices is certainly important, but it is not obvious that other species' "music" is less linked to their species-wide practices than human music is to our own. Moreover, animals seem to vocalize to express emotions in a manner similar to that of human beings, as Patrik Juslin and Petri Laukka indicate:

Given phylogenetic continuity of vocal expression and cross-species similarity in the kinds of situations that generate vocal expression, it is interesting to ask whether there is any evidence of cross-species universality of vocal expression. Limited evidence of this kind has indeed been found (Scherer, 1985; Snowdon, 2003). For instance, E. S. Morton (1977) noted that "birds and mammals use harsh, relatively low-frequency sounds when hostile, and higher-frequency, more pure tonelike sound when frightened, appeasing, or approaching in a friendly manner" (p. 855; see also Ohala, 1983). Another general principle, proposed by Jürgens (1979), is that increasing aversiveness of primate vocal calls is correlated with pitch, total pitch range, and irregularity of pitch contours. These features have also been associated with negative emotions in human vocal expression (Davitz, 1964b: Scherer, 1986).[68]

Perhaps Hodges's point is like that of Walter Freeman, who comments, "Birds, whales, and cicadas 'sing' and 'signal,' but they do not manifest the richness of compassion and understanding that we experience in speaking and singing with one another."[69] But isn't Freeman's judgment that animals' sounds fail to display compassion and understanding based on his observation that they do not indicate these things to *us*? Should we expect animals to express their sense of mutual affinity to other members of their respective species in the precise manner that we do?

Hodges acknowledges that animals use sounds in connection with "social communication and in courtship and mating rituals."[70] Some animal species employ music quite remarkably in this connection. A wide variety of bird species (most commonly tropical species that form long-term monogamous pair bonds) engage in complicated duets between a male and a female. Peter J. B. Slater remarks that some of these duets "have phenomenal precision of timing . . . the birds fitting their sounds together so precisely that it is hard to believe that more than one individual is involved."[71] Mated pairs of gibbons also sing duets in "relatively rigid, precisely timed, and complex vocal interactions to produce well-patterned duets."[72] These duets often climax with acrobatic display on the part of one or both partners, as well as piloerection (hair bristling) and branch shaking.[73] Surely such behavior should count as "involvement."

Yet another argument for denying that nonhuman animals have music is that they lack the originality and creativity that we associate with human music-making. Many songbirds do not show the same kind of musical creativity that human beings display. The songs many bird species learn are fixed quite early; a bird in one of these species is not able learn new songs after a certain stage in its development. It is also common among songbirds that songs are learned by directly copying the songs of older birds. Many songbirds are also less flexible with respect to pitch than human beings. John Sloboda presumably has such considerations in mind when he claims, "the functions of music for man find no parallel in the animal world; many of the most highly patterned sound behaviours (e.g., bird song) are relatively rigid intra-specific signals of territory, aggression, warning, etc."[74] But certain songbirds do have flexibility with respect to pitch, allowing for some individual variation in songs. Some birds also develop regional "dialects," again indicating some room for departure from rigid adherence to fixed patterns.[75] For that matter, human infants are initially inflexible (and people with perfect pitch remain relatively inflexible into adult life). Jenny Saffran claims that babies are like starlings, "who can switch from relying on absolute pitch cues to using relative pitch cues when necessitated by the structure of the task."[76]

Human beings do seem to be more creative in their musical productions than animals, but we cannot say that musical creativity is restricted to human beings. Katharine Payne describes humpback whale song as being highly structured, complex, variously contoured, multithematic, and structured in a manner akin to rhyming. Very rarely does a humpback whale sing alone. In a particular population of humpback whales, the males (the exclusive singers of the species) are all singing the same song at any given time, a song that differs from that of other groups within the species. Moreover, the song being sung evolves as the singing progresses. Gradual changes, which are picked up by the entire singing group, emerge. Payne describes the results of her research:

> Our analysis eventually included all the phrases from all the songs we collected from three decades in North Atlantic and Pacific humpback populations. The results suggest that the whales have an ever expanding number of ways to modify the structure of their notes, phrases, and themes. Each theme continually changes in its own way and at its own ever-changing rate, apparently as the consequence of decisions (whether conscious or unconscious) that are shared by all the singers. At any given time all the singers seem to agree which themes are stable and which are changing. For those that are changing they agree as to which aspects are changing and which are not, and how and to what extent they are changing.[77]

However, it is fair to say that human beings exhibit a kind of creativity that animals, at least apparently, do not. Human beings manipulate meaningful sounds into larger structures that produce further, emergent meanings. Peter Marler points out that while some birds and whales order their vocalizations creatively by recombining sounds ("phonocoding" in his parlance), the recombination of sound patterns along with the assignment of meaning to the elements of the signal ("lexicoding") is unique to human beings.[78] Aniruddh

Patel points out that human music involves something further: the emergence of new meanings as a consequence of these recombinations.[79]

Are lexicoding and consequent emergent meaning essential to music? This seems to be the crux of the issue with regard to whether animals have music. If one argues that music requires multiple levels of hierarchical syntactical organization, of the sort that is displayed in language, human beings do seem to have a monopoly. In Western tonal music, for example, hierarchies relate scales, chords, and keys, and events are also organized hierarchically, with certain pitches being of greater structural importance for a particular passage of music. Syntactical ordering of the elements also affects the meaning, something that is apparently not the case in other animals' sonic communications.[80] If one requires this kind of hierarchical organization and meaning-affecting syntax of anything termed *music*, human music will be the only music by default.[81]

I do not think this amounts to a sufficient reason to discount animal music, however. In the first place, it is unclear to me that all instances of human song are so complex that hierarchical organization is clearly involved. W. Jay Dowling and Dane Harwood describe certain cultures, including that of the native Hawaiians, in which certain chants move back and forth between two pitches.[82] Would this meet the bar for *music* if multilevel hierarchical organization is required? My guess is that those who insist on human music's uniqueness because of its structural hierarchies with emergent meanings would not insist upon such complexity in every instance, only in *music* taken as a whole. But if two-pitch chants are acknowledged to be music, it strikes me as arbitrary to exclude sonic productions by animals that may be considerably more complicated.

Another reason for resisting the temptation to refuse the term *music* to animal sounds categorically is that we can't know the animal's perspective. We may feel comfortable enough attributing the meaning "This is my territory" to certain animal vocalizations. But we don't know whether or not the meaning experienced by the animal is monodimensional. Affective meanings such as joy, self-expression, responsiveness to some change in the environment, and interactive engagement with other animals and their sounds are all levels of meaning that might be experienced by a vocalizing animal. Some of the dimensions of meaning in human music are experienced from the first person point of view.[83] To posit that animal vocalizations "mean only one thing" is to ignore the subjective aspect of meaning that the animals themselves may experience.[84]

Naturally, we are going to evaluate from our own point(s) of view. But from a human perspective, the animation and aliveness of animals' vocalizations seems engaging in itself. We recognize enough similarity to our music to refer to many of them as "song," and these songs are often structurally interesting to us. Many of us find at least some animal vocalizations worthy of aesthetic contemplation.[85] If one understands *music* broadly, these are grounds for applying the term to at least some of these animal sounds.

SPECIES PRIDE

Reviewing the arguments against animal music, we observe the following alleged criteria of musicality: melody, scales, capacity for musical experience, intelligent design, complexity of musical structure, subtlety of response, aesthetic pleasure, creativity, involvement, expressiveness, and the rearrangement of meaningful elements to produce new meanings. Only the last appears to be unique to human music. Yet assuming that these arguments reflect sensibilities that are more widespread than the sources quoted, I see them as evidence that we take pride in our musicality as displaying our kind of intelligence and sensitivity. Scruton expresses this straightforwardly: "only rational beings make and listen to music . . . our music is the music of upright, earth-bound, active, love-hungry beings. Words move, music moves, 'so as to reach into the silence'—so as to claim for our humanity the speechless space surrounding us."[86] We hear ourselves in music, and we are gratified by the sense of ourselves that results.

The case of the *Voyager* space probe suggests that the philosophers just considered are not idiosyncratic in thinking that music expresses our species nature. In 1977 the National Aeronautics and Space Administration (NASA) launched its Voyager program, with enough fuel and electric power to operate until 2020. It sent two spacecraft with the mission of exploring the outer solar system and beyond. Recognizing that the Voyager satellites could be the first human artifacts to reach intelligent beings elsewhere in the universe, NASA pondered what gesture should be sent to these unknown beings to express who we are. The conclusion reached was that we should send the sounds of our world, our verbal greetings and our music.[87]

And so a gold-plated twelve-inch copper phonograph record was attached to each of the *Voyager* spacecrafts, along with a needle and symbolic instructions for playing the record. The record includes 115 analog depictions of things on earth, recordings of sounds,[88] greetings in fifty-five languages, and also a ninety-minute recording of twenty-seven pieces of music.[89] On first encounter, alien beings will not know the translations of our words, but they might find some meaning in the sounds. The music (selected by a committee chaired by Carl Sagan) is a potpourri of the music of our "sphere": several works or movements from the Western classical tradition (by Bach, Mozart, Beethoven, and Stravinsky, including the "Sacrificial Dance" from *The Rite of Spring*), instances of jazz ("Melancholy Blues," by Louis Armstrong), rhythm and blues (by Chuck Berry), and the blues ("Dark Was the Night" by Blind Willie Johnson), as well as works from Java, Senegal, Zaire, Aboriginal Australia, Mexico, New Guinea, Japan, Georgia, Peru, Azerbaijan, Bulgaria, the Navajo Nation, the Solomon Islands, China, and India. Music—a more universal language than it has ever been before.

Or is it? At this point in history, the Western world acknowledges its common humanity with people across the globe, but it is only beginning to recognize the common humanity of the world's music. Despite his musical ethnocentrism, Scruton describes aesthetic experience in universal terms:

> The aesthetic experience is a lived encounter between object and subject, in which the subject takes on a universal significance. The meaning that I find in the object is the meaning that it has for all who live like me, for all members of my "imagined community," who share our "first-person plural" and whose joys and sufferings are mirrored in me.[90]

I agree with Scruton that music engenders a sense of shared experience. Music, as most of us think of it, is what "we" have; hence the many grounds on which some deny the existence of animal music. At issue, though, is how large a group this "we" is. The song of a bird or a whale, I am convinced, can already make us aware of sharing a world with other sentient beings, and enjoyably at that. If this is so, shouldn't human music show us even more compellingly that we share the world with other human beings?

CHAPTER 3

What's Involved in Sounding Human?

I hope they're as human as they sound.   DR. BONNELL, *The Invasion of the Body Snatchers*

Dr. Bonnell, a character in the 1956 film *The Invasion of the Body Snatchers*,[1] finds himself increasingly isolated as alien body snatchers separate people's souls and bodies, replacing their souls with robotlike minds. At a certain point, Bonnell hears music and is encouraged to think that there might still be other human beings in the vicinity. This is when he utters the statement in the epigraph, "I hope they're as human as they sound." He soon discovers to his horror that he has only heard the radio of a truck that is now driven by one of the snatched bodies.

What is it to sound human? Is there even a generic way of sounding human, as there is a generic way of sounding like a gibbon or a humpback whale? Can we use sound to recognize others of our species, as many songbirds do? Ethnomusicologist Bruno Nettl contends that human individuals can almost always recognize other cultures' music as music, and that they are thereby recognizing what can be termed "musical universals."[2]

In 1974 a Sumerian song from approximately 1400 BC (probably a hymn to Nikkal, the wife of the Hurrian moon god), which had been decoded from cuneiform on clay tablets, was performed for an American audience. Sandra Trehub reports, "Listeners at the song's North American premiere did not hear the exotic melody that they had anticipated; what they heard, instead, sounded like an ordinary lullaby, hymn, or folk song."[3] Surely, one of the remarkable aspects of music is its ability to traverse time. When we hear the music of Josquin, Bach, or Beethoven, we hear living impulses from those very composers, despite their historical distance. We literally *hear* Josquin or Bach or Beethoven. And surely there is something seemingly magical about music transmitted from 1400 BC. Through it those dead for several millennia sing to us, as if alive.

John Blacking raised the issue of whether there is a universal way of sounding human in his groundbreaking book *How Musical Is Man?* His answer is that musicality is a basic part of our human inheritance, and that it is only because we have allowed our natural abilities to atrophy that we are not all active performers:

> A variety of circumstances and taboos . . . have suppressed the innate talents of millions of people. That is what concerns me most, because I believe that music-making is a special activity that has had, and could continue to have, important consequences for the full development of human potential.[4]

Despite his distress about our failure to claim our musical inheritance, however, Blacking is sanguine about the prospect for cross-cultural musical communication on the basis of our common perceptual abilities:

> Our own experience suggests that there are some possibilities of cross-cultural communication. I am convinced that the explanation is to be found in the fact that at the level of deep structures in music there are elements that are common to the human psyche, although that may not appear in the surface structures.[5]

As is no doubt obvious, I am sympathetic to Blacking's views. Indeed, he emphasizes one of the major points that I am defending in this book, the centrality of musical capacity in members of the human species. I also agree that the common character of human music is greater than divergent surface features might indicate. In any event, if music is a central aspect of human experience, cross-cultural evidence should support this. We should be able to find what social scientists call "species-invariant traits" pertaining to musicality in individuals of various cultures. Without a common denominator, the claim that musicality is basic to human nature will not be very convincing.

ACOUSTICS AND UNIVERSALITY

Insofar as music is constructed of sounds displaying certain frequency patterns, we might think that the science of acoustics ensures a common basis for musical experience across cultures. For example, it has sometimes been argued that natural acoustics determines what would be an acceptable cadence, the end to a phrase or melody. How plausible is the idea that acoustics will show us which features of music are universal?

We should first consider the way acoustics explains consonance. In the West Pythagoras is credited with the discovery that vibrating strings of lengths in simple ratios to one another produce pleasing, harmonious intervals. Moreover, a vibrating string produces not only a single tone but also numerous "harmonics," or overtones. When we hear middle C, for example, we hear in addition to the fundamental tone, middle C, the frequencies that are multiples of 2, 3, 4, for example, times the fundamental frequency. Thus we hear the C above middle C, the G above that, and so on. This is because in addition to vibrating as a whole, each half of the string also vibrates, as does each half of these halves, and so on. Each of these vibrating subsections of the string generates a tone as well, and these tones generated by the vibrations of subcomponents of the string are called *overtones*. The overtones are less prominent than the basic tone, the fundamental, but we hear a blend of the fundamental and its overtones as a single sound. Within this blend, a particular overtone is more evident the more closely it relates to the fundamental.[6]

When two tones are sounded simultaneously, the particular distance between the pitches is called an interval.[7] We hear in the interval the fundamental and the overtone series of each of the tones. If one of the fundamental tones corresponds to one of the first several overtones of the other, the interval will tend to be perceived as consonant. Another way of expressing the tones' relationship is to say that two tones will tend to be heard as consonant if many of the tones in their overtone series overlap. These acoustic principles, dealing as they do with the physics of sound, apply to music throughout the world. Hence, one might expect basic consonances, intervals formed of tones with simple frequency ratios, to be the same in music across the globe.

Even an appeal to these basics as the core of what is universal, however, is not straightforward. Perception of consonance is highly context dependent. The range of acceptable consonances in a musical tradition is subject to change. The perfect consonance of the fourth (strings resonating in the ratio of 3:4) was considered relatively dissonant in some periods of Western music. The Western musical tradition has shifted considerably since 1600, when thirds were considered too dissonant to use in a cadence.

Dowling and Harwood consider the changes in Western perceptions of dissonance to reflect a psychological principle articulated by Harry Helson. Helson endorses the theory that in any sensory modality, we prefer stimuli that differ from our adaptation level (the level to which we are accustomed) by a small amount.[8] Dowling and Harwood comment:

As listeners adapt to greater amounts of tonal dissonance, there is a gradual shift along the continuum. Helson's model also explains why a shift toward greater consonance is sometimes attractive—for example, Stravinsky's backing away in the 1920s from the dissonances of *Rite of Spring*.[9]

The Rite of Spring is the rhythmically jabbing, harmonically jarring ballet of 1913 that provoked a riot when it was first performed in Paris; by contrast, Stravinsky's works from around 1923 are commonly described as "neoclassical" because of their inclusion of techniques and idiomatic tendencies from earlier, less dissonant times.[10]

Lerdahl and Jackendoff observe that the analysis of consonance in terms of the overtone series is of limited usefulness. They point out that "there is no way to derive the minor triad from the overtone series," although the minor triad has been taken as sufficiently consonant to be used in the final cadence in Western classical music since the eighteenth century. They conclude, "derivation from the overtone series is neither a sufficient nor a necessary condition for consonance, even in the musical idiom most familiar to us."[11] Patel reiterates this point, noting that that although the octave (an interval with a 2:1 frequency ratio) is interpreted as "the same again" virtually everywhere, and the fifth (with an interval with a 2:3 frequency ratio) is an important interval in most cultures' music, the relationship between the overtone series and the scales of many cultures is not very strong.[12]

Moreover, pentatonic scales, commonly taken to be the most universal among scales, are not understood the same way in various cultures.[13] Some cultures use semitones,[14] some require particular ornaments,[15] the intervals and their sequence differ, and the relative hierarchy of tones within the pentatonic scale varies across societies.[16] Most importantly, different musical cultures use different methods of tuning to determine the exact pitches used in the scale.

During the baroque period, the West began using tempered tuning, which is not based on strict acoustics but modifies acoustically pure intervals slightly in order to facilitate transposition and modulation from one key to another.[17] The form of tempering used in Western music is called "equal temperament."[18] In natural acoustics F-sharp and G-flat are not identical, but tempering makes it so. The consequence is that in a scale tuned according to equal temperament, the ratios of frequency vibrations for the intervals among the tones are not precisely the simple ratios that Pythagoras identified. They are, however, close enough that the ear tolerates them. The octave is kept acoustically pure, the fourth and fifth are tuned in a way that slightly fudges the simple ratios between the frequencies of vibrations, and other intervals are modified to a greater degree. Tempered tuning is employed in the now standard tuning of the piano.

The motivation for tempered tuning stems from a surprising fact about the harmonic system. Successive modulation from one key to its nearest neighbor does not, in nature, return one to exactly the same key.

One can get the point by attempting to go through the circle of fifths, the series of tones produced by successive moves up a fifth. If one starts on the tone of C, the series goes C-G-D-A-E-B-F#-C#-G#-D#-A#-E#(F)-B#(C). In order to keep the sequence of tones within an octave, for practicality, this sequence can also be thought of as involving successive leaps up a fifth and down a fourth; the descending leap of a fourth lands one on the lower octave relative of the tone one would reach by leaping up a fifth. Through this process, one returns to the same key on the piano in twelve moves. Without some distortion of natural tuning, however, E# and F would not be equivalent, nor would B# and C. In other words, the pitch one arrived at would not be the same as that produced by the first piano key.[19]

The circle of fifths can also be characterized in terms of key proximity. Let us consider the keys in the Western diatonic system, that is, the system in which the distances between notes in the scale come in two sizes, distances of whole tones and of semitones, with no two successive half steps and no more than three successive whole steps. Keys in this system are more or less close to each other depending on how many of the tones in the scale of one key are also included in that of the other. The closest keys have only one differing tone. This relationship obtains between keys whose tonics are a fifth apart and a fourth apart. Thus G major and F major are the closest keys to C major, because each requires only one change from the tones used in C major.

Tempering is possible because our ears, as we will shortly consider further, are willing to interpret intervals that are less than acoustically perfect as close enough. This enables us to hear equal-tempered tuning (the specific tempering system used in the West) without having a sense that something is out of tune. We deliberately tune fifths to produce one beat per second. A beat, in this usage, is an interference of sound waves that produces a recurrent audible intensification of sound, a regular cycle in which the sound gets louder periodically. The faster the beats, the more unpleasant we tend to find it. We in the West take one beat per second as acceptable, even though the beats can be perceived.

The reason those of us accustomed to Western music do not usually notice the beats inherent in tempered tuning is that this pattern of beats conforms to our pattern of expectation. Gaining familiarity with any musical tradition involves developing mental templates, or schemata, for the way the music ought to sound, and the schemata we develop in acquiring familiarity with Western music include those for scales based on equal-tempered tuning.[20] Other societies may use different schemata for tuning, constructing scales on different bases than we do. Cultural schemata for tuning may also differ with respect to how standardized tuning is across the range of instruments.[21]

Unfortunately for cross-cultural musical understanding, we may well hear music from cultures with tuning systems unlike ours as out of tune, just as they might hear our music that way. Alternatively, if the discrepancy is not too vast, we might distort what we are hearing so that it conforms to our schema for pitch. Y. R. Chao, who was both a linguist and a musician, described such a case in his own experience:

> The writer once heard a piece of music and interpreted it as here in major and there in minor and its notes as being *do*, *re*, *mi*, etc., only being slightly "off," but subsequently learned to his surprise that it was a scale of seven equal steps in the octave. The illusion persisted even after he was told. He had forced his own intervals into the new scale. . . .[22]

Recognition of the role of culture in music should lead us to recognize that acoustics do not ensure that everyone will experience the same piece of music in the same way. As Stephen Davies observes, musically significant features of a piece of music may not even be perceptible if one has internalized a different sense of tuning. Davies takes Javanese music as an example:

> To someone raised on the major scale, almost all the intervals of the Javanese *slendro* scale sound so horribly out of tune on first hearing that no sense can be made of the different relationships holding between them. To such a person, a shift from the mode (or *patet*) of *manyura* to *nem* does not sound like a modulation at all. And, for such a person, unused from Western music to the cadential function of long-lasting, gong-punctuated structures, the colotomic pattern is likely to be missed altogether, even if the sound of gong *agung* is unmistakable.[23]

Acoustics will not ensure cross-cultural musical comfort. We need another basis for determining species-invariant musical traits. In other words, we need to ascertain what traits, if any, amount to musical universals.

SEEKING MUSICAL UNIVERSALS

The quest for universal musical characteristics of human beings is fraught with difficulties, however. To begin with, different disciplines have different criteria for universals. Philosophers, sometimes postulating that universals exist on a different, more abstract plane than the material world, will typically refuse to call a trait universal with respect to a particular set or group unless it appears in every possible individual instance. A single counterexample can be sufficient to jettison a firmly accepted assertion.[24] By contrast, anthropologists, concerning themselves with real-world cases, are much more comfortable accepting as universals traits that are characteristic of members of a group, though not exhibited in every case. Mantle Hood, for example, straightforwardly proposes,

> let us be content in defining "universals in music" as those attributes of music that *approach* worldwide distribution. . . . In other words, let us accept "universality" in the sense of "high probability of occurrence." Another analogy: babies are born with two arms and two legs—almost always.[25]

Hood's point is that we tend to view cases that depart from the "universal" as involving some disability. The "universal" is thus a normative paradigm. Given that I am concerned with real-world musical experience, I will be employing this weak standard for a universal in what follows. Even using this weak standard of (more or less) species invariance, the number of such universals is small.[26]

If we decide provisionally to accept as universals what most philosophers would at most allow are "near-universals," what evidence should we use to establish them? How much evidence is necessary to allow the induction that a particular musical capacity is universal, in a rough sense? And even if we agree on the nature of the evidence, what does it show? Evidence must be subject to analysis, and the most suggestive hints require speculation and extrapolation. But speculation and extrapolation can go wrong. What kind of evidence is sufficient to establish that a right or wrong step has been taken?

Presumably we will be on reasonably firm ground if we seek universals in standard human perceptual mechanisms. To be a member of the human species is fundamentally to fulfill certain biological criteria. As we shall see, many alleged musical universals are rooted in human sensory perception. They therefore seem good candidates for what human beings have in common, at least to the extent that they share the same sensory capabilities. (Some of the universals that have been proposed, however, are not uniquely dependent on auditory perception but would also be involved in tactile pattern recognition. They would therefore apply to the perceptions of deaf individuals as well as to hearing ones.)

For the remainder of this chapter, I will focus on various "musical universals" that empirical evidence seems to support thus far. I will not insert quotation marks around the expression in the remainder of my discussion, although we should keep in mind that cross-cultural research is at a sufficiently preliminary stage that some revisions to the list may become warranted.

Taken together, musical universals provide a degree of perceptual access into foreign music.[27] At the same time, some of them ensure a certain amount of difficulty adjusting to music that contrasts with familiar music, particularly in connection with pitch. Even if we all use scales and categories in our perception of music, the fact that cultures make use of different ones means that mental schemata for interpreting incoming musical signals are not universally the same. The use of schemata in our musical processing, in fact, ensures that there are perceptual barriers restricting the ease of access to music that departs sufficiently from what we have learned to expect.

PROCESSING UNIVERSALS

I will initially distinguish between universals of musical perception and universals of musical structure.[28] The former we would expect to apply to the basic operations involved in perceiving music (assuming the requisite sensory modalities). The latter may apply on a certain level of generality to instances of music that are stylistically diverse on another level. We will consider proposed universals in each of these categories, beginning with universals of musical processing. I will go on to suggest that these universal processes alone already establish an illusion that has an impact on our sense that music has meaning, the impression that music "moves" in a manner akin to our own activity.

Several universals relating to the perceptual processing of what Lerdahl and Jackendoff call "the musical surface" have been identified.[29] Harwood terms these "processing universals."[30] I will list a number of them, briefly explaining where appropriate, and then comment on the extent to which they might ground a sense of common human experience.

1. We distinguish signals from noise.[31] Cultures in general distinguish between music and nonmusic. Albert Bregman points out that perceptually,

"tones (sounds whose waveforms repeat cyclically) will often segregate from noises."[32] The acoustic characteristics of what is deemed "noise," however, differ from culture to culture.[33] Robert Walker points out that

> the sound of an automobile braking may become periodic and may, therefore, have pitch purely acoustically, as would a wolf howl or a dog bark. However, our learning and experience operate on the information from the auditory perceptual mechanism in such a way as to enable us to distinguish clearly between those categories of periodic sounds that we know as being musical, according to our own particular culture, and those that acoustically have similar periodic function but do not belong to the sound world we call "music." To this extent one may say that just as acoustical dissonance is not the same as musical dissonance, so acoustic pitch is, de facto, not necessarily the same as musical pitch.[34]

2. Sounds that are candidates for being incorporated into music must be within the vibration range of human pitch perception, which is most accurate between 100 and 1,000 Hz.[35]

3. We perceive musical information in "chunks." In other words, when we perceive an unfolding musical stream, our mind grasps it as a sequence of units or events.[36]

4. We perceive a tone and its counterpart an octave away (tones vibrating in a frequency ratio of 2:1) as "functionally equivalent."[37] Even three-month-old babies accept the substitution of one tone by its octave counterpart without showing signs of being startled.[38] This phenomenon is called *octave equivalence*. One consequence of octave equivalence is that men and women singing an octave apart, in most societies, are taken to be singing in unison.[39]

5. We stretch octaves. This means that at higher frequency ranges, an interval of frequencies vibrating in a ratio slightly greater than 2:1 (i.e., somewhat larger than an acoustic octave) is perceived as an octave. In lower-frequency ranges, by contrast, the ratio of tones accepted as an octave is slightly smaller than 2:1.[40]

6. Musical signals are organized in terms of *melodic contour*.[41] We grasp and remember a musical sequence as having a certain shape. Harwood describes contour as a "potent perceptual 'chunking' mechanism in memory for melodies."[42] Awareness of contour appears to begin early in life. Chang and Trehub found that five-month-old babies' heart rates, which decelerate when startled, decelerated when melodies they had become adapted to changed contour.[43]

7. *Melodic fission* occurs. This means that a single line of sequential pitches is heard as two lines, a high line and a low line, when the pitches alternate across a relatively wide intervallic distance.[44] As an example, we might consider the melody of "Joy to the World," which is simply the descending major scale. Let us imagine two tones that begin and end the opening descending melody of "Joy to the World," to which the words are "Joy to the world, the Lord is come." If we imagine just those two tones, one after the other, without the intervening ones, what we have in mind is a descending leap of an octave. If the next note we imagine is the tone that is conjoined with the word "to" in this Christmas carol, followed by another tone an octave lower than it, we have begun a sequence that could be continued down the major scale, with each tone followed by its counterpart an octave below it. Melodic fission means that we perceive this going back and forth between a higher set of tones and a lower set of tones as creating two lines, or two descending minor scales, instead of a single line that is constantly leaping. Bach strikingly exploits melodic fission in his works for solo violin and solo cello, creating the impression of multiple melodic lines by going rapidly back and forth between registers (i.e., distinct areas of the range of pitches).[45]

8. We accept an acoustically deviant tone as the nearest pitch in the scale, so long as it is sufficiently close. This can be referred to as the phenomenon of *pitch proximity*. Our ears are rather tolerant of acoustic imperfection. As long as a tone is sufficiently close to a pitch within the scale, we will hear it as that pitch. Another way of putting this point is that we perceive pitches *categorically*, that is, we tend to hear pitches as conforming to notes of the scale even if they are somewhat sharp or flat (although past a certain point, we notice that they are not on target, and at some point the discrepancy is great enough that we do not hear it even as a malformed instance of the intended tone).[46] This perceptual tendency has enabled those of us accustomed to tempered tuning to develop a schema for pitch that makes the acoustical beats produced unnoticeable.[47]

9. We prefer and more easily remember intervals and sequences of tones with frequencies in *small-integer ratios* with one another (relative consonances) to those in frequency relationships of *larger-integer ratios* (relative dissonances).[48] We perceive the former as relatively stable and the latter as relatively instable. (In light of the previous point, we should note that the frequencies heard only need to approximate those in small-integer ratios to be perceived as relatively consonant.)

Western musical analysis since the Renaissance has counted as "perfect consonances" those intervals comprised of tones whose frequencies of vibration are in simple ratios with one another. These correlate with strings whose lengths stand in simple ratios to one another. The perfect consequences are the octave (with a 1:2 ratio), the (perfect) fifth (with a 2:3 ratio), and the (perfect) fourth (with a 3:4 ratio). At the other end of the spectrum are intervals composed of tones whose frequencies of vibration stand in very large-integer ratios to one another. The frequency ratio for the tritone (the augmented fourth or diminished fifth, an unstable interval referred to as "the devil in music") is 45:32.[49] (One can hear our tempered version of this interval by playing C and the nearest F-sharp/G-flat on the piano.) Experimental studies have provided some evidence of cross-cultural agreement that the fourth and fifth are more consonant than the tritone.[50]

10. *Temporal patterns* are more important for processing and remembering musical sequences than are specific timing cues.[51] In other words, we pay more attention to overall timing patterns than to the timing of individual musical events.

11. With few exceptions, human music makes use of *scales, frameworks of discrete pitches*, typically with *uneven step size*.[52] Isabelle Peretz considers "the encoding of pitch along musical scales" to be one of two anchoring points used by the brain to process music. (The other is "the ascription of a regular beat to incoming events."[53]) The use of scales with definite steps seems to be a near-universal, at least. This does not imply that all cultures utilize an explicit *concept* of a scale, but most utilize stable pitch contrasts, even if the number of pitches utilized varies widely.[54]

Five other universals further characterize the scale frameworks used in music.

12. Virtually all scales are restricted to *five* to *seven* tones.[55] This is consistent with George Miller's principle that our short-term memory can manage "7 plus or minus 2" items of information.[56] Some psychologists have suggested that the number of items in the scale is as restricted as it is because of this limitation of memory; but Burns and Ward think this is exaggerated, since competent Western musicians can usually keep track of the twelve tones of the chromatic scale. Still, even they think there is an upper limit of how many tones we can keep track of, and the use of scales ranging from five to seven tones per octave is widespread.[57]

13. Pitches are organized *hierarchically* within the scale.[58] In other words, scales include both a pitch that is most stable, called "the tonic" in Western music, and others that are less stable, each to a different degree.[59]

14. The temporal lengths of tones are typically uneven.[60] This tendency, coupled with the tendency to employ scales of discrete tones, may explain why

Western music was for centuries successfully notated by means of neumes, the signs used to notate liturgical chant from around the ninth century. Neumes indicate that the melody should rise or fall, and show only two durations, long and short.[61]

15. Rhythm is more basic for making judgments of similarity of musical patterns than pitch,[62] and we tend to normalize rhythm.[63] In other words, as Lerdahl and Jackendoff point out, the listener "normally . . . treats . . . local deviations from the metrical pattern as if they did not exist; a certain amount of metrical inexactness is tolerated in the service of emphasizing grouping or gestural patterns."[64] Thus we tend to hear less than regular intervals as regular, up to a point. We also tend to hear temporal intervals as half or twice as long as previous intervals, even when they approximate such durations very inexactly.[65] According to Sloboda, this is because we categorize rhythm and have "a limited set of categories for describing durations of notes." Given a specific duration for a particular note, "all the other symbols acquire a defined duration which is exactly double, or half of that standard."[66] Thus our musical notation and terminology reflect our categorical perception of duration.

16. Tempo keeping seems to be proportional, on the basis of low integer ratios.[67] This means that sections within musical performances display tempos that relate to one another in simple proportions (e.g., 1:1, 2:1, and 3:1). This is the case even when performance is interrupted by rest periods. David Epstein found evidence that these results hold cross-culturally.[68] He proposes that proportional tempo keeping may provide an aesthetic constraint on musical performance, establishing one criterion for aesthetic success.[69] This pattern suggests that Leibniz is onto something when he writes that music is "an unconscious exercise in arithmetic in which the mind does not know it is counting."[70]

In addition to these universals formulated in relation to music, we can include others that are more generally applicable to human cognition. The principles of Gestalt psychology concern the ways that we group perceptions together into objects and coherent shapes, which, Dowling and Harwood suggest, "seem to describe aspects of stimulus organization that arise automatically from the operation of the sensory systems, without involving more complex cognitive systems such as memory."[71] Musicologist Leonard Meyer contends that Gestalt principles should be included in any roster of universals involved in processing music:

The universals central for music theory are not those of physics or acoustics but those of human psychology—principles such as the following: proximity between stimuli tends to create connection, disjunction results in separation; orderly processes imply continuation to a point of relative stability; a return to patterns previously presented enhances closure; and, because of the requirements of memory, music tends to have considerable redundancy and is often hierarchically structured.[72]

By "hierarchically structured," Meyer means that music is patterned in layers, with "higher," more encompassing patterns subsuming those on lower layers. For example, measures subsume individual notes; phrases subsume measures; sections subsume phrases; and so forth.[73]

Glenn Schellenberg provides experimental support for the claim that Gestalt principles are universal in a study that compared melodic expectancy among American and Chinese listeners, using Chinese and British melodies. Two Gestalt principles that applied to all the subjects, regardless of national background, were the expectation that melodies would be composed of small intervals ("pitch proximity") and the expectation that a leap in one direction would be followed by pitch movement in the opposite direction ("pitch reversal").[74] Consider, for example, "The Star-Spangled Banner." The first phrase ("Oh say, can you see") involves relatively small steps between tones. The second ("By the dawn's early light") does, too, except for the leap down as one sings "early." This leap is followed immediately by two small ascending steps, an instance of pitch reversal. The third phrase similarly involves a leap, this time an ascending leap (at the word "proudly"), which is followed by small steps in the opposite direction.[75]

The first of Meyer's principles (disjunction in stimuli results in separation) is evident in melodic fission. This is a specific manifestation of the Gestalt "principle of proximity," which holds that objects that are close together are perceived as grouped together.[76] The second of Meyer's principles is an application of the basic law of Gestalt psychology, the law of "good continuance," or *prägnanz*, which he defines as follows: "A shape or pattern will, other things being equal, tend to be continued in its initial mode of operation."[77] Meyer's third principle is an instance of the Gestalt "principle of closure," which holds that objects that are physically incomplete will be perceptually filled in. (For example, we will tend to see an incomplete circle as a circle, even though it is not physically closed up.) The fourth deals with musical structures, which we will consider shortly.

Of course, further empirical evidence might show that some of what are now thought to be universals are the result of incomplete evidence. Patel describes an investigation in which he participated that called into question a long-standing belief about a universal. The belief held that the grouping pattern for linguistic and music chunks of a short duration followed by a long one was a universal perceptual law. Inconveniently for the belief, a large number of Japanese subjects indicated that they heard the reverse pattern.[78] Huron also points out that evidence has not sustained the theory, premised on Gestalt theory and defended by both Meyer and musicologist Eugene Narmour, that listeners prefer a melody that moves along a scale but skips a tone to backtrack to "fill in" the gap that has been left.[79] Such findings indicate the need for considerably more empirical work before we can rest content with our theories about what constitute universals.[80]

For the moment, however, let us consider the processing universals so far discussed and the way these already suggest a basis for recognizing something familiar in even quite foreign music. I will suggest that even if some of these purported universals prove to be less than ubiquitous, the evidence so far suggests that the list indicates features of musical perception and widespread practices (such as scale use) that accommodate them. These features, I will go on to argue, also underlie our tendency to experience music as "behaving" or "acting" in a manner that we associate with our own activities. If this is so, perceptual tendencies that appear to be common across cultures already take us a long way toward a shared ground for associating meanings from our extramusical experience with music.

MUSICAL PERCEPTION AND HEARING ACTIVITY IN MUSIC

Certain of the seemingly universal perceptual processes we have considered are particularly important for awareness of sharing a common world with other human beings. In the vast majority of instances, music seems to resemble human activity and draws attention to unfolding temporality, both features of our experience that we have in common with other human beings. Both, too, depend on the way we perceive music. I will defer most of my discussion of music's reflection of our temporal experience until chapter 8. Here I will consider the ways that musical perception overdetermines our tendency to find a strong resemblance between music and human activity.

Certainly the fact that we move when making music would already incline us to associate music with human behavior. In any context in which musical performance is live, performers and listeners experience the music as a result of human movement.[81] Even in cases in which music is not live, I suspect that we usually think of the music in this way so long as we have any sense of how it is produced (although the production of music by means of computers might make the connection a bit less obvious).

But we connect music with our nonmusical activity as well, and what I will argue here is that some of the perceptual processes considered above are particularly relevant for this association. First, music suggests movement through the changes of state we refer to in terms of consonance and dissonance. We prefer intervals with frequency ratios of simple integers, which we experience as consonant, and we expect more dissonant intervals to give way to more consonant ones. This is the case not only for dissonant intervals that are performed simultaneously (harmonic dissonances), but also for dissonant intervals that are performed sequentially (melodic dissonances).[82] Consonance and dissonance are often defined in terms of relative tendency to movement or repose, stability or instability, with dissonance tending toward resolution in a consonance.[83]

We tend to experience patterns of dissonance and consonance in terms of tension and relaxation. We feel tension and relaxation ourselves in response to the degrees of tension among the intervals, and we also tend to objectify tension and relaxation as features of the music. Accordingly, we easily sense a similarity between the behavior of music and our activity, for we notice recurrent tensions, followed by partial or complete resolutions of those tensions in music. These resemble our own patterns of exertion and relaxation. For example, we follow moments of exertion (lifting a heavy weight, for example) with moments of relaxation. These may be temporary (as when we lift a weight, set it down, lift it again, and so on) or they may be relatively enduring (as when we leave the gym entirely). We should note, however, that a sense of relative tension among intervals depends upon the hierarchical organization of pitches within a scale, which may not be immediately obvious to the listener who is unfamiliar with the system through which the scale is constructed. We have also observed earlier that what counts as consonance, although premised on frequency ratios that are simple, is relative to a musical system.

Nevertheless, besides sequences of consonances and dissonances, one of the most basic ways that human beings organize what they hear as music is melodic contour, and contour is also among the means by which music suggests relative tension and relaxation and the change of states this involves. We sense that a melodic line reveals more and less effort, in accordance with changes in the relative height of pitches. The fact that higher pitches in one's vocal range are more difficult to sing than lower pitches may be a factor in the correlation of higher pitches with greater effort. The fact that Western and a number of other cultures use the straightforwardly spatial metaphor of height in reference to pitch also supports the tendency to consider music as resembling our effortful activity; we speak of "reaching" for "high" notes, for example.

Patel suggests a third basis for associating music with human activity. He proposes that an inherent tension between two features of perception may be operative in the impression of animation. One is the expectation of proximity in tones that are similar; the other is the fact that neighbors in pitch may be quite different with respect to their hierarchical roles in relation to the centering tone. In the case of Western tonal music, the hierarchical roles amount to stability within a key; but Patel points out that pitch hierarchies arise in any music that is organized around a tonal center. Melody, he submits, is animated in part by the psychological pull between these two principles.[84]

A fourth ground on which we experience music as active like ourselves is the analogy that we observe between pitch space and the space of our activities. That we do suppose such an analogy is suggested by the very fact that many cultures speak of pitches in spatial terms.[85] We also have the impression while listening that music is filling space, the very space in which we literally operate.[86] We tend to associate spatial position with sound as well, for we use acoustics to localize sound sources laterally in space.[87]

Charles Nussbaum indicates a neurophysiological basis for the analogy that we make between musical space and the space in which we act. On the basis of the close relationship between the auditory system and the motor system, according to Nussbaum, music makes use of the same system we use to interact with the external spatial world. In the spatial case, we mentally model the features of the environment to prepare ourselves to act in it. Nussbaum claims that we do the same thing with music, representing "virtual layouts and scenarios in an imaginary musical space in which the listener acts (off-line)." In the case of music, we mentally "represent virtual layouts and scenarios in an imaginary musical space in which the listener acts (off-line)."[88] We are exploring a virtual space when we listen to music, and our motor systems are stimulated by it (as is evident from our tendency to swing and sway with music).

The engagement of our motor systems suggests an explanation for the fact that we tend to interpret rhythm in kinetic terms. Soundtracks underscoring the movements of cartoon characters exploit this association of musical rhythms with the rhythms of active agents. This, too, inclines us to consider the music as active in much the way that we are.

Fifth, we locate ourselves within the unfolding music much as we locate ourselves in the space in which we act. The unevenness of both the steps within the vast majority of human scales and the temporal lengths of tones gives us a sense of position within music, a position from which we can move by steps and leaps. We might compare the pitch and rhythmic spectrums to two axes of a grid extending indefinitely in both directions (just as the spatial continuum is often modeled as grids extending indefinitely in three dimensions). If pitch and rhythmic increments were absolutely even in their respective spheres, locations in music would be no more distinctive with respect to each other than are the spaces of a checkerboard. John Sloboda compares the function of scales and rhythms in this respect: "Scale and rhythm perform the same essential function, that of dividing up the pitch and time continua into discrete and re-identifiable locations, on which backdrop all the essential dialectical activities (tension-resolution, motion-rest), can flourish."[89] The fact that in many cultures' music some tones are more structural in a melody and others ornamental might psychologically reinforce the sense of moving by steps from one definite position to another.[90]

Sixth, musical entrainment also encourages us to associate music with our actions. Entrainment is the synchronization of one's biological activity (including our physical movements) with an externally produced rhythm, such as that of a metronome or another person.[91] Apparently unlike other animals, human beings are able to deliberately adjust the rhythm of their own movements to concur with the pulse of something outside themselves.[92] People can march in formation, perform music in accordance with composers' tempo indications, and conjoin their strength in common tasks by means of entrainment. Nietzsche makes the point that music can be a tool of politics for this reason: "Rhythm is a compulsion; it engenders an unconquerable urge to yield and join in; not only our feet follow the beat but the soul does, too."[93]

Because music can and often does entrain many listeners at once, it is a powerful means of synchronizing our activity. Work songs and marching songs, two globally widespread phenomena, illustrate the impact of music for entraining and coordinating the actions of many human beings. Such interpersonal synchronization also effects a strong sense of connection with other participants. Phenomenologist Alfred Schutz describes the social bond established among performers and listeners through music's synchronization of their multilayered impression of time. He observes,

> On the one hand, there is the inner time in which the flux of musical events unfolds, a dimension in which each performer re-creates in polythetic[94] steps the musical thought of the (possibly anonymous) composer and by which he

is also connected to the listener. On the other hand, making music together is an event in outer time, presupposing also a face-to-face relationship, that is, a community of space, and it is this dimension which unifies the fluxes of inner time and warrants their synchronization into a vivid present.[95]

A seventh possible experiential basis for relating music to our own activity is a reference within the performance of musical phrases to the speeding up and slowing down involved in our locomotion. Bruno Repp found that within musical phrases performers tend to speed up at the beginning and to get slower toward the end. He suggests that this derives from our patterns of physical movement.[96] If this is so, music literally mimics our physical behavior.

The universal and quasi-universal features of our musical perception not only encourage comparison between the activity of music and our own behavior; their doing so serves as a ground for further associations between music and extramusical meaning. Because musical perception itself leads us to compare music to our own modus operandi, it encourages us to identify with music even as listeners, as Nussbaum explains:

> The internal representations employed in recovering the musical structure from the musical surface specify motor hierarchies and action plans, which, in turn, *put the listener's body into off-line motor states that specify virtual movements through a virtual terrain or a scenario possessing certain features.*[97]

We feel as though the movements of the music are our own movements because our mental representations of music involve enacting virtual movements in accordance with it. Music's relationship to the systems by which we navigate our world also ultimately provides a basis for the many dimensions of meaning that music has for us and for our sense of its relevance to extramusical content. "Musical modeling of nonmusical domains," Nussbaum claims, "is pervasive, because musical experience is fundamentally bodily, gestural, and simulational in significance."[98] In other words, because music engages our bodily systems for relating to the world, we model many features of the world in terms of it.

The resemblances between music and our own activity are significant for a number of reasons. First, they suggest a basis for recognizing commonalities between ourselves and others whose minds, like ours, relate music to their own activity and exploration of the world. Second, they provide grounding for musical associations with extramusical meaning, a topic that we shall consider further in a later chapter. Third, and most relevant to our topic here, they offer an initial way of relating to music that is disorientingly foreign.

Can we really recognize our own activity in unfamiliar foreign music? We can to some extent. That is, we can recognize in such music activity akin to our own to the extent that we can discover melodies whose contours suggest various levels of exertion and relaxation, entrain to a regular rhythm, locate ourselves within patterns of uneven pitches and rhythmic patterns, and mentally represent the musical signal in terms of layouts and scenarios in virtual musical space. Music's reflection of features of our own activity, largely on the basis of relatively universal features of musical perception, encourages us to identify with its movement. The animation of music, with which we can identify, provides a basis for our feeling to some degree at home in unfamiliar music.

Nevertheless, processing universals are not the only aspects of music that affect our sense of comfort. We have already considered the potential difficulties that arise when the schemata we bring to an experience of music deviate from those utilized in the structuring of the music. Cross-cultural intelligibility is not ensured by the processing universals. In fact, the universals of pitch proximity and the employment of scales almost ensure the opposite—that sometimes we will distort what we hear more or less automatically, conflating it with what we expect to hear.

In the following chapter we will consider further complications for the project of cross-cultural understanding of music. On the one hand, we will note some of the quasi-universal tendencies that shape musical structure, which should help us to recognize familiar features in music that is structured in unfamiliar ways. On the other hand, we will find that evaluative and interpretive approaches to many aspects of music are culturally relative. We will reach the unsurprising conclusion that although we can enjoy much foreign music, we may not be sure what it means, at least to those who produce it. However, I will suggest that some of the obstacles to understanding can be ameliorated and, with persistence, overcome.

CHAPTER 4

Cross-Cultural Understanding

Hearing something new is embarrassing and difficult for the ear;
foreign music we do not hear well.

FRIEDRICH NIETZSCHE, *Beyond Good and Evil*

In *Silent Night: The Story of the World War I Christmas Truce,* Stanley Weintraub recounts the tale of combatants on both sides of the front line putting aside their weapons and celebrating Christmas together in December 1914.[1] A striking feature of the spontaneous gestures of goodwill at many points along the front line was how often they were facilitated by song. "It was with shared traditions and song that the two sides approached one another," Weintraub observes.

> Yuletide carols initiated a tentative courtship that further developed through physical contact and ultimately the sharing of the soldiers' most valued commodities—food and tobacco and such souvenirs as uniform buttons and insignia.... Everywhere, Christmas ritual—especially song—eased the anxiety and fear of initial contact.[2]

At times song was used to transform the struggle with the enemy into something more like sport. One Seaforth Highlanders regiment officer wrote home about a challenge from the Germans to sing and of the irreverent renditions of "Who Were You with Last Night?" and "Tipperary" his side sang in response. He goes on to register his surprise when "the enemy played 'Home Sweet Home,' and 'God Save the King,' at 2:30 A.M.!'" Weintraub also reports Lieutenant Sir Edward Hulse's claim in a letter to his mother that "his 2nd Scots Guards 'assaulted' the Germans with carols." Hulse remarked, "we are going to give the enemy every conceivable song in harmony from carols to Tipperary.... Our object will be to [shout] down the now too-familiar strains of *Deutschland über alles* and the *Wacht am Rhein* we hear from their trenches every evening."[3]

Certainly this episode indicates that the same music can be appreciated—even be a source of inspiration—across national boundaries. But it hardly demonstrates that the same music is intelligible across the boundaries of musical cultures. As far as "Silent Night" is concerned, German, French, English, and American societies are all the same musical culture. Are there grounds for believing that music penetrates hearts and minds across musical traditions?

We have already seen that a number of features of musical perception appear to be characteristic of the species. Thus we can expect them to impact the way music is organized, even though they are insufficient to dictate musical structure in detail. Directly, we will look at some "structural universals" of music—characteristics that typify the way people organize music in all or most cultures. These are "universals" in a weaker sense than the processing universals described in the previous chapter; they are widespread patterns, but they do not necessarily apply to all human music. Still, they can also often facilitate comprehension of much foreign music in that they indicate patterns that should be familiar to members of most musical cultures.

Nevertheless, as I argue in the previous chapter, certain factors stand in the way of the listener who seeks to understand alien music. In the latter part of this chapter, we will consider some of these, beginning with the fact that some of a culture's grounds for evaluating music are not always superficially obvious. After discussing some of the obstacles to cross-cultural musical understanding, I will conclude this chapter with some preliminary considerations of how these obstacles might be overcome.

STRUCTURAL UNIVERSALS

Musical cultures seem to converge in some of their choices about how to structure pieces of music. Lerdahl and Jackendoff propose a direct relationship between the processing universals described in the previous chapters and the sorts of musical structures societies construct:

> Musical idioms will tend to develop along lines that enable listeners to make use of their abilities to organize musical signals. Therefore, if there is some kind of organization that is especially "natural" (that is, favored by musical cognitive capacity), we should expect this sort of organization to be widespread among musical idioms.

They add the important qualification, "On the other hand, we do not expect all idioms to exploit all aspects of musical cognition equally."[4]

As we noted in the last chapter, Meyer mentions one cross-cultural regularity—considerable redundancy and usually hierarchical organization. Ethnomusicologists, psychologists, and philosophers have indicated other "universals" of this sort:

1. Music is made in "pieces" or "utterances." Bruno Nettl observes, "One does not simply 'sing,' but one sings something. Music is composed of artifacts, although cultures differ greatly in their views of what constitutes such an artifact."[5] Stephen Davies observes, "I do not know of any culture lacking musical works for performance—that is repeatable pieces with titles or identifying descriptions."[6]

2. Melodies in all cultures tend to be constructed on the basis of fairly small successive intervals. The chief melodic intervals in melodic progressions tend to be in the range of the major second (though the exact interval depends on the tuning system); it is "usually no greater than 3–4 semitones," according to Harwood.[7] Meyer claims that "intervals smaller than a half step almost always serve to inflect structural tones" because of the limitations of human perception. Although microtonal scales are theoretically possible, Meyer observes, "to the best of my knowledge, no scales of this sort have ever become shared cultural constraints."[8]

3. Most musical cultures employ a centering tone (a tonic) or some kind of tendency.[9] Cultures usually devise music in such a way that the listener has a clear conception of the ultimate destination of a piece.[10] Drones and frequent recurrence of a pitch are among the means by which such a reference pitch is established.[11]

4. Musical utterances tend to descend in pitch at the end.[12] David Huron terms the tendency of melodies to move downward via small intervals "step declination."[13]

5. Internal repetition is typical within musical utterances.[14]

6. Use of loud, fast, accelerating patterns in high registers appears to be a "universal" device expressing emotional excitement.[15] (In general, some prosodic cues for emotional expression seem to be constant across speech and language and to hold cross-culturally. We will consider universal cues for emotional expression in later chapters.)

7. Rhythmic structures depend on tones with varying lengths and varying dynamic emphases.[16] In particular, pulse or meter makes the rhythmic pattern asymmetrical, creating an impression of location within the beat.[17]

8. One might include the nearly universal tendency to construct rhythms on the basis of patterns of twos and threes.[18] John Chernoff points out that this tendency is at work even within rhythmically complex African music. "In spite of what we think, most African music is in some common variety of duple or triple time (like 4/4 or 12/8) and not in the 7/4 or 5/4 that many Westerners have thought they might have heard. Music in 7/4 time would be very difficult to dance to."[19]

9. Emphasis on the interval of the fifth is a near-universal.[20]

Some of these structural universals further contribute to music's capacity to reflect our activity, which we considered in the previous chapter. The very fact that music tends to be formulated in pieces enables one to have a sense of completion, usually combined with a sense of at least relative relaxation. Relaxation is also conveyed by the decline in pitch at the end of a piece. Melodies tend to be constructed in small steps, and this reinforces awareness of the precise tones available in the scale across a particular span of pitch space. Going to the adjacent scale tone or the next is the most typical melodic movement; thus we become particularly aware of where the specific steps of the scale are. The device of a centering tone facilitates the impression of a sense of direction in music, as well as the sense of relative relaxation when this pitch occurs. Rhythmic structure, which indicates regularity in the passage of time, depends on the uneven durations of tones, which we considered previously.

Musical structure is also ubiquitously affected by the human psychological tendency to habituate to any persistent stimulus.[21] A repeated pattern, for example, recedes into the attentional background. Perhaps this explains the "law of three" observed by many composers in the West.[22] The law of three states that an exact repetition or sequence should be repeated no more than three times if one is to maintain the attention of the audience. The reason for this may be that a third appearance of a pattern is noteworthy; one recognizes that a stable trend is in place. On the fourth statement, however, the mind only confirms its judgment that a regularity has been introduced. Having recognized the presence of a reiterated pattern, one's attention is no longer required to make sense of that part of the musical signal. The *tihai* phenomenon in Hindustani music involves an exact reiteration of a pattern so that it is stated three times consecutively, with the effect of a relative climax. The repetition gives the *tihai* pattern particular emphasis. Perhaps this is another reflection of the optimality in cases of repetition of three consecutive statements of a pattern.

Scholars differ with respect to whether universals are evident in any larger formal structures in music. Harwood is dubious.[23] Nettl, however, contends that there is a near-universal "simplest style." It "consists of songs that have a short phrase repeated several or many times, with minor variations, using three or four pitches within a range of a fifth."[24] This type of music, which Nettl thinks is archaic, is frequently used in ritual and remains the primary kind of music in some societies. Mâche proposes another ubiquitous style, "pentatonic polyphony on a drone," which he takes to be so widespread that it might be classed as a universal.[25]

UNIVERSALS OF EVALUATION

Transcultural and Pancultural Universals

Perceptual and structural universals do not exhaust the range of possible musical universals. Analyzing the universal dimensions of aesthetic experience, Wilfried van Damme suggests that there may be evaluative universals. He distinguishes between what he calls "transcultural universals" and "pancultural universals." Transcultural universals are "*stimulus properties* which as such would seem to appeal to all human beings, regardless of cultural background." Pancultural universals, by contrast, are evaluative criteria, "*principles* that are found to be operative in evaluating stimuli in all (pan) cultures," whether or not the stimuli themselves are similar.[26]

Van Damme submits that what most people consider to be "real universals" are those of the transcultural sort. He cites several candidates for transcultural universals in visual aesthetic appreciation, which are apparent in many cultures and for which counterexamples are virtually nonexistent. These include symmetry and balance, clarity, smoothness, brightness, and novelty. However, he also observes that divergent aesthetic values may actually reflect the same underlying principle (a pancultural universal if the principle holds across cultures). The diverse cultural standards of ideal human body weight, for example, may all reflect a high evaluation of "health and material well-being." Van Damme concludes from this that although there may not be transcultural agreement in evaluating a particular person's physical weight, there is pancultural agreement that a person's weight should correlate with health and physical well-being. He proposes that there is such a pancultural universal: the regularity that "people in a particular culture find attractive those visual stimuli which in terms of that culture aptly signify its sociocultural ideals."[27] He defines sociocultural values or ideals as "those qualities which, in a given culture or society, are more or less communally conceived to be worth striving for individually and collectively, and which as such are explicitly or implicitly held up as guidelines or objectives."[28] The same societal ideal may be expressed in diverse images.

Applying Van Damme's distinction to music, we might expect some universal standards for positive evaluation, even if musical cultures apply them to works that differ markedly. Among the transcultural universals for visual appearance that Van Damme lists, symmetry, balance, and clarity, at least, would seem potentially applicable to music as well. Novelty might apply, too, although considering the seemingly universal tendency to value repetition in music (presumably another transcultural universal), novelty is apparently considered desirable only to a limited degree.

Diversity among Cultural Ideals

Despite some similarities, various cultures nevertheless seem to have different ideals for evaluating the stimulus properties of music. We find a musical illustration of such differences in the evaluative standards of Javanese and Balinese musical culture. As William Malm describes the difference, "the generally sedate quality of Javanese music is completely shattered by the boisterous brilliance of the Balinese sound."[29] Although the instruments used in the two musical cultures are fairly similar, Balinese gamelan performers create a "shimmering" effect by precisely tuning groups of instruments at approximately 7 hertz apart, with the effect that when instruments from both groups play the same note, they produce approximately seven beats per second.[30] The Javanese aim at an even, balanced sound that has been compared to a river flowing over a pebbled bottom. Balinese musicians, by contrast, aim at fiery, brilliant effects and dramatic contrast. Their music is jagged, dramatic, irregular, and unbalanced. Balinese singers sometimes practice on rocky beaches in order to create the desired vocal quality.[31]

Cultural differences with respect to ideals for vocal music can have perceptual repercussions. Robert Walker points out the contrast between the sound qualities valued by the Western tradition and by some Native American societies. Western singers are "trained to produce high levels of spectral energy" so as to produce a ringing tone, while Native Americans of the Pacific Northwest concentrate energy at a lower energy level.[32] Walker considers each of these ideals for vocal sound contextually appropriate. The Western approach, which results in a wide range of harmonics, is suitable to public performance, in which the aim is to hear the singer above accompanying instruments. The vocal ideal of the Kwakiutl tribe, by contrast, is appropriate for their "intimate, personal, and intensely spiritual music," which "serves personal totemistic needs rather than public performance functions." Walker observes that the environment also encourages this ideal, for the music is usually sung outdoors, and in the rainforest in which the Kwakiutl live, higher frequencies fade quickly.[33]

Within the West, different ideals for vocal music have been upheld at different periods in history. A treatise from the early thirteenth century alleging to represent the views of "the ancient Holy Fathers" claimed that by upholding its precepts for singing "the offering of our praises becomes pleasant and agreeable unto God"; among these were the precepts to sing naturally, with a clear, full, and steady voice.[34] By contrast, controlled vibrato and emphasis on individual timbre were admired and commonplace in nineteenth- and twentieth-century vocal performance.

Music's Reflection of Social Ideals

Alan Lomax suggests that cultural differences in preferred vocal style reflect different conceptions of how individuals should interact. He contrasts American Indian and European vocal styles, which he correlates with their different respective emphases on collective cooperative activity and individualistic assertion. American Indian vocal style is "strikingly muscular in character," according to Lomax, typically "throaty, husky, sometimes grating, rich in nasal overtones, and produced at the normal speaking pitch" with occasional high-pitched yelps, although the Plains Indian style tends to maintain a high-pitched tone throughout. Although used for ritual, healing, mnemonics, and shamanistic trance, the majority of Native American music is employed with dance, and for this reason is emphatically rhythmic and regular. The European area from which colonizers came tends toward a "high-pitched, often harsh and strident" vocal quality, "delivered from a tight throat with great vocal tension," and "suitable for the presentation of long and highly decorated melodic line." Lomax summarizes: "Control and individualism are the key descriptive terms here. Cooperative music-making is achieved only by groups of adepts," that is, by experts, usually professional musicians.[35]

Lomax's theory that a society's song style is correlated with social factors supports the notion that music reflects sociocultural ideals. He contends, "musical styles may be symbols of basic human value systems which function at the unconscious level and evolve with glacial slowness because the basic social patterns which produce them also evolve slowly." Lomax developed a technique that he terms "cantometrics," a coding of generic style features characteristic of the music of particular societies.[36] Cantometrics considers both "the phenomena described by European music notation—melody, rhythm, harmony interval size, etc.," and other factors, such as the size, social structure, leadership roles, integration of the music-making group, the kinds of embellishments employed, and the vocal tone quality typically adopted.[37]

One of Lomax's most striking proposals is that musical style is correlated with sexual mores regarding the behavior of women, with a more relaxed vocal style corresponding to greater permissiveness and a higher status of women. In an article in which he considers the typical song style in various cultures, focusing in detail on the regions of Spain and Italy, he concludes:

> In those societies considered, the sexual code, the position of women, and the treatment of children seem to be the social patterns most clearly linked with musical style. Where women are made into chattels, as they have been during recent history in most areas of high culture, their feelings of melancholy and frustration have determined that the entire music of the various societies take on a nostalgic or agonized character, in singing style, melodic type, and emotional content. The women in these societies fix the early musical preferences of the young, so that when these children become adults they experience a pleasurable recall of childhood emotions associated with their mothers and their mothers' sad songs; thus a sorrowful music fills them with a feeling of security and they find it beautiful and pleasurable.[38]

Lomax's account of the origins of the tense, vocally constricted, plaintive style is obviously speculative. One might alternatively suppose that general attitudes toward the body correlate with the extent of a culture's insistence on bodily control and with its level of sexual repression.

Perhaps less contentiously, Lomax considers the presence or absence of a dominating leader in a musical style to reflect a society's ideals for social organization, hierarchical or otherwise. He describes Western Europe folk song as being mainly organized with a leader dominating a passive audience (noting the similar pattern of symphony orchestras, where the conductor gets extreme compliance from the orchestra as well as the audience). This pattern is essentially the normative ideal for interaction in the same region.[39]

Music, according to Lomax, is a symbol of a society's general orientation toward the world. Referring to the Pygmy and Bushmen of Africa, whose way of life is similar in most particulars, Lomax reports that their musical style symbolizes their idyllically cooperative and tolerant lifestyle.

This extraordinary degree of vocal relaxation, which occurs rarely in the world as an over-all vocal style, seems to be a psycho-physiological set, which symbolizes openness, nonrepressiveness, and an unconstricted approach to the communication of emotion. . . . The vocal empathy of the Pygmies seems to be matched by the cooperative style of their culture. . . . Even their melodies are shared pleasures, just as are all tasks, all property, and all social responsibilities. The only parallel in our coding system is found at the peak of Western European contrapuntal writing, where again all the separate interests of a variegated musical community are subordinated to a desire to sing together with a united voice about universal human values.[40]

Lomax's cantometric theory has generated considerable critical response. As Steven Feld summarizes the lines of criticism:

Sample size and time depth, compatibility of song data with social structural data, psychocultural reductionism, inferential history, reading correlation as causation, intracultural and areal variability, and the extent to which the coding system normalized raters in ways which constrain the accuracy of pattern judgment were all causes of critical discussion surrounding this monumental work.[41]

Feld emphasizes the further problem of limiting the base for constructing a cultural profile to ten songs.[42] Lomax justifies this strategy on the ground that song styles in a culture are highly redundant, but one consequence may be the exaggeration of cultural homogeneity. More methodologically, his cantometric method has been criticized for using the same test, the chi-square test, on the same data over and over in generating his various correlations, making it more likely that the statistically improbable will appear to be a serious probability.[43]

Even his critics, however, acknowledge that Lomax is on to something important in correlating musical style with cultural norms for interpersonal behavior. Edwin Erickson, who reanalyzed Lomax's data using a cluster approach, did not find many of the clusters of societal arrangements to be correlated consistently with musical variables. However, he did find cross-cultural correlations between a constricted vocal style and sexual repressiveness, between polyphonic singing and gender equality, and between interlocking counterpoint and small-scale gathering societies. He also found correlations between societal complexity and the number of musical instruments typically employed.[44] Feld acknowledges the aptness of seeing musical structure as a model of social structure, even while denying a one-to-one structural isomorphism: "For any given society, everything that is socially salient will not necessarily be musically marked. But for all societies, anything that is musically salient will undoubtedly be socially marked, albeit in a great variety of ways, some more superfluous than others."[45]

Two important corollaries emerge from the idea that music reflects cultural ideals. One is that the reflection of cultural ideals may enhance both the enjoyment and the meaning that musical participants (both performers and listeners) find in music. Van Damme suggests that visual images may be especially gratifying when they consolidate sociocultural ideals into a form that is particularly dense with meaning for the beholder.

> The gratification or pleasure involved may be seen to derive from the fact that visual metaphors of sociocultural ideals are able to elicit a condensed manifold of meaning that the enculturated mind of the perceiver has come to favourably assess. The intensified welcoming of such a range of positively evaluated meaning, cogently signified by a visual stimulus, may then be regarded as particularly gratifying.[46]

I submit that the musical "image," too, can offer gratification on similar grounds, and that this helps account for both its emotional power and the complications involved in appreciating music from another culture.

For example, consider the presentation of Schiller's "Ode to Joy" in the fourth movement of Beethoven's Ninth Symphony (op. 125). Halting statements of what will become the basic melody of the ode in several lower instrumental voices prepare one for the initial outburst of the human voice. After the voice states the first verse of the ode, other voices join in, deriving their musical material from the song's melody. Schopenhauer (apparently taking the structure of his society's music for granted) proposed that the vocal registers conjoined in music are analogous to the great chain of being from inorganic nature to the human being; these analogies strike me as fairly persuasive in the context of this movement. I find it easy to imagine that Schopenhauer built his analogies with this movement in mind, when he describes the various voices as different levels manifesting the will, the fundamental reality in his metaphysical view:

> Those nearer to the bass are . . . the still inorganic bodies manifesting themselves, however, in many ways. Those that are higher represent to me the plant and animal worlds. . . . But all these bass-notes and ripienos that constitute the

harmony, lack that sequence and continuity of progress which belong only to the upper voice that sings the *melody*. . . . Finally, in the *melody*, in the high, singing, principle voice, leading the whole and progressing with unrestrained freedom, in the uninterrupted significant connexion of *one* thought from beginning to end, and expressing a whole, I recognize the highest grade of the will's objectification, the intellectual life and endeavour of man. . . . Melody . . . relates the most secret history of the intellectually enlightened will, portrays every agitation, every effort, every movement of the will.[47]

Even if one is not convinced by Schopenhauer's account, the impression that the whole panoply of nature gradually erupts into the joy that is explicitly described in the ode amplifies the emotional content of Schiller's poem and the gratification of participating in it, whether as performer or listener. Moreover, this ideal of coordinated, harmonious interplay of every vital entity is an image of the ethical ideal of highly structured industrialized societies. Very likely the impact of the enthusiastic conviviality and cooperation embodied in the fourth movement of Beethoven's Ninth figured prominently in the European Union's selection of the music for the "Ode to Joy" as its anthem.[48]

We are also in a position to recognize a second corollary to the fact that music reflects cultural ideals. The difference between surface characteristics of musical style and the underlying preferences that give rise to them suggests a rather surprising fact about musical universals. Insofar as musical universals include preferences that can manifest in a variety of ways, the universal character of music promotes diversity, not conformity. The range of musical universals (perceptual, structural, and evaluative) underdetermines particular musical structures. The universals are, accordingly, compatible with enormous musical variety. The widely diverging styles we hear in the music of the world, then, are exactly what we might predict.[49] *A consequence of musical preference universals, then, is the vast variety of music.*

The picture is complicated still further by the fact that in today's world, in which few musical cultures are homogenous, we would be hard pressed to categorize many cultures as having a single set of evaluative ideals for music. These days few societies, if any, are musically homogenous or immersed exclusively in the traditional music of their ancestors. The widespread availability of recording and playback technology has acquainted much of the world with Western music. Visiting New Caledonia some time back, I saw a local group on television performing John Lennon's song, "Imagine," and recognized that the song might be in the repertoire of local groups everywhere. The era of "world music" is not without imperialistic tendencies, particularly among those who steer the music business, and well-situated Western musicians no doubt exert more musical influence on musicians in the developing world than the other way around. "Imagine" is played everywhere, but traditional New Caledonian songs are not. The nonreciprocity in these encounters of cultures gives us reason to be concerned about the preservation of traditional musical cultures.[50] In relation to evaluative principles, the current situation of musical exchange raises new questions about the grounds for universal convergence where it exists. It would be worthwhile to try to determine the degree to which evaluative principles applied to music are being transformed by these encounters, and, conversely, how much the application of different cultures' evaluative standards is affecting the performance of transplanted music.[51]

The popularity of rock music throughout the world suggests the possibility that evaluative standards are changing or broadening in some places, but it is hard to tell which of several possible descriptions is more accurate. Some of these possibilities are:

1. Rock music is sufficiently malleable (or has few enough intrinsic characteristics) to be adapted to suit a variety of cultural evaluative preferences. (The development of the rock opera, for example, might be seen as such an adaptation. The Who's *Tommy*, while expressing "traditional" rock values such as musical energy and strong backbeat, nevertheless incorporates tendencies that are valued in other musical styles, such as complex vocal harmonies and elaborate instrumentals. In connection with cultural interaction, the question to the point for our purposes here is whether at least some of the same evaluative standards applied to traditional music are also satisfied by rock.)

2. Rock music is promoting new musical values in communities where they didn't exist before, often supplanting previous values. (This was one of the complaints of opponents of early rock 'n' roll. This is also the concern of those who worry about the fate of other musical forms and traditions that appear to have declining audiences.[52])

3. Rock music reflects pancultural values that are also expressed in traditional forms of music (such as the value placed on music that encourages physical entrainment and participation).

4. Rock music widens the range of musical values that are appreciated within given societies, but does not (or need not) supplant those that were already present. (In other words, audiences are capable of appreciating various kinds of music and applying differential values appropriate to these various types.)

5. All of the above.

Thomas Turino offers reasons to think that musical imports might extend the scope of musical appreciation without supplanting previous musical values. He also draws attention to certain values of long standing that apply to participatory music across many traditions, though they are not necessarily evident in all types of music in the respective cultures. Such values, he suggests, speak to general psychological needs and can be satisfied by music to which one is a relative newcomer.

Turino contends that criteria for evaluating music can and do vary within societies, depending on what type of music is being evaluated. Evaluative criteria differ depending on which of four subcategories, or "fields," an instance of music belongs to: presentational music, participatory music, "high fidelity music" (which aims at accuracy in representing a live performance), and "studio audio art" (which aims to create a new sonic product that does not correspond to an actual live performance). Each of these subcategories has its own profile of preferences for certain kinds of sound qualities. Participatory music, which aims at the inclusion of as many as possible, is successful when it achieves a "wall of sound" and "densely overlapping textures, wide tunings, consistently loud volume and buzzy timbres." These ideals typify participatory music across cultures, according to Turino.[53] By contrast, studio audio art is liberated from the aspiration of involving people in performing together in real time and is valued more highly in accordance with the control and precision it exhibits in shaping the sonic object.[54]

While relativizing evaluative criteria to the subcategory of music involved in a particular case, Turino stresses the ubiquitous tendency of people to engage in participatory music-making. Different societies and smaller cohorts of individuals vary in how they value the four fields (that is, subcategories) of music. For example, presentational music (music performed for an audience that does not participate) is the predominant field in the contemporary United States. Nevertheless—and this is one of Turino's major points—participatory music-making is widespread throughout the world because it serves the human need for deep connection with other people.[55] The values endemic to participatory music—good social interaction, provisions to make newcomers comfortable and easily able to participate (such as a high degree of repetition, dense textures that cloak individuals contributions, formal predictability, redundant rhythm, room for a variety of levels of skill and experience (with both "an ever expanding ceiling of challenges" to keep the interest of the experienced as well as simple roles that novices can play), and deliberate efforts not to exclude others—are conducive to social bonding in a powerful way, and Turino argues that they are exhibited in this type of music throughout the world.[56] In that he believes that participatory music is valued in all societies to some extent, these values seem to be transcultural in one sense. At the same time, they are not appropriate to other subcategories of music that exist within the same society, such as presentational performance or studio audio art.

The upshot of our consideration of evaluative universals is that while some cross-cultural standards for evaluation do seem to exist, they do not exhaust the grounds on which instances of music are assessed within their cultures of origin. Part of the challenge of learning any form of seriously foreign music includes the discovery of what standards of evaluation are appropriate in the cultural context, and not all of these are cross-culturally evident. Nevertheless, the apparent existence of evaluative universals give us reason to think that at least some familiar values will be relevant for coming to understand what a culture esteems in its music.

CROSS-CULTURAL INTELLIGIBILITY

Impediments

The diversity of ways in which cultures shape their musical styles can be impediments to cross-cultural musical understanding. This need not be an absolute obstacle, however, even if we inevitably do bring our encultured expectations to bear on foreign music. Nicholas Cook rightly suggests that although we will need considerable exposure to another culture's music to really understand it, we can enjoy it on some level in the meantime.[57]

Davies points out that one kind of enjoyment of foreign music is not, strictly speaking, *musical* enjoyment.

> A person who listens to Balinese Gendèr Wayang, neither knowing nor caring why the sounds follow each other in the order they do, is someone who interests herself not in the music, but in the noise it makes. . . . If she is unable to anticipate what might or should be played next, feels no sense of closure on the completion of a piece, is incapable of identifying recurrence of material or of recognizing similarities and differences between parts of a work or between different works, then she does not appreciate the music qua music, though the music causes her enjoyment. This remains true in the case in which, rather than being indifferent to its organization, she radically misperceives the principles governing its generation. This is the position of an Occidental who listens to these Balinese pieces in terms of the musical conventions with which she is most familiar, those of tonal, Western music.[58]

Davies suggests some of the desiderata for understanding foreign music: (1) having some sense of why one musical event follows another, (2) being able to anticipate what musical event might follow, (3) having a sense of closure at the end of a piece of music, (4) recognizing material that recurs, (5) recognizing similarities and differences among the parts of the a piece, (6) recognizing similarities and differences among different works, and (7) not superimposing the presuppositions of one's own musical background on foreign music.

But what if we are simply unable to orient ourselves in foreign music? What obstacles stand in our way? A number of factors may be at work. One of these is discomfort in response to an unfamiliar timbre, the use of idiophones,[59] or even vocal techniques not employed in the music of one's own culture. When I first heard the sound of a didgeridoo, I did not immediately recognize that the sound came from a musical instrument. I thought that it might be computerized sound used to create an evocative soundscape for the movie I was watching. I was rather fascinated in this case, but I can imagine being disconcerted. The growling buzzyness characteristic of chants by Tibetan monks or the music played on the mbira (the African thumb piano) also differ markedly from timbres and vocal ideals in Western music, and it might sound disturbingly alien to someone who is only familiar with Western music.[60] While this basis for discomfort is superficial, it may still be a real impediment to attentive appreciation.

Two other interference factors derive directly from the nature of musical perception. We might find either the tuning system or the basic way of organizing the structure of the music too far removed from our instilled expectations. As we have noted, psychologists of music point out that memory for musical features involves schemas developed over time.[61] These include general knowledge of scales and allowable intervals, for example, and of how music behaves, as well as more specific knowledge, established while listening, of how the particular piece of music is behaving. While one is listening to music, therefore, one taps both long-term and short-term memory.

To claim that we have acquired schemata for scales implies that we are geared to the type of tuning our society uses. Being accustomed to the scales of one's own musical culture can seriously interfere with enjoying or even processing the intervals in another culture's music. Marc Perlman and Carol Krumhansl experimentally confirmed that many musicians among their subjects, from both Java and the West, assimilated intervals to "a set of interval standards," although some of the musicians from both cultures were able to identify the interval size of unfamiliar intervals with considerable accuracy."[62] Michael Lynch and Rebecca Eilers similarly indicate that culturally ingrained schemata can pose a problem for those who listen to unfamiliar foreign music.

> When a Western adult . . . listens to melodies based on non-Western scales . . . the intervals of the melodies will not necessarily match those of a culturally familiar schema, and this mismatch may cause the listener difficulty in processing and determining the interval structure of the melodies.[63]

Lynch and Eilers's experimental research suggests that children between the ages of ten and thirteen, whether or not they have been musically trained, already have sufficient acculturation with respect to the musical scales of their own culture that they are unable to identify mistuning in a nonnative scale. Western adult musicians were better able to identify mistunings in non-Western scales than the children, but they did less well than they did in identifying mistunings in Western scales.[64] David Huron claims that listeners "commonly . . . will form a broad category of 'otherness' into which all deviant stimuli are, by default, indiscriminately assigned."[65] Possibly the inability of the children studied to discriminate mistunings in nonnative scales stems from employment of this generalized category.

As an example of a case in which internalized schemata are misleading, consider the *tala* (or tempo) *tintal* in North Indian classical music. *Tintal* employs a cycle of sixteen beats. Westerners, who are accustomed to music in 4/4 time, tend to find this *tala* relatively accessible (by comparison, say, with *ektal*, which employs a cycle of twelve beats, or *dhamar*, which employs a cycle of fourteen beats); but they also tend to *hear tintal* as 4/4 time.[66] To hear *tintal* this way is to misunderstand the rhythmic cycle, which involves relative stress (referred to as *tali*, meaning "clap") on beats 1, 5, and 13, antistress (referred to as *khali*, meaning "empty") on beat 9, and a powerful gravitational impulse toward beat 1 (referred to as the *sam*, the most important beat structurally).[67] A Westerner hearing *tintal* as 4/4 time would think of the 9th beat as stressed, while in *tintal* it is the least stressed beat in the cycle. Even if Western musical training is something of a boon for learning Indian music, in that one has learned to recognize countable meter in the first place, it can also misdirect attention if the limits of its applicability are not recognized. Huron proposes that it is "difficult to form a new schema when the new context differs only slightly from an already established schema."[68] The difficulty with *tintal* for Western listeners is not that it is so different from any familiar rhythm but that it is too much like one of them.

The perceptual challenge posed by alien tuning may be more disorienting than one might at first expect. The reason for this is that when we hear a tone, as we have noted earlier, we do not hear a single pitch only, but we also hear many overtones. When one does not hear the fundamental tone as being in a familiar scale, one may have difficulty determining which of the many pitches heard actually is the fundamental.[69] Moreover, mismatch negativity, a brain wave response to perceived deviance, is evident even in cases in which the music is being ignored.[70]

The organization of musical structures elsewhere in the world may also be difficult to follow if they are unlike those with which one is familiar. Even seemingly observable patterns such as rhythm are not as immune to subjective factors as one might think. Pandora Hopkins's 1982 study of three master musicians of other cultures (from India, Greece, and the United States, respectively) listening to Norwegian *hardingfele* (fiddle) music demonstrates the musicians' use of interpretational frameworks in attempting to identify the rhythmic pattern in foreign music.

> The restructuring process resulted in the trying out of new and different possibilities—mental templates. . . . It is especially significant that this restructuring process was carried out by each musician according to the path already established in his or her initial responses to the material, determined, of course, by experience.[71]

All of these grounds for possible confusion or disorientation in foreign music may be correlated with cultural ideals and beliefs, themselves not necessarily familiar. Music's symbolic role in reflecting alien cultural ideals and assumptions is a fourth possible cause for difficulty in relating to foreign music, even if it is not perceptually disorienting. If music is a symbolic reflection and reinstatement of the network of roles within one's society, a foreign listener could conceivably find the style of interaction rather alien.[72]

Such characteristics are not necessarily disorienting. The characteristics to which Lomax attends are evident in the surface features of songs from a given culture. One need not reorient one's musical schemata in order to hear or recognize them. Moreover, different contexts within one's experience might call for different modes of interaction, acquainting one with other possibilities than that which predominates in one's cultural style of interaction. Although industrial societies tend toward hierarchical organization, this does not mean that situations the call for relatively egalitarian interaction—jury deliberation for example—are entirely lacking. Even if one might recognize that a style differs markedly from any evident in one's own society, this does not necessarily mean that it is hard to process. Nevertheless, the particular musical "image" of optimal human interaction can be startling. This is demonstrated by Feld's example, discussed in chapter 2, of Christian missionaries encountering Kaluli music and hearing, not a musical reflection of their favored interpersonal style, but hopeless unmusicality.

A fifth aspect of foreign music that can disturb a listener is alien ornamentation. The rapid yodel in some Hindustani vocal music might strike a Westerner as off-putting, perhaps especially if he or she cannot imagine how one could make one's voice produce it. Foreign ornament, however, may strike a listener as more familiar than alienating. Some features of musical ornamentation, although characteristic of a particular culture, may also have widespread currency throughout the world.

Ornament style, however, even when employing basic geometric pattern, sometimes serves as a signature for a particular culture (the Swiss yodel, for example). When an ornament style is recognizably that of a particular foreign culture, it may seem especially prominent. In this case, ornament style may assist the process of familiarization with another culture's music, even if one is becoming familiar with features that are distinctively foreign. One of the intriguing aspects of cultural ornament style is that it seems to permeate the various arts. The gesture of the Balinese dancer in which fingers are tilted back toward the wrist resembles the ornaments at the edges of many Balinese roofs and sculptures. Music, too, exhibits analogies with visual nuances of a culture's creative output. For example, the inverted turn ornament common in Irish music (in which a tone is sequentially decorated by its upper and lower neighbor tones) might be seen as resembling the visual pattern of the Celtic line (evident, for instance, on Celtic crosses), which curves to cross itself in one direction and then the opposite.

This reinforcement of particular ornamental tendencies across various arts can serve to reinforce a template or help the uninitiated become sensitized to a new template. It thus does not necessarily provoke a sense of alienation from a foreign culture, but it can actually help one to become more comfortable in it as one gains a sense of ease in the culture more generally. Nevertheless, the greatest comfort in recognizing such parallels is reserved for those who see the culture in question as their own. E. M. Forster's character Dr. Aziz in *A Passage to India* experiences a moment of soothing recognition along these lines. He steps into a mosque that he has always liked, and the narrator describes his state of mind.

A mosque by winning his approval let loose his imagination. The temple of another creed, Hindu, Christian, or Greek, would have bored him and failed to awaken his sense of beauty. Here was Islam, his own country, more than a Faith, more than a battle-cry, more, much more . . . Islam, an attitude toward life both exquisite and durable, where his body and his thoughts found their home.[73]

Like the mosque for Dr. Aziz, a society's ornament styles are signs of being at home to members of the culture. Nevertheless, Forster, a non-Muslim, is imaginatively projecting himself into the mind of someone from another religious and cultural background even to develop this character.[74]

Orienting Oneself in Foreign Music

Thus far we have considered several aspects of foreign music that may interfere with one's ability to easily relate to it. Among these are unfamiliar timbres, foreign tuning, exotic musical organization, alien symbolic contents, and disturbing ornamentation. To what extent can we overcome these difficulties?

One way is to develop new schemata that are appropriate for the type of unfamiliar music we encounter. Patel points out that "listeners unfamiliar with a new music are nevertheless sensitive to the statistical distributions of tones within the music, and can infer some structural relations on this basis."[75]

According to David Huron, we can and do develop new schemata for music. He contends that we utilize a variety of schemata in many contexts and often learn quickly that a schema is inappropriate in context. It doesn't take long to switch schema in such a context—this is precisely what we do when we scan radio stations, recognizing diverse styles as we hit upon various stations. Huron reports on an experiment by David Perrot and Robert Gjerdingen, which showed that listeners can often determine musical type in 250 milliseconds.[76] Huron attributes the acquisition of schemata for multiple types of music to statistical learning, that is, learning the basic characteristics of a style simply by means of exposure.[77] Huron suggests that failures in expectations are often the triggers that lead listeners to shift schema. They are also, he speculates, the basis for developing new schemata: "The persistent failure of expectations might well raise the alarm that a novel cognitive environment has been encountered and that the listener's existing palette of schemata is inadequate."[78]

The possibility of developing a new schema, however, depends on sufficient exposure for the type in question. If a Westerner's exposure is too limited, the person is likely to apply a general category such as "the rest" or "the exotic" to non-Western music instead of schemata appropriate to particular non-Western styles. Even if the person is able to discriminate with a bit more sophistication, insufficient exposure will result in failure to develop new schemata for specific foreign styles.[79]

The most obvious solution to these problems is to become conversant with particular unfamiliar musical idioms. Becoming acquainted with a culture's music is akin to learning a foreign language. The more one immerses oneself, the easier the process. Sometimes one will discover some features that resemble those of one's own culture's music. Davies mentions, for example, that

> the music of Africa, south of the Sahara, is easily approached by Westerners because it so often employs the equivalent of the major scale for its tonal organization. In addition, anyone familiar with the techniques of repeated motivic variation in folk, pop, and jazz musics, as well as in some "classical" music, will not find it difficult to understand how music for the *mbira* or *likembe* is put together.[80]

Such fortunate coincidences facilitate the project of gaining one's bearings, although it is important not to assume that music that is alike in some respects will be alike in all respects, as we noted above. Whether or not one is assisted by the presence of some familiar features, accounts provided by ethnomusicologists and others about how a culture's music is structured are useful tools that can assist the novice listener in knowing what to look for. Developing familiarity with another culture's music, however, is inevitably a gradual process.[81]

Prelinguistic infants are initially able to discriminate many more phonetic contrasts than they are later. As they learn a language, they appear to become desensitized to contrasts not employed in their mother tongue. Some experimental evidence suggests that infants learn to discriminate intervals in native scales more effectively than unfamiliar ones, but Trainor and Trehub have criticized the construction of the experiments that purportedly showed this.[82] If this pattern can be confirmed, it would show that a perceptual advantage for interpreting one's native music begins early. But this would not demonstrate that the challenge of learning to understand a foreign music is insurmountable.

As a matter of fact, experimental evidence seems to show just the opposite. Patel describes the emerging view as being "that the mental framework for sound perception is not a frozen thing in the mind, but is adaptive and is constantly tuning itself."[83] Huron, along with Paul von Hippel and David Harnish, offers some empirical evidence that statistical learning leads to improved performance in being able to predict the next tone in a foreign melody. Studying both Balinese and American subjects, who were presented with tones in Balinese scales and asked to bet on what the subsequent note would be, Huron and his colleagues found that Balinese subjects did considerably better than their American counterparts, which is unsurprising. However, American subjects became considerably more certain as to what the next note would be in a short time period. At about ten tones into the melody, the American subjects showed comparable confidence in guessing the next note as their Balinese counterparts.[84] Huron concludes that this experiment shows that the American subjects were making rapid headway in orienting themselves to the Balinese music: "Either the American musicians were able to adapt quickly to the unfamiliar music, or they were able to successfully apply intuitions formed by their extensive experience with Western music—or both."[85]

Even before very much exposure, the previously discussed fact that we experience music as animated can help guide our focus in alien music. We can ask ourselves, "How does it move?" In endeavoring to answer this question, we will tend to isolate particular streams in the music, distinguished perhaps by relative distance from each other in auditory space, or perhaps by distinctive timbres. We will also pay attention to whether or not there is a regular pulse, and whether a pattern of strong beats is recognizable.

Turino's characterization of participatory music suggests that music in that category is designed to facilitate acquaintance with the music for those who are unfamiliar with it. Presumably the transition is easier for those who are accustomed to the general style than for those who are not, but no previous experience is presupposed. This would suggest that a culture's participatory forms would be particularly inviting points of entry for foreigners to begin getting oriented in the culture's music. The evaluative universals, in general, offer bases for beginning to enjoy music that is significantly foreign. Both transcultural universals—such as the preference for symmetry, balance, and clarity—and pancultural universals—such as the preference for displays of vitality—can direct what we attempt to hear in foreign music as well as offer bases for taking pleasure in it.

Cultural Familiarity

The upshot of this and the previous chapter is that there are characteristic ways of sounding human. Even though the "universals" are at most constraints, with the consequence that music is extremely diverse, the general profile of human music is sufficient to afford us a way into foreign music. Of course, nothing can replace experience as a means of deepening one's understanding.

In efforts to understand music of types that are made in reidentifiable pieces, Davies emphasizes the importance of familiarity with the type of which it is an instance. For example, "because of differences between the conventions characterizing suites, symphonies, sonatas, concertos, and the like, hearing the work as the work it is involves hearing it in terms of conventions that apply to it as a symphony, as a concerto, or whatever."[86] While this principle is applicable to making acquaintance with musical forms in one's own culture, it is also relevant to efforts to understand unfamiliar music from other societies. Greater acquaintance with the music of a culture can help one to pick out what is predictable in generic terms as well as what musical events are surprising.

Getting acquainted with another culture more generally is also important for gaining deeper understanding of its music. The tendency to conjoin musical patterns with extramusical contents is a common denominator of human musical experience. This tendency of music is often exploited in rituals and in other contexts, most obviously by means of the apparently universal tendency to conjoin some music with words.[87] Harwood suggests that if there is anything that might be called a universal in such practices, it is music's symbolic role.

> Those theories of ritual which do suggest how music (and language) might play critical roles . . . stress the symbolic function: music occurs in ritual because it "signifies" other non-musical concepts involving human affect and communication.[88]

The symbolisms that cultures wed to music, however, are rarely transparent to outsiders. Thus the universality of musical symbolism is of mixed benefit for making sense of alien music.

One might simply fail to recognize a way that music is connected to other content within a foreign culture. Or one might learn something about content that the culture's music is conjoined with and be alienated by the specifics. After hearing and greatly enjoying Rhoma Irama's popular hit in 1980s Indonesia, "Sahabat" ("Friends"), I was moved to read the lyrics, provided by the CD insert. Then I was startled to discover that their theme was that one can only find true friends among those who share one's religion, specifically, Islam.[89] Music conjoined with messages that exclude one as an audience member may certainly interfere with cross-cultural musical enjoyment.

Alternatively, if the symbolic character of music is recognized, it can enrich our understanding of foreign music. Learning more about the culture that produced the music is likely to make the music more intelligible to a foreign listener. One might also discover musical associations with common human themes (such as longing or mourning) that one can relate to one's own experience. Some symbolisms may be cross-culturally common, grounded in some of the universals considered above. The association of music with human animation, for example, might be elaborated into more specific symbols that can be understood by outsiders without much difficulty.

Music's symbolic role is important for our purposes. It suggests an important interface between the universal and the culturally specific, since the content that music is taken to symbolize will presumably be culturally shaped, even if some aspects are more common. The idea of music as a symbol, however, also returns us to the theme with which we opened, the notion of music as a language. If music is symbolic, is it symbolic in anything like the way that language is? I will consider this question obliquely in the following chapter by reversing it: does language communicate like music does, or in some other way?

CHAPTER 5

The Music of Language

People suppose that words are different from the peeps of baby birds, but is there any difference, or isn't there?

CHUANG TZU, *The Complete Works of Chuang Tzu*

I wondered whether music might not be the unique example of what might have been—if the invention of language, the formation of words, the analysis of ideas had not intervened—the means of communication between souls.

MARCEL PROUST, *Remembrance of Things Past*

From the folk saying with which we began in chapter 1 to the contemporary psychology lab, music has often been compared to a language, particularly in connection with its universal aspects. "Music . . . is a kind of language which we speak and understand yet cannot translate," observes Eduard Hanslick.[1] Claude Lévi-Strauss, too, refers to music as "the only language with the contradictory attributes of being at once intelligible and untranslatable."[2] Wittgenstein is equivocal: "Music, some music at least, makes us want to call it a language; but some music of course doesn't."[3] Theodor Adorno characterizes music as "the most eloquent of all languages" even as he endeavors to explicate the dissimilarities between the two modalities.[4]

How plausible is this characterization of music as a language? That depends on what is meant and on how literally it is intended. Clearly, music and language have much in common. They both involve sound addressed to hearing and have rules for combining elements. The resulting strings of sound events are meaningful,[5] and both link human beings to the external world. Music and language have enough in common to justify metaphoric comparison.

But despite their similarities, the two modes are also different in ways that neuropsychology increasingly specifies. Patients with amusia (the loss of certain musical abilities) due to brain lesions do not necessarily develop aphasia (an inability to speak), nor do those with aphasia necessarily develop amusia.[6]

This suggests neurological dissociability of the two systems.[7] The two modes seem to involve separate brain areas, even if there is considerable overlap in the areas engaged.[8] Evolutionary theorists also stress the differences in the way the two systems operate, often arguing that language has evolutionary priority (in terms of importance), although there is much debate about whether either, neither, or both are evolutionary adaptations.[9]

As modes of communication, speech and music differ in their means and in what is communicated. Wittgenstein proposes, "one says of a piece of music: 'This is like some sentence, but what sentence is it like?'"[10] We can ask other questions, too. What in music resembles vocabulary? Where are music's parts of speech?

One might, I suppose, claim that music has affinity with a particular part of speech, specifically the preposition. Sequences of music have directionality, and the various ways this directionality proceeds might be described in terms of prepositions (above, beyond, during, etc.). The differences among musical idioms might also be compared to the different usage of equivalent prepositions in various languages. The prepositions used in one's native language feel "natural," while dissenting usage in foreign languages seems mildly perverse. I imagine that the *up* is appropriate in the expression *pick up*. Indeed, I can rationalize it, in that I do lift something when I pick it up. But what of the *up* in *shut up!*? Does it literally command one to lift one's jaw? The German pronouns *auf* (on, upon, at, in) and *zu* (to, toward, up) used for *open* and *shut* (shortened forms of *aufmachen* and *zumachen*) strike me, by contrast, as merely conventional, but I doubt that this is the impression of most native German speakers.[11]

Even if music might be compared to a language of prepositions, this would be a *language* in a very strange sense. A language with only one part of speech is unlike the languages people speak. Natural languages involve systematic interconnections among words assuming different roles. How would the terms in our all-preposition language be strung together? "Around, up, below, around." At most this seems like a series of directions to be followed. This string of words would have meaning only in conjunction with much that is implicitly understood.

And yet the *language* notion of music has taken root. It is particularly strong in recent times when many linguists and philosophers take language as the model for thought. I am convinced that music's centrality to human life is often obscured by the dominance of a linguistic model. If one describes music as a language, it is far too easy to assume that its role in human life is sufficiently investigated by elaborating its parallels with linguistic structures and meanings. Music's uniqueness can too easily be overlooked when it is examined through analytic grids designed in efforts to understand language.

In this chapter I will suggest that the linguistic model obscures some aspects of music's communicative powers. For example, music more holistically communicates an overall sense of intentional orientation than does language. At the same time, using language as a model for music obscures the extent to which linguistic communication relies on musical characteristics. While it may be true that our experience with language can illuminate certain features of music, it is also true that our experience with music can reveal certain features of language, features that are often underappreciated.

In order to draw attention to these omissions, I will engage in a thought experiment. I will reverse the model of the language-music comparison, suggesting, along with composer and musical semiotician David Lidov, that we might justly call language a music.[12] Lidov observes that a reversal of this sort is a bit facetious: "To claim today that musicology should encompass linguistics rather than the reverse can only be a literary ploy." Nevertheless, he concludes, "the musical aspect of speech is truly of its essence."[13]

I grant that my discussion in this chapter is a bit tongue in cheek, but my purposes are serious. One of these is to indicate that music has different communicative strengths than language, even though the two modes draw on some of the same capabilities. The other is to show that these strengths facilitate communication across language groups, supporting the suggestion that "music" can be a means by which we bridge our cultural barriers.

COMMON CHARACTERISTICS

Music and language are both universal human practices, and they share many characteristics.[14] Insofar as these are *shared* characteristics, they offer at least as much a warrant for claiming that language is a music as for claiming that music is a language. In what follows I will take spoken language to be the paradigmatic case, as I take performed music as paradigmatic.[15]

If we return to the list of musical processing universals discussed in chapter 3, we find that many of those not dealing with precise pitch are relevant to language perception as well. The first three are uncontroversially important for perceiving language.

1. We make a distinction between signals and noise, and we certainly make a distinction between spoken language and noise. Joseph P. Swain observes that languages, like music, exclude certain sounds. "Completely banned from all languages are laughs, whistles, and other vocal products that are simply

deemed to be nonlinguistic."[16] We do not make a similar distinction between music and language; we use the same stream of sound as both music and language in any song with words. We do not make the distinction between speech and noise, however, in the same way in every language. A study of brain response to speech and nonspeech suggested a differential response to clicks between Zulu and English speakers. The brains of Zulu speakers, who employ clicks in their language, responded to them as they did other speech sounds, while English speakers' brains did not.[17]

2. Human pitch perception is most accurate in the vibration range between 100 and 1,000 Hz. This universal determines the basic range in which spoken language can be understood as well as the basic range for musical sound.

3. We perceive linguistic information in "chunks." After some familiarization infants are able to distinguish between sequences of consonant-vowel clusters that are commonly used and those that are unusual. This suggests that they recognize spoken language in chunks and develop familiarity with those that occur frequently.[18]

Several other "universal" features of musical perception are also applicable to language, although this might not be immediately obvious in every case. Stating these perceptual factors as linguistic universals, they are as follows:

1. Linguistic signals are organized in terms of *melodic contour.*
2. *Categorical perception* is involved in our apprehension of phonemes and temporal intervals.[19]
3. Frameworks of *discrete scale pitches* are utilized, typically with uneven step size.
4. *Durations* of syllables are typically uneven.
5. *Rhythm* is more basic for making judgments of similarity of pattern than pitch.[20]
6. We employ *Gestalt principles* in grouping linguistic strings.

Let us consider these one by one.

Melodic Contour

Melodic contour is important in linguistic communication.[21] One occasionally has difficulty understanding one's native language when spoken by a person with a foreign accent. Sometimes the speaker's using nonstandard contour in shaping their words and phrases causes this. In Japan I experienced the other side of this situation. I was not getting the reaction I expected when I attempted to say thank you—*Domo aragato*. I was pronouncing *aragato* with an accent on the penultimate syllable, a typical accent pattern in Spanish, a language with which I am more familiar. I began to notice that the Japanese pronounce the word with an even stress on all the syllables. When I weighted the syllables more evenly in pronouncing *aragato*, the Japanese to whom I spoke seemed to understand me.

Melody also appears to express emotion in a similar way in both language and music.[22] Patrik Juslin and Petri Laukka, using 1,095 data points, suggest that rising pitch contours may correlate with "'active' emotions (e.g., happiness, anger, fear)" and falling contours with sadness and tenderness, which are less active.[23] More generally, emotion is conveyed by the similar prosodic cues in speech and music.[24] Prosody has to do with melodic nuances of speech, and it involves those features of vocal expression that are described as "tone of voice." It includes, as Steven Brown summarizes, "the local risings and fallings, quickenings and slowings, and loudenings and softenings that are involved in expressively conveying our meanings in a pragmatic sense."[25]

Juslin and Laukka show that similar patterns of "speech rate/vocal intensity, vocal intensity/sound level, and high frequency energy" are used to convey the same emotions in speech and in music. They found that "low pitch was associated with sadness in both vocal expression and musical compositions . . . whereas high pitch as was associated with happiness in both vocal expression and musical compositions." Fear and anger tend to be associated with high pitch, and tenderness with low pitch. They note a discrepancy between music and speech in expression of fear, since it is "commonly associated with high intensity in vocal expression, albeit low intensity (sound level) in music performance." They suggest, however, that the explanation for this divergence may be a function of experimental structure: studies of music performance may have focused on expressions of mild fear, while vocal expression studies may have focused on panic fear.[26]

The human neurological system is highly specialized for recognizing tone of voice. Psychologist Isabelle Peretz has established that this recognition is dissociable from both evaluation of the emotional content of facial expression and from recognition of semantic information.[27] Patel suggests that the main difference between speech and song contours is that speech contours rarely attract attention and tend not to be very intricate. Citing Simon Shaheen's characterization of melody as "a group of notes that are in love with each other," Patel submits that by contrast "a speech melody is a loose affiliation of tones (or pitch movements) that work together to get a job done."[28]

In addition to its value for word recognition and emotional expression, prosody in language is also important for conveying information about syntax.[29] Prosody apparently helps listeners parse incoming speech, a matter of particular importance in the case of ambiguous sentences (e.g., "The girl met the husband of the woman who was on steroids"). Prosody helps disambiguate such statements by indicating grouping patterns.[30] S. G. Nooteboom and J. G. Kruyt asked subjects to indicate the acceptability of accent patterns for presenting new information. Their results indicate that subjects expected new information to be indicated by acoustical emphasis.[31]

Categorical Perception

Categorical perception applies to language as well as to music. Just as we tend to hear both pitches and durations categorically in music, we also categorically perceive the phonemes of language. Sloboda observes, "From sounds which vary continuously on a number of dimensions we extract a few categories into which all normal speech sounds are assigned."[32] Some training seems to be required before listeners perceive pitch categorically, while exposure (presumably in early life) seems to be sufficient to develop categorical perception of the phonemes of one's native language.[33]

We tend to utilize the habits we have for segmenting speech even in cases of listening to a language we don't understand.[34] One consequence is that we have difficulty hearing certain distinctions in languages that divide up the sound continuum in an unfamiliar manner.[35] In some languages, duration is also organized categorically. For example, in Dutch, long and short vowels are distinguished in this way. Categorical perception is so important in speech that according to Nelson Goodman, syntax would be impossible without it.[36]

We normalize irregularities in both language and music by inserting sounds that make the acoustic signal easier to recognize. In experiments conducted by Richard M. Warren and Roslyn P. Warren, subjects were told that a phoneme would be missing from a recorded sentence. The sentence used the word "legislatures," but in the recording the first /s/ was replaced with noise. The subjects did not register the phoneme as missing, and instead heard the word "legislatures." Similarly, when subjects were presented with noise before "eel" in various sentential contexts, they variously heard "'wheel,' 'heel,' 'peel,' and 'meal,' to complete the sentence in the most sensible way."[37]

In both speech and music, listeners similarly insert a sound to clarify the harmonic situation in the phenomenon of the missing fundamental. This is the case in which a number of the harmonics of a tone (the fundamental) are heard, but the tone itself is not presented. Despite the absence of the tone, the human ear hears the fundamental, so long as it is in the frequency range of about 20–2,000 Hz.[38] Dowling and Harwood point out that this phenomenon occurs frequently in our everyday experience, for "telephones do not transmit the fundamental frequencies of male speakers, and yet that has no effect on the perceived pitches of their voices over the phone."[39] The number of harmonics necessary to produce this effect varies; fewer are required if one is hearing fairly low-numbered harmonics, that is, early harmonics within the overtone series.[40]

Discrete Scale Pitches

The idea that language utilizes scales of discrete pitches as frameworks may seem improbable, at least for languages such as English that are not "tonal" languages. A tonal language is a language in which the relative pitch and inflection affect the meaning of a word. Mandarin Chinese, or *putonghua*, is an example of a tonal language. It has four tones, and distinct words are produced when what would in English be the "same" syllable is pronounced in the various tones. *Ma* when pronounced with the first (high, level) tone can mean, among other things, *mother*.[41] Pronounced with the second (ascending) tone, *ma* can mean *hemp*. Pronounced with the third (dipping) tone (a low tone that descends and then quickly reascends), *ma* can mean *horse*. Pronounced with the fourth tone (which descends from a high beginning) *ma* can mean *to scold*.[42]

However, according to the consensus theory in phonology, the autosegmental theory of intonation, pitch plays an important role as a semantic device in nontonal languages as well as in tonal ones. The autosegmental theory resolved a debate about whether intonation is a matter of movement between discrete pitch levels or whether it involves pitch movement, without reference to level tones. The autosegmental theory, as Steven Brown characterizes it, claims that "phonological events should be modeled as sequential movements between discrete pitch levels, often only two levels, High and Low, and that all movements between them should be reduced to the status of transitions, rather than primary phonological events of importance."[43] In other words, specific levels of pitch are of primary importance. They serve as targets, with movement between them amounting simply to a means of getting from one to another.

The autosegmental theory implies that level tones are central to intonational languages, and thus that the use of tones is not unique to tonal languages (which, we should note, sometimes employ nonlevel tones). It also regards "all spoken utterances as series of steps from one level tone to the next."[44] Brown cites studies showing that speakers of the same language tend to standardize their pitches when reading the same passage.[45] The conclusion to be drawn, he claims, is that "speech, like music, is based on scales consisting of discrete pitch levels. The major difference between speech and music in this regard is that these scales change quite a bit during speech (e.g., when pitch levels change) and thus so do the level tones themselves."[46]

As Brown observes, some intonational languages move between just two pitches. This pattern resembles those musical cultures mentioned in chapter 3 that utilize only two tones in their music. In tonal languages, more scale pitches are often utilized. In Mandarin Chinese, employing four tones, we can easily distinguish at least a high, a low, and perhaps two more moderate pitches (the target pitch of the ascending and descending tones). Cantonese, which uses nine tones, includes a middle pitch area as well.[47] The number of pitches in a speech scale seems, however, to abide by a restriction in number of pitches, as would be expected given the limits of individuals' comfortable speaking range.

Uneven Syllable Lengths

The duration of syllables in speech is typically uneven. Bruce Richman observes that both music-making and speaking depend on the ability to repeat sequences exactly. He emphasizes that speech, like music, uses formulaic patterns, or "open-slot formulas."[48] To develop the ability for exact repetition in either case, one must attend to a regular beat, which presupposes uneven temporal durations.[49] Those of us who used memorized dialogues to learn a foreign language have experienced firsthand the usefulness of such formulas. Once a dialogue is memorized, each of its sentences serves as a template for constructing novel statements in the new language. The uneven syllable lengths in speech, as in music, make possible the distinctive rhythmic patterns on which phrasing and open-slot formulas depend.

Rhythm

Although I know of no direct evidence, it seems plausible that temporal patterns are more important for remembering linguistic sequences than specific timing cues. Indeed, a frequently taught mnemonic device for memorizing strings of words is to repeat them in a distinctive rhythm. I can still recite about half of a memorized list of English prepositions, and I am fairly certain that my recall depends on the rhythmic pattern my eighth grade teacher taught our class to use. Janellen Huttenlocher and Deborah Burke show that grouping series of digits into rhythmic groupings improved the memories of children four to eleven years of age for the sequences.[50]

In any case, rhythm is fundamental to linguistic communication. A number of studies indicate that individuals synchronize their "gestures, postures, and rapidly changing body movements" to the speech rhythm, usually without being aware that they are doing so.[51] Successful everyday conversation depends on rhythm, as Stanford Gregory demonstrates.[52] The rhythm of successful talk generates solidarity among participants, who tune in to a common rhythm of speech. People tend to doubt they are being comprehended if the conversational rhythm is broken.[53]

On the basis of films of interactions, William Condon and Louis Sander observe such conversational synchrony across cultures.

> Interactional synchrony appears with frame-by-frame analysis as the precise dancelike sharing of micro-body-motion patterns of change between speaker and listener. Like self-synchrony, it has been observed in all normal human interaction thus far studied, including films of Mayans, Kung Bushmen, Eskimos, among others. It has also been observed in group behavior, for example, seven listeners moving in synchrony with an eighth who was talking.[54]

Gestalt Principles

Gestalt grouping patterns should apply to speech as well as to music.[55] Lerdahl applies the principles formulated in his and Jackendoff's generative musical grammar to poetry. The meter of both poetry and music involves a hierarchy of beats, with beats at one level being subdivided into two to three beats at the level below. This means that although cultures differ in which metrical patterns they prefer, "cultural variation on poetic and musical meters is intrinsically limited," for "the possible combinations of two and three, across or within levels, are very small."[56] The tendency to construct musical rhythms on the basis of patterns of twos and threes corresponds to a comparable tendency in language.

Other Similarities

In addition to these characteristics of perception that are applicable to speech and music, the two modes of communication are linked by certain other similarities. Like music, speech involves rules for conjoining elements, collectively termed "combinatorial syntax." Brown offers the following characterization of combinatorial syntax: "a limited repertoire of discrete units is chosen out of an infinite number of possible acoustic elements, such that phrases are generated through combinatorial arrangements of these unitary elements." On the level of syntax, then, music and language both have a grammar.[57]

To this we can add the relevance of context for the acoustic properties of both musical tones and phonemes. Swain observes that the production of a particular phoneme depends on what is before or after it, and he offers the persuasive example of the way "I have to" sounds in practice like "I hafta," which he analyzes as follows:

> The conversion occurs because the vocal tract is getting ready to pronounce /t/ in the next word, which is a voiceless consonant. If the voicing does not "turn off," /t/ will come out /d/, and usually the voicing cuts out prematurely to ensure that this does not happen. This extremely common phenomenon, called co-articulation, does not impair listener comprehension in the slightest, but it does imply that sound items cannot operate in a completely primitive manner, from the ground up.[58]

The many parallels just discussed may suggest some of the ways that music and language are on a par. But is there any ground for tipping the balance toward claiming, as I propose, that language is a music instead of the reverse? Yes, there is. Language presupposes musical sensitivities, both developmentally and operationally.

LANGUAGE PRESUPPOSES MUSICAL CAPABILITIES

Language relies on our musical capacities. To begin with, our first steps toward learning language depend on its musical characteristics. Musical sensitivity is evident earlier, and we learn language, initially, through its "musical" features, such as pitch and rhythm patterns and melodic contour, features that infants attend to.[59] Recognition of these characteristics is developmentally a prerequisite to learning meaningful language. Developmental psychologist Hanus Papousek claims that "musical elements . . . pave the way to linguistic capacities earlier than phonetic elements."[60] According to Dowling and Harwood, "Nine-month-olds have been observed to babble using the sentence intonation contours of adult English."[61] I suspect that many people besides myself have witnessed prelinguistic toddlers mimic telephone conversations on exactly this basis.

Not only do babies pay most attention to the melodic characteristics of language; caregivers also go out of their way to emphasize these musical characteristics of speech when they speak to infants.[62] Trehub describes this infant-directed style of speaking, or "motherese."

> Caregivers the world over enhance their vocal messages to prelinguistic infants by making them more musical than usual. They use simple but distinctive pitch contours but articulate words poorly; they raise their pitch level, slow their tempo, and make their utterances more rhythmic and repetitive compared with their conventional speech patterns. . . . In general, playful speech to infants embodies high pitch and expanded pitch contours that are rising or rise-fall in shape; soothing speech involves low pitch, a reduced pitch range, and pitch contours that are level or falling. . . .
>
> The pervasiveness of musical features in infant-directed utterances led several investigators to characterize these utterances as melodies.[63]

As examples of this kind of infant-directed speech, one might consider the utterances of television's *Teletubbies*, a series aimed at children as young as one year old. Although the *Teletubbies* seem to be speaking, at times their speech is hard to distinguish from singing.[64] Some theorists have suggested that babies seem to have innate predispositions to attend to the exaggerated intonation that this infant-directed speech employs.

Such patterns of prosody are strongly correlated with specific communicative intentions. For example, caregivers use descending pitch to soothe a baby; rising pitch to attract attention and provoke a response; and bell-shaped pitch contour to maintain attention. Infant behavioral responses to these prosody patterns vary appropriately. Although comparative linguistic studies have been limited, they have nevertheless supported the hypothesis that prosodic patterns are used to convey communicative intentions across language groups.[65]

Musical features of caregivers' speech and behavior, such as rhythm and style of movement, also enable infants to attune themselves to their caregivers.[66] Insofar as the development of speech depends upon a sense of interaction with another person, the engagement of these musical characteristics is necessarily a prolegomena to language. Condon and Sander studied newborns and concluded that they are rhythmically entrained to their caregivers' speech:

If the infant, from the beginning, moves in precise, shared rhythm with the organization of the speech structure of his culture, then he participates developmentally through complex, sociobiological entrainment processes in millions of repetitions of linguistic forms long before he will later use them in speaking and communicating. By the time he begins to speak he may already have laid down within himself the form and structure of the language system of his culture. This would encompass a multiplicity of interlocking aspects: rhythmic and syntactic "hierarchies," suprasegmental features, paralinguistic nuances, not to mention body-motion styles and rhythms.[67]

On this view, our communication with other human beings, whatever system it employs, presupposes the bond effected by the musical capacity for rhythmic entrainment.

In a series of experiments by Jacques Mehler and his colleagues, infants as young as four days old were able to distinguish their native language from a different language, while they were unable to distinguish utterances in two foreign languages.[68] The babies were more aroused by utterances in the native language, as indicated by the faster rate at which they sucked on their pacifiers. On the basis of several studies indicating that some sound from speech reaches infants in utero, although reduced in frequency range and intensity,[69] Mehler and his colleagues tested very young infants with highly filtered versions of recordings in the native language and one that was nonnative. The infants were able to discriminate preferentially in favor of their native language. This suggests that prosodic cues play an important role in the infants' responses, since those were the only cues available on the filtered tapes. The experimenters conclude that prosody is sufficient for infants to discriminate the two languages.[70]

Adults, too, understand other speakers largely by virtue of the rhythmic and melodic characteristics of their speech. We have already noted that the importance of melodic contour for speech comprehension is evident in the difficulty we have in understanding someone with a radically different accent. Anne Fernald, Rainer Banse and Klaus Scherer, and others have conducted experiments to determine whether adults could determine communicative intent in speech electronically filtered so that the words were unintelligible.[71] Fernald's experiment demonstrated that adults more easily recognize communicative intent through the exaggerated intonations of infant-directed speech than through adult-directed speech, and that consistent patterns of prosodic cues convey intents such as warning or comforting.[72] Banse and Scherer found good recognition of intended emotions in the vocal qualities of actors speaking meaningless "words" composed of Indo-European phonemes, although certain emotions, in particular shame and disgust, were not easily recognized using exclusively vocal cues.

The Neo-Futurists, a Chicago theater group, demonstrate the extent to which intonation conveys communicative intent in a production called *Too Much Light Makes the Baby Go Blind*, which is actually thirty plays in sixty minutes. In one of these plays, two actors interact for two minutes. Their lines consist only of descriptions of utterance types, spoken with the inflection appropriate to the type. For example, the actors would say, in appropriate intonation, "agreement," "overconfident statement," "elaborated defensive excuse," "self-assured agreement as denial," and "aggressive childish insult." One has the impression of a real interaction because the actors use prosody to convey the communicative intent in each utterance.[73] The play impresses one as extremely witty because it underscores the near irrelevance of the specific words, so long as their affective intent is conveyed.

That musical factors have priority in matters of comprehension is indicated by cases in which the accents or contour patterns of words are distorted to preserve musical shape and pattern. William Bright cites examples from the Navajo and from the Lushai of northwest India.[74]

> Although the latter have a tonal language, they sometimes allow musical pitch patterns to override word pitch completely, so that a word which has rising pitch in speech may have any type of falling or level pitch in singing.... This is true not only in modern songs, which often copy European melodies, but also in traditional songs. The Lushai claim, however, that they can understand the meanings of song lyrics even when the word pitches are effaced in this way.[75]

A study by Stefan Koelsch and his colleagues contends that music can even suggest specific verbal content by activating brain mechanisms that are involved in processing word meaning.[76] Koelsch and his colleagues consider whether music can prime meaning for particular words, as sentences in language can. Priming means presenting a stimulus that facilitates the subsequent processing of another stimulus. A sentence can prime the processing of words that have related meaning. For example, a sentence about boating might prime the word *water*. In the Koelsch study, experimenters wanted to determine whether presenting a sequence of music could facilitate the processing of particular words, as they suspected. "Intuitively, it seems plausible that certain passages of Beethoven's symphonies prime the word *hero*, rather than the word *flea*."[77] Their findings confirm that music can suggest particu-

lar verbal meanings when the musical sounds resemble the sounds or qualities of objects, or when they resemble prosodic or gestural cues. In addition,
they found that musical styles or forms could prime meaning for associated
words (such as a hymn priming *devotion*)."[78] Other musical means that allegedly convey specific verbal content are the use of instruments that mimic
speech patterns (such as talking drums) and whistled speech. Patel notes that
the latter has been alleged to convey very specific messages about what should
be done in a particular situation, and that the "speech" of *krar*, a five-stringed
instrument, in southwest Ethiopia is used to describe the position of objects
by imitating the tones used in speech.[79]

Besides the fact that musical factors facilitate the acquisition and comprehension of language, another reason suggests that music may be a more deep-
seated communication system than language. Extensive evidence shows that
many patients who lose the ability to speak can express themselves by singing.[80] Words that are unavailable to them in the form of speech can nevertheless
be accessed while they are singing. A study by Martin Albert, Robert Sparks,
and Nancy Helm, for example, describes patients with Broca's aphasia (the
inability to speak due to lesions in the part of the brain termed Broca's area)
who could nevertheless learn to sing what they wanted to communicate.[81]

Musical ability is presupposed in language acquisition, involved in linguistic communication among adults, and is a means whereby speech-deprived
patients can express their thoughts. On the basis of this evidence, I concur
with ethnomusicologist Charles Seeger when he claims, "Music, though not
a universal language, is without question more nearly universal in all senses of
the word, including world-wide perspective, than speech."[82]

THE ENTRENCHMENT OF THE MUSIC
AS LANGUAGE MODEL

Historical Background

Why, then, does the MUSIC AS LANGUAGE model continue to hold sway, while
David Lidov and I are able to suggest the LANGUAGE AS MUSIC metaphor
only provocatively? A confluence of intellectual developments has promoted
the tendency to see music on the model of languages. The rise of instrumental
music in the eighteenth century was a development that many found hard
to understand. Prior to the eighteenth century, the assumption was that music served important educational purposes, usually accomplished through
words set to music. The comparison of music to language gained prominence

in this context, for it was offered as an apology for instrumental music on its own.[83]

Several developments in twentieth-century anglophone philosophy have also encouraged the tendency to think of music as a language, among them Wittgenstein's analysis of language games. A language, according to Wittgenstein, is like a game in which the significance of each element is established by the entire practice that constitutes the game. Similarly, the meaning of the word comes from the way it is used, not from its correspondence with a thing in the world or some mental idea. Language learning involves becoming initiated into the rules of the "game"; that is, one learns the contexts in which particular expressions are used and how words relate to people's actions. Meaning is not something to be discovered by philosophical analysis; instead, it is evident in the way people use words within particular communities. If one adopts Wittgenstein's account of language as a practice within a community's way of life, the suggestion that music is a language would emphasize music's acquisition of meaning by virtue of the way it functions in a social context.

Another trend that has encouraged the "language" view of music is the position of some contemporary philosophers that language is a formal system. Like natural languages, on this view, artificial languages have well-defined rules for the use of the symbols of the language and for indicating when strings of symbols can be take as equivalent. The grammaticality and interpretation of any string of symbols in such a language is established according to whether it follows those rules. An interpretation of a string of symbols in an artificial language is typically a string of symbols itself. Artificial languages invite comparison with music in that neither tracks objects and occurrences in the external world, as natural languages do. They also can be said to refer in the same way: just as strings of formal language refer to other such strings, a musical "utterance" refers to other music.

A comparison of music to formal language in this way, however, illustrates the way that the model emphasizes some features of music at the expense of others. The features of music that seem most relevant if one emphasizes this comparison are its formal, systematic, and rule-governed characteristics. What is left out is the actual performance of music, the context, and the performer's communicative gestures.

J. L. Austin's speech act theory is a third development in twentieth-century philosophy of language that has encouraged a comparison of language and music.[84] Austin's claims that language plays many social functions in addition to transferring information, such as performing an action (e.g., making a vow) or affecting the listener (e.g., persuading or irritating the person), strike some philosophers as relevant to music. Music can similarly accomplish certain extramusical goals (e.g., alerting), and it often affects the listener's state of mind.

In linguistics, Noam Chomsky's overthrow of the empirical theory of language acquisition in favor of a theory of an inherited linguistic faculty has also reinforced the language model of music (as well as providing new motivation for considering the universal features of music). Chomsky holds that human minds all recognize certain relational patterns that they express in language, using an innate grammar of transformation rules that operate in all languages. These are rules that enable one to change the surface structure of an utterance without changing its meaning. In addition to enabling us to learn a language, according to Chomsky, they enable us to form novel utterances within it.

The idea of an innate faculty of music, akin to the Chomskian faculty of language, was proposed by Leonard Bernstein in his series of Norton Lectures at Harvard, titled *The Unanswered Question*.[85] He argues that we inherit musical transformation rules as well as linguistic ones, and thus have an innate grammar of music.[86] Bernstein compares elements of music to those of language, the note being like a phoneme, the motive like a noun, the notes added to chords like adjectives, and rhythm like a verb.[87] The natural sentence is like the musical phrase. Music and language both have syntax, and importantly, a sequence of musical events, like a string of language, has meaning that can be preserved despite changes in the musical surface. Thus composers are able to develop thematic material by deleting, extending, ambiguating, transposing, ornamenting, and such, without listeners losing track of its relationship to the originally stated theme.

Inspired by Bernstein, musicologist Fred Lerdahl and linguist Ray Jackendoff set out to formulate our innate musical grammar. Their impressive study, *A Generative Theory of Tonal Music*, articulates principles used by experienced listeners to make sense of tonal music. Listeners analyze musical input at several levels, from small-scale patterns of pitch and rhythm to highly abstract levels of structure.[88] The grammar Lerdahl and Jackendoff present involves rules for analyzing incoming "musical signals" in terms of structural patterns of time span, meter, grouping, and pitch prolongation. In practice the process is mostly unconscious, Lerdahl and Jackendoff assert, but listeners process the music they hear by applying these principles.

The grammatical rules Lerdahl and Jackendoff articulate are various, including both syntactic rules, which determine when a particular musical sequence is well formed, and preference rules, which determine what tones or structures listeners prefer to hear. They base these rules on principles of Gestalt psychology, which they take to be universal despite the restricted focus of their discussion (tonal music). Lerdahl and Jackendoff present tree analyses of works and passages of music, akin to the type of analysis that linguists give to sentences, showing the relative dominance and subordination relations of the musical elements. Their work reinforces the tendency to compare music to language and to describe it in terms of such linguistic notions as grammar and syntax.[89]

Along similar lines, I should mention the inspiration that some have drawn from the field of semiotics, the systematic study of signs and signification, in articulating an interpretation of music as a kind of language.[90] Some semioticians (e.g., Roland Barthes) interpret music as a language of gestures, while others (e.g., Jean-Jacques Nattiez) focus on the deep structure that they believe can be ascertained through careful analysis of the surface characteristics of music.[91] In any case, the semiotic approach to music encourages the application of the terminology of semantics, syntax, and pragmatics to music.

A further intellectual development that has helped to entrench the language model of music is recent work on metaphor by linguist George Lakoff and philosopher Mark Johnson. They propose that we make use of basic conceptual metaphors in structuring our experience, such as ARGUMENT IS WAR and MIND IS A MACHINE.[92] Inspired by their work, musicologist Justin London has explicitly suggested that the notion "MUSIC IS LANGUAGE" is such a metaphor, enabling us to make our way in music.[93]

Language as More Important

The idea of music as a type of language is also reinforced, by the recent growth of interest in the evolution of language. Given that music and language utilize similar human capabilities, efforts to ascertain the evolutionary history of language commonly compare the two systems, often concluding from their dissimilarities that language is a more foundational feature of human life. Steven Pinker takes this tack in his popular book *How the Mind Works*, where he claims that music is "auditory cheesecake, an exquisite confection crafted to tickle the sensitive spots of at least six of our mental faculties," which he goes on to itemize.[94] Despite its multifaceted ability to entertain, Pinker concludes that music, unlike language, is really inessential to human experience:

> As far as biological cause and effect are concerned, music is useless. It shows no signs of design for attaining a goal such as long life, grandchildren, or accu-

rate perception and prediction of the world. Compared with language, vision, social reasoning, and physical know-how, music could vanish from our species and the rest of our lifestyle would be virtually unchanged.[95]

The claim that music is useless is a veritable mantra. In *The Principles of Psychology*, William James claims that "susceptibility to music . . . has no zoological utility."[96] In *The Life of Reason*, George Santayana asserts, "Music is essentially useless, as is life."[97] Charles Darwin remarks in *The Descent of Man*, "As neither the enjoyment nor the capacity of producing musical notes are faculties of the least use to man in reference to his daily habit of life, they must be ranked amongst the most mysterious with which he is endowed."[98]

Music's supposed uselessness is not necessarily intended as disparaging, however, as Santayana's comment suggests.[99] But most of those who, like Pinker, think that music is an evolutionary by-product stress its costliness from the standpoint of survival. It makes those who practice it more evident at a distance, and hence more vulnerable to predators. Musical expertise takes considerable time and effort to cultivate, both of which might be spent on more obviously useful pursuits.

I will not engage in the debate about music's evolutionary status here.[100] Instead I will consider one of the grounds on which music is sometimes compared unfavorably to language in terms of its usefulness as a mode of communication, the fact that music lacks the kind of semantics that language has. Items in music do not seem to refer to objects and events in the world by means of a systematically meaningful vocabulary.[101] Neurologist R. A. Henson observes that "the capacity of musical language to represent exactly is extremely limited in contrast with speech."[102]

The upshot for many in the current era is that when it is compared to language, music seems to be a deficient language. The main thing we find useful in language is its ability to refer systematically to particular meanings. Those who consider music to be "useless" usually consider language to be our fundamental tool, seemingly because language can embody precise meanings.

Some theorists are not willing to concede that music lacks semantics. One tack is to claim that music does have a kind of semantics, an "affective semantics" that connects musical sound to specific emotional character. Along these lines Diana Raffman refers to music's "quasi-semantics" with respect to the emotional feelings that particular musical structures inspire.[103] Jean Molino similarly contends that music involves rhythmo-affective semantics, "which involves the body, its movements, and the fundamental emotions that are associated with them."[104] Others acknowledge certain semantic resources in music, such as the ability to take on wordlike meanings (as is the case with Wagner's leitmotifs) and its ability to refer to other music.[105]

One's inclination to consider music as having semantics on any of these grounds probably depends on how strictly one wants to define "semantics." Graham McFee contends that insofar as music is meaning-bearing, it has semantics: "as with meaning for words, attributing meaning to music is ascribing a semantics."[106] But this is an overly permissive use of the term. On this point I agree with Scruton, who argues that to demonstrate a musical semantics would require showing how musical structures connect with particular meanings.[107]

If music lacks a full-blown semantics, does that render music an almost-language, a language wannabe that doesn't mean anything? Not at all. Granted, music does not encode meaning in a manner comparable to the way that language does. But this is not necessarily a disadvantage for music. If we acknowledge the difference between the two systems, we should acknowledge their different virtues.

I am hardly the first to suggest that music's lack of a robust semantics is no deficiency. Historically, in fact, those who attended to this lack often thought it redounded to music's stature. The idea of music's ineffability—its untranslatability into words—has often been taken as a symptom of an inadequacy on the part of language. Although the suggestion that music is a language was offered as a defense of the legitimacy of instrumental music, music's nonsemantic character became associated by some late eighteenth-century and many Romantic theorists with "spontaneity, immediacy, prereflexivity." Such thinkers construed these characteristics as grounds for valuing music as superior to language, communicating in immediacy what language could only convey in a mediated way.[108] E. T. A. Hoffmann expresses this view, albeit through his own version of the MUSIC IS LANGUAGE metaphor: "Is not music the mysterious language of a distant realm of spirits, whose wondrous accents, echoing within us, awaken us to a higher, more intensive life?"[109]

This association of music with prearticulate experience stands in tension with the view, defended by Felix Mendelssohn and Susanne Langer, that music communicates with greater precision than language, though this view could be based on the idea that the sensuous surface of music, but not language, communicates the topography of feeling.[110] Importantly, the Romantics' praise for musical ineffability reverses the evaluation of thinkers such as Hegel and many of his eighteenth-century predecessors, who judged both music and language in terms of their ability to articulate the structures of reality in objective terms and gave the laurels to language.[111] As Andrew Bowie sums up this view:

> For eighteenth-century representational theories there is always a verbal equivalent of what music says, the apparently non-representational aspect of music being catered for by an underlying representational or mimetic conception of language as that which can render explicit what is only implicit in the music.[112]

The Romantics' view, by contrast, celebrated music's sensuous directness, holding the conceptual clarity of language to be achieved at the sacrifice of the prelinguistic and prereflective. John Hamilton describes the praise of music's ineffability as preserving a distinction between language and music in order "to protect the nonsemantic from the crime of symbolization."[113] The Romantics' enthusiasm for music's seeming resistance to conceptual confinement, as opposed to the tidy classification schemes of language, is akin to their fascination with the sublime as opposed to the beautiful.

In contemporary times, Leonard Bernstein and Diana Raffman are among those who see music's lack of a languagelike semantics as an asset. Bernstein does not hesitate to use the term "semantics" in reference to music, although he does not use the term in a technical sense.[114] He means that music has genuine meanings. In his argument that music shows remarkable parallels with language, he claims that it is more like poetry than everyday speech. Music lacks the denotative character of language but retains the connotative, and this, he argues, is where its poetic character lies.[115] Music's lack of a distinct vocabulary, coupled with its insinuation of tensions that could be resolved in a variety of ways, makes it ambiguous and thereby particularly expressive. Even poetic language is more expressively restricted than music. When poetry involves ambiguity, because multiple alternative meaning structures are at work, the meaning structures must remain more or less compatible to avoid a mixed metaphor. Music has fewer restrictions in this respect, since one does not have explicit denotative meaning structures that must be reconcilable.

Raffman similarly rejects the idea that music's lack of semantics is a liability for music. She accepts the language metaphor but argues that music is a language that bypasses semantics.[116] Indeed, her explicit concern is with musical ineffability, music's ability to provoke experiences that exceed our linguistic capacity. Raffman distinguishes three types of musical ineffability. *Structural ineffability* is the impossibility of definitively articulating certain high-level structural characteristics of a piece of music, caused by the fact that at the most abstract level, musical structure is susceptible to multiple analyses (and thus to different interpretations in performance). *Feeling ineffability* is the listener's inability to articulate the sensory-perceptual "feel" of a performed piece of music to someone who does not have the same sensory-perceptual experience.

The kind of ineffability of most interest to Raffman is *nuance ineffability*, the impossibility of linguistically articulating the details of musical performance that occur on the level of differences too fine-grained to be captured by the analytical framework of musical grammar.[117] These differences are thus in principle ineffable. The discriminations our perceptual apparatus can make and our memories for nuance are both limited, so we are not able to reidentify nuances or categorize them into types to the extent that would be necessary to systematize what we know of them.

As the very topic of musical ineffability suggests, the breakdown of the analogy between music and language is the point at which Raffman's model becomes most interesting. She denies that there is a level for language that is comparable to the nuance level of music. Actually, I think there is such a level, but only for spoken language. The nuances of the way a particular individual articulates a given phrase in language are fine-grained in a way that is comparable to musical articulation.[118] This is so, in my view, because language at this point is functioning musically. In other words, the nuances occur with respect to the shaping of the sounds rather than the shaping of meaning.

Language functions musically (as opposed to referentially) in some other ways as well. In discussing the relevance of Austin's speech act theory for music, London claims that even absolute music can perform what Austin defines as the "behabitive" class of speech acts.[119] This is a miscellaneous class that includes, according to Austin, speech acts that "have to do with attitudes and social *behaviour*."[120] London mentions "warnings, threats, greetings, etc." He notes that these "often involve little or no propositional content" and are performed in the present tense. He also contends that these are

> speech acts which are strongly marked by intonation as well as other paralinguistic features. . . . Thus behabitives . . . require the listener to attend to the "musical" qualities (pitch, tone of voice, loudness, rhythm, and articulation) of the locution in order to comprehend the illocutionary act.[121]

In my opinion, these are cases in which language functions like music. The same is true in the case of some Russian soldiers in Leo Tolstoy's *War and Peace* mimicking the phonetic sounds and intonations of French while pseudo-addressing French soldiers for their own amusement. Tolstoy tells us that "the soldiers burst into a roar of such hearty, jovial laughter that the French could not help joining them."[122] A similar example is John Searle's account of an American soldier who recited a line from Goethe in order to convince his Italian captors that he was a German soldier (a ploy that works only if he is right in assuming that his captors do not speak German).[123] Referring to this example, London observes, "Thus while it is important that the American soldier's utterance have the appropriate phonological form (both in its phonetic content and in its overall intonation), it need not have *any* particular syntactic or semantic form."[124] The crucial feature of the soldiers' utterances in both examples is the sound, not the linguistic meaning.

London remarks, "There is not any sense of 'reference' involved in the American's German babbling, but there is a sense of signification: when the American produces German-sounding language (in the given context) this expression counts as a sign of his Germanness."[125] Such "signification" is not specifically linguistic. Making music from an identifiable culture, or even using a particular instrument, can achieve signification (e.g., a bagpipe to show Celtic identification, or a balalaika to indicate being Russian). The characters performing the "Marseillaise" in the movie *Casablanca* signify their French identification whether they are singing (and using French words) or playing an instrument.[126] To adapt a remark from Nietzsche that was cited earlier, we don't need to take their *word* for it. We recognize their sound.

An interesting musical case in which words are used in this manner is that of an instance of a song in the language of an idealized "old country" that the musical participants do not speak. Ethnomusicologist Ron Ernoff asserts:

> I was told often by Cajuns, many of whom did not speak Cajun French, that "the words make the song beautiful." With the marked demise of the use of Cajun French in Louisiana, this aesthetic evaluation inevitably can refer more to the sound shape of the words, to their sound sense, than to their semantic sense. For example, even though he did speak Cajun French, Cajun fiddler Dennis McGee was purported to have used 'words for rhythm and sound more than to present a story.'"[127]

Ernoff notes a similar pattern among native Hawaiians, who value songs that are sung in Hawaiian, even when they do not speak the language themselves.[128] One might also consider the use of nonvernacular languages in some religious traditions, for example Sanskrit, Pali, Hebrew, and Latin. These languages can have profound emotional impact on the religious participant even in the absence of knowledge of the words' meaning.

Meaningful words of language can be employed musically in yet another way. Frits Staal notes a particular type of language use in which verbal meaning is of little importance. This is the case of the mantra, an untranslatable word or a string of words repeated over and over in ritual contexts without concern for whether the words are meaningful or meaningless. "While form, in a natural language, is at most as important as meaning, the form of mantras is more important than their meaning." Staal compares mantras to bird songs, which are similarly hard to explain in terms of a particular function (though functional accounts abound). The meanings of bird songs vary with context.[129] Staal cites Konrad Lorenz, who argues that "acquired motor skills . . . are forever being performed for their own sake in the obvious absence of any other motivating or reinforcing factors. Indeed, the very concept of play is based on this fact to a large extent."[130] Staal concludes:

> The similarity between mantras and bird songs is due not to common function, but to common non-functionality. Mantras and bird songs share not only certain structural properties, but also lack of an inherent or absolute purpose. It is precisely these features that express the common characteristic of both as essentially satisfying, pleasurable and playful.[131]

Although music and language diverge where semantics are concerned, I agree with Bernstein and Raffman that music's lack of a full-blown semantics reflects specific virtues of music. Besides the virtues they describe—music's poetic suggestiveness, its capacity to convey feelings too precise and nuances too particular for linguistic capture—I see another: music's openness to acquired and multiple meanings. Thomas Turino describes the accumulation of meaning that the same musical signs can collect as a consequence of their use in various contexts as "semantic snowballing."[132] John Blacking and Alan Merriam both contend that music is intrinsically polysemic, in that the same musical pattern can be conjoined with multiple meanings.[133]

Ian Cross also stresses music's polysemy, claiming that "music has the capacity to lack consensual reference; it can be about something, but its aboutness can vary from context to context and even within context."[134] Using cross-modal comparisons of a sort that we consider further in the next chapter, Cross describes music's inherent polysemy as essential to its role in cognitive development:

If music is *about* anything, it exhibits . . . a "transposable aboutness." And it is conceivable that music's "transposable aboutness" is exploited in infancy and childhood as a means of forming connections and interrelations between different domains of infant and childhood competence such as the social, biological, and mechanical. To give a crude example; the arc of a ball thrown through the air, the prosodic contour of a comforting utterance, the trajectory of a swallow as it hawks an insect, the pendular ballistics of a limb swung in purposive movement, might, for a child, each underlie the significances of a single musical phrase or proto-musical behaviour on different occasions. Indeed, these heterogeneous incidents may be bound together simultaneously. . . . Hence one and the same musical activity might, at one and the same time, be about the trajectory of a body in space, the dynamic emergence or signification of an affective state, the achievement of a goal and the unfolding of an embodied perspective.[135]

Music's polysemy stands in tension with the virtue celebrated by the Romantics when they acclaimed music's freedom from the straitjacket of conceptualization. Nevertheless, music's lack of an assigned semantics affords it both capacities. It can convey impressions of immediate sensuous experience, and it can acquire multiple layers of meaning. What is remarkable is that it can do both at the same time.[136]

Music can be replete with meaning because it is not limited by denotation. Its availability for metaphoric and associative meaning enables it to play a remarkable range of roles, some of which we considered in chapter 2. Music can map both the landscape and our various cognitive domains. It is tremendously flexible in terms of what meanings can conjoin with it. Music does not lack meaning by comparison with language; its meaning is less restricted.

WHAT CAN THE MUSICAL MODEL
OF LANGUAGE DO FOR US?

Although ample justification exists for reversing the MUSIC IS LANGUAGE framework, this framework endures. One reason is that the characterization of music as a language is reinforced by the kinds of comparisons it activates. Swain's book, *Musical Languages*, abounds in discussions of the many ways one can use the metaphor of music as a language to draw attention to features of music. But what is to recommend consideration of language as a music? Does the reversal of the cliché actually do any work for us?

One thing the music model of language might do is alert us to the acoustic potentials of speech—for example, to the ways in which our speaking can be beautiful and melodious, and ways in which it can fail to be. It can also remind us of the importance of rhythmic pattern in speech communication, emphasized by Gregory, Condon, and others.

A second benefit I see in the music model of language is that it counters the easy assumption that language is an adequate model of thought. This would be a major contribution to the philosophy of language.

Philosophers frequently characterize the contents of thought as propositions, understood in terms of linguistic clauses (e.g., "that Mary likes Fred") but as conveyable by a variety of sentences. On this view we take various "propositional attitudes" toward these contents, such as "believing that" or "desiring that." One has the tendency, in recent anglophone philosophy, to take these two specific propositional attitudes—believing and desiring—as the most important kinds.

Music, by contrast, does not typically involve propositional content, and even if Swain is right that Wagner uses the leitmotif at times to construct veritable musical propositions, this is not the typical musical case.[137] Does music therefore reflect thought less aptly than language? I would say no. If anything, music reflects thought's specific modalities more accurately than language. Language can state that a person approaches some content reverently, but music can convey the thought-tone of reverence.

I would hardly deny that some thoughts, some of them spoken, do involve the expression of beliefs and desires in propositional form. But this is hardly the full extent of thought. Often we take attitudes toward other contents besides propositions. The reigning perspective in philosophy of language is that language is designed to convey propositions. But this is only one of the functions of language. Significantly, if language were only designed to convey propositions, its prosodic elements would be of minimal importance. At most, they would clarify the propositional attitude. But even this role would be trivialized by much recent philosophical discussion, for the set of propositional attitudes of concern to philosophers has tended to be truncated to the small set of beliefs and desires.

"A lovely girl—ah!" is certainly a thought, and sometimes a thought expressed in language, but I think it would be ludicrous to restate this in terms of a standard propositional attitude taken toward a proposition. How might one reconstruct the thought in these terms? "I believe that a girl exists and that she is present and that she is lovely and I desire the continued presence of the girl, etc." For good reason we do not ordinarily express our ideas in the strung-out mode of predicate calculus. Not only is it absurdly explicit. It does not even express the statement's actual content. It fails to reflect the focus of the statement, and it insists on "beliefs" where none may be present. One can imagine the lovely girl, or recall her, or consider the archetype of a lovely girl, without having any particular lovely girl completely in mind.

In my opinion, the nuanced contents of music reflect much of our thinking life more aptly than does language, because it draws attention to various ways of holding mental content in mind. Music, as Lidov puts it, appears to "think out loud."[138] One can meditate upon a motive or theme; one can find its recurrence oppressive; one can linger over it; one can start to see reflections of it everywhere. Focus on propositions may be useful for analyzing the power of language to convey explicit information, but it does not indicate the manner in which a flow of thought occurs. Music can reveal both tonal attitudes of thought and the character of whole streams of thought, whether they are halting or straightforward, meandering or rushing. The pace is a part of the thought, sometimes trivially so, but sometimes importantly. A conclusion drawn hesitantly is not the same conclusion as one articulated in the same words but reached in a leap or as the crest of a volley of ideas. The LANGUAGE IS MUSIC framework can help us attend to these differences and thereby reflect our thought more accurately.

Finally, the LANGUAGE IS MUSIC model can remind us of the contextual layers that modify linguistic meaning, for these are the bases by which musical meaning becomes in any way specific. Feld analyzes the "interpretive moves" that listeners make in the course of relating to a piece of music. These interpretive moves are judgments, involving "the action of pattern discovery as experience is organized by the juxtapositions, interactions, or choices in time when we encounter and engage obviously symbolic objects of performances."[139] In other words, the broader circumstances in which we encounter music, including the many societal decisions about what contexts, occasions, and associations are appropriate to music of a certain sort, affect our sense of its significance.

Among the types of "interpretive moves" Feld envisions are references of particular features of music to: *locations* (understood from a subjective perspective); *categories* (which assign the item to particular classes of things, and perhaps subclasses as well); *associations* (with what Feld describes as imagery—"visual, musical, or verbal"); *reflections* (having to do with "some personal and social conditions [like political attitudes, patriotism, nationalism] and related experiences where things like this can be heard, mediated or live"); and *evaluations* ("instantly finding this funny, distasteful, inappropriate, or immoral").[140] Societies (and particular individuals) interpret music in terms of its relationship to locations, categories, associations, reflections, and evaluations relevant to the listener.

These interpretive moves have corollaries in the linguistic case, corollaries that are usually lost sight of by philosophers. I note a slang word in an utterance, and this leads me to infer where the speaker is from. For example, I judge that someone asking me, "Would you like some brekky?" is Australian (although accent, another musical aspect of language, might make this judgment more definitive). Or perhaps a word pronounced a certain way tips me off, for example, the dropped *r* in the speech of Bostonians, New Zealanders, or Australians. Certain buzzwords lead me to associate a speaker with certain contexts. A sprinkling of terms such as "propositional attitudes," "bare particulars," and "rigid designators" would lead me to associate the speaker with twentieth-century analytic philosophy. "Whatever!" pronounced with a certain exasperated inflection might stir up associations with the San Fernando Valley. It might also lead me to reflect on the oddity that an expression denotatively suggesting the speaker's deference to another person is actually a retort.[141] I might go on to judge the speaker as rather rude or as a hothead on this basis. In *My Fair Lady* Eliza Dolittle's elegant pronunciation of statements in lower-class diction is funny because we relate both the pronunciation and the diction to the circumstances in which each seems appropriate. Only thus are we able to recognize their incongruity. By looking at the way we relate ourselves to music and thereby determine what meanings it has for us, we can become more aware of the way we similarly assess the meanings linguistic utterances have for us, and not just the meanings they have denotatively.

Language is often touted as our great species achievement, as both the product of our intelligence and the way we express this intelligence. Fair enough—but language is not our only aptitude that fits this description. Music is similarly the product and expression of the kinds of minds we have. If we are interested in our species nature, we should not attend to language at the expense of music, for music reveals some features of our minds and souls more clearly than does language when it is understood in terms of entrenched structural models that underplay its musical characteristics. Such models also shortchange the ways in which the meanings associated with linguistic expressions derive from listeners' (or readers') interpretive efforts to relate themselves to what is said (or written). To understand our use of language, we would do well to pursue musical models. To understand ourselves, we cannot dispense with music.

Importantly, some of the musical characteristics of language, those involved in prosody, apply cross-culturally; and these same characteristics are evident in music as well. Apart from semantic information, the acoustic codes that are cross-culturally evident in both language and music convey considerable information about attitudes and affect.

Music cross-culturally intimates something further in the absence of semantic information—a sense of a broader world beyond music. I will argue for this claim in the following chapter. I will contend that as a consequence of its biological depth and the salience of its signal to multiple senses, music galvanizes the entire sensorium, which is the means through which we experience the larger world. One consequence is that music prompts synesthetic associations in those who experience it. Music's enlivening of our sensory faculties, I will argue, primes us for attending to the larger world that is both our musical and our extramusical environment. One consequence is our readiness to link music with extramusical content, a tendency that is cross-culturally prevalent. As we shall see, however, this cross-cultural power results in a proliferation of associated meanings that are often not cross-culturally accessible.

CHAPTER 6

Musical Synesthesia

> In the Dionysian dithyramb man is incited to the greatest exaltation of all his symbolic
> faculties; something never before experienced struggles for utterance.... The essence
> of nature is now to be expressed symbolically; we need a new world of symbols; and the
> entire symbolism of the body is called into play.
>
> FRIEDRICH NIETZSCHE, *The Birth of Tragedy*

Marcel Proust describes the experience of tasting a madeleine, a kind of French cookie, as conjuring memories of the entire world he once inhabited.

> And suddenly the memory returns. The taste was that of the little crumb of madeleine which on Sunday mornings at Combray (because on those mornings I did not go out before church-time), when I went to say good day to her in her bed room, my aunt Léonie used to give me, dipping it first in her own cup of real or lime-flower tea.... And once I had recognized the taste ... immediately the old grey house upon the street, where her room was, rose up like the scenery of a theatre to attach itself to the pavilion.[1]

Like the taste of the madeleine in Proust's memoir, musical experience incites us to respond as if to a whole perceptual world. In transporting us beyond the streams of auditory and tactile input to an impression of the larger sensorium, music effects a type of synesthesia.

This tendency of music to elicit the listener's imaginative projection of a full sensory "world" in connection with music is one of the common bases for the human experience of music. Musical synesthesia is thus one of the aspects of musical experience that contributes to its being universally so powerful. At the same time, however, cultural differences in the interpretation of the extra-auditory world with which music is connected renders the interpretations connected to musical synesthesia culturally divergent. This synesthetic character of musical experience is evident in the universal tendency to model nonmusical phenomena through music. However, although synesthetic associations and the use of these in forming musical symbolisms and models appear to operate across the human species, the cultural variety of specific symbolisms and models limits the extent to which musical synesthesia serves as a basis for cross-cultural communication.

SYNESTHESIA IN EVERYDAY LIFE

What is synesthesia? In the loosest sense, the term *synesthesia* connotes any cross-modal connection. More strictly, synesthesia refers to unusual phenomenological associations of perceptual material from one sensory mode with perceptual material in another. I will include among sensory modes certain other kinds of perceptual awareness besides that associated with the five senses taken individually. Among these will be the kinesthetic sense and a general sense of spatiality. I will refer to synesthesia strictly defined as "idiopathic synesthesia," for it is highly individual in its manifestations.[2] When I use *synesthesia* without a qualifying adjective, I will use the term in a broad sense to include any cross-sensory association.

Idiopathic synesthesia involves individually specific experiences in which sensation in one mode automatically brings with it sensory experience in another.[3] The most common type of idiopathic synesthesia is often called "colored hearing," or "psychochromasthesia," usually involving spontaneous perception of patches of color, termed "photisms," in conjunction with hearing particular sounds.[4] For some individuals the relevant sounds are musical; for others it may be certain vowels, consonants, or phonemes.[5] The Walt Disney movie *Fantasia* offers a hint of what this type of synesthesia is like for those who have not experienced it. Early in the film, an orchestra begins to play. Gradually the screen focuses on the movements of the violin bows, which turn into a completely abstract pattern of lines, and eventually into flecks that pulsate, even appear and disappear, along with the rhythm of the music.

Not everyone is an idiopathic synesthete, but synesthesia in a loose sense is a common experience. Virtually everyone understands references to "brightness" and "darkness" in reference to sound as well as visual appearance. Lawrence Marks, Robin Hammeal, and Marc Bornstein suggest that there is a basis for this in the neurophysiological similarity of the visual and auditory systems.[6] Davies observes that certain timbres have a synesthetic character: "The trumpet's upper notes are bright and the clarinet's low register is dark; the tone of the celesta is ethereal, while high string harmonics are brittle."[7]

Aristotle had already considered such qualities, which he termed "common sensibles." The common sensibles (movement, magnitude, and number) are perceived multimodally.[8] Aristotle describes them as follows.

> The senses perceive each other's special objects incidentally; not because the percipient sense is this or that special sense, but because all form a unity: this incidental perception takes place whenever sense is directed at one and the same moment to two disparate qualities in one and the same object, e.g. to the bitterness and the yellowness of bile; the assertion of the identity of both cannot be the act of either of the senses; hence the illusion of sense, e.g. the belief that if a thing is yellow it is bile.[9]

More recent philosophers, Maurice Merleau-Ponty and Charles Hartshorne, also contend that cross-modal experience is common. Merleau-Ponty claims that synesthesia is actually the normal condition of human perception, and he suggests a number of instances of cross-modal experience in everyday life:

> The senses intercommunicate by opening on to the structure of the thing. One sees the hardness and brittleness of glass, and when, with a tinkling sound, it breaks, this sound is conveyed by the visible glass. One sees the springiness of steel, the ductility of red-hot steel, the hardness of a plane blade, the softness of shavings. . . . The form of a fold in linen or cotton shows us the resilience or dryness of the fibre, the coldness or warmth of the material. . . . In the jerk of the twig from which a bird has just flown, we read its flexibility or elasticity, and it is thus that a branch of an apple-tree or a birch are immediately distinguishable.[10]

Hartshorne offers another example of everyday synesthesia, suggesting that the burden of proof is on the person who considers the sensory characteristics of ice cream separable. "What blind dogmatism to deny that in the eating of ice-cream the senses of taste, of cold, of smoothness, of smell, are all so interblended, and far indeed from absolutely heterogeneous, that it is not decided kinship but significant difference of quality that is hard to detect."[11]

Presumably such everyday synesthesia was what Franz Liszt, while Weimar *Kappelmeister*, intended to evoke when, according to anecdotal report, he urged his musicians: "'more pink here, if you please'; or . . . 'that is too black'; or 'here I want it all azure.'"[12]

Psychologist Lawrence Marks defends the idea that synesthesia, understood broadly, is an occurrence with which everyone is familiar, arguing that synesthesia is essential to cognitive development. Synesthesia is akin to all cross-modal metaphor and to abstract verbal meaning, each of which depend on analogy. Synesthesia becomes a relevant stage in the developmental shift from recognizing similarity in the same domain to recognizing it in another, a shift that is presupposed by abstract reasoning. "Similarities among the qualities of a single sense progress to similarities among qualities of different senses, which in turn progress to similarities and resemblances that transcend simple sensory properties and partake of the myriad relationships that the mind can construct."[13]

Along with his colleagues Hammeal and Bornstein, Marks suggests that early synesthesia continues even after children learn to distinguish sensation among the sensory modes. Young children find cross-sensory metaphors among the easiest metaphors to understand, and children continue to prefer perceptually based metaphor long past the stage at which they require them.[14] Marks, Hammeal, and Bornstein speculate that

> "stumbling onto" cross-modal similarities can precipitate a subsequent search for other similarities within diverse domains—in our view, the very crux of metaphor. . . . If so, then cross-sensory metaphors . . . may provide one key to understanding more generally the establishment in childhood of metaphoric competences.[15]

Marks postulates a synesthetic stage, which is not lost in childhood, but continues into adulthood, though perhaps diminished in its importance and salience.[16] Richard Cytowic similarly argues that a synesthetic stage (in a loose sense) is involved throughout life in the normal perception of objects. When we perceive an object, we form an image of it in our minds. We do not imme-diately connect a detailed representation to the object; instead, we go through a series of refinements to our mental image as we attempt to map it onto the object that is observed (a series that unfolds at lightning speed). Eventually the image is sufficiently elaborated and coincident with the data we observe that it is finally exteriorized (i.e., projected as an entity in the external world), at which point we take it to be an accurate reflection of the object. Cytowic suggests that synesthesia involves the same processes we all use in object rep-resentation, but halted at an earlier stage.

> Just as in the microgeny of word finding there is a point at which "table" and "chair" have a covalence, and either one could come out in a task of naming

a four-legged piece of furniture, so too in the normal unfolding of object perception the generic form may be inadequately constrained such that it carries additional information that detaches into reality and becomes externalized as a perception in another mode, hence synesthesia.[17]

We experience everyday cross-modal connections very early in life. Considerable evidence suggests that three-month-old infants already connect brightness in sound with visual brightness.[18] Marks, Hammeal, and Bornstein note that one-year-olds are sensitive to "several auditory-visual correspondences, notably a correspondence between rising versus falling pitch and upward versus downward-pointing areas."[19] Here we already encounter a music-related synesthetic association (one that may be culturally relative, given that some cultures reverse what others, including ours, term *high* and *low* notes). Another, however, is more noteworthy in connection with the topic of this book. Psychologist Daniel Stern suggests that the emotional and social development of infants depends on their perception of the behavior of their caregivers. Significantly for my purposes, this perception is initially not limited to one or two sensory streams.

According to Stern, infants experience their caregivers in terms of "vitality affects"—dynamic, amodal, kinetic characteristics[20]—before they experience them as identifiable individuals. The "underlying feature" of the vitality affects is what Stern calls "activation contour." Various experiences can be characterized by a similar dynamic description if they share "similar envelopes of neural firings," even if these occur "in different parts of the nervous system."

> Because activation contours (such as "rushes" of thought, feeling, or action) can apply to any kind of behavior or sentience, an activation contour can be abstracted from one kind of behavior and can exist in some amodal form so that it can apply to another kind of overt behavior or mental process. These abstract representations may then permit intermodal correspondences to be made between similar activation contours expressed in diverse behavioral manifestations. Extremely diverse events may thus be yoked, so long as they share the quality of feeling that is being called a vitality affect.[21]

Infants recognize the vitality affects in the context of interacting with their own bodies and with the behaviors of others in their environment.

Stern explicitly proposes that vitality affects also demonstrate how disparate kinds of experiences—such as music and extramusical content—can be yoked. According to Stern, infants develop a sense of being with other people by attuning themselves to these vitality affects. Attunement to the vitality affects depends importantly on infants' "musical" sensitivity to rhythm, which itself engages multiple sensory modes.[22] Our original sense of being related to others, then, presupposes a basic musical capacity, one that fuses the streams of our sensory perception into impressions of another being as a whole, a point that we will return to in chapter 8.

EVERYDAY SYNESTHESIA AND MUSIC

We have prima facie grounds for thinking that synesthesia is relevant to musical experience. We seem to perceive music multimodally. The fact that deaf people are able to respond to music through the sense of touch is one indication of multimodal perception. Music is particularly suited to invite synesthetic response. It prominently features "amodal sensory qualities," E. M. von Hornbostel's term for such qualities as brightness, darkness, and roughness, which are recognizable by more than one sense.[23] The vocabularies of many cultures in connection with music indicate cross-modal associations. As we noted previously, many cultures describe pitch in terms of spatial images— *high* and *low*. The cross-cultural employment of such terms suggests that multisensory engagement with music is both common and not restricted to a single culture. Some Western societies correlate musical keys with sensations geared to other senses, too. The German use of *dür* and *moll* (hard and soft) to refer to major and minor keys is a case in point. The Kota tribe of south India use olfactory metaphors for music.[24] The Aboriginal peoples of Australia refer to recognizing a song through its taste or smell.[25] The Kaluli of Papua New Guinea employ the cross-modal metaphors of "lift-up-over sounding" and "hardness" to describe their musical ideal.[26]

We also respond to music multimodally. We feel like dancing, or at least moving, along with most music. Nietzsche describes our muscular response to music in his account of the Dionysian dithyramb, although he notes that our movements are typically inhibited.

> Music, as we understand it today, is . . . a total excitement and a total discharge of the affects, but even so only the remnant of a much fuller world of expression of the affects, a mere residue of the Dionysian histrionicism. To make music possible as a separate art, a number of senses, especially the muscle sense, have been immobilized (at least relatively, for to a certain degree all rhythm still appeals to our muscles).[27]

The impact of music on our musculature—the tendency to tap a foot or rock one's torso with music—is familiar to all of us.[28] I have seen infants too young to talk bouncing their whole bodies in accord with musical beat. Elvis Presley's gyrations are only a more extreme case of the rhythmic movements to music we are all disposed to make. We learn to suppress these inclinations in the Western concert hall, but many of us catch ourselves swaying a bit or pulsing a toe along with the music in spite of ourselves. In such situations, we associate the art of sound with our kinesthetic awareness.

We might recall here Charles Nussbaum's account of how music's kinesthetic involvement is basic to the way our brains represent music, specifically, as virtual layouts and environments that we mentally navigate in the same way that we navigate external space.[29] We noted earlier Nussbaum's suggestion that our overall bodily involvement with music is the basis for the ubiquitous phenomenon of modeling nonmusical domains in music. One instance of such modeling is the impression of music mimicking our activity, discussed in chapter 4.

Our kinesthetic response to music, like kinesthetic response in general, presupposes the communication of the senses. Gestalt psychologist W. S. Boernstein draws on Hornbostel's conception of "amodal sensory qualities" in his account of kinesthesia. Boernstein emphasizes the role played by physical tonus, the state of mild tension in which the organs of a living body are maintained, and also a means by which the modalities communicate. Because of this systemic tension, stimulation of one organ has an impact on others. Boernstein suggests that the integration of the effects of the multiple sensory modes and amodal sensory stimulation on physical tonus is crucial for spatial orientation, a precondition of internalized movement.[30] Physical tonus is thus involved in all sensory experience, and Boernstein considers the connection between the senses and motor functions to be essential to the perception of the amodal sensory qualities.[31] The stimulation of amodal sensory qualities, kinesthetic sensation (which integrates physical tonus), and the naturalness of conceiving of music in terms of space (both metaphorically and through physical movement) shed light on why music makes us feel like dancing or otherwise moving along with it.

Besides impact on physical tonus, music activates the limbic system, which is located in the lower brainstem and the areas just above it. On the basis of his experiments with idiopathic synesthetes, Cytowic concludes that the hippocampus, central to the limbic system, is particularly involved in such synesthesia. The hippocampus allows the sensory modalities to communicate with one another, because it is the point at which both external and internal sensory inputs converge before being transferred to the cortex. Cytowic notes that after analysis by the cortex, the inputs return to the limbic system, which determines what is important enough to attend to.[32] The limbic system is the emotional core of the nervous system, and it is crucial in forming novel reactions, making value judgments, and experiencing emotion.

Music's physical appeal is obvious, but one might still doubt that cross-modal stimulation is involved. Music, narrowly conceived, is addressed to audition, and secondarily to touch. However, I propose that music's appeal to the auditory and tactile senses is precisely what inspires cross-modal imagery and response across the sensorium as a whole.

Music is organized so as to be particularly salient to our senses of hearing and touch. Although music seems to address itself only to this limited range of senses, the clarity and immediacy of its presence in these domains suggests to our awareness that we are encountering a reality that transcends our own bodies. Because our senses normally operate together, the sensory intensity of the experience that we have in connection with music, I suggest, stimulates the rest of the sensorium as well.[33] Although most of us are not idiopathic synesthetes who see photons in connection with music, our minds are still disposed to form or seek content for the full range of our senses.[34] Thus we use cross-modal imagery in our speech about music, and we are so inclined to move with music that we often do so unawares.

What is going on when we are inclined to conjure responses in other sensory modes in connection with our experience of music? I submit that music encourages such associations, perhaps paradoxically, because it is addressed to a limited range of senses. Because music is designed to make pattern salient, we perceive it as having particular immediacy. Normally, our perception of sounds is but one of several ways that we experience the larger world. In the usual case, our senses operate in tandem. Occasionally we focus on one sense in particular, for example when we are having our eyes tested, but generally speaking, hearing and touch, like our other senses, are among multiple means we use together to orient ourselves to the world. Because music is so salient to us, it makes us strongly aware of connection with a larger reality. This sense of connection enlivens our other senses at the same time, motivating us to respond with our entire bodies to music that engages us. We experience our perception of sound in the case of music as connecting us to the very world that we experience through the range of our senses.[35]

THE UNIVERSAL DIMENSIONS OF SYNESTHESIA

Synesthetic responses to music are ubiquitous, and we might wonder how much they might serve as a basis for cross-cultural communication. The role that vitality affects appear to have in infant development, with the rhythmic sensitivity that this implies, suggests some common ground on which musical interaction might be built.[36] Music researcher Manfred Clynes connects synesthetic potential for expression with what he takes to be universal emotional states, suggesting a hard-wired basis for emotional communication across cultures. He suggests that much of our expressive behavior in connection with music is linked to what he calls "sentic states," specific emotional states that he contends are universal. These sentic states can be expressed through various "output modalities," including "a variety of motor modes: gestures, tone of voice, facial expression, a dance step, musical phrase, etc."[37] Clynes claims that human beings are hard-wired to use "precise elements of communication faithful to specific qualities and also to recognize these elements when communicated by others" across this range of sensory modes. In several series of experiments, Clynes found consistent patterns in the vertical and horizontal components of the finger pressure subjects would use to tactilely express particular emotional states. He monitored head position, respiration, and heart rate, which were also common across subjects attempting to express the same emotional state. Clynes found the same patterns across studies in the United States, Japan, rural Mexico, and Bali. He concludes that the correlation between particular affect and motor expression is inherent in the human nervous system. Although one might wish for further empirical research to demonstrate the same commonalities in different modalities and across additional cultures, Clynes's research is suggestive for an understanding of how synesthetic response might further cross-cultural communication.[38]

Although our disposition to synesthetic response appears to be a typical human tendency, the particulars that are conjoined with music can be culturally, even individually specific.[39] (This is evident whenever we conjoin music and language.) How do these particulars become conjoined? One obvious way is through convention. For example, the cross-modal images used to describe music—the height of pitches and the brightness of tone, for example—are acquired in the context of learning other culturally standard ways to refer to things. But many of the symbolisms or modelings associated with music seem entrenched. One hears them in the music. How do cultural conventions come to be so tenacious that they come to seem "natural"?

A musical case of such a "natural" association is the Western tendency to hear music in major keys as "happy" and music in minor keys as "sad." I am frequently asked, when I mention my interest in the universal characteristics of music to Westerners, if music in major keys really does turn out to sound happy all around the world. I reply that not only do many cultures have no major keys, the correlation of happy/sad with major/minor is not even long-standing in the West. Nor is it consistent even in relatively recent music. Consider "Lili Marlene," a song about a soldier separated from his lover by the war, popular among both Allied and German soldiers during World War II. Although it does end with the image of Lili's face remaining in the soldier's dreams and his hopes to return someday, it is a melancholy song—and yet it is in a major key.[40] My conversational partners are often astonished by my answer. That major is happy and minor is sad just sounds natural to them. Where does this sense of "natural" come from?

Judith Becker suggests an answer to this question in her work on the nature of trance experiences.[41] She describes trance behavior in a number of cultures, behavior that varies remarkably. For example, a fifteenth-century peasant woman in the boot heel of Italy (Apulia) is bitten by a tarantula spider (or believes she has been bitten) during the hot months of the summer.[42] She goes into a stuporous depressive trance, for which the cure is dancing the tarantella. The woman's family hires musicians, who try various pieces of music until they hit one that prompts the woman to dance. She dances, wildly, often obscenely, perhaps going into the marketplace with the musicians, where others (including relapsed former patients) might join her. The dance continues until she drops from exhaustion. Another of Becker's examples of culturally distinctive trances comes from Bali. When the community is out of equilibrium, the Barong/Rangda ritual is performed to restore balance. This ceremony produces trance in the young men who are present, all of whom dance a *kris* (knife) dance, in which they stab themselves with knives. Considering that trancing individuals are not using everyday consciousness, but indeed are in an altered state of which they will likely have no memory, how do the trancers go into the culturally appropriate type of trance? Why did the Italian woman who believed herself to be bitten by a tarantula dance the tarantella instead of stabbing herself with a knife?

Becker calls the sequence of culturally expected behaviors during trance the cultural "script." She refers to Gerald Edelman's theory of neuronal group selection to explain how these scripts become so internalized that they direct the behavior of individuals in trance states. This theory was proposed in part to explain why areas all over the brain are activated by sensory stimuli, not just those that are specialized with respect to the sense in question. Edelman contends that bundles of neurons in the mind are activated together in an operational unit, and that groups of such bundles, called maps, can become connected with each other. Bundles that interact with each other frequently enough develop into "classification couples," groups of neurons that will be simultaneously activated when the stimulus that initially connected them occurs. The appropriate kind of stimulus, exciting a certain group or groups of neurons, will also excite other groups that have habitually been activated at the same time. The result is that "the initial perceptual stimulus comes, through structural coupling in a ritual context, to excite large areas of the brain with no necessary connection with the original perception."[43] This, according to Becker, is why trancers have the specific experiences that their cultures prescribe. Referring directly to music as a stimulus, Becker asserts,

> the auditory system . . . consists of neuronal groupings, each responding to a different aspect of the incoming signal, that is, timbre, pitch, loudness, melody, rhythm, harmony, stress, and so on. Through reentrant or looping processes, that is, synaptic connections going to many other parts of the brain, we are simultaneously, or so it seems, aware of the last time we heard this piece, or one like it, as well as concomitant feelings of joy, sadness, or even fear. . . . In this way, a particular sensory stimulus acts as physiological metonym—one part (music) invokes the whole mythology and its accompanying behavior and emotional feel.[44]

Becker's account, suggesting how associations formed in connection with music come to be engaged automatically, is applicable to the culturally specific synesthetic experiences we have in connection with music. Our Western association of major and minor with happy and sad has become part of our cognitive mapping. These associations seem natural because the appropriate neuronal groups linked to the happy/sad opposition, being habitually triggered at the same time, have come to fire automatically when we hear music in major or minor keys. Had we been musically raised in a society without major or minor keys, or without the same emotional pairings, these associations, even if we could recognize them, would not seem "natural" at all.[45]

Becker's account also provides an explanation of why cross-modal connections with music are typical of human beings. Our initial social bonding and our cognitive development depends on our being able to link perceptions from our various sensory modalities. Insofar as music is perceptually salient, but salient primarily for hearing and touch, I have argued, it enables and encourages associations with objects and processes that may be primarily salient for other modalities. Particular associations, sufficiently repeated (by virtue of being frequently encountered in the environment where music-making occurs), become deeply ingrained in the sense of being neurologically coupled. Forming deeply ingrained associations with music is a universal propensity. The multimodal images used to talk about music in various societies offer evidence of this tendency.

If "stumbling onto" cross-modal metaphors is the norm, however, we have no reason to think that the cross-modal associations formed in connection with music will be universal. The variation among cross-modal images used by different societies indicates that although the tendency to employ such images may be universal, the images themselves are not.[46] Indeed, we have no reason to expect all such associations to be shared by entire cultures. Those who experienced Bugs Bunny's version of Wagnerian opera may commonly connect "The Ride of the Valkyries" with Bugs Bunny, but this would hardly be the standard across American society. Perhaps others from my grade school class that was exposed to classical music while we were supposed to consume our lunch without talking share my association of "The Hebrides" with these strange circumstances, but I recognize that this reaction is unusual to the point of idiosyncrasy.

Music serves to connect us with the external world and motivates us to forge associations along multiple sensory lines. In this respect, it bears a noteworthy resemblance to language. A significant difference however, is that language requires conventional (i.e., established and standardized) associations between words and those things to which they refer. The associations between aspects of music and aspects of extramusical experience seem in some cases to be as "natural" as the meanings of words seem to someone fluent in a particular language. But as we have seen, divergent backgrounds can result in divergent associations, even with the same particular music. Extramusical associations with features of music are not as established and standardized as the denotations of words.

Feld's analysis of the "interpretive moves" that listeners employ in response to music provides an explanation of why societies will inevitably differ with respect to what images they conjoin with music.[47] He suggests, quite plausibly, that all musical listening involves the listener's active efforts to relate the music to his or her broader experience. Feld maintains that we foreground and background various aspects of music, making judgments that relate them to a whole schema of relations to other, often extramusical concerns. Feld emphasizes the extent to which many interpretive judgments are specific to social groups, which makes sense, given that one's sense of group membership often depends on shared location, classification schemes, backgrounds, experiences, metaphors, and values. Thus, for example, the Aboriginal Australians connect songs with particular contours of the landscape, as we considered in chapter 2, while many Westerners associate organ music with ritual experiences in Christian churches.

Feld's account would also seem to imply, however, that differences in individual backgrounds, whether or not they conform to specific group patterns, will have significant impact on the way particular individuals will interpret the music they hear. The unique set of an individual's personal experiences may influence which locations, categories, associations, reflections, and evaluations that individual will draw upon in interpreting music as personally relevant.[48] Thus music comes to have both personal meaning and shared meanings, or what Constantijn Koopman and Stephen Davies call "meaning-for-us."[49]

CONCLUSION

Music draws attention to our participation in a larger world, in part through its powerful multimodal appeal. However, its synesthetic potential enables considerable cross-cultural diversity in the more detailed associations between music and the larger world. Once again, as with musical preference universals, variety is the consequence of an underlying commonality.

The closest we have come so far to a basis in music for cross-cultural comprehension has been music's communication of affect. The grounds for the variant of the adage that termed music the universal language of *emotion* seem evident. Thus far, we have emphasized prosody as a universal basis for emotional communication through music as well as speech. I will suggest in the following two chapters that other features of music yield cross-cultural emotional communication as well.

CHAPTER 7

A Song in Your Heart

Music has charms to soothe a savage breast.   WILLIAM CONGREVE, *The Mourning Bride*

Music is joy.   HSÜN TZU (XUNZI), *Basic Writings*

MUSIC AS EMOTIONAL

A traditional basis for asserting the centrality of music to human nature is its relation to the emotions. Deryck Cooke straightforwardly claims, "music is, properly speaking, a language of the emotions, akin to speech."[1] Beethoven, he notes, wrote on the manuscript of *Missa Solemnis*, "From the heart—may it go back—to the heart!"[2] Psychologist Carroll C. Pratt also claims that music is a language of the emotions that is "unequalled in this regard by any other art."[3]

The idea that music has a special relationship to emotion is not uniquely Western. According to the "Great Preface" in the Chinese *Book of Songs* (*The Shih Jing*),[4]

The feelings move inwardly, and are embodied in words. When words are insufficient for them, recourse is had to sighs and exclamations. When sighs and exclamations are insufficient for them, recourse is had to the prolonged utterances of song. When those prolonged utterances of song are insufficient for them, unconsciously the hands begin to move and the feet to dance.[5]

When the ancient Confucian philosopher Xunzi claims that "music is joy," he is not only expressing his own opinion. He is pointing out that the Chinese character for music is identical to that for joy.

Joy is only one of the emotions that cultures commonly link with music. The twelve *dastgāh*, or modes, of the Persian musical system are associated with various emotional tones.[6] The ragas[7] used in classical Indian music (both Hindustani and Karnatic[8]) are similarly associated with particular moods, as well as with times of the day. According to Rowell, "the tradition of *rāga* has become one of the primary means by which Indian culture has become sensitized and perhaps even instructed in emotive life."[9]

The Temiar of Malaysia describe the heartbeatlike rhythm of their bamboo percussion as "moving one's heart to longing."[10] Steven Feld describes the Kaluli of Papua New Guinea as singing with the purpose of moving listeners to "feel sorrow for the performer," whose songs typically involve recalling and lamenting someone who has died.[11] Music is a primary means of expressing grief throughout the world.[12]

A common theme across cultures is that music renders participants emotionally open (regardless of whether they are performing or listening). Medieval philosopher and mystic Al-Ghazali (1058–1111) claims of the Qu'ran, poetry, and serious music, "There is no way of extracting their hidden things save by the flint and steel of listening to music and singing, and there is no entry into the heart save by the antechamber of the ears."[13] Gilbert Rouget observes that the association of music and emotion is so strong in the Arabic world that *tarab*, the Arabic word for musical emotion, "has in fact come to signify music."[14]

Association with emotion seems at least a near-universal in connection with music. But how are emotions and music related? First, I will consider some of Western philosophy's answers to this question and suggest that the competing answers need not be seen as mutually exclusive. Instead, we should recognize that listeners can relate to music in a fluid manner that allows for varying degrees of identification or detachment. The various competing theories tend to focus on different ways the listener can engage with music.

Second, I will consider the question of the object of musically aroused emotion. Emotion is often said to require an object, for example, something at which one is angry when one experiences anger. But how is an object provided when emotion is aroused by music? Is one angry, for example, at the music? I will argue that in musically aroused emotion, the object is typically vague. Our attention is certainly not focused on as clearly structured an object as we encounter in everyday emotional experience.

I will go on to suggest that the listener's fluid relationship to the emotional character of music as well as the typical lack of a definite object of emotion enable music to prime listeners for a relatively open-ended empathetic stance that can encourage feelings of affinity with others with whom one does not usually feel connected. I will then discuss the extent to which musical expressiveness and arousal of emotion transcend cultural boundaries and to what extent they are more restricted.

The relationship of music and emotion has traditionally received at least three different explanations in the West, although many thinkers combine more than one of them. Some theorists claim that music imitates or cognitively represents emotion, because of either natural resemblances or conventional associations between features of music and characteristics of emotions and/or their behavioral manifestations. Others argue that music expresses emotion.[15] A third group holds that music arouses emotion in musical participants. I will discuss each of these positions in turn, noting some parallel positions formulated outside the West.

1. Music Imitates (or Cognitively Represents) Emotion

The idea that music imitates emotion may strike us as a highly abstract thesis, but this was taken for granted at an earlier point in Western history, when music was not sharply differentiated from other activities, such as dance, poetic presentation, and theatrical performance (as it remains in much of the world). Thus Plato, whose character Socrates argues that music imitates (as well as arouses) emotion, seems to have believed that the character and rhythms of music resemble the characters and rhythms of human beings in the grip of certain feelings, a view that seems quite plausible when the music goes along with the movements of an actor or dancer.[16] Medieval Islamic thinker Ibn Sina (980–1037) proposed an alternative imitation theory, according to which the basis of our delight in music is the resemblance between the appearance and disappearance of motives and themes in music and the comings and goings of beloved individuals.[17] In the Renaissance and early Baroque a debate ensued over whether Plato associated imitative qualities with the mode (i.e., the scale) or the specific melodic fragment.[18] But even these later theorists did not expect the imitation to be established by the music alone; they assumed that music would be linked with texts and, in the case of opera, action.

The eighteenth century saw both renewed defense of imitation theory and the inception of doubts as to its plausibility.[19] The doctrine that the fine arts in general were inherently imitative, a view ascribed to Aristotle, motivated a defense of music's imitative powers, and emotion was typically taken to be the object of imitation. However, as instrumental music developed into a phenomenon in its own right, this categorization began to strike some theorists as dubious. Adam Smith (1723–1790), for example, reveals skepticism.

> Instrumental Music . . . though it may, no doubt, be considered in some respects as an imitative art, is certainly less so than any other which merits that appellation; it can imitate but a few objects, and even these so imperfectly, that without the accompaniment of some other art, its imitation is scarce ever intelligible: imitation is by no means essential to it, and the principal effect which it is capable of producing arises from powers altogether different from those of imitation.[20]

James Beattie (1735–1803) goes further and contends that music should not be considered among the imitative arts, for its power is its ability to affect listeners, not to represent anything.[21]

A more recent critic of imitation theory has had perhaps the strongest influence on subsequent Western philosophical views on the music-emotion connection. Eduard Hanslick (1825–1904) sought to debunk the fashionable theories of his day concerning music's relation to emotion, including the view that music represents emotion. In *On the Musically Beautiful* (1854), he asserts: "The representation of a specific feeling or emotional state is not at all among the characteristic powers of music."[22] The only ideas that music can represent with its own resources, according to Hanslick, are "those ideas which relate to audible changes in strength, motion, and proportion," including ideas "of increasing and diminishing, acceleration and deceleration, clever interweavings, simple progressions and the like."[23] Music's content is not emotion, but "tonally moving forms."[24] We can use emotional terms to describe the character of passages of music—they reflect our felt experience and "indeed" Hanslick adds, "we cannot do without them." Strictly, however, we should keep in mind that "we are using them only figuratively."[25]

Thus shared dynamic character leads people to associate particular emotions with music, according to Hanslick. Several emotions might share the same dynamic, however, and this enables people to associate the same passage of music with a variety of emotional states.[26] Hanslick also observes that composers frequently use the same passages of music to express different emotions. (We might think of the music for "Greensleeves," which has amorous words attributed to that wife-killer Henry VIII, but is also utilized as a Christmas hymn.) Because particular musical passages are not uniquely correlated with definite emotional content, Hanslick concludes that the imitation theory (and the broader view that music represents emotion to the mind) should be rejected.[27]

Some who accept Hanslick's position that music and emotions share dynamical characteristics have drawn the opposite conclusion, a route that is available to them because they do not take representation to require, as does Hanslick, a one-to-one correspondence between a musical passage and a particular emotion.[28] Susanne K. Langer is among these thinkers.[29] She characterizes music as a "presentational" (as opposed to "discursive") symbol of emotional life, with which it is isomorphic. Music presents the "logical form" of human feeling.[30] "Logical form," in this case, means such patterns as "motion and rest, of tension and release, of agreement and disagreement, preparation, fulfillment, excitation, sudden change, etc.," which characterize both music and "inner life."[31]

2. Music Expresses Emotion

Although often conjoined with the view that music imitates or cognitively represents emotions, the view that music expresses emotions is a distinct account of the music-emotion connection.[32] The expression theory has a long track record in the West, and it had particularly enthusiastic adherents among those who elaborated specific correspondences between musical elements and passions in the sixteenth through eighteenth centuries and among the Romantics.[33]

The expressiveness of music is broadly accepted around the world.[34] In the fall of 2004, Haitian victims of Hurricane Jean were shown on a CNN clip singing about their tribulations, including their lack of food.[35] In Japanese Noh theater harsh music, punctuated by cries, is used before a ghostly character appears on stage to express both the attachment that is pulling the ghost through the gap separating the living and the dead and the pain that is caused by this crossing. In ancient China, as the previously cited passage from the "Great Preface" of the Chinese *Book of Songs* (*The Shih Jing*) attests, music was considered an outgrowth of a natural human need for emotional expression and an enhancement to the expressive power of words.[36] Xunzi similarly contends with respect to music, "Man must have his joy, and joy must have its expression."[37]

Expression theory also has its opponents. Igor Stravinsky claimed, "music is, by its very nature, essentially powerless to express anything at all."[38] Hanslick argues, "Music consists of tonal sequences, tonal forms; these have no other content than themselves."[39] China, too, had its Hanslick or, perhaps more accurately, its Langer.[40] Although he considered musical patterns to be revelatory of "patterns of mind and nature," the neo-Daoist Ji Kang rejected the correlation schemes devised during the Han dynasty to link particular sounds with particular emotions.[41]

The idea that music expresses emotion has led some philosophers to ask whose emotion is expressed. The obvious candidates are the composer or the performer, but the activities of composing and performing are not necessarily expressive activities. The technical details of writing or performing music are quite absorbing in themselves, and attention to these may be incompatible with giving complete attention to emotional expression. Moreover, both composers and performers are able to concentrate on producing music, even quite moving music, when their personal emotional states are quite different from those expressed by the music. But if the emotion expressed in music is not that of the composer or the performer, whose is it?

Eighteenth- and nineteenth-century defenders of expression theory, including J. G. Herder, C. P. E. Bach, and Heinrich Heine, held that the composer expressed his own emotions through music, but that these were not his emotions as a particular individual. Instead, they were universal emotions, expressive of the "intelligible self," the noumenal self, independent of particular circumstances and motives that differentiate individuals from each other.[42] Music, expressive of such a self, conveyed universal emotions that anyone could understand, because everyone was such a self.[43] One might compare this view to that of eleventh-century Kashmiri Shaivite Abhinavagupta, who held that the true savor (*rasa*) of the emotion (*bhāva*) produced by the performing arts arises only when one experiences it in its essence, as a universal mode of experience.[44]

In the twentieth century, however, artistic concepts of expression in the West have focused on the artist's personal emotions, although the supposition is usually that human drives and their vicissitudes are sufficiently similar to render such expression communicative to others. By contrast, twentieth-century Western philosophy became suspicious of the notion of emotional communication on any basis besides intersubjective awareness of a particular person's behavior (including speech). For some time, under the influence of Ludwig Wittgenstein, anglophone philosophy took the postulation of mental states to be unwarranted. In this respect, philosophy seemed more concerned to avoid speculating beyond what is provable than to acknowledge the possibility of communicating anything beyond what is observed in behavior. While many contemporary philosophers reject the proscription on reference to mental states, debate continues to emphasize external behavior and what is intersubjectively verifiable.

A growing number of musicologists and philosophers have recently urged a kind of restoration of a sense of a person behind musical expression. They do not, however, propose that the emotions expressed are the occurrent emotions of the composer or performer. Somewhat resembling adherents of eighteenth-century expressionism, these theorists propose that the communicator of musically expressed emotions is not the particular individual who composes or performs, but a more abstract and more universal character, a persona, particular to music.[45]

As Jerrold Levinson characterizes the notion, the persona is "the individual indefinitely imaged as the subject of the state being expressed."[46] This seems a reasonable answer if one considers that *persona* means mask, or the face one presents to the world. The persona is not the full-fledged character, but the personality as it appears. If we take the putative musical persona to be something like this, it would be the hypothetical person who experiences the apparent emotions expressed in music, with no further characterization than that.[47] Superficially, "someone's" emotions are expressed; the persona is, essentially, that "someone." Levinson has associated the persona with the sense of human intentionality and agency that we recognize in music. I am inclined to agree with him: we do interpret music, for the most part, as human communication, even in instrumental music, in which the source of the communication is minimally identified. The persona is the *mask*, or placeholder, for this source.

The persona is something of a persona non grata to many philosophers of music, Davies and Kivy among them. They hold that musical expression is *in* the music; we need not posit some person to whom the expressiveness belongs. Music is expressive by virtue of its resemblance to the kind of behavior or utterance characteristic of a person experiencing an emotion.[48] Hence the persona is unnecessary.

Davies and Kivy diverge in their further grounds for criticizing the persona idea. Davies acknowledges that a listener might contemplate a work of music in terms of a persona; he objects to the idea that imagining a persona is necessary for a full understanding of the work and doubts that music constrains the imagined narrative enough for it to be useful for illuminating what specific music is expressing.[49] Kivy, by contrast, dislikes the very idea of the persona, primarily on the ground that it is too vague to be very helpful. "The musical persona is such a vague, abstract, shadowy being that even 'its' sex cannot be determined,"[50] he complains.

No doubt Kivy is right that the musical persona is ungendered, but I think this vagueness is a virtue, enabling listeners and performers with various personal traits to identify with it. The fact that the musical persona is in many respects devoid of detail allows the listener the possibility of an unobstructed vicarious joining in with the movement of the music, including the expressive movement. Once again, I suggest that a type of vagueness in music is a virtue. Because the persona does not have specific traits besides those exemplified in its behavior, many of the situating characteristics that identify individuals in everyday life are lacking, along with the interference these sometimes present for empathetic identification with others. And the modes of movement that music conveys are not restricted to persons of any particular body type, a fact that yields considerable delight in childhood games of imitating animals. A petite preschooler can display a lumbering gait, for example. The postulation of a largely indefinite persona reflects the fact that musically expressed emotion can be, but need not be, recognized by anyone and everyone participating in the musical experience—including composer, performer, and listener.[51] Whether or not imaging a persona's experience will lead to convergence in judgments about what a given piece of music is expressing is another question.

Aaron Ridley rightly suggests that some works of music are more likely than others to suggest an impression of a persona doing the expressing, and that the responsiveness of the individual listener plays an important role in the experience of a work of music.[52] Importantly, Ridley acknowledges transformations of the listener's affective response over the course a particular experience of music. He suggests that initially the feeling state expressed by a musical persona may strike us as "out there" and as "a state of mind that is not ours . . . but the persona's."[53] We may well sympathize with this state of mind, but this somewhat distanced entertaining of the persona's feeling often gives way to a more identified empathetic response. "It seems reasonable," claims Ridley, "to describe the net effect upon the responsive audience as empathetic rather than sympathetic in nature . . . even though the persona to whom the person . . . may be said empathetically to respond has been partly constructed by him, on sympathetic grounds."[54]

What strikes me as particularly important about these observations is their acknowledgment that a listener's affective perspective on the music can vary over the course of a particular work. We may listen from a primarily intellectual state of mind, in which case we may not respond to the expressive content with either sympathy or empathy.[55] Instead, we occupy a relatively detached perspective. At such moments the music is no less expressive, but we don't particularly identify the expression with our own individual state. Even if we are responsive on an intellectual level, as Ridley notes, we may shift from an initially somewhat distanced attitude toward a more fully empathetic one. I would add that our attention and stance can shift over the course of listening to music, particularly while listening to long and complex works.[56] Sometimes we are particularly identifying with the emotions expressed. At other times we may occupy a relatively detached perspective on the music and its emotional content. At such moments the music is no less expressive, but we don't particularly identify the expression with our own individual state.

I think the notion of a persona is useful for suggesting the range of relationships we can take toward musically expressed emotion. At times we identify with the persona (in which case we do not take the detached analytical view in which the term or impression *persona* would likely come to mind). At other times, we are more emotionally detached from the music, and the term *persona* is serviceable for indicating a sense that the expressive content pertains to beings like us, categorically considered.

3. Music Arouses Emotion

Cultures appear to be fairly unanimous in the belief that music can arouse emotion. We have already mentioned the Kaluli of Papua New Guinea and the Temiar of Malaysia, and the texts of ancient China, as well as the raga system of Indian music. Merriam reports that members of the Basongye tribe of Africa believe that even outside of its cultural context, music can arouse emotion.[57] Tuamotus, a Polynesia people, believe that mana, or the supernatural power of the ancestors, is conveyed through their music. Mana is more than emotion, but emotional nonetheless.[58] Anthony Seeger similarly reports of the Suyá people of the Amazon rainforest: "Suyá singing arouses sadness in some and creates euphoria in the rest."[59]

Music's power to influence emotion is one of the key reasons that Chinese philosophers typically believe that music has significant ethical influence. They often emphasize music's potential as a means of emotional regulation.[60] The neo-Confucian thinker Chou Tun-I (Zhou Dunyi) observes, "As the sound of music is calm, the heart of the listener becomes peaceful, and as the words of the music are good, those who sing them will admire them. The result will be that customs are transformed and mores are changed."[61] The ancient "Record of Music" and the Confucian tradition generally emphasize the importance of structuring music in accordance with right principles so that the influence it exerts is good.[62]

Like Chinese philosophy, Indian thought takes for granted that music arouses emotion. The classical text that elaborates on the connection is the *Nātyaśāstra*. Insofar as it provides techniques for achieving a basic emotional tone in performance, the *Nātyaśāstra* offers a theory of emotional imitation through the arts, including music; but it is primarily concerned with arousing emotion in the audience. The aim in performance is to arouse one or more *bhāvas*, or basic emotional states.[63] Ideally, however, performances arouse one of eight *rasas*, each of which is the universalized flavor or savor corresponding to one of the *bhāvas*.[64]

Ancient Greek philosophers also held that music arouses emotion. The Pythagoreans may have originated the Greek idea that music could have ethical effects, that is, an impact on listeners' spiritual state that would influence their behavior. This idea was linked to the notion that each tribe or city-state had its own characteristic mode, and that the modes themselves had an impact on the character of the people. Damon of Athens (fl. 460 BCE), Plato, and Aristotle all endorsed this view, commonly called the *ethos* theory.[65]

Many of the great Islamic philosophers of the Middle Ages explicitly endorse some version of arousal theory. Al-Kindi (ca. 800–870) contends that although the emotional impact of particular instruments is culturally relative, some music can instill courage, strength, military fervor, or delight in any listener.[66] Al-Farabi (d. ca. 950) stresses both the expressive function of music and its ability to communicate the emotions expressed to listeners.[67] He classifies the affects linked to music into three categories: affects that make the soul stronger (e.g., anger and hostility), affects that soften the soul (e.g., fear and mercy), and affects between the other two categories (e.g., calm).[68] Ibn Sina suggests that the listener's soul conforms to the affective quality of the music heard. He also claims that music (and sound in general) can help release intense emotions and tranquilize disruptive ones.[69] Al-Ghazali contends that music can arouse various emotions, both energizing and relaxing ones, and it can stir the spiritually prepared person to longing for God, the highest potential of music.[70]

Like many medieval Islamic thinkers, seventeenth- and eighteenth-century European theorists often emphasized music's power to arouse feeling and held that the emotions expressed in music were the ones aroused in the listener.[71] The idea that listeners mirror emotions expressed in music continues to hold sway, but this view is hard to verify empirically. Experimental subjects may describe their emotional responses to music inaccurately because they read into the music what they think they are supposed to feel on the basis of "demand characteristics," cues that indicate what the researcher wants to find.[72] Listeners may also identify the emotions they think a musical passage expresses as their own feelings, even if they have not really experienced these emotions.[73]

Music's arousal of emotion is probably widely taken for granted, but some theorists have challenged the view. Langer denies that music arouses emotion, even though it symbolizes emotional life. Composer Paul Hindemith argues that emotions aroused by music are not real, but apparent. "The emotions which music evokes are not feelings, but they are the images, memories of feelings."[74] Psychologist Carroll C. Pratt, while acknowledging that some listeners do feel aroused by the emotion expressed by music, contends that most listeners (and all who are sophisticated) do not.[75] Peter Kivy similarly rejects the view that listeners typically mirror expressed emotion (though he is decidedly in the minority).[76] The lack of unanimity among listeners is one of the principle arguments against the arousal view: not everyone seems to experience the emotions that are allegedly aroused.[77]

One of the most innovative accounts of the music-emotion relationship, that of Leonard B. Meyer, deflects this criticism. Meyer's theory is based on the idea that as we listen to music in a familiar style, we have certain expectations of the way the music will proceed. "Affect or emotion-felt is aroused," argues Meyer, "when an expectation—a tendency to respond—activated by the musical stimulus situation, is temporarily inhibited or permanently blocked."[78] According to Meyer, listeners typically have affective responses at points in the music where their expectations are thwarted. Alternatively, a listener may approach the music less emotively and more analytically, attending to the way it has been structured and noting the points at which it takes a surprising turn. These are the points at which affect predictably occurs.

Meyer's indication of alternative approaches that a listener can take to music, with different impacts on affective response, strikes me as important and surprisingly underappreciated. If the arousal of emotion depends in part on a listener's attitude in approaching the music, there should be no mystery as to why one listener experiences musically induced emotion while another one does not. Meyer makes the important point that alternative types of engagement can be taken toward the same piece of music. Although Meyer emphasizes different personality types and educational backgrounds as inclining listeners toward different orientations toward the music, his point acknowledges the possibility that listeners can be flexible in their focus, a point that I will make much of in what follows.

One of the ingenious features of Meyer's theory is its attempt to connect affective response with objective features of a musical work: "granted listeners who have developed reaction patterns appropriate to the work in question, the structure of the affective response to a piece of music can be studied by examining the music itself . . . deviations can be regarded as emotional or affective stimuli."[79] If Meyer's strategy succeeds, it dispenses with the need to track the subjective reactions of particular listeners. As long as a listener is sufficiently habituated to the style of a piece of music, his or her emotional responses will correspond to its structural features (unless the listener defuses these by rationalizing them).

Meyer's theory of the mechanism for musical arousal of emotion is only one of many. Even if we restrict our attention to the emotional impact of intramusical developments, we need not limit ourselves to the fulfillment or nonfulfillment of expectations. Early in our exposure to a style of music, for example, before our expectations have become very detailed, emotions of satisfaction can be aroused by virtue of our tracking a trajectory of music and recognizing its gradual development of clear form. The goal-directed character of many cultures' music (as we noted in chapter 3) is one structural component that can give shape to a piece of music. Many musical forms across the world encourage a gradual sense of the music "taking shape." For example, the *alap* in Hindustani music, which involves a rhythmically free exploration of the raga (scale-melody) on which a piece is constructed, typically gives way to a section with a steady pulse (the *jor*), and later reaches a stage characterized by a definite rhythmic cycle imposed by a drum (*jhala*).

The purposive growth and renewal that are experienced in the unfolding of a musical form are also emotionally satisfying. Japanese music tends to be organized in a sequence that moves from relative rhythmic freedom (*jo*) toward greater rhythmic regularity (*ha*) and ultimately toward a conclusion in which density is intensified (*kyū*).[80] In many forms of Western classical music, particularly in sonata-allegro form, preliminary statements of themes give way to more exploratory development of some of their features, ultimately to give way to a recapitulation, typically in the tonic key. The move from the development (in which bits of the form are allowed to evolve on their own) to the recapitulation signals a new level of integration in which the earliest statements of themes are renewed but are more replete with meaning by virtue of the elaboration of its elements over the course of the development. The structure follows the course of what John Dewey analyzes as meaningful experience generally: the evolution of themes in tension with each other toward a new integration. The development of form enables participants to undergo an integral experience that runs its course to a culmination and aftermath, just as valued experiences in life do. By sharing the shape of many meaningful developments within life itself, the musical piece resonates with meaningful experience in life generally.[81] In this way, it stimulates a sense of life through musical means.

Other mechanisms for arousal are not based on musical structure. Patrik Juslin and Daniel Västfjäll indicate multiple mechanisms that can act independently or in tandem:

1. Brain stem reflexes (the arousal of the nervous system by acoustic effects);
2. Evaluative conditioning (the pairing of "positive" and "negative" stimuli in music with other positive or negative stimuli);
3. Emotional contagion (emotional mirroring or mimicry of the emotions seemingly expressed in the music);
4. Visual imagery (which is conjured by the listener in connection with music, and which itself has affective associations);
5. Episodic Memory (personal associations that have affective character);
6. Musical expectancy (the type of structural expectancy that Meyer describes); and
7. Cognitive appraisal (the sense that the music may positively or negative affect one's goals or plans).[82]

Because these arousal mechanisms may operate in combination, and because they operate at different levels of mental functioning and interact at different levels, Juslin and Västfjäll suggest that mixed emotions may arise in connection with music.[83] I will discuss their research further in connection with the cultural variation in musical arousal of emotion.

4. Music Induces Moods or Feelings

A fourth candidate for an explanation view of music's relationship to emotion should be mentioned. This is the position that music arouses moods or "feelings" instead of emotions. The motivation for this view is largely theoretical. Emotion is often analyzed as requiring an object.[84] Indeed, one of Kivy's grounds for denying that music evokes "garden-variety" emotions is the argument that emotion must have an object, and music does not present an appropriate object for such responses. One alternative response to Kivy is to claim that music elicits moods, which do not take objects. Moods simply set an affective tone for experience of whatever sort.

The difficulty with this approach is that there is no consensus on how to distinguish emotions and moods, although a number of criteria have been suggested. Sloboda and Juslin contend that moods are lingering conditions, while emotions are relatively brief; that moods, unlike emotions, cannot be identified by means of a particular stimulus event; and that moods do not have distinctive facial expressions, while emotions do.[85] All of these points are controversial, however. While psychological experiments tend to define emotion operationally, as brief episodes, emotions can certainly be extended over time. Some emotions, such as resentment, even seem to be long-termed by definition.[86] Although moods may develop in the absence of a defining precipitating event, they sometimes do commence as a response to some occurrence. I recall several friends becoming depressed by the murder of John Lennon, and many Americans became jumpy after the terrorist attack on the World Trade Center on September 11, 2001. As for the emotions having distinctive facial displays, a theory proposed by Darwin and developed in great detail by Paul Ekman, even Ekman sometimes suggests that a distinct correlation applies only to affect programs, which in turn specify only basic emotions. This would imply that nonbasic emotions are not distinguishable on the basis of identifiable facial expression; and the display of nonbasic emotions is generally acknowledged to admit of culturally relativity.[87] Ekman's point, of course, assumes that one can distinguish between basic and nonbasic emotions, a matter that is itself controversial.[88]

R. J. Davidson suggests another way of putting the distinction between emotions and moods: "emotions bias action, whereas moods bias cognition."[89] In other words, emotions function to assist an individual's action readiness, while moods influence the way information, both incoming and remembered, is processed.[90] But surely moods affect action readiness. A person in a chipper mood is more geared to energetic action than one who is despondent. Emotions influence the processing of information, too. Anger at a particular person, for example, can certainly affect whether some new instance of behavior on that person's part appears as evidence of his or her bad character.

Aaron Ridley, taking emotions to require objects, contends that music arouses feelings, not emotions, but I think his category of "feelings" amounts to what other theorists often mean by "moods." Ridley holds that feelings "do not take particular material objects but instead consist in a tendency to regard things in general as fitting the description given by the relevant formal objects."[91] Feelings "color our world," and such world-coloring affect is what we experience in connection with music.[92] Ridley does not contend that musically aroused feeling lacks an object, but he considers it a generalized object, not a particular material one. He submits, however, that "some feelings can be interpreted as attitudes of a certain kind, where an attitude is a tendency to regard things in a particular way, often an evaluative way."[93]

Certain philosophers who deny that moods lack objects take a similar approach to the issue of the affective object. Robert C. Solomon contends that moods have objects, but that their object is the world in general. He sees emotions and moods as being different domains along a continuum.[94] Martha Nussbaum similarly argues that some emotions have "a highly general object (fear of unnamed and unnamable dangers, hope for something good)," which music can embody.[95] Gabriela Husain, William Thompson, and Glenn Schellenberg propose that moods and emotions lie on a continuum, defining moods as "relatively long-lasting emotions."[96] Neurologist Antonio Damasio also rejects a strong distinction between emotions and moods; he calls moods "background emotions."[97]

Another alternative is to deny that emotions must take objects. On this basis, Colin Radford challenges those who defend the idea that sad music does not necessarily make us sad.

> Only people confused by philosophical theory about the emotions would say this cannot be sadness or, if it is, that it is unintelligible (and so probably it is not sadness!). For sadness cannot only lack an object, it can lack any obvious cause, and can be experienced in situations in which there is no focused attention, or if there is, we cannot see why our focusing on that should do anything more than coincide with the onset of our sadness. People who are sad may be puzzled as to why they are feeling sad, and what they are feeling sad about, and why it overcame them as they heard the clock strike, stepped off the bus, etc. Everyone is familiar with these experiences.[98]

Radford concludes that this demonstrates that an emotion need not have a particular object. A defender of the view that emotions take objects might reply that sadness is sometimes a mood (e.g., in music, where it lacks a definite object), although sometimes it is an emotion, or that one's sadness may have an object that one recognizes only unconsciously.[99] In any case, the contention that music arouses moods is sufficiently vague, and the criteria of the emotion/mood distinction sufficiently debatable, that the mood theory has not been a leading contender in the debate about music's relation to the affective domain.

A Proposal: All of the Above

Which of the accounts just considered is right? My answer is, "All of them." At least sometimes music has each of these relationships to emotion. Fortunately, these candidates are not mutually exclusive. The connection between emotion and music depends on the participant's perspective, and one's sense of one's position in relation to the music is fluid, particularly if one is a listener. Music flows, and so does our relationship to it. One can move back and forth among the possibilities described by the various emotion-music theories. Each alternative suggests a particular relationship between the perceiver or performer and the music, and one can shift from one relationship to another during the course of listening or performing a single piece of music.

Imitation/representation theory suggests a relatively detached point of view in which a listener recognizes similarities between features of music and features of emotional experience. Some listeners will find resemblance between the structural forms of music and some features of emotions along the lines of Hanslick's account. But a more common basis for finding imitation of emotion in music arises as a consequence of the context of music. When music is used to accompany dance, drama, or film, for example, it seems to underscore the resemblance between the music's movements and those of emotionally motivated actors. In these contexts the resemblance between music and emotional surges, and that between music and behavior, seem unquestionably parallel, although I doubt that most audience members contemplate the resemblance dispassionately for extended periods.

Does such resemblance provide evidence in favor of imitation or expression theory? I would say, "Both," depending on whether one is more abstractly observing the parallel forms (noting the music's imitation of or resemblance to emotional experience) or whether one is more generically empathetic (appreciating the similarity between the music and the behavior of a person with whom one might empathize). In general, I think the various music-emotion theories operate along a continuum, with the imitation/representation theory corresponding to a relatively disinterested mode of listening, expression theory corresponding to a somewhat more engaged mode (in that one is appreciating the kinship between the music and the behavior of an agent with whom one might empathize), and arousal theory corresponding to a highly empathetic mode of engaged listening.

The mood theory also seems an apt description of some cases of music arousing affect. This is evident when music is enlisted in connection with dance, drama, and film. Usually the reasons for employing music in these contexts are to arouse the emotions and to stimulate the physiology of audience members. But this often works so effectively because music first stimulates general moods or background emotional tones. Once the mood is induced, the audience is primed for the arousal of emotion. The case is very similar to the Pavlovian case of the low two-note cello motif in the movie *Jaws*.[100] After an association is established between this motif and sharks swimming in the deep, the motif primes audience members to jump at any hint of a surprise, for they expect a shark to appear.

Musical soundtracks are geared to emotional arousal. For example, sighing wails of the bagpipe early on during the film *Titanic*[101] prime the audience for the poignant emotions the plot will provoke. The association of such poignancy with sweeping violin music is so common that a clichéd way of indicating that a person is expressing self-pity is to play "air-violin," a wordless sarcasm suggesting "How sad!" In the case of such soundtracks, the music is prompting a mood, not an emotion, but at the same time it is priming one for the experience of emotions on cue. The use of "mood music" in everyday life is another case in which the mood set by music primes the occurrence of kindred emotion.

The very same similarities that justify a comparison between musical and emotional patterns—which underlies imitation theory—strongly suggest a basis for music's ability to arouse emotion. Meyer is right in claiming that interpretive distance distinguishes emotional from analytic attention to music. He observes that one can listen from a detached analytical point of view or from a more engaged stance in which one is receptive to emotional arousal. The imitation/representation point of view presupposes the more detached point of view; the expression view presupposes a less detached outlook; and the arousal view presupposes an engaged one, which enables more direct identification with the music's movement than the other two stances.

Davies points out that it is quite common for a person who recognizes similarities between musical patterns and the patterns of behavior typical of some kinds of emotion to feel the emotion in question, even though other emotional responses are possible as well.[102] A mirroring relationship between expressed and aroused emotion is presupposed by the common tendency to reinforce one's occurrent emotion (or mood) with music that expresses it. In this case, however, the emotion is not newly aroused by the music. The teenager who reinforces an alienated feeling by listening to music that expresses alienation (almost always texted music) uses the feeling as the principle of selection in choosing music for listening. But the chosen music effectively adds fuel to the feeling. The music in this case is something of a two-way mirror for the emotion, both reflecting and renewing it.

I suspect that mirroring emotion in connection with musical experience is more common than mirroring other people's emotion in everyday life. In daily life one often occupies some specific role or set of roles (even if they are temporary) with respect to someone who displays emotional behavior. Such roles help to determine what emotional response is appropriate, for emotional appropriateness is often a matter of interpersonal positioning. Sometimes emotional mirroring is called for, but sometimes it is not. For example, if someone behaves angrily toward you, you may have a response that is not merely mirroring, even if you are moved to anger as well. You may feel fear if the angry person is perceived as a real threat, or contempt if the angry person is not.

In the case of music, however, one is usually not in a specific role or position vis-à-vis another person that determines the dramatically appropriate response. Accordingly, the possibility of mirroring the emotion suggested by the music—a purely empathetic response—is not blocked by one's own practical stance toward another person who is behaving. (Conceivably, one could stand in some kind of relationship with another performer or a composer that might restrict one's responses, such as competitive rivalry or close personal attachment. But these are not, I think, the usual circumstances of either performers or listeners.)

Common as the mirroring response is, it does not preclude other stances a listener might take toward emotion expressed through music.[103] One can imaginatively move around the music's emotional terrain. One can shift back and forth between a less engaged and a more empathetic mode of relating, to the point of identifying with the music. Efforts to adjudicate among the theories of music's relation to emotion usually ignore the fact that the listener is able to relate to the music in a fluid way, moving back and forth between the extremes of emotionally identifying with the music and taking an analytic approach to music as an object.

Performers while practicing often experience such shifts when they go back and forth between playing a passage as they might perform it, in an emotionally engaged manner, but analytically alert to flaws in their playing, enough to be able to stop and attend to those areas that need specific work. Performers in ensembles, particularly in improvisatory contexts, maintain a dynamic equilibrium between involvement and keen attention to other performers. Paul Berliner describes the situation of improvisatory performers:

> Listening is typically a dynamic activity and performers continually adopt different perspectives on the musical patterns that surround them. Their constantly fluctuating powers of concentration, the extraordinary volume of detail requiring them to absorb material selectively and developments in their own parts that periodically demand full attention, together create a ka-

leidophonic essence of each artist's perception of the collective performance. Moreover ... improvisers sometimes deliberately shift focus within the music's dazzling texture to derive stimulation from different players.[104]

Similarly, it is possible for a listener to attend emotionally to an unfolding piece of music, sometimes being more detached and taking the music as an object of emotional display, sometimes focusing on the music as animate (perhaps semiconsciously thinking of the music as tracking the experience of an agent), and sometimes feeling emotional identification with music. The various types of theories describe alternative possibilities that a listener or performer might take up at different moments.

I do not mean to suggest that listeners and even performers are lurching from one state to another, overcome by emotional arousal at one moment and completely switching gears at another. Such shifts may happen, but I doubt that this is typical. Instead, what I am suggesting is more akin to Paul Thom's notion of "playful attention" during the course of a performance. Describing the situation in the context of musical performance, Thom plausibly suggests that audience members can and optimally do engage in active play of attention over the course of listening. He itemizes six types of playful attention that can factor into a listener's activity of interpreting the work.

1. "An audience's attention can play between the performer's present action and recollected past actions or anticipated future ones.
2. "An audience's attention can play between one performer and another.
3. "An audience's attention can play between content and vehicle.
4. "An audience's attention may play between a particular performance as a whole and another performance of the same work.
5. "The audience's attention can play between aspects of the performance and aspects of their own lives.
6. "An audience's attention can play between what occurs inside the performance space and what has occurred or may occur outside it."[105]

Some of these types of attentive play require a somewhat detached outlook—attention playing between content and vehicle, for example—although it would be possible to do so while largely mirroring the expressive content and flashing occasionally on how glad one is to be present for a performance that conveys it with such skill. Others of the types of attentive play—for example, the comparison of the present performance with another performance of the same work—probably necessitate sufficient distance that one is not at the moment of comparison fully identifying with the music. It would be possible, for example, to relate the present performance to another one in terms of technique or in terms of the affective feel of the performance, or to compare the two performances, sequentially, in both respects as different features draw one's attention or come to mind. Although one might compare aspects of the performance to things going on in one's life in a dispassionate way, I suspect that often such comparisons involve emotional assent. Each of the types that Thom mentions admit of variety with respect to the extent of detachment involved. Importantly for my purposes, Thom points to the fact that shifts in attention occur for even "consummate" audience members. In fact, he considers such active mental engagement with the music to be the hallmark of consummate listening.

Fluidity in the focus of immediate attention while attending to music is suggested, too, by reports of listeners. Alf Gabrielsson, in a study of strong emotion in connection with music, quotes a young woman who had attended a performance of Mahler's unfinished Tenth Symphony, reconstructed.

> The orchestra is breaking out in a warmth that is fascinatingly painful. I remember tears filling my eyes. I felt as if I understood a message, from one time to another, from one human to another. I sat as if turned to stone, with my fingers gripping the armrest. After a while I became quite dizzy. Then I realized that I had forgotten to breathe. . . . The last movement opens with eleven beats of an enormous wooden club against the largest bass drum. The effect is horrible. A flute, followed by the strings, starts hesitatingly to develop a melody, but it is suddenly crushed by the beat of the wooden club. I was totally taken by surprise. Each time the club beat, I was seized by terror. Each time an instrument began to sound, doubtfully, I anticipated the hit of the wooden club, I mourned. Here, too, I felt like I was a receiver of a message . . . I felt like I had not missed a single note . . . the feeling of being spoken to, strongly and directly, lived inside me.[106]

The young woman, admittedly giving an after-the-fact report, suggests that she comes out of a state of extreme absorption enough to realize at one point that she has forgotten to breathe. The impression of receiving a message, which she mentions more than once, seems to imply a different degree of identification with the music's behavior than is indicated by her claim that she was "seized by terror." I suspect that in much of our emotional lives we have occasion to move from a state of unself-conscious emoting to a slightly more analytical condition of reflecting on what we are feeling. Alternatively, sometimes we are bracing ourselves with steadying "thoughts" when we feel a surge of inchoate feeling rising to awareness, only to find that surge overwhelming our composure. I see no reason to think that our focus is completely steady in music, any more than it is in these cases.

I emphasize the fluidity of the listener's emotional engagement as well as the relative freedom from situational features that would inhibit mirroring of expressed emotions because both are relevant to the musical participant's relative freedom to empathize through music, regardless of practical positions vis-à-vis particular individuals in nonmusical everyday contexts. The ability to relate without attention to ordinary roles is one of the reasons that music is particularly conducive to forging emotional connections even among strangers.

CROSS-CULTURAL SIMILARITIES

Theorists who emphasize listeners' differences with regard to emotional recognition and arousal through music presumably refer mainly to individuals with similar cultural backgrounds. We might surmise that differences would be more obvious cross-culturally, and this expectation, as we shall see, is empirically justified. However, there is evidence of much cross-cultural convergence at least in recognizing emotional expression in music. The interrelation of emotion and prosody appears to be shared cross-culturally.[107] Juslin and Laukka, in their previously cited study, found specific patterns of acoustic cues for particular emotions, regardless of culture. They point out that listeners recognized the emotion performers aimed to express, with particularly strong cross-cultural correlations for anger and sadness.[108]

Juslin elsewhere notes that the same acoustic codes are used cross-culturally for "songs of different 'emotional' types (e.g., mourning, love, war, lullaby)," and that this enables people to recognize these song-types in other cultures' music. "Mourning songs," he observes, "usually have a slow tempo, low sound level, and soft timbre, whereas festive songs have a fast tempo, high sound level, and bright timbre."[109] He concludes that "some aspects of music (e.g., tonality, melody, and harmony) are relatively more culture-specific, whereas other aspects . . . are more culture-independent (because they are based on nonverbal communication of emotion)."[110]

In a series of experiments Laura-Lee Balkwill and William Thompson investigated listeners' ability to recognize intended emotion in unfamiliar music.[111] In one study musical excerpts in Hindustani ragas were presented to Canadian subjects, who rated them in terms of tempo, rhythmic and melodic complexity, pitch range, and the emotions of anger, joy, sadness, and peacefulness. These subjects' judgments of joy, anger, and sadness (but not peacefulness) correlated significantly who had those of listeners with considerable experience with Hindustani music.[112] Another study, which involved experiments with subjects from Japan and Canada, corroborates the general finding that subjects from outside a musical culture could be fairly accurate in recognizing intended emotional expression.[113]

Balkwill and Thompson took pitch range, tempo, and rhythmic and melodic complexity to be straightforwardly perceptual cues and considered the emotional associations with the ragas to be enculturated cues, though they acknowledge that the two types of cues can be redundant. The distinction between the two types may not be as sharp as the experimenters hypothesize, given the influence that learned schemata may have on perception. What sounds deviant from the point of view of an uninitiated listener may not sound deviant from the point of view of a musical insider, and yet the impression of deviance may seem perceptually evident. Such an impression could well have an impact on the listener's ability to recognize emotional content, distracting attention from such content or prompting affective response.

Hanslick, with his insistence on absolute agreement, would probably be unimpressed by these convergences, given that experimenters offer their subjects a limited number of available emotion categories, so that responses within the same categorical range is taken to be agreement. Contemporary psychologists do not, however, take the establishment of constant regularities in spontaneous judgments of emotions expressed to be a reasonable goal. Juslin, for example, postulates that the apparently species-invariant acoustic cues for expressing emotions were selected by evolution for clear communication of broad emotion categories, not for nuances.[114]

If we do want more specificity than broad emotion terms provide, we may well emphasize cultural—and individual—differences, or at least grant their significance. One's views about cross-cultural correlations regarding musically expressed or aroused emotions depend in part on one's willingness to grant context a role in specifying particular emotions. The specific affective associations with particular ragas are evident only to the extent that one has absorbed these conventions, for example, even if the general emotion tone of a particular raga is more widely recognizable.

A particular difficulty that attends efforts to determine the extent of cross-cultural convergence in emotional expression is the fact that cultures do not categorize emotions in the same way. Marc Benamou, studying the use of affective terms to describe the expressive character of music among Western and Javanese subjects, ascertained that some Javanese emotion terms did not straightforwardly correspond to Western categories.[115] This raises some doubts about how much we can trust studies that purport to compare cultures. Presumably, we can assume that when Javanese subjects report expressiveness in music using words for which English-speaking subjects have no term, the two groups of subjects are not recognizing the same expressive content. But more generally, we should be alert to the possibility that imperfect translations lead us to imagine greater agreement about musical expression than we would find if we had a more nuanced sense of the way the terms are used in the respective languages.

With regard to musical arousal, we cannot assume that the sharing of emotions by listeners extends to nuances of experience. In the first place, much about the emotional experience of listening to music is listener specific. Such factors as disposition to mirror expressed emotions (on the basis of the listening stance that the listener adopts, which may be influenced by temperamental factors), mental imagery, personal associations, and connection with the listener's own goals can differ from one individual to another. The specific level of empathy adopted in a given listening experience can also affect how arousal mechanisms might interact.

Moreover, as we have already noted, one's responses can shift as one interacts with the music, just as the emotions expressed are not constant, but sequential. This may help to explain why many find it difficult to articulate the emotions aroused in precise terms and why listeners may spontaneously choose different emotion terms in labeling the emotion(s) aroused. The fluidity with which listeners can move from one degree of emotional distance or empathy to another renders the emotional character of a particular encounter with a piece of music (as performed by oneself or by others) nonstandardizable.

Another reason that the arousal of emotion by a specific piece of music cannot be precisely delimited is that performance variables can have a powerful impact on emotional arousal. To a significant extent arousal is performance-specific, not work-specific. Charles Keil analyzes the affective impact of aspects of performance in terms of vital drive and participatory discrepancies.[116] Vital drive is a term Keil borrows from André Hodeir, who contends that it is a part of "swing" and characterizes it in terms of "rhythmic fluidity."[117] In jazz, Keil observes, "To the extent that the rhythms conflict with or 'exhibit' the pulse without destroying it altogether, we have engendered feeling, and for a solo to grow the feeling must accumulate."[118] Vital drive is missing from Meyer's analysis of emotion in music, Keil comments, and he offers the following principle to supplement it: "Paralleling Meyer then, the greater the processual tension and gestural uncertainty a jazz piece has the higher its value."[119]

Participatory discrepancies are those nuanced deviations from precision in articulating the rhythms and pitches in music as notated or otherwise abstractly indicated. These, according to Keil, are the points at which we gain an affective impression of another human being. They also explain why human performance moves us while a computer reading a score with mechanical precision usually does not. Keil asserts provocatively, "Music, to be personally involving and socially valuable, must be 'out of time' and 'out of tune.'"[120] He is not particularly interested in offering labels for the emotions aroused by participatory discrepancies or vital drive. He seems to see the affective upshot of participatory discrepancies as the "feelingful" recognition of other human beings, who share and express emotion with individual precision.[121]

We will have occasion in the following chapter to consider further the feelingful recognition of others in connection with music. For now, I will conclude this one by moving back from our grounds for doubting that the nuances of emotional arousal are identical for any two individuals toward the more optimistic view we are likely to take if we accept broader emotional categorizations. A rather surprising aspect of emotional arousal in connection with music is the common association of music with happiness or joy, despite the fact that music can arouse other, more specific emotions, including some that are far from cheerful. Judith Becker points out:

> "Happiness," meaning some kind of strong positive emotion, is the feeling most frequently cited in connection with music listening and may constitute one of the universals of cross-cultural studies of music and emotion. From the "polka happiness" of the Polish-American parties of Chicago . . . to the !Kung of the Kalahari desert: "Being at a dance makes our hearts happy" . . . to the Basongye of the Congo who "make music in order to be happy" . . . to the extroverted joy of a Pentecostal musical service music has the ability to make people feel good.[122]

In a study of the musical arousal of emotion by Juslin, Laukka, and their colleagues, 1,500 adult Swedish citizens similarly ranked happiness the emotion they experience most commonly in connection with music.[123] What should we make of this?

We could follow the tendency among psychologists to analyze in terms of valence, that is, in terms of positive or negative emotion. We might, accordingly, consider the characterization of music as arousing happiness, even alongside more disturbing emotions, as indicating an overall positive valence for musical experience. The notion of valence would not, however, be very informative in this context. One problem with valence is that the positive/negative poles are not consistently defined. Are they equivalent to pleasure and pain? To "desirable" and "undesirable"? To conducing to and interfering with well-being? To stimulating approach and avoidance?[124]

Another problem is that various levels of musical detail might be related to valence. For example, dissonance might be perceived as "negative" in the sense of requiring movement (and hence suggesting a kind of aversion), while consonance might be perceived as "positive" because it does not. Anne Blood and Robert Zatorre point out, however, that the positive affect that coincides with chills while listening to music involves different brain structures than those related to consonance and dissonance. Moreover, the pleasure associated with consonance is mild by comparison to that involved with chills. If valence is interpreted in terms of listener enjoyment, it appears that listeners enjoy music that is sad as well as music that is happy.[125] Husain and her colleagues suggest the further complication that "positive" and "negative" moods may be influenced by different neurotransmitters that may be activated.[126]

Perhaps a more straightforward psychological explanation of the association of music with joy and happiness concerns the activation of brain structures. Blood and Zatorre, conducting PET studies of subjects who experienced "chills of varying intensity while listening," found brain activation patterns associated with euphoria and/or pleasant emotion, including that involved in cocaine use. "Activity in these regions in relation to reward processes is known to involve dopamine and opioid systems, as well as other neurotransmitters."[127] They suggest that the physiological reward system is engaged (and not differentially on the basis of consonance and dissonance). They conclude:

> Music recruits neural systems of reward and emotion similar to those known to respond specifically to biologically relevant stimuli, such as food and sex, and those that are artificially activated by drugs of abuse. . . . Activation of these brain systems in response to a stimulus as abstract as music may represent an emergent property of the complexity of human cognition. Perhaps as formation of anatomical and functional links between phylogenically older, survival-related brain systems and newer, more cognitive systems increased our general capacity to assign meaning to abstract stimuli, our capacity to derive pleasure from these stimuli also increased.[128]

Reference to "the reward systems," while perhaps accurate, contrasts with the outpouring of affect in the descriptions of those who are deeply moved by music. Many philosophers and scientists may urge caution in ascribing everyday emotion terms to music, but the musical participant rarely seems concerned to restrict his or her emotional vocabulary.[129] Recall the previously cited passage from a study by Alf Gabrielsson, quoting a young woman who described her responses to a performance of Mahler's unfinished Tenth Symphony. This woman's report of the emotions she experienced in listening to Mahler emphasizes an aspect of emotion we have not yet attended to, the impression that music involves emotional communication. ("I felt like I was a receiver of a message . . . I felt like I had not missed a single note . . . the feeling of being spoken to, strongly and directly, lived inside me.")

Despite the variability of emotions experienced, the association with "happiness" seems to be basic to what draws people to music. Besides the physiological impact of music on the rewards system, I submit that part of what grounds this association of music and happiness is our sense of interpersonal participation in something larger than ourselves. Even if we are listeners, we gain "that quickened sense of life" that Walter Pater describes as the ambition of the arts, and a sense that we are dynamically involved in the living world that surrounds us.[130]

In the following chapter I will defend the idea that music impresses upon us a powerful awareness of sharing life with others in the world, and that this awareness is a source of basic security. I will argue that one of music's cross-cultural emotional functions is to evoke and reinforce feelings of security, and that this depends both on specieswide aspects of musical perception and on culturally specific associations. In promoting feelings of security, musical experience reinforces our sense of comfort in the world, replenishes our sense of life, and invigorates our recognition that we share a world with others.

CHAPTER 8

Comfort and Joy

Music . . . it's a form of communication and reassurance of feelings . . .
what I get out of music is a feeling that I'm not alone.

ERIC CLAPTON, *Official Tour Program 1998*

ONTOLOGICAL SECURITY

Let us return for a moment to the musical mission of the Voyager project.
In packing a selection of the world's music and the means to play it on the
Voyager spacecraft, the United States' space program expressed openness to
the possibility of encountering intelligent life elsewhere in the universe. This
gesture says to any beings with the ingenuity to use these devices, "If you
have minds like ours, we want you to know it. You are not alone—and neither
are we."

What does it mean to be alone in the world? Most often, people use this
expression to describe someone bereft of family. Our very concern for such
people indicates that they are not alone in the most extreme sense. But we recognize that a person experiencing new loss or multiple losses often feels that
isolated. What such individuals feel is the lack of sharing on intimate terms
the texture of the world they experience. Their sense of "we" as a supportive
awareness has been undercut. They no longer feel connected because of the
absence of others they belong with and to. To be alone in the world is to be
devastated.

Although healthy individuals can come to feel separate from the world as
a consequence of major losses, mental health generally involves confidence in
having a place within the larger world. R. D. Laing describes individuals who
have a basic sense of belonging to the same world as others as being "ontologically secure."

A basically ontologically secure person will encounter all the hazards of life, social, ethical, spiritual, biological, from a centrally firm sense of his own and other people's reality and identity. It is often difficult for a person with such a sense of his integral selfhood and personal identity, of the permanency of things, of the reliability of natural processes, of the substantiality of natural processes, of the substantiality of others, to transpose himself into the world of an individual whose experiences may be utterly lacking in any unquestionable self-validating certainties.[1]

According to Laing, the lack of ontological security is a form of profound psychological disturbance. He describes schizoid and schizophrenic individuals as lacking this basic sense. "There is a loss of 'vital contact' with the world."[2] Interestingly, Laing describes one of his psychotic patients as being at ease only in musical circumstances. "There was only one situation as far as I could judge in which he could let himself go without anxiety at not recovering himself again, and that was in listening to jazz." Laing describes music (as well as quasi-mystical experience of God) as a special case in which some schizoid and schizophrenic patients can do what they are otherwise almost completely incapable of doing—overcoming a sense of deep isolation and a desperate need for protection.[3]

Provisionally, I submit that one of music's most basic emotional functions is to help to establish a sense of ontological security in the participant and to reinforce feelings of security more generally. What this implies is that music does not just serve as entertainment or replenishment in our leisure time. Music makes important contributions to psychological health.

At this point I am shifting from a consideration of features of music as it is structured and experienced by human beings to some of the functions it serves. I think this is a warranted shift for two reasons. First, features of our musical capacities and the ubiquitous tendencies for structuring music enable some of its functions. The rhythmic entrainment that music with regular rhythm brings about, for instance, enables the use of music to coordinate activities as well as to promote feelings of solidarity with others who are perceived to be part of the musical company (however broadly this extends). Second, in that such functions are elaborations on our natural musical capacities, they reveal something about the universal aspects of music, even if it is important to keep in mind that music can be used in a variety of ways, some of which are far from humanizing. Indeed, one of my reasons for raising the question of how far the universal aspects of human musicality go is to prompt further consideration of how we might use it in more beneficial ways.

I will offer a number of prima facie arguments to show that music is implicated in participants' feelings of security (whether the participant is a performer or a listener), and that it functions to affect these feelings in human societies across the world. I will begin by considering some reasons for thinking that music helps to establish a sense of ontological security, and then discuss other grounds for thinking that music reinforces feelings of security in other respects.

In arguing that an important function of music is to promote feelings of security, I am challenging the view, advocated by Theodor Adorno, that we should be dubious of music that promotes a sense of comfort and security. According to Adorno, music supports a politically undesirable attitude of passive contentment with the status quo. I think that Adorno fails to acknowledge the important role that music plays in promoting a more basic kind of comfort, specifically a basic comfort as being a participant within the social world. Thus I think there is a vital sociopolitical role to be played by music that listeners find comforting. I agree with Adorno that music, like all art, can help people to push beyond their usual ways of seeing things, and that it can inspire them to reenvision possibilities in the social sphere. But if music accomplishes these things, these accomplishments are premised upon the support it offers for listeners' basic sense of security, not upon the lack of this sense. In other words, those who can be persuaded to move beyond their comfort zone are individuals who are already deeply secure, and music has the virtue of instilling the security as well as providing the persuasion.

If one accepts this view, then Adorno's objection to music encouraging contentment appears wrongheaded. Music can get through people's defenses, but it can only do so because music—that is, music in a style with which one has developed a sense of familiarity—promotes a sense of basic security. One of the effects of music's conservatism—that tendency to repetition that is so typical of music but would be distressing in most other arts—is to engender or reinforce a sense of background stability as well as confidence that humanity and one's own society will continue into the future. Music can shake people up and encourage change, but this only works effectively, I am convinced, when music supports the belief that one is ultimately safe.

I will defend the claim that music serves to help establish and reinforce feelings of security, including ontological security. I will defend this claim by drawing attention to a number of features of music that produce feelings of security. Some are particularly related to a sense of sharing the world with other beings like ourselves; others encourage feelings of being at home in and supported by the world; still others draw attention to the participant's specific network of relationships in a particular culture and life story. Although such feelings of security are not in practice sharply divided, I will organize my discussion in terms of these three categories. The first category links music to ontological security; the second to existential security (the sense of being at home in the world); and the third to a sense of belonging (in relation to some particular social membership).

I will begin by discussing aspects of music in the first category: the physiology of hearing and the previously noted connection of musical sensitivities to the establishment of security in infancy. In the second category I will consider the conservatism of music, music's attainment of form, and music's intimation of continuity into the future, features of musical experience that promote a sense that the larger world is supportive and is our home. This category also reinforces a sense of ontological security in that the world that one securely inhabits is also a world shared with other people. The third group includes the role of music in developing a sense membership within one's society and its role as a means of intergenerational communication. I will consider some objections to the view that music is conducive to the participant's deep-seated sense of security and conclude with a consideration of how the feelings of security afforded by music impact our sense of connection with the human world beyond our society.

In preview: obviously, if foreign music that clashes with a listener's expectations can be experienced as jarring, not all music will impart a sense of repose to any given listener. The claims I will make about music promoting feelings of security presuppose that the music is in a style that is familiar (or becoming so). Thus in this chapter I am not addressing the ease of acquiring comfort in an unfamiliar musical style or system; instead, I am considering an emotional aspect of music that I think typifies experience with music to which one is accustomed, an aspect that I think holds for individuals across cultures, so long as we are talking about their experiences with familiar (preferably deeply familiar) music.

Music's relationship to our sense of psychological security cuts two ways in connection with the notion of universality. Music that is in a familiar style may be profoundly comforting. So may music in a style that is akin to what we are used to (a lullaby from almost anywhere is likely to sound familiar enough). However, this does not imply every kind of foreign music will have similar effects. In fact, the reassurance that music in a familiar idiom offers may reinforce the disturbance caused by music that is radically unlike what one is expecting. My discussion in this chapter is not aimed at demonstrating that one will gain psychological support from music that is startlingly foreign.

Instead, my purpose is to indicate that musical experience encourages feelings of comfort in the social world, which one may consider to be open-ended or, alternatively, take to be confined to one's own social group. Music hooks into our feelings of being secure members of our social world, and this, I submit, is one of the reasons that music can so powerfully impress us with our mutual affinity. What is unsettled here is who the "us" is in this formulation. Music can forge bonds across usual cultural boundaries. It can also reinforce the sense that those boundaries are barriers. What seems one of music's universal roles in human experience—its promotion of feelings of security—can, ironically, serve highly divisive ends.

MUSICAL BASES FOR ONTOLOGICAL SECURITY

A Modified Definition of Ontological Security

I will begin my account of the ways music impinges on our feelings of security with a consideration of music's relationship to ontological security. Before doing so, however, I must deal with a problematic feature of Laing's account of ontological security, which renders it unserviceable for cross-cultural discussion. I will then suggest a modified definition that retains the spirit of Laing's notion while being more versatile.

The problem is that Laing describes ontological security and its lack in terms endemic to the Western worldview. He speaks in the passage characterizing ontological security, cited above, of "his own and other people's reality," "the permanency of things," "the substantiality of natural processes," and "the substantiality of others." Some cultures, or religious traditions within these cultures, particularly in Asia, would reject all of these formulations. Buddhism, for example, sees the world as fluid, not substantial. It also denies the reality and substantiality of the self and the permanence of anything. According to the Buddhist view, suffering arises because of the false belief that each of us is a substantial self, distinct from other selves. Buddhism teaches that nothing has independent existence. We are not separate beings, but temporary configurations, aggregates of causes and effects, within an ever-changing flux. Accordingly, there is no self. Neither apparent entities nor their conditions are permanent. The contents of flux that we experience are not ultimately real; the only reality is the metaphysical substrate (and, according to some Buddhists, the causal chains that produce the appearances of "things"). We and all other temporary configurations are interdependent moments within the whole. This has a direct consequence for Buddhist ethics. We cannot harm another sentient being without harming ourselves, for we are not distinct from one another. The only attitude that is consistent with the proper understanding of reality is compassion for all that lives and feels.

The Buddhist account is coherent and accepted by millions of people throughout the world, many of whom seem psychologically healthy and supported in their health by Buddhism. This being the case, Laing's description of ontological security is inadequate for a cross-cultural description of psychological and spiritual well-being. I will use the expression "ontological security" in this discussion with a somewhat different meaning from that indicated by Laing. Instead of claiming that an ontologically secure person has "a centrally firm sense of his own and other people's reality and identity," I will claim that such a person has "a centrally firm sense" that he or she has the same ontological status as other people. In other words, the person senses that he or she occupies the same order of being as other people and shares the encountered world with them (whether that world is ultimately "real" or "unreal"). On the basis of this conviction, the person feels confident of living in a *shared* world, whatever his or her articulate views about the nature of that world or that sharing might be. I will also include as part of my understanding of ontological security a basic confidence that the world—both the world of nature and the social world—provides support for one's being (whether or not one considers that being to be real or only relative to a larger reality).

This account is, I think, compatible with the Buddhist view that human beings occupy the same ontological status with one another—the status of nonselves that are continuously changing and are interdependent with one another and the entire texture of reality—and that they share phenomenal "reality" with one another, even though it is not real in an ultimate sense. I think my modified definition is compatible with other worldviews that deny substantial reality and/or permanence to the self as well.

With this modified definition of ontological security in mind, then, let us consider two aspects of musical experience that promote it, the physiology of hearing and music's relationship to the vitality affects.

The Physiology of Hearing

The physiology of hearing as utilized in music has a number of features that support a sense of securely being in the world with others like ourselves. In the first place, our auditory system is conjoined with our vestibular system, the system for balance, which provides a sense of security in our movement through the environment. Hearing thus implicates our sense of balance, which is crucial to our feeling of being able to make stable movements through the world.

Second, hearing brings us into connection with the living world around us. We feel ensconced by music; it surrounds us. The same music that we internalize through our ears pervades the environment outside us. Furthermore, we use hearing to recognize other agents, their locations, and their activities. Our auditory system alerts us to the presence, number, and movements of other entities within the environment. Albert Bregman indicates the variety of cues and the regularities with which the auditory system organizes them. For instance, "Unrelated sounds seldom start or stop at exactly the same time," and "many changes that take place in an acoustic event will affect all the components of the resulting sound in the same way and at the same time."[4] Hence the detection of unsynchronized auditory cues suggests the presence of multiple agents and/or events. Changes of sounds from the same source tend to be gradual, so a sudden change suggests the beginning of a new event. The auditory system also tracks the frequency components of sound emerging from the same source. If the frequency components are multiples of the same fundamental, they are likely to originate with the same source.[5]

The perceptual mechanism for alerting the brain to the presence of another agent is considerably faster than that of the visual system. Within the inner ear, hair cells, which operate in bundles, receive sound vibrations mechanically. This tightens the filaments that connect the channels of adjacent hairs, which result in the openings of these channels. This enables the entry of the ions that initiate the transmission of sound signals to the brain. This process happens within five to ten microseconds of the vibrations hitting the hairs within the inner ear. This is up to one thousand times as fast as the eye opens its channel to allow transmission of light signals to the brain.[6] This suggests that the auditory sense is primary for recognizing the presence of other animated beings.

Hearing also produces coordinated activity with others through rhythmic entrainment, the synchronization of our actions with externally produced rhythms, such as those of a metronome or another person. Human beings can deliberately choose to synchronize with a particular external rhythm (as we noted in chapter 3), but we also tend to join in with others' rhythms subliminally. In both cases, entrainment enhances a sense of mutuality, whether or not one is consciously focusing on this sense. According to Judith Becker, "Bodies and brains synchronize gestures, muscle actions, breathing, and brain waves while enveloped in music."[7] Newborns already engage in rhythmic entrainment. This means that from the beginning of our lives, our physiology inclines us to mutual experience through sound.

The physiology of hearing discloses our connection to the larger environment, our sharing that world with other agents, and our capacity for attuning the dynamics of our behavior with them. By conveying these aspects of our relationship to a world and beings beyond ourselves, music helps to develop a sense of securely sharing a world with other people.

Vitality Affects

We have already considered the early development of awareness of other people by means of vitality affects.[8] We observed in chapter 6 that the vitality affects are "amodal," kinetic characteristics that infants recognize in their caregivers before they recognize them as definite individuals. We also noted that vitality affects are crucial to the process by which mother and infant adjust the timing and contour of their expressive acts and movements to each other to achieve what Daniel Stern calls "attunement."[9]

Stern distinguishes the vitality effects from traditionally named emotions, such as anger, joy, sadness, which he calls "categorical affects" and which seem to correspond to Kivy's "garden-variety emotions." Unlike these labeled affects, vitality affects are "those dynamic, kinetic qualities of feeling that distinguish animate from inanimate and that correspond to the momentary changes in feeling states involved in the organic process of being alive."[10] The vitality affects do not lend themselves to our usual emotional lexicon but

> are better captured by dynamic, kinetic terms, such as "surging," "fading away," "fleeting," "explosive," "crescendo," "decrescendo," "bursting," "drawn out," and so on. These qualities of experience are most certainly sensible to infants and of great daily, even momentary, importance. It is these feelings that will be elicited by changes in motivational states, appetites, and tensions.[11]

Through the vitality affects, an infant develops a sense of its mother as a unified being (as opposed to sensing her breasts, arms, and such, as separate entities). Stern points out that because mothers engage in specific affect displays toward their infants only discontinuously ("perhaps every thirty to ninety seconds"), "affective tracking or attuning with another could not occur as a continuous process if it were limited to categorical affects. . . . Attunement feels more like an unbroken process."[12] Vitality affects can accomplish attunement because "they are manifest in all behavior and can thus be an almost omnipresent subject of attunement."[13] Because they attend all behavior, besides enabling the infant to bond and synchronize with its caregiver, the vitality affects are also the means by which we gain a sense of being "with" another person at any stage of life.

The vitality affects are involved in the experience of listening to music, which according to Stern revives the state of the infant attuning itself to its caregiver. He suggests that "an unmeasurable wave of feeling evoked by music" can feel like a "rush" even in the absence of a sense that a particular categorical emotional label would be appropriate. Music is an example "par excellence of the expressiveness of the vitality affects."[14] The listener's experience is akin to that of the infant perceiving its mother, which involves the direct perception of vitality affects rather than specific acts.[15] Adults relating to music are effectively doing what they did as infants when they attuned to vitality affects. They are experiencing themselves in secure rapport with others. By enabling people to attune the timing and contour of their behavior with each other's, music draws attention to their shared sphere of activity.

POTENTIAL OBJECTIONS

Before considering other ways in which music promotes feelings of security, I should consider some possible objections that might be made to my suggestion that music encourages a sense of ontological security. One potential counter is that ontological security is not itself an emotion. In fact, I have no problem with describing ontological security as a mood or an affective background, although I am inclined to accept the view mentioned in the previous chapter that emotions and moods are not sharply differentiated. Ontological security does have an object, namely, the world, including its many inhabitants. However, I think one can be ontologically secure without any conscious attention to this fact, and in such cases it might be reasonable to deny that the person is experiencing an episodic emotion. One is more likely to be conscious of one's insecurity than of one's security. It may be worthwhile to distinguish a background sense of ontological security and a conscious or quasi-conscious appreciation of this condition. For the fortunately contented person, music may arouse this sense of appreciation. But the state of feeling ontologically secure is not episodic in the case of the fortunate person for whom ontological security is a way of life.

There are, however, several further challenges to the idea that music instills and supports ontological security that deserve further comment. One is the question of how this view is compatible with the fact that music can suggest or arouse so-called negative emotions, such as sadness. This is particularly obvious in one of the cross-cultural ritual functions of music: to express grief. A second problem is the fact that music is often used to make one more open and vulnerable, particular to transformed conceptions of oneself. If this is so, it may be difficult to see how music encourages a sense of secure participation in the order of being in which one finds oneself.

In response to the challenge that the negative emotions aroused by music do not seem compatible with ontological security, I would suggest that this charge reflects a misunderstanding of what this sense of security amounts to. Recall Laing's characterization of ontological security as enabling a person to "encounter all the hazards of life, social, ethical, spiritual, biological," on the basis of "a centrally firm sense," which I describe as the sense that he or she occupies the same order of being as other people and shares the encountered world with them. Ontological security is the presupposition of being able to confront disturbing emotions without being devastated by them. A person who is ontologically secure is not immune to disturbing emotional experiences. Ontological security, the sense of being securely situated in the same order of being that others inhabit, is vital to the background confidence one needs to cope with disturbing emotions, but it isn't a panacea that prevents experiencing such emotions in the first place.

Nevertheless, the experience of supposedly "negative" (i.e., unpleasant) emotions in connection with music contrasts with the experience of these emotions in everyday life. We take satisfaction in musical reflections of fear, sadness, and such, although we do not particularly enjoy these emotions in relation to ordinary events.[16] Freud's account of mastery in *Beyond the Pleasure Principle* suggests a reason why music can be enjoyable despite the range of emotions it expresses. Freud describes his small grandson's game of hiding objects and then "finding" them and raises the question of why he found this game enjoyable. Freud sees a connection between the game of hiding objects and another game, a game of peek-a-boo in which the child found another person whom he was initially unable to see. The moment of being unable to see the other person in the game, an older person who helped care for the child, was reminiscent of situations in which his mother left him alone, Freud suggests, and he argues that this similarity is not accidental but indeed crucial to the enjoyment of the game. In the circumstance of being left alone by his mother, the small child was frightened, and he was greatly relieved when she returned. Freud argues that his grandson, in making a game out of what had been an upsetting situation, has taken control of the situation. He has made a game of the whole cycle of losing sight of his mother but then seeing her again. The game reflects his discovery that the disappearance of his mother is something he can expect to be temporary.[17]

In many cases, the experience through music of emotions that would usually be distressing represents a similar scenario. By deliberately exposing oneself to emotions that might be disturbing, but savoring their progress and ultimate resolution, one expresses one's sense of mastery. In this respect, one asserts a sense of deep security in the face of challenges to one's repose.[18]

Let us now turn to the second challenge to my suggestion that music instills and reinforces a sense of ontological security: that posed by the use of music to transcend or undermine one's usual sense of self. Certainly, the use of music to achieve ecstatic experience is cross-culturally widespread. Although Gilbert Rouget indicates that music is not essential to induce trance, a state in which one is "outside" one's usual self, most deliberate efforts to provoke trance do involve music.[19] Becker takes the potential for trance to be universal, and she suggests that most of us have had "near trance" experiences in connection with music.[20] She suggests that a transformed sense of self is typical in trance and trancelike states, such that an expanded sense of self replaces the ordinary one.

Becker points out that some cultures expect music to result in a transformed conception of self while others expect the dissolution of any sense of self. Comparing the perspectives of listeners from Western cultures and the audiences for Hindustani classical music, she suggests, "In one case, the listener may be exploring the emotional nuances of his or her inner self or identifying with the emotional interiors presented by the music. In the other, the listener is trying to bring about a kind of 'sea' change, a different self altogether, one that comes closer to divinity."[21]

Sometimes the latter sort of experience involves a sense of dissociating from the body. David Henderson describes the devotional songs (*bhajans*) of Nepalese musicians in the Kathmandu Valley, which he claims can sometimes yield experiences of oneness with the divine that transcend emotion.[22] In this condition, the participants become dissociated from their bodies.[23] The understanding that the *bhajan* participants have of their experience reflects a particular religious interpretation of the nature of consciousness, which holds that the true Self is the same for all individuals.[24] Recognition that all are ultimately the same Self enables one to dissociate from one's illusory sense of holding a definite position in relation to the rest of the net of worldly entities and to become a pure witness of reality. Understood in this way the experience of the *bhajan* participants certainly includes the sense of sharing one's ontological status with others, even while interpreting one's usual sense of one's own and others' reality as deficient. This interpretation holds that one not only shares one's status with others, but also that one is actually the same being as they are.

Most Western individuals do not hold the same view of either musical experience or the nature of God, but they too experience transformations in the sense of self and the world in connection with music, sometimes involving a loss of self-awareness. On the basis of an empirical study of 103 subjects, Robert Panzarella analyzes the ecstatic state they experienced in connection with works of art. These include altered perception, in which the world is considered "better, more beautiful than had been thought before"; ecstatic physical and quasi-physical responses (including sensations of floating); loss of connection with the environment; and a sense of merging with the artistic object.[25]

Marcia Herndon and Norma McLeod consider the "shifting [of] personal awareness" to be a basic capacity of music.[26] They contrast two kinds of powerful experiences available through music: "flash," which involves heightened awareness of being present in an event, sometimes to the exclusion of awareness of anything else in the environment, and "flow," in which one loses self-awareness and any sense of separation from the object.[27]

Whether or not loss of self-awareness is involved, such ecstatic states typically involve the elimination of a sense of division between one's own ego and other people. This effect is an aspect of hāl,[28] the ecstatic emotional state to which Persian performers aspire, described here by Dariouche Safvate:

> Hāl is an intense state of the soul, it is the interior fire, which must animate the artist like the mystic. . . . When he attains the high point of this state, the artist plays with an extraordinary facility of execution. His sound changes. The musical phrase liberates its secret. The creativity gushes forth. It seems that the very essence of the music manifests itself delivered from the usual interferences of the human personality. The world becomes transfigured, unveiling its marvelous visages, and across an ineffable transparency which abolishes the actual barriers between the musician and his auditor, offers itself to the direct comprehension of every being capable of sensing. Hāl is the fruit of authenticity. The authentic musician is he who plays or sings under the force of an irresistible interior impulse.[29]

Ravi Shankar similarly describes his experiences performing music in terms of transcending a narrow sense of self in favor of an expanded, affiliative awareness of connection.

> When with control and concentration, I have cut myself off from the outside world, I step on to the threshold of the *raga* with feelings of humility, reverence, and awe. To me, a *raga* is like a living person, and to establish that intimate oneness is achieved, it is the most ecstatic and exhilarating moment, like the supreme heights of the act of love or worship. In these miraculous moments, when I am so much aware of the great powers surging within me and all around me, sympathetic and sensitive listeners are feeling the same vibrations. It is a strange mixture of all the intense emotions—pathos, joy, peace, spirituality, eroticism, all flowing together. It is like feeling God . . . The miracle of our music is in the beautiful rapport that occurs when a deeply spiritual musician performs for a receptive and sympathetic group of listeners.[30]

Once again, to interpret such ecstatic experiences as offering counterexamples to the claim that music establishes and reinforces a sense of ontological security is to misunderstand the nature of ontological security. Ontological security is, as defined above, a firm sense that one occupies the same order of being as other people and shares the encountered world with them. This sense enables one to cope with distress of various sorts; it also obviates the need for a fundamentally defensive approach to reality. Ecstatic experiences of music presuppose sufficient lack of defensiveness that one can allow the boundaries between oneself and others to be less rigid, or to subside altogether. A sense of ontological security might make one more, not less, prone to experiences of self-transcendence.

Music offers altered states within everyday life. In the "near-trance" experiences that Becker describes, we experience our bodies as offering no resistance to consciousness, as empowered in extraordinary ways. We transcend our everyday impressions of ourselves and the world. This does not remove us from the secure sense of occupying the same order of being as others, but it does transform our sense of that order.

Shankar's description of his ecstatic experience through music, even while it obliterates the sense of distinction between self and others, nevertheless emphasizes the sense of shared being with them. Such descriptions do not refute the claim that music supports a sense of ontological security but instead articulate it in terms suited to the speakers' religious traditions.

Such spiritualized accounts of transcending the small self through music suggest that Alexander Pope was mistaken to suggest disdain when he writes,

> As some to church repair,
> Not for the doctrine, but the music there.[31]

One would not be entirely wrong to go to church for the music if the purpose of going to church is to tune in to what is larger than one's individual ego. While the qualitative character of the altered sense of self and the doctrinal interpretations of what is involved differ, music's accomplishment is to attune us with what is beyond ourselves. By building and reinforcing ontological security, music facilitates secure participation in a world with other, fellow beings. What begins in an infant's sense of being with its mother expands to open-ended spiritual rapport.

MUSICAL BASES FOR EXISTENTIAL SECURITY

The Conservatism of Music

Besides helping to construct and reinforce a sense of sharing the world with others, music also promotes a sense of being at home in that world. One of the means by which it fosters this sense is its "conservative" character. Music is conservative in the sense that it makes use of an unusual amount of repetition by comparison with other human pursuits.[32] The familiar is comforting, and music characteristically presents the familiar over and over again. Thomas Turino describes that the tendency of music toward redundancy, which he notes is particularly strong in music designed to promote participation, creates "security in constancy."[33]

Repetition in music occurs on multiple levels. Musical works are often structured on the basis of repeated phrases, themselves perhaps composed of repeated motives or patterns. Musical forms commonly involve repetition of whole passages or sections. This is obvious in any song with a refrain, or in any Western work with the indication "da capo," which means that a whole section should be repeated verbatim.

People also enjoy the repetition of entire musical works. The very notion of a work of music implies that an extended musical structure is preserved for repeated performance, and such preservation occurs in most musical cultures.[34] The history of Christian liturgical music from the seventh to the thirteenth centuries gives pride of place to preserved chant melodies. The *cantus firmus* (literally, fixed song, or chant) was the basis for the music of the Mass, with stylistic innovations occurring around it. The fixed tune is also basic in jazz, where improvisation commonly amounts to a meditation on a pregiven song. The phenomenon of "the old favorite" further reveals our attachment to long familiar pieces of music, and in the era of modern recording, certain performances become "old favorites" as well. Well-known rock musicians have often been annoyed at how much audiences want their live performances to sound like the record.[35] Symphony orchestras are sometimes similarly frustrated by the strong demand for the same popular works within the repertoire, which limits the number of less well known works they can perform in their programs if they are to satisfy the audience.

Besides the repetition of musical patterns and musical works, music is also conservative in that particular cultures' preferred musical styles are also resistant to change. Thus in addition to promoting a sense of being at home in the world, the conservatism of music also fortifies feelings of being at home in one's particular society. Alan Lomax contends that musical style is so tenacious because music instills a sense of security in a society's members.

> From the point of view of its social function, the primary effect of music is to give the listener a feeling of security, for it symbolizes the place where he was born, his earliest childhood satisfactions, his religious experience, his pleasure in community doings, his courtship and his work—any or all of these personality-shaping experiences. As soon as the familiar sound pattern is established, he is prepared to laugh, to weep, to dance, to fight, to worship. His heart is opened.[36]

Lomax goes on to observe, "An art so deeply rooted in the security patterns of the community should not, in theory, be subject to rapid change, and in fact this seems to be the case."[37] Jay Dowling and Dane Harwood concur that musical style is one of the most stable of cultural phenomena, surviving migrations and change in a society's economic organization.[38] (Turino points out, however, that largely repetitive music also offers challenges for more experienced participants, who would lose interest if it were merely repetitive.)

Surely, though, we don't enjoy excessive repetition. We generally want a fair amount of novelty in our experience. Why do we enjoy so much repetition in music? Why aren't we bored instead? Many answers have been suggested. One is that in societies that encourage musical participation, where much of the enjoyment depends on mutual engagement in the music, repetition facilitates learning and enables newcomers to join in. Besides the "security in constancy" noted above, Turino observes that such music tends toward dense textures in which particular contributions do not stand out, which results in "a cloaking of individual contributions." These two effects together "create comfort for participants," even those who are novices.[39]

A second explanation for the pleasure taken in musical redundancy is that given the human tendency to associate music with other concerns in living, repeated music is new each time because of the new situation in which it occurs.[40] The new situation includes both the immediate context of music-making and the particular temporal trajectory leading up to this point.

A third explanation is that we need a background of repetition in order to recognize novelty when it occurs. This is an important argument for Leonard Meyer, whose theory that music arouses affect through deviation from the expected requires that deviation be noticeable.[41] The precondition for a strong sense of expectation is sufficient familiarity with musical conventions, and this depends on repetition (whether of musical motives, basic forms, or of specific works).

A fourth reason proposed for our enjoyment of musical repetition is that it enables us to enjoy the novelty that enters our musical experience through the subtle differences in performances of the same work.[42] Fifth, we may simply enjoy the twists and turns of the musical work as we do a good story, even if we have experienced it before.[43]

John Sloboda and Patrik Juslin propose a sixth possible explanation: there may be a module for processing music (i.e., a network of "hard-wired" responses) that is sealed off from other aspects of cognition. If so, this processor would not have conscious access to stored memory for comparison of what is presently being heard to what is remembered from previous hearings. Such a processor would always hear the piece "for the first time," even if we are consciously aware of having heard the piece before.[44]

All these answers suggest that the preference for repetition must be explained in terms of desire for novelty. This ignores the fact that human beings do experience emotional satisfaction from repetition in its own right. Robert Zajonc indicates that mere repetition makes people (and chickens and monkeys) feel better. He cites a number of experiments, both his own and those of others, that demonstrate a preference for phenomena that have been encountered previously over those that have not.[45] Among the studies he considers is one W. R. Wilson conducted, which presented pairs of sequences of musical tones to subjects and asked which in each pair they preferred and which they had heard previously. The result was that subjects preferred sequences they had in fact heard previously, and that this was independent of whether or not they consciously recognized it as familiar.[46] Experiments conducted by Zajonc and colleagues corroborate that subjects show preference on the basis of previous exposure even when the exposure is too brief for them to recognize the stimuli. Subjects also prefer stimuli that resemble those previously encountered, even when the specific stimuli are novel. Zajonc concludes, "One would suppose that the effect documented here must be well known in the advertising industry."[47]

Certainly, I have found in my own experience that mere repetition is enough to warm me up to a piece of pop music, even if my first reaction was that it was a rip-off of some other, "better" work.[48] I have also discovered that intimate familiarity with a piece of music makes me particularly eager to hear each musical event as it unfolds. When I hear a recording of a piano work that I have at one time performed, for example, my attention becomes riveted. I have difficulty attending to conversation. This is so even if the volume is low and the music is being utilized as background music (not an uncommon situation in certain restaurants).

On such occasions I feel something akin to bated expectation for the next musical event at every moment. Although I know exactly what the next chord or melodic element will be, I feel an almost magnetic desire to hear it. My only comparable experience occurred in childhood, when I wanted to hear a well-known story exactly as I had heard it every time before. At every moment during a story, I was eager to hear the very next detail. I awaited even the arrival of the Wicked Witch in "Sleeping Beauty" with something akin to desire, even though I hated and feared her, so long as she appeared at the precisely correct moment.

In his book *Musical Elaborations*, Edward Said also observes that prior familiarity with a work of music conditions and heightens his response upon hearing it. During a concert in Carnegie Hall, Said reports, Alfred Brendel performed a transcription of a Brahms sextet. Said found this part of the recital of particular interest, for he was well acquainted with the original sextet.

> Strangely, I think the effort of correspondence held me much more rigorously to the music than is usually the case: I assimilated, I actively bound my hearing to, an earlier but still lively experience of the score with Brendel's performance.[49]

Nietzsche aptly describes the phenomenon of enjoying musical repetition. Familiarity breeds not contempt, but love.

This is what happens to us in music: First one has to *learn to hear* a figure and melody at all, to detect and distinguish it, to isolate it and delimit it as a separate life. Then it requires some exertion and good will to *tolerate* it in spite of its strangeness, to be patient with its appearance and expression, and kindhearted about its oddity. Finally there comes a moment when we are *used* to it, when we wait for it, when we sense that we should miss it if it were missing; and now it continues to compel and enchant us relentlessly until we have become its humble and enraptured lovers who desire nothing better from the world than it and only it.[50]

Nietzsche's comment draws attention to another way in which sufficient novelty attaches to music that we hear again and again. We develop a kind of personal relationship with it, and we enjoy the development of this experience. This suggestion combines two of the explanations for enjoying reheard music offered above. We experience novelty because we bring to each hearing the different relationship we have to it; and we enjoy reexperiencing the twists and turns of *this* particular work.

The familiar is comforting, and music characteristically presents the familiar over and over again. Rather than emphasizing the way repetition serves as the background for recognizing novelty, we might stress, as Nietzsche does, the way repetition enables us to learn to feel at home with what is new. And as Ibn Sina observed, the return of a familiar theme is not unlike the return of an old friend.

Continuity in Time

Perhaps the most striking ways that music encourages a sense of safety within the world is the impression it gives of the present continuing steadily into the future. Music conveys the possibility of things continuing well, a possibility that is important to us as intentional beings who project ourselves into the future. Through music we experience temporally extended courses that satisfy in their unfolding, and this draws attention to our own nature as temporal beings with trajectories that might be similarly fulfilling. Alan Merriam aptly describes the reassurance that music provides when he claims in the passage cited above that music is "a normal and solid activity which assures the members of society that the world continues in its proper path."

Several features of musical experience serve to draw our attention to the steady continuation toward the future. These include (1) the perceptual character of music, which requires recognition of temporal continuity; (2) the cross-cultural tendency to divide the pitch continuum into discrete steps and to use tones of varying durations, ensuring the recognition of change; (3) the connection between our musical perception and a more general sense of ourselves as continuing in time; and (4) myths about music that encourage this association.

Musical perception involves the recognition of characteristics of sequences. The ability to synthesize sequentially presented groups of notes and then to be able to characterize properties of the entire group, such as the waxing or waning of frequency level, is essential to musical perception. Patients who lose or never have this ability hear music as a succession of discrete, unrelated events, described by some of them as "noise."[51]

Recognition of continuity is involved in one of the basic Gestalt principles that apply to melodic organization, the principle of *prägnanz*, or "good continuation." As we noted in chapter 3, this principle claims, in Meyer's characterization, that "a shape or pattern will, other things being equal, tend to be continued in its initial mode of operation."[52] Our musical expectations, so vital in our recognition of musical surprises, are structured on this principle.[53] Charles Sanders Peirce similarly emphasizes the importance of continuity for the perception of melody: "to perceive it [melody] there must be some continuity of consciousness which makes the events of a lapse of time present to us."[54]

The tensions and resolutions, as well as the general sense of motion conveyed by music, all depend on our awareness that musical events are organized sequentially in time yet perceived as connected. Resolution tendencies, our sense that a relative dissonance needs to give way to a more consonant chord or interval, presuppose our experiencing music as projecting into the future.[55] Victor Zuckerkandl observes, "we could not hear the melody as motion if we did not hear it as continuous."[56]

The cross-cultural tendency to divide the musical gamut into distinct increments, which we considered in chapter 3, also guarantees that we have an impression of steps from one musical event to another. By dividing up the continuum of pitch possibilities into discrete intervals, a musical system ensures the recognition of movement along the continuum. The differential pitches of a given scale provide signposts, as it were, for a melody's shifting from one level of vibrational frequency to another. Because the continuum is divided in this way, we are able to recognize the melody's progressive "stepping" through a pattern of distinguishable frequencies. The sense of proceeding by definite steps is reinforced by the tendency to utilize tones of varying temporal durations. Because we have a sense of location in musical space, we are able to have an impression of music traversing that space. Again, a process that we engage in while listening to music presupposes at least implicit awareness of temporal continuity.

This suggestion may seem at odds with the idea that music often results in experiences of "flow," in which time seems to drop away, being replaced by an impression of a continuous "now."[57] In the most intense of such cases, I grant that a sense of being directed toward the future is likely to be muted, if part of one's consciousness at all. However, the very term *flow* suggests a movement forward in time. Moreover, often when someone refers to having lost track of time, it is the time of everyday routine that disappears from consciousness. The continuous "now" that participants sometimes claim to experience is not a lack of temporal continuity but a lack of a resistant temporal order (of the sort we experience when we are "fighting time" or trying to keep up) that contrasts with the pace of one's own activity.

While a listener need not be consciously aware of attending to music's continuation through time, the fact that one must be doing so to experience music means that we at least preconsciously apprehend continuation. Zuckerkandl describes this apprehension as an experience of "futurity" in music,[58] suggesting that musical perception is integrally connected with our extramusical sense of continuity in time. Reports that music can counter the disorienting effects of dissociative disorders support this suggestion. Oliver Sacks offers a number of such cases, including the famous "man who mistook his wife for a hat." This man, a musician who had suffered damage to the visual areas of the brain, was unable to integrate visual details into a whole, with the consequence that he had difficulty recognizing individual people or things. He oriented himself in the world by means of singing. Sacks reports the explanation given by the man's wife.

> He does everything singing to himself. But if he is interrupted and loses the thread, he comes to a complete stop, doesn't know his clothes—or his own body. He sings all the time—eating songs, dressing songs, bathing songs, everything. He can't do anything unless he makes it a song.[59]

The continuity exhibited by music has struck some philosophers as making us particularly aware of ourselves as temporal beings. Monroe Beardsley contends, for example, that our sense of music's profundity and its impact on us depends on its reflection of the basic patterns of our existence in time.

> The idea that music exemplifies—indeed, exploits and glories in—aspects of change that are among the most fundamental and pervasive characteristics of

living seems to be true. . . . Because these patterns or modes of continuation are such general features of all experience, I . . . call them metaphysical . . . the metaphysical modes of continuation that are deeply apprehended in music must account for much of its capacity to move us.[60]

The numerous myths that involve music in the creation and maintenance of the world suggest that many of the world's peoples have strongly associated the continuity of music and a sense of the world continuing well. Among these are the Aboriginal Australian myths that the creator-god made the world by beating the oceans with a reed and that a primordial crocodile drumming its stomach with its tail made the world harmonious. The Pima Indians in Arizona believe that their songs were "given in the beginning," being sung "by the Creator and other mythical personages" and handed down since then.[61] The Andaman Islanders hold that music preserves living things through the night. The Pawnee believe that the morning star sings each morning as it tosses the sun up to light the day.[62] According to Vedic metaphysical theory, the vital energy manifest in sound is the same energy that created and sustains the world. Lewis Rowell points out that ancient Indian thought also considers music a form a sacrifice and holds that "as the direct result of . . . sacrifice, time is established and maintained in its proper course."[63] Rabbi Israel Sarug's Kabbalistic text, *Commentary on Luria's Songs*, attributes to music the power to make the sun rise and move.[64]

Music depends upon our implicit sense of continuity in time, and it presents perceptible patterns within this continuity. This suggests order within the flow of time, a comforting impression for those, like us, who move along with its march into the future. Many of music's patterns, moreover, are repetitive, offering reassurance that the future need not be unprecedented, but can itself be a region where we are at home, even surrounded by friends. Merriam does not overstate the case when he claims that music offers reassurance that the world continues in its proper course. In the experience of music, we also encounter a world full of life. Pieces of music reach endings, but we sense that we have recognized something ongoing when we start another musical experience. As we experience music, we appreciate a life that flows on and on.

MUSICAL SUPPORT FOR A SENSE OF BELONGING

The Sense of Membership

The relative conservatism of music facilitates its serving as a symbol of a continuing community. Music promotes feelings of affinity with other people, as we have already suggested in discussing the vitality affects. These two potentials together make music a powerful means for promoting feelings of membership in a particular community. As Dowling and Harwood observe, "Songs are emblems of society and culture, and they form an important part of the self-image of members of society."[65] The music of one's society can make one aware of one's membership and help one to feel a part of the group. This is also the case with respect to music affiliated with any other community to which one might belong, including religious sects, high schools and colleges, political parties, and such. Merriam concludes: "Music is in a sense a summatory activity for the expression of values, a means whereby the heart of the psychology of a culture is exposed without many of the protective mechanisms which surround other cultural activities."[66]

The shared physicality and pleasure of musical experience is crucial to music's power to bond participants within a musical context, as we have observed above. The fact that music can cement feelings of group membership does not obviously suggest that it furthers a sense of connection with those outside that group, however. In fact, insofar as group membership implies the existence of an out-group, those individuals who do not belong, music can apparently aggravate a sense that the world is divided between "us" and "them." In partisan uses of music for propagandistic purposes, this is often exactly what music does.

However, that the musical experience creates enjoyable feelings of connectedness among people is important, for the participants in a musical experience need not be part of the same community in other circumstances. This is important because music serves to create feelings of comfortable membership, and while this is clearly the case within particular societies and organizations that use music to create this feeling, the sense of membership can extend beyond one's own society to an open-ended community of others. Contemporary recording technology enables anyone with access to it to share music with a potentially global community, and musical solidarity can extend broadly. Although much of the time participants are not attending to this widespread sharing, their attention could at any point be so directed, and sometime it is (as, for instance, when a radio announcer brings the extent of the audience to listeners' attention). When thought of in this way, music suggests membership in the human community at large. Thus the same mechanism through which music reinforces membership in one's community of long standing can encourage a sense of membership beyond one's usual social group.

Transgenerational Communication

In addition to being able to create solidarity among individuals dispersed in space, music also facilitates emotional connections across time. Members of different generations who are assembled together in a musical audience come to feel connected through the kind of pleasurable sharing just described, as the Confucian thinker Xunzi observes.

> When music is performed in the ancestral temple of the ruler, and the ruler and his ministers, superiors and inferiors, listen to it together, there are none who are not filled with a spirit of harmonious reverence. When it is performed within the household, and father and sons, elder and younger brothers listen to it together, there are none who are not filled with a spirit of harmonious kinship. And when it is performed in the community, and old people and young together listen to it, there are none who are not filled with a spirit of harmonious obedience.[67]

Music also forges a sense of transgenerational connection through its preservation of cultural memory. This may be less apparent in the present-day industrialized world, in which generation gaps are often expressed by means of music, than it was in previous times, when musical events were relatively rare but attended by the entire community. Nevertheless, the preservation of musical works through time makes possible the communication of one generation's musical ideas with succeeding generations.

Music even enables the living to commune with the dead. Consider the impression one sometimes has of a work from the distant past, or even from a century or two ago. We can justifiably consider ourselves to be in contact with Bach, for example, through his music. The eerie feeling provoked by hearing the recorded duet between Natalie Cole and her deceased father Nat King Cole stems from this sense of generations speaking across time and across the divide of death.[68] Although this duet depends on recently invented recording technologies, any musical culture that preserves musical works that are performed again and again has opportunities to bridge the worlds of the living and the dead.

The sense of security produced by such transgenerational communication is primarily focused on generations within a society with which one is already affiliated. Music returns us home to our societies and our now-dead ancestors. It promotes awareness of the continuity of the past to the present and a sense that further continuity is not only possible but is the route we are already on. While focused on the continuity of one's particular society, feelings of security on this basis also reinforce the existential sense that the world has continued safely forward thus far and will continue to do so.

I have suggested several bases for feeling a sense of security in connection with music. The physiology of hearing makes us feel supported by a living world that we share. Our experience of musical dynamism outside our bodies is the original means whereby we become aware of and bond with distinct agents in the social world. Music's conservatism—its repetitive nature—offers the comfort of the familiar as well as reassurance to participants who are non-experts. It also facilitates a sense of community membership, with the protection that involves. Our sense of having secure bearings, both personally and culturally, is facilitated by music's support and enlivening of our memories and histories. And music offers us a secure place within historical time while still enabling us to encounter previous generations.

Besides prosodic cues, music impacts us emotionally in two other ways that permeate cultural divisions: it communicates vitality and engages our sense of connection with the larger environment and those within it. The kind of bonding that results can powerfully impress us with our shared life and relation to other people. Even though such feelings are most effectively engaged by a style with which we are quite familiar, they can link us to others who may be outside the community with which we typically associate. The music we consider most deeply our own offers us sufficient comfort with our place in the order of things that it can facilitate our explorations of the larger human world. Although my main point in this book is that we should acknowledge and get acquainted with the range of music beyond our ken, the considerations offered in this chapter show that insofar as we have assimilated the features of *some* musical style, making some particular musical style our own, our previous musical experience provides an emotionally secure basis for doing so.

CHAPTER 9

Beyond Ethnocentrism

THE PROBLEM OF SECTARIAN MUSIC

Thus far I have been presenting my grounds for optimism about music as a means of promoting cross-cultural understanding and a palpable sense of our common humanity. However, an obvious problem is that music can reinforce ethnic and sectarian divisions. It does this, moreover, through exactly the mechanisms that make it a vehicle for forging bonds of sympathy. The entrainment that gives us a physical sense of connection with the larger musical audience can also reinforce sectarian bonds when that audience is circumscribed. The thrill of sharing life with an open-ended throng of fellow human beings can secure the political solidarity of groups with hostile regard for those who do not share the same hallowed cause, and the physically inciting power of music can be channeled into violence. One of the most disturbing moments in Michael Moore's film *Fahrenheit 9/11* is an interview with a United States soldier in Iraq who describes the way he and other soldiers would get themselves psyched for battle: "You know you're going into the fight to begin with, and you got a good song behind you."[1] The lyrics of the soldier's preferred song urge a blazing roof to keep burning. That and the strong beat are presumably enough to prime him to kill.

Musical complexity and lyrical wit are hardly necessary for a song to be effective in mobilizing forces or rallying the party. The kitsch song sung by a young Nazi in the movie *Cabaret*, "Tomorrow Belongs to Me," with its easy singability and its cliché references to nature and the new day ahead, typifies the propaganda song.[2] Such songs are catchy, easy to entrain to. With the right context and/or lyrics, entrainment is directed toward defending one's side against all comers.

The facile ways in which political "spin" can be applied to music should come as no surprise in light of the features of music that we have just considered. Security achieved through redundancy, pleasure attained through entrainment, a musically provoked sense of membership in a larger social group, and the sense of movement toward the future can all be harnessed to achieve sectarian ends.

Music's connection with feelings of security, considered in the previous chapter, also suggests challenges for the idea that the universal features of music can help us to develop a greater sense of human affinity. Ontological security—the secure conviction that we share a world with other beings like ourselves—and existential security—the sense that we are at home in the world—are both quite compatible with feeling our kinship with people who are unlike ourselves. In fact, it would seem that one would feel vastly more secure if one felt such affinity. However, music's ability to facilitate such feelings of security depends on one's comfort with the music. Music that is too startling or alien sounding is not likely to encourage a sense that one is at home, or even the sense that one is encountering beings like oneself.

Music's promotion of a sense of belonging, more disturbingly, reinforces the splintering of the human world into separate groups, often groups who stand in enmity with each other. One defining feature of group identification is that it establishes a clear delineation between those who are inside the group and those who are not. Political identities depend on securing boundaries. Martin Stokes makes this point when he characterizes ethnicity, one of the most common bases for sectarian identification in our contemporary world.

> Ethnicities are to be understood in terms of the construction, maintenance and negotiation of boundaries, and not on the "putative" social essences which fill the gaps within them. Ethnic boundaries define and maintain social identities, which can only exist in "a context of opposition and relativities."[3]

Music's role in fortifying one's secure sense of membership in a society, accordingly, involves implicit reference to groups that are excluded.

Are we left in the ironical position that the upshot of music's universal character is that music promotes ethnocentricity? Some uses of music do exactly that. Fortunately, music also affords opportunities for the development of mutual sympathy among strangers who do not necessarily share any ethnic or sectarian affiliation. I will describe a situation within my own musical culture that I found very moving in this connection and then consider ways that members of different cultures might similarly share a sense of connection through music, building on the universal features and potential uses that I have been discussing in this book.

THE FLASH MOB

While recently visiting my family in Kansas City in December, I had planned with my sister Jeanine to attend the annual performance of Handel's *Messiah* presented by the high school we had attended. The concert was at 3:00 p.m. the Sunday before Christmas, but Jeanine suggested that she pick me up an hour early so we could participate in a musical "flash mob" that was in the works. A flash mob is a bit like a surprise party, except that the participants are mostly strangers and the surprise is not aimed at any one individual. The participants come together as a group only for this particular occasion with the aim of jointly bursting into song (or some other specific activity).⁴ A member of a church choir in Kansas City had heard of such events in a few other cities where sudden choral renditions of the Hallelujah Chorus had startled the unaware, and she wanted to try such an event locally. The appointed time was 2:00 p.m. and the designated place was Crown Center, a popular mall that brims with shoppers during the Christmas season. The organizer sent messages to alert the grapevine via e-mail and Facebook, and these were passed along in various ways. Jeanine was among those who had learned of the plans through e-mail, and she wanted to be involved. I was game.

As it turned out, between flash mob enthusiasts and the Christmas shoppers, the traffic around the shopping center was at an impasse. Jeanine, who was driving, urged me to go on in. "There's no point in both of us missing it," she said. So I went in without her. A few minutes later Jeanine called me on my cell phone to say that the parking situation was hopeless, but she asked me to keep the line open so she could hear what transpired.

At 2:00, the pianist who had been playing background Christmas music paused, the cue for the flash mob to begin. About four hundred people joined in—and maybe Jeanine wasn't the only one who was singing along in a car. The sound of the Chorus resonated through the large atrium, while the shopping center's multistory escalators were rather comically packed with people going up and down and belting out "King of kings! And Lord of lords!" Even if you weren't entirely sure which part you were singing (first soprano? second soprano?), it was no disaster. All of the parts were there in strength, carrying along anyone who lost track.

After the last "Hallelujah" had finished resonating, I walked out of the mall to the street. When Jeanine, who had been circling, picked me up, I felt a little as though I were jumping into a getaway car. And yet I was thoroughly refreshed, part of me still mentally thundering, "Hal–le–lu–jah!"

For many reasons, the flash mob story is likely to seem inappropriate to my purposes. It involves a song that many people within Kansas City—and the United States as a whole—probably could not sing in such circumstances, despite their familiarity with how it sounds, because they have never done so previously. The Chorus is sectarian in that it celebrates the birth of Jesus, an event of unique importance to Christians. The Kansas City flash mob was probably relatively homogenous, in that word spread largely from members of one church choir to those of others. I only knew about it because my sister told me about it, and she heard because she is herself a church musician. The Chorus is in Western tonality and epitomizes Western functional harmony. The whole event is a far cry from an encounter between mutually foreign musical cultures.

All of this is true, and yet I think the impact of the event was to spread joy and mirth throughout an open-ended public, including not only those at Crown Center, but also those who have been "present" after the fact via YouTube videos. Moreover, the potential for joining in is not all or nothing. The Hallelujah Chorus, while many people have never performed it, is widely familiar. After all, it has been used in advertisements promoting pain relief products.[5] As for its cultural narrowness, the Hallelujah Chorus is a great work in the Western classical repertoire, the sectarian associations largely submerged in popular imagination.[6] Possibly some other work would have done as well and been less associated with a particular religion. The "Ode to Joy" from Beethoven's Ninth Symphony comes to mind, though that would have made serious musical demands on some particular singer with a strong baritone voice.

Of course, a surprise performance of the Hallelujah Chorus is not a case of cultural encounter, but several features of this event suggest some desiderata for live musical encounters among strangers, some of them characteristic of participatory music of the sort that Thomas Turino describes. First, the flash mob was a *participatory* event open to anyone who cared to participate. The aim was to encourage participation by as many people as possible. The dense texture cloaked any fumblings in individual contributions. Because one could drop in and out of the singing, it made room for performers with varying degrees of skill. I have no way of knowing whether anyone surprised by the singing joined in, but everyone was welcome to take part. To sing the whole chorus required knowing one's part from beginning to end, but I can imagine someone who only knew the final volley of hallelujahs joining in at that last stage, or someone singing bits of the work, shifting parts from time to time to stay in one's vocal range.

Second, again in keeping with Turino's characterization of participatory music, the event created a powerful *physical impact*. The redundant rhythm provided a steady impetus that synchronized the throng. The ambient sounds ensured a buzzy quality to the environment; the videos of the event posted on YouTube pick up sounds of cutlery being used at the food court on the edge of the atrium. The effect was perhaps not a wall of sound—the dispersion of participants through the extended space was more like an arena of sound, with the loudness characteristic of participatory music-making. Awareness of one's whole body resonating in tandem with an untold number of others and of the palpable vibrations emanating from those who were physically proximate was exhilarating.

Third, not surprisingly the event was conducive to a feeling of *social bonding*. The organizer, interviewed on National Public Radio's *All Things Considered*, said that some people wanted to continue singing together when it was all over, although no one had figured out how to coordinate this, so the group eventually dispersed. The reluctance for the event to end strikes me as evidence of group bonding. In my own case, I was proud to hear the segment on National Public Radio's *All Things Considered* about "our" flash mob. If Hume is right that we take pride only in what we associate with our own identity, this feeling demonstrates my sense of identification, perhaps more striking in that I was a happenstance participant who had not resided in Kansas City for over thirty years.

Participants in the flash mob, like other music-making experiences, would have experienced the release of the neurotransmitter oxytocin, which has been linked to heightened states of trust and the reduction of fear.[7] My suggestion that such experiences are humanizing in the sense of encouraging feelings of affinity toward other participants is to this extent supported by contemporary neuroscience.

Fourth, the flash mob achieved its apparent purpose—to spread joy by means of *emotional contagion*. Simply to be present in a context in which so many people engaged in the display of energy required to sing the Hallelujah Chorus would, I suspect, be enough to produce affective arousal. The aptness of the music for the joyous sentiment the words convey is one of the reasons the Hallelujah Chorus is so popular. In this situation, the obvious enjoyment the singers were taking in the experience would likely prompt emotional mirroring on the part of those who witnessed it. Online reactions to Hallelujah Chorus flash mobs suggest that those who have been present—and even those who observed them online—have typically found them extremely moving. According to Steve Jalsevac, in an article about the YouTube video of the flash mob in Ontario, Canada, on November 17, 2001 (the flash mob that inspired others in a number of cities, including Kansas City), by December 17 the video had been seen 22,500,000 times, and posts of positive comments vastly outweighed posts of negative ones, 48,868 to 1,075. One comment notes, "You can clearly see people crying. . . . This is the most intense video I've ever seen on YouTube."[8]

Fifth, the flash mob was evocative because it was a case of *large-scale cooperation* that was completely *voluntary*. Every participant could take pleasure in his or her own contribution to the event in part because it was uncoerced, an act of one's own will. In that sense, each person could "own" the event in a way that one cannot in the case of more obligatory efforts. This situation encouraged a feeling of optimism about what human beings can do if they set their minds to it, even without some compelling authority.

Granted, someone did conduct in the case of the Kansas City flash mob, but this conducting role was completely facilitative. Most people were in no position to see the conductor anyway. In other words, even if Western orchestras with conductors embody Western society's tendency toward top-down organization, in this case, the conductor was just another participant, directing traffic for those who cared to pay attention, but hardly in control of the situation. The scene was relatively egalitarian. One of the pleasures of the flash mob was the breakdown in usual social roles (particular jobs and socioeconomic status) that rendered everyone a fellow singer.[9] The idea that the conductor was just one more participant was echoed in the behavior of one of the food court patrons, visible in one of the videos, who "conducted" at his table for his own amusement as his own way of participating.

THE VALUE OF CROSS-CULTURAL
MUSICAL ENCOUNTERS

One might ask at this point how the experience of the flash mob has anything to do with cross-cultural contact through music. If one can get the humanizing benefits that I have been touting through music from our own culture, why should we think we have anything to gain from encounters with star-tlingly foreign music? And how could encounters with alien music result in anything like the musical camaraderie of a mob of midwestern choir members singing one of their all-time favorites?

Encounter with foreign music is important, I think, because it extends our feelings of sympathy and relatedness toward those we perceive as alien. In this sense, it is valuable for one of the educational desiderata that Richard Rorty describes, that of acquainting "people of different kinds with one another so that they are less tempted to think of those different from themselves as only quasi-human."[10] Familiar music can expand our sense of human connected-ness, of course, as I argued in the last chapter. Singing in the flash mob in-spired feelings of solidarity among a large number of strangers. Nevertheless, the strangers were in many ways homogenous, to the point of sharing certain repertoire. While it is certainly desirable to have occasions that arouse feel-ings of kinship and deflate suspicion among social classes within one society, a felt recognition of common humanity across cultural boundaries would be even more striking and might help to mitigate the hostilities that are driving forces in global politics.

At least, cross-cultural musical exchange can make inroads against preju-dice that will not be accomplished by musical solidarity that remains narrowly intracultural.[11] While I think that events such as the flash mob do promote a sense of general goodwill, not limited to other participants or members of a single religion, there is some danger that the generalized sense of connection will subtly reinforce ethnocentrism. Probably many Westerners are moved in a positive way by the fact that many East Asians, in particular, have taken up and achieved virtuosity in Western music; and likely this does enhance these Westerners' feeling of a generalized kinship with these musicians, a sense that "they are like us." But how many Westerners give East Asians the opportunity for similar reactions because they have sought virtuosity in a traditional Asian music? More worrisomely, I fear there may be others like the bigot I once met on a plane who told me that he had seen an African dance performance and asked himself, "Are these human beings?"

Encounters with music beyond our own cultural comfort zone can, I am convinced, lead to exactly the opposite of this man's reaction. Instead of dis-paraging difference with racist rationalizations about how it seems more in-stinct than art, or simply ignoring musical achievements from other cultures because they aren't accomplishments we're accustomed to, there are other possibilities. We might instead be impressed, even humbled by the music of other cultures, and still recognize that we are of the same sort as they are. Of course this requires that we have real encounters with foreign music, and avoid knee-jerk tendencies to dismiss it because it "sounds like noise" to us.

Gaining some appreciation of significantly foreign music can have other benefits for us in addition to a sense of closer connection with people from other cultures. As one is learning how to make sense of a particular type of music, one reenters the stance of a child getting oriented toward the world. The mental operation of dropping one's habitual musical schemata because they are unusable can be a refreshing experience. The relaxation of expectations in the musical case and the positive results of gaining greater understanding encourages more general willingness to adopt an open stance, which in turn may translate into a lessening of a guardedness toward people we don't know.

In any case, exploring new patterns in music amounts to investigating alternative ways to navigate. Learning new music is learning new ways to move as well as hitherto unexplored ways of charting a course. As Charles Nussbaum tells us, we engage our capacity to represent space when we are finding our way in music. Gaining our bearings in alien music amounts quite literally to expanding our horizons. Some of our discoveries might be merely enjoyable excursions. But at times the impact of our adventures may be a whole new perspective on what music can mean in our lives. The recognition, for Westerners, that there are whole cultures who see music as primarily participatory, who see serious music-making as a "natural" part of life, and who do not think of music-making as a special skill or the province of experts, can reorient their attitude toward music and its place in their lives. John Blacking's *How Musical Is Man?* is testimony to such a revolution in his musical outlook as a consequence of spending time among the Venda people of Africa.

Even if the discovery of other musical possibilities does not change our musical behavior, learning new music has an impact on our sense of identity, as any learning does. As we develop new abilities, we attach them to our sense of self. As we widen the circle of those we care about, our extended relational network becomes part of our identity, too. If we care about music makers whose cultures are alien, we've expanded this network and our sense of relatedness somewhat further. If this seems too abstract or far-fetched, reflect on the role that music played in improving the status of African Americans in the United States since World War II. Participatory songs, in particular "We Shall Overcome," were vital to making the civil rights movement a movement.[12] But even before that, the growing enthusiasm of white audiences for music by black music makers had an impact on the way African Americans were perceived by the white population. Musical appreciation entailed empathy. My suggestion here is that empathy through music can happen again. All we need is love, and perhaps open-minded attention to foreign music can be a start.

To some degree, these benefits of making cultural contact through music are available with only a bit of individual determination and a little steady effort. This is not to say that we will warm up to seriously foreign music as quickly as white Americans developed a taste for Nat King Cole's singing style. However, as I have been arguing, the universals of musical perception and the common musical techniques that have grown out of them represent a starting point for approaching other cultures' music; we learn statistically (i.e., through exposure and pattern recognition) to form new musical schemata. The fact that people communicate verbally, too, can help us understand what is happening in unfamiliar music. Those initiated in another musical vernacular can help us make sense of what is happening, and ethnomusicologists have devoted entire careers to assisting comprehension across musical cultures.

Of course, the fact that accustomed musical schemata can make our experience of some music more jarring at first is bound to be a hindrance if not an outright deterrent. For this reason I think it would be highly desirable on a societal scale to forestall discouragement by exposing children early on to a wide variety of music and musical sounds. The best way to facilitate understanding foreign music is to educate children in a wide range of the world's musical styles. If children hear diverse music from an early age, they will quite naturally develop schemata for many types, much as children can develop templates for multiple languages if early in life they are exposed to them on a regular basis. Children who learn several languages in this way do not get confused about which language is which—they learn which terms and utterances belong to which language. Similarly, children who hear many types of music early in life are able to distinguish which tones and structural possibilities are appropriate for each. Exposing children to the sounds of various instruments, vocal styles, and idioms early in life would preempt their developing perceptual biases that impede appreciation of music from outside their native cultures. If I am right in thinking that music can encourage feelings of security, and if general psychological security makes it easier to move outside one's comfort zone, even a modest degree of familiarity with diverse musical possibilities in childhood should enable deeper appreciation of multiple musical systems than is experienced by those of us who encounter music from foreign musical cultures later in life.

One objection to my contention that we would benefit by even a little bit of attention to foreign music is likely to be that I am encouraging dilettantism toward foreign music. It may sound as though I am encouraging people to rest content if they can make a little headway in orienting themselves in music they find initially incomprehensible. This is not my intention, although I do think that we should resist the idea that we have to be experts or be assimilated into a culture to gain anything of value from its music. I do think that at the beginning of one's exposure to significantly foreign music, one should not be frustrated if one has only minimal awareness of what is going on, but my point is not that one should stay there. In suggesting that we should learn more about the music of other cultures, I am proposing an ongoing project, though one that is recreational, need not be systematic, and probably would be more a pastime than a focused undertaking. I have argued that the results are likely to be beneficial and enjoyable, and I suspect those who set out to explore foreign music will find the effort worthwhile.

The difference between making some sense of significantly foreign music and understanding original work in one's own musical vernacular is in many ways a matter of degree. In both cases one attempts to relate the music to a schema one has already assimilated, and if that effort fails, one sets to work looking for patterns that may become basic to a new schema. Usually we don't have to learn a new schema for original works in our own culture's music, but some music pushes the boundaries of what its audience is prepared for. We may think that the perceptual demands of music from outside one's cultural framework are unlike any that are met with inside one's musical culture (particularly when different tuning systems are involved), but I suspect that isn't always true. I have met a person who was well educated in music of the Western classical tradition who nevertheless had trouble following "early" music, such as music of the Renaissance, because it didn't have the kind of chordal harmonic structure to which she was accustomed. The innovations in music history have all made intellectual demands on the part of those who engaged with it.

Distinctive musical styles within what we think of as a "culture"—jazz and rock being two that are part of American music culture—may also be unfamiliar to many of its members, and may thus require them to develop new schemata. And even if one develops schemata for musical subcultures, new works can still render them inapplicable. John Coltrane's "Ascension" is an example of jazz that even jazz aficionados of the era might have found hard to comprehend.[13]

No doubt it is true that we will never have the same understanding of another culture's music as would a member of that culture. We will also never have the same understanding of a work of music as the person who composed or improvised it, or have an identical musical autobiography with that of any-one else. This means that the commonality of musical background we share with anyone is always a matter of degree. The fact that we share some aspects of our processing of music with all other members of our species means that we always approach another culture's music with something in common.[14]

How do we go about having a real encounter with other cultures' music? In comparing the sense of greater empathy ideally occasioned by cross-cultural musical encounter to the sense of goodwill encouraged by the flash mob, I am contending that live music-making, especially when it involves elements of participation and inclusiveness, can be an effective means for creating a feeling of mutuality. The physical immediacy of the flash mob is rare enough within American musical culture(s) and subculture(s). The circumstances in which one can attend performances by music-makers from other societies who present music from their own cultures are for most of us uncommon, and participatory activity in connection with such an event rarer still. This does not mitigate the value and importance of such experiences, however. The physical intensity of mutually resonating (whether one's own participation is overt or inward), the emotional communication (in which behavioral cues of performers supplement those that may be suggested by the music itself), the bonding that shared music in general facilitates, the fun that music and sharing enjoyment typically involves, the noncoercive character of the typical musical situation—all of these features of live musical performance or partici-patory music are conducive to strong feelings of affinity.

Nevertheless, many other kinds of cross-cultural musical encounters can also be worthwhile. Some of these are:

- music-making by members of multiple musical cultures, where the differ-ent cultures' performance styles blend in the production of music;
- performances that include works from various cultures, whether in au-thentic or in culturally adapted performance styles;
- music-making that fuses stylistic features of different musical cultures together (Ravi Shankar's *Symphony*, performed with the London Philhar-monic, is an example);
- participatory music-making in a style that is endemic to a particular musi-cal culture but includes participants from outside it;
- participatory music-making that invites contributions in multiple musical styles;
- one or more persons listening to recordings of music from a musical culture of which they are not members;

- people from a different musical culture appropriating a musical style or aspects of a musical style foreign to all of them;
- and listening to recordings or watching video presentations of such appropriations.

I want to stress the importance of experiences with recorded music, for recordings are the primary means through which most of us experience foreign music.[15] I am convinced that while recordings offer the impression of human connection less palpably than live music, encountering music through recordings still fosters a sense of human kinship. Listeners in the contemporary world, it is true, may assert their membership in one musical audience as opposed to another, as was evident in the music skirmishes between generations in many households before iPods and ear buds were common implements for listening. Nevertheless, even in the privacy that iPods afford, recorded music produces a sense of being connected with others, at the very least with the musicians who made the recordings. As we have observed, we tend to mirror emotions that we take to be expressed in the music. Even if we don't directly mirror emotion, we tend to identify with the aurally perceived physical gestures and the impression of effort.

In the case of music with lyrics, the range of those with whom one consciously identifies can be restricted, and not only because lyrics are always in some language, and perhaps not a familiar one. A listener who has been let down in love might identify very directly with the imagined character (the persona, strictly speaking) in a blues ballad singing that his wife has done him wrong, and not feel very close to anyone who might fall into the category of betrayers.[16] Identification with the personae of songs, however, is not restricted to those whose alleged circumstances resemble a position one has occupied. Probably everyone who has ever been unhappy in love can feel sympathy for the blues persona just described. One can feel empathy for the persona of Cher's 1973 hit "Half-Breed" even if one is not of mixed ethnicity or has never been picked on for such a reason.

As we have noted, our imaginations are relatively free to play while listening to music, given the fact that when we engage with music we are typically less tied to particular roles than we are in most circumstances in everyday life. We can imaginatively take on the perspective expressed in the lyrics, lamenting, bragging, or triumphing along with the persona. Even if the music is connected with our situation in some sense (as marching songs may be for a soldier or religious songs may be for a worshipper), commonly songs offer room for some imaginative play, not stipulating the details of a situation in an inflexible way.[17]

In addition to the persona of the lyrics to a song (who is fictional or, minimally, stylized), I think we often feel connected to a much larger swath of humanity while listening to singing. We sometimes sing along, and sometimes do this with others. A student in one of my aesthetics classes told the charming story of singing along with a song while she was driving and pulling up to a stoplight next to another person singing along with the same song. They smiled at each other and kept singing. Although most of us do not have such serendipitous experiences while singing with recordings, I suspect that we often have a half-conscious feeling of singing along with the rest of the world.[18]

Recorded music can help us to hear what the rest of the world is singing; recorded music can also enable us to hear the same musical patterns and articulations again and again, which can help us to develop schemata appropriate to what has been hitherto incomprehensible. At this point in history recordings are indispensable if we are to get better acquainted with music from outside our culture. Best of all—if music is to further a sense being kin to music-makers from distant parts of the globe—would be to experience both recorded music, which assists familiarity, and live encounters with music-makers, whose vitality we can hear and feel and see.

Music is a relatively nonthreatening mode of cultural encounter whereby we can extend the sense of fellow feeling beyond our usual imaginative boundaries. The other arts also offer opportunities for being touched by a sense of our common humanity, all the more piquant when the source is temporally and spatially distant. A love poem from antiquity, a tale of war and passion from one of humanity's great epics, or a vignette from Sei Shonagon's pillow book touchingly reminds us of our kinship, psychologically, with people who lived a millennium or longer ago. In this sense literature is like music, but music's immediacy is singular. It neither requires nor allows for translation, and it communicates with urgency because it is so direct. Its physical impact is massive, and we feel its rhythms entraining ours. Quite literally, music gets under our skin. It should be no surprise, then, that it can make us feel like blood brothers of those with whom we share it.

CONCLUSION

When we reflect on some of the conclusions reached in this exploration of musical universality, irony may seem to abound. We share perceptual mechanisms and processes, but the result is that we develop mental schemata that make some foreign music sound strange. We share some universal preferences, but most are not on the surface, and their compatibility with many structural possibilities results in musical diversity, not similarity. Music's impact on our sense of security and its power to create group cohesion makes it serviceable for sectarian purposes.

Yet it takes only an antique tune in a pentatonic scale—the Sumerian melody described in chapter 3, for example—to remind us what fragile, transient things we are and how close we are to ancestors remote in time and space. "What a piece of work is man," marvels Hamlet, "how infinite in faculties . . . in action how like an angel, in apprehension how like a god!"[19] And how amazing is our music, as vast as human possibility, yet addressed to our peculiarities. As varied as our music is, as varied as we are, we all sound human. If anything about music is universal, that certainly is.

NOTES

CHAPTER 1

1. Nietzsche, *The Gay Science*, §80, 134–35.

2. Cirignola, "WOMAD: A Celebration of Cultural Diversity."

3. Darwin, *The Descent of Man*, 462; citing *The Nile Tributaries of Abyssinia* (1867), 203.

4. The term *tonality* refers to the system used in the West since the latter seventeenth century. Tonal music employs the major-minor scheme and makes use of seven-tone scales, the tones of which stand in different degrees of stability. Major and minor keys can be constructed on any of the twelve tones of the chromatic scale (the twelve tones within an octave, which correspond to the piano keys within an octave). Within a key, the tonic, the root tone of a scale, is the tone of greatest stability. Chords constructed from the available tones similarly have different degrees of stability, and they can be arranged to heighten and manipulate tensions. The tonic chord, the chord with greatest stability, is built on the tonic, and it is the chord toward which multivoiced tonal music aims. The tonal system allows for modulation from key to key, and it is associated with tempered tuning, tuning that slightly modifies acoustically pure intervals in order to minimize the dissonances that would otherwise occur as a consequence of multiple modulations from key to key.

5. Hullah, *The History of Modern Music*, 9.

6. See Becker, "Is Western Art Music Superior?," 341–59.

7. See Scruton, *The Aesthetics of Music*. Scruton views himself as a defender of Western civilization, and in this effort this elegant book, clearly a labor of love, elaborates on the power of the Western tonal system and on the role that music plays in articulating cultural values. Despite the fact that my first mention of this book is in the context of criticizing one of its points, I greatly admire it, particularly for its defense of music's ethical role.

8. Ibid., 266.

9. Ibid., 239.

10. Scruton, "The Eclipse of Listening," 53. For a discussion of the debate over whether

Western tuning is "natural," see Lerdahl and Jackendoff, *A Generative Theory of Tonal Music*, 290–96. Although they accept the view that "tonality reflects an innate organization of the pitch structure of music" (290), they conclude that "tonality is not simply man's response to physical facts about sound. . . . The mind is not simply following the physical path of least resistance, as the overtone hypothesis would have it, but is creating its own way of organizing pitch combinations into coherent patterns" (293).

11. Rosen, "Classical Music in Twilight," 53–54.

12. My thanks to Jay Garfield for drawing this incident to my attention. Cf. Solomon, *The Joy of Philosophy*, 69.

13. Sachs, *The Wellsprings of Music*, 218.

14. See Rowell, *Thinking about Music*, 192–93.

15. See DeWoskin, *A Song for One or Two*, 101–24.

16. Sorrell, *A Guide to the Gamelan*, 1.

17. For a description of this gamelan, see Lockspeiser, *Debussy: His Life and Mind*, 1:115.

18. Dowling and Harwood point out that instruments in Indonesian gamelan orchestras need to be retuned frequently, and that this involves several kinds of physical modifications. See *Music Cognition*, 103.

19. Lockspeiser, *Debussy: His Life and Mind*, 1:115.

20. George Harrison first introduced the sitar into the Beatles' music in "Norwegian Wood" on the 1965 album *Rubber Soul* (EMI/Parlophone). The members of Ladysmith Black Mambazo are not the only African musicians with whom Paul Simon collaborated on *Graceland* (Warner Bros. Records, 1986). Others include Bakithi Kumalo, Ray Phiri, Demola Adepoju, Youssou N'Dour, Isaac Mtshali, Morris Goldberg, and the groups Stimela, Tau Ea Matsekha, General M. D. Shirinda and the Gaza Sisters, and the Boyoyo Boys band. Presumably Ladysmith Black Mambazo's appearance drew particular attention because of the furor that arose over Simon's collaborating with anyone from South Africa during the era of apartheid. Simon had already made use of "non-Western" style on Simon and Garfunkel's *Bridge over Troubled Waters*, in "El Condor Pasa," an Andean folk song. For discussion of some of the issues surrounding Simon's appropriations, as well as the general problem of whether Western appropriation of non-Western music benefits those from whom the music is borrowed, see Charles Hamm, "Graceland Revisited," and Feld, "Notes on 'World Beat.'"

21. Stephen Davies notes that there is considerable tension within the field of ethnomusicology between those in anthropology and those affiliated with music departments, with the latter sometimes dismissing the musical sensitivity of the former (personal communication).

22. Huron, *Sweet Anticipation*, 379.

23. Stephen Davies is one of these noteworthy exceptions. See, for example, *Musical Works and Performances*, 254–94, and "Life Is a Passacaglia."

24. Kivy, *Sound Sentiment*, 94. Kivy contrasts the listening expectations of someone whose musical background is Western and geared to a mainly harmonic way of organizing polyphonic music with the semitone as the smallest available interval, with those of the person whose expectations were developed by Indian music, which is organized mainly horizontally and includes microtones. Kivy's paradigm of "Western" music is clearly based on models later than the Renaissance, when choral music was also organized horizontally, with the melodic lines

of different voices having relative independence of one another. Kivy also overemphasizes the role of microtones in Indian music. Although the tones available for a raga, and particularly for required ornaments, include tones at intervals less than a semitone, ragas are formed in discrete steps, with approximately the same number of tones as Western scales. Ragas must include at least five tones, and many have seven tones, sometimes with differences between ascending and descending versions. The use of these variants is comparable to the common employment of different versions of the ascending and descending statements of the minor scale in Western music. This implies that only very seldom is a tone succeeded by a microtonally proximate tone, and then almost always when one of the tones ornaments another. Thus the danger of microtones interfering with general perception of musical contour, which Kivy contends would be a serious problem for Western listeners, does not seem to be significant. Moreover, the structure of most Hindustani music involves an initial section (the *alap*) in which the raga is explored, familiarizing even the novice listener with its basic shape, before a more freewheeling exposition occurs. See Rowell, *Music and Musical Thought in Early India*, 42, 80, 147, and 168; and Dowling and Harwood, *Music Cognition*, 120.

25. Jerrold Levinson similarly notes that scholarly expertise on matters of musical structure has distorted scholars' understanding of the actual experience of most listeners. See Levinson, *Music in the Moment*. Many ethnomusicologists have also criticized scholars for excessively focusing on the musically elite. See Blacking, *How Musical Is Man?*

26. I discuss music's ethical impact in Higgins, *The Music of Our Lives*.

27. See London, "Musical and Linguistic Speech Acts," and Lidov, *Is Language a Music?*

28. Daniel Barenboim, Reith Lectures 2006, Lecture 1.

29. Aniruddh Patel indicates such a case. The supposedly "universal law" in the perception of both speech and music that "a lengthened sound tends to mark the end of a group," has been undercut by recent evidence that English and Japanese speakers differ in their respective groupings of tones, with English speakers perceiving in accordance with the predicted short-long pattern, but Japanese speakers perceiving in accordance with the contrasting pattern of long-short. See Patel, *Music, Language, and the Brain*, hereafter indicated as *MLB*, 169–73.

30. See *MLB*, 319–20. For an illuminating discussion of the sense of motion in music, see Clarke, *Ways of Listening*, 62–90. Clarke argues that the sense of movement is fictional and an inevitable by-product of the fact that our auditory systems are fine-tuned for detecting motion. See also Scruton, *The Aesthetics of Music*, 19; Lidov, *Is Language a Music?*, 120 and 146.

31. Dame Evelyn Glennie's performance career indicates that the deaf are not inherently prevented by their disability from engaging with music even at a very high level. Glennie, who has been deaf since the age of twelve, is a virtuoso percussionist, able to perform solos with a symphony orchestra. She often performs barefoot to enhance her tactile experience of the music. My thanks to Stephen Davies for suggesting this example. We should also note that Beethoven's deafness did not prevent him from composing masterpieces (though admittedly his deafness was acquired late in life).

32. See Sacks, *Musicophilia*, 98–119. See also Sacks, *The Man Who Mistook His Wife for a Hat and Other Clinical Tales*.

33. See Blacking, *How Musical Is Man?*

34. The ambivalent role of recording technology is complicated, and a topic worthy of

analysis. It both enables amateur performers to make their music available to others beyond their immediate environment and promotes the idea of music as a product that only a subset of the population produces.

35. See Zatorre and Halpern, "Mental Concerts." Cf. Davies, "Perceiving Melodies and Perceiving Musical Colors."

36. No doubt, many who hear background music are not actively engaged but may in fact attempt to tune it out. I do not mean to include this kind of passive or resistant "consumption" (if one can even call it that) as "listening."

37. See Mehler et al., "A Precursor of Language Acquisition in Young Infants," 143–78.

CHAPTER 2

1. Aristotle, *Politics*, 8.7.1341b.1.35–40, 1315.

2. Ibid., 8.7.1340a.1.4, 1311.

3. Ibid., 8.7.1341a.1.12–15, 1313.

4. See *MLB*, 100. Patel notes, however, that some species, such as frogs and some insects, do synchronize their calls with each other.

5. For a discussion of such views, see Kivy, "Platonism in Music."

6. See, for example, Cook, *Music, Imagination, and Culture*, 223. See also Scruton, *The Aesthetics of Music*, 3–6. In making the case that music is not identical to physical sound, Scruton makes use of a thought experiment imagining a "music room," in which we hear music in the absence of vibrations or a sound source. He suggests that the imaginability of such a scenario demonstrates the distinguishability of music and physical reality, and he goes on to argue that listeners hear "sounds apart from the material world" (221). This move is illegitimate in my opinion. The fact that we use our minds to organize and make sense of sounds that we hear as music does not mean the sounds themselves are immaterial. We can obviously imagine sounds apart from a physical sound source; we do that every time we imagine music in our heads. But this does not mean that the music we are imagining, were it actual, would be separate from the material world. Scruton is also right that the systemic grid of tonal space is not identical to the Newtonian grid, which we mentally impose on physical space in order to determine relative distances among things in the world. Thus the way we organize musical events in sound space is not the same as the way we map the spatial organization of the instruments of the orchestra; but this does not mean that we dissociate music from our actual environment. We hear the *world* as resounding, not just our mental space.

7. See Goehr, *The Imaginary Museum of Musical Works*, 89–95. Goehr's argument derives from Morris Weitz's case for considering "art" an open concept. See Weitz, "The Role of Theory in Aesthetics."

8. Blacking, *How Musical Is Man?*, 10.

9. This might suggest that I should define music simply as "organized sound," Edgar Varèse's characterization. I opt for Blacking's, despite the fact that it appears to exclude animal music, because I want to reflect the fact that the imposition of order relevant to the notion of music comes from human beings, if only in their interpretation of environmental sound "as mu-

sic." Strictly, then, I would not need to modify Blacking's definition to include animal sounds. Because "humanly organized sound" connotes the external production of sounds by human beings, however, I make explicit reference to animals in my rather awkward-sounding coda to Blacking's formulation.

10. Because I consider "humanly organized sound" to include any sounds that we can hear as organized, I think environmental sound can fit Blacking's definition of music, as can computer music and other kinds of music generated by machines. If one prefers to interpret "humanly organized sound" as restricted to the production of sounds and not the interpretation of sounds that are heard, computer and other machine music might still be included on the grounds that human beings produced the machines that produce the music, though admittedly this is production at one remove.

11. One of these is likely Jerrold Levinson, who seeks "a set of conditions that are necessary and sufficient" for an instance being music. He contends, "We will have succeeded if *all and only* those things that, on reflection and after consulting our intuitions, we are willing to count as music—in the primary (i.e., artistic) sense—satisfy the proposed conditions." Not surprisingly, he rejects both "organized sound" and "humanly organized sound" as definitions of music. Levinson, "The Concept of Music," 268 and 270.

12. See Cantrick, "If the Semantics of Music Theorizing Is Broke, Let's Fix It," 245-46. Although unlikely to be sympathetic to my freewheeling attitude toward the scope of the term *music*, Robert Cantrick raises a point that suggests another motivation for not demanding a hard and fast definition. He argues that it is difficult to establish that any particular sound is musical because recognizing a sound as musical depends on the context of a particular natural language that makes reference to music, specifically, by means of technical terms within ordinary language.

> . . . when theorizing about art music in Europe during several centuries before the twentieth, one *knows* that any sound is musical only if it is in a *key*.
> . . . when theorizing about art music in the Arab Middle East during several centuries before the twentieth, one *knows* that any sound is musical only if it is in a *maqām*.
> . . . when theorizing about art music in the Hindustani tradition of north India during several centuries before the twentieth, one *knows* that any sound is musical only if it is in a *thāt*. (245-46)

I disagree with Cantrick's suggestion that the mediation of technical language or the context it theoretically indicates is necessary to recognize that a particular sound is musical. A sound's appearance in the culture's relevant musical context is evidence that the sound is musical, but I do not think that one can only consider a sound musical if one observes that it occurs in a context such as *key*. This would seem to exclude the sounds of many percussive instruments from being musical because they are not pitched. It would also rule out expressive deviations from the pitches indicated in such contexts. Nevertheless, I think that Cantrick is right to suggest that listeners within a given musical culture tend to presuppose, on the basis of hearing a sound they take to be musical, that it can be accommodated within the larger matrix within which musical sounds occur, and that such matrices cannot be assumed to be the same across cultures.

13. For an interesting discussion of whether John Cage's *4′33″* should be considered music, see Davies, *Themes in the Philosophy of Music*, 11–29. Arthur Danto's account that "an atmosphere of theory" determines what sort of things count as art in a given time and place was designed for just such cases. See Danto, *The Transfiguration of the Commonplace*, 135. For a critical response to this view, see Davies, "Life Is a Passacaglia."

14. The philosopher in question is Paul Griffiths.

15. Although individuals sometimes have idiosyncratic understandings of the criteria for a classificatory definition, the evaluative nature of an honorific definition of a word is more obviously susceptible to idiosyncratic or privately subjective judgments as to whether the word applies to a particular case.

16. Feld, "Sound Structure as Social Structure," 390 and 393.

17. Cage's *4′33″* would not appear be music on this definition, which is a limitation. However, we might construe this work as urging us to listen to environmental sounds as if they were organized. In this case, Cage would implicitly be relying on a notion of music as organized sound, though "humanly" organized only in the listener's imposition of an interpretive frame.

18. This opposes the view of some theorists, such as Levinson, who do think that music needs to be appreciated for its own sake to count as music. See "The Concept of Music," 273, where Levinson defines music as "sounds temporally organized by a person for the purpose of enriching or intensifying experience through active engagement (e.g., listening, dancing, performing) with the sounds regarded primarily, or in significant measure, as sounds." Although he does allow that some other purposeful activity is going on besides appreciating the sounds for their own sake, he does not seem overly concerned to include all non-Western phenomena that I would pretheoretically call music: "But if a phenomenon in another culture with some resemblance to music simply *cannot* be encompassed in the broadest notion of music we can discover in our own conceptual scheme, then it is a confusion to say, for instance, out of misplaced liberality, that it is at least music 'to them'" (269n).

19. The New Caledonian crow (*Corvus moneduloides*) customizes twigs and leaves to make them more useful for digging food out of crevices. See Weir, Chappell, and Kacelnik, "Shaping of Hooks in New Caledonian Crows," 981. See also Hunt and Gray, "Diversification and Cumulative Evolution in New Caledonian Crow Tool Manufacture." Reports have also been made of tool use among chimps, orangutans, and Galapagos woodpecker finches. See Visalberghi and McGrew, "*Cebus* meets *Pan*."

20. *MLB*, 10. Patel denies we have evidence that the meaning of humpback whale song is associated with the sequencing of elements; and he contends that their songs "always seem to mean the same thing, in other words, a combination of a sexual advertisement to females and an intermale dominance display." Similarly, he considers birdsong to be confined to a limited range of meanings. Appropriately, however, he cautiously phrases his points, referring to how the situation "appears" (to us).

21. Kant, *The Critique of Judgment*, 94. See Parret, "Kant on Music and the Hierarchy of the Arts," 257.

22. See Hartshorne, "Metaphysics Contributes to Ornithology," 127–28, 131, and 133.

23. Feld, "Sound Structure as Social Structure," 395. See also Feld, "Aesthetics as Iconicity

of Style, or 'Lift-up-over Sounding,'" 88; and Feld, *Sound and Sentiment*, 181: "Song is communication from a bird's point of view, communication of one who becomes a bird."

24. My thanks to Stephen Davies for drawing my attention to this musical practice. His source was an unpublished paper by John Fisher, "The New Guinea Drone Beetle vs. the Teutonic Symphony Orchestra: Beholding Music Cross-Culturally," presented to the American Society for Aesthetics, Asilomar, California, April 1994.

25. For example, hear Kate Bush, "Moving," on *The Kick Inside* (1977), EMI SW-17003.

26. Trevor Wishart, *Vox 5* (1986). Cf. McAdams and Matzkin, "The Roots of Musical Variation in Perceptual Similarity and Invariance," 81.

27. See Feld, "Aesthetics as Iconicity of Style, or 'Lift-up-over Sounding,'" 88. See also Feld, "Sound Structure as Social Structure," 395.

28. Paul Lansky, *Homebrew* (1992), BCD 9035 Bridge.

29. See Allen, *Philosophies of Music History*, 51. Cf. Herzog, "Music in the Thinking of the American Indian," 9. Herzog also points out that many Native American tribes hold that songs were given by the Creator at the beginning of creation, or even before creation emerged.

30. See Allen, *Philosophies of Music History*, 51 and 5–7. Cf. Nasr, "Islam and Music," 221.

31. Lucretius, *On the Nature of Things* (*De Rerum Natura*), Book V, lines 1379–412, pp. 174–75.

32. For further discussion of theories of the divine origins of music, see Allen, *Philosophies of Music History*, 12, 24, 52.

33. Miller, "Evolution of Human Music through Sexual Selection," 330. Miller goes on to qualify this statement, however, in that he acknowledges that in 1773 Daines Barrington, claiming that birdsong must be functional for the birds, proposed that it is useful in territorial competition among males.

34. Darwin, *The Descent of Man*, 571.

35. Armstrong, in *New York Times*, July 7, 1971, 41.

36. Graham, "The Value of Music," 151.

37. Slater, "Birdsong Repertoires," 60: "Although animals may not share music in the strict sense with us, there is no doubt that some of them do have complex and beautiful vocal displays."

38. Darwin, *The Descent of Man*, 568; citing Waterhouse, from W. C. L. Martin's *General Introduction to Natural History of Mamm. Animals*, 1841, 432; Owen, *Anatomy of Vertebrates*, 3:600.

39. Darwin, *The Descent of Man*, 568; citing Lockwood, *American Naturalist*, 761.

40. Graham, "The Value of Music," 150.

41. Gordon's argument also ignores the "musicality" that the Kaluli of Papua New Guinea find in waterfalls, with which they often sing. See Feld, "Waterfalls of Song: An Acoustemology of Place Resounding in Bosavi, Papua New Guinea," 132–34.

42. Whaling, "What's behind a Song?," 65–67.

43. Merker, "Synchronous Chorusing and Human Origins," 321. The report he mentions is Boesch, "Symbolic Communication in Wild Chimpanzees?," 83.

44. Maconie, *The Second Sense*, 3.

45. See Marler, "Origins of Music and Speech," 33.

46. Falk, "Hominid Brain Evolution and the Origins of Music," 210; referring to Schaller, *The Mountain Gorilla*, 223, 226.

47. Falk, "Hominid Brain Evolution and the Origins of Music," 210. See also Goodall, *The Chimpanzees of Gombe*, 133; and Schaller, *The Mountain Gorilla*, 226.

48. Darwin, *The Descent of Man*, 460–61.

49. Scruton, *The Aesthetics of Music*, 160. Scruton is clearly asserting the superiority of human beings. He comments, "Appearances can cease to matter to us only by beginning to dominate our lives, as they dominate the lives of animals. The person who cannot contemplate appearances, surrenders to the trajectory of getting and begetting which makes each merely animal life dispensable" (370).

50. Radford, "Emotions and Music," 74.

51. Hanslick, *On the Musically Beautiful*, 62. Hanslick's statement is not praise for the power of music; he is rejecting the view that music has a positive moral effect on listeners. He goes on, "But is it really so commendable to be a music lover in such company?" Reports of music's effects on animals are nothing new. Varro (Marcus Terentius Varro, 116–27 BCE) claimed that the Gauls reported that the playing of timbrels tamed a lion. See Schueller, *The Idea of Music*, 111.

52. Shaw, *Keeping Mozart in Mind*, 240. The seals apparently dislike fast music, for they disappear when the violinist plays jigs or similar music. They seem to prefer slow, melodic music.

53. See Lerdahl and Jackendoff, *A Generative Theory of Tonal Music*, 290. See Wright et al., "Music Perception and Octave Generalization in Rhesus Monkeys," 291–307. Rhesus monkeys recognized songs transposed by an octave, but did not recognize the same songs transposed at other intervals. See also Fishman et al., "Consonance and Dissonance of Musical Chords: Neural Correlates in Auditory Cortex of Monkeys and Humans," 2761–88, which provides evidence of similar cortical response patterns to consonance and dissonance in human beings and macaques. My thanks to Stephen Davies for drawing these references to my attention.

54. See Shehadi, *Philosophies of Music in Medieval Islam*, 27, 60, and 120. See also Becker, *Deep Listeners*, 79.

55. Charles Darwin, *The Descent of Man*, 569n.

56. Ibid., 568–69; citing Mr. R. Brown, in *Proceedings of the Zoological Society*, 1868, 410.

57. See Juslin and Laukka, "Communication of Emotions in Vocal Expression and Music Performance," 773.

58. Mâche, "The Necessity of and Problems with a Universal Musicology," 475–77.

59. Slater, "Birdsong Repertoires," 60.

60. Wolfgang Welsch pursues a similar line of argument in "Animal Aesthetics." See also Miller, "Evolution of Human Music through Sexual Selection," 341–44; Staal, "Mantras and Bird Songs," 555; and Mâche, "The Necessity of and Problems with a Universal Musicology," 478.

61. Darwin, *Descent of Man*, 569.

62. Hartshorne, "Metaphysics Contributes to Ornithology," 127–28, 131, 133.

63. Music's strength as a mnemonic depends on its connection with very basic sensory operations. Klaus Scherer and Marcel Zentner propose that music may be so effective in causing recollection of emotional experiences because "music, like odours, may be treated at lower

levels of the brain that are particularly resistant to modifications by later input, contrary to cortically based episodic memory" ("Emotional Effects of Music: Production Rules," 369).

64. Chernoff, *African Rhythm and African Sensibility*, 35.

65. See Ellis, *Aboriginal Music, Education for Living*, 59 and 126; Chatwin, *The Songlines*, 13–14 and 108; Dowling and Harwood, *Music Cognition*, 234; and Roberts, *Ancient Hawaiian Music*.

66. See Rudinow, *Soul Music*, 173–95. See also McAllester, *Enemy Way Music*; Roseman, *Healing Sounds from the Malaysian Rainforest*; Ellis, *Aboriginal Music*; and de Muris, *Summa Musicae*, III, 195b.

67. Hodges, "Human Musicality," 31.

68. Juslin and Laukka, "Communication of Emotions in Vocal Expression and Music Performance," 773. They cite Snowden, "Expression of Emotion in Nonhuman Animals"; Jürgens, "Vocalization as an Emotion Indicator"; Davitz, "Personality, Perceptual, and Cognitive Correlates of Emotional Sensitivity"; Scherer, "Vocal Affect Signalling"; Scherer, "Vocal Affect Expression"; Morton, "On the Occurrence and Significance of Motivation-Structural Rules in Some Birds and Mammal Sounds"; and Ohala, "Cross-Language Use of Pitch."

69. Freeman, "A Neurobiological Role of Music in Social Bonding," 412.

70. See Hodges, "Neuromusical Research," 209.

71. Slater, "Birdsong Repertoires," 57.

72. Giessmann, "Gibbon Songs and Human Music from an Evolutionary Perspective," 103.

73. Ibid., 107.

74. Sloboda, *The Musical Mind*, 18.

75. See *MLB*, 243; and Balaban, "Bird Song Syntax."

76. Saffran, "Mechanisms of Musical Memory in Infancy," 38.

77. Payne, "The Progressively Changing Songs of Humpback Whales," 139.

78. Marler, "Origins of Music and Speech," 31 and 41. See also *MLB*, 244–59; and Hodges, "Neuromusical Research," 208.

79. *MLB*, 244.

80. See ibid., 244–59.

81. That is, unless you want to characterize music produced by machines such as computers as outside the purview of "human music," in which case there would be two categories: human music and machine music.

82. Dowling and Harwood, *Music Cognition*, 90–91.

83. See Koopman and Davies, "Musical Meaning in a Broader Perspective," 268–71.

84. It is also to ignore the fact that some animals, such as vervet monkeys, do signal different referents depending on the situation. See Marler, Evans, and Hauser, "Animal Signals: Reference, Motivation or Both?" Strangely, Patel considers meaning within animal music to be restricted to a single message, or at most to a very restricted one: "animal songs always advertise the same set of things, including readiness to mate, territorial warnings, and social status" (*MLB*, 356). Clearly, he is taking "meaning" to be objective and evident to us in these statements.

85. Kant makes the interesting point that we can find beauty in the song of a bird, but that

this would be spoiled for us if we discovered that a human being were producing the music. See Kant, *Critique of Judgment*, 94.

86. Scruton, *The Aesthetics of Music*, 171–72.

87. According to the National Aeronautics and Space Administration website, "One of the purposes was to send a message to extraterrestrials who might find the spacecraft as the spacecraft journeyed through interstellar space." http://voyager.jpl.nasa.gov/spacecraft/languages/background.html.

88. The sounds of a volcanic eruption, a rocket takeoff, animals, a mother and child, meteorological phenomena, the ocean surf, laughter, a kiss, human speech and movement, fire, tools, machines, Morse code, life signs, pulsar, and the music of the spheres were all included.

89. Printed greetings from President Jimmy Carter and United Nations Secretary General Kurt Waldheim were also sent with the two spacecraft.

90. Scruton, *The Aesthetics of Music*, 460.

CHAPTER 3

1. *Invasion of the Body Snatchers*, directed by Don Siegel, 1956.

2. Nettl, "On the Question of Universals," 3.

3. Trehub, "Human Processing Predispositions and Musical Universals," 441. She suggests that the familiar feeling may have come from "the apparent diatonicity of the underlying scale." See also Kilmer, Crocker, and Brown, *Sounds from Silence*; Trehub, "Musical Predispositions in Infancy," 9; Trehub, Unyk, and Trainor, "Adults Identify Infant-Directed Music across Cultures"; Unyk et al., "Lullabies and Simplicity."

4. Blacking, "Can Musical Universals Be Heard?," 22.

5. Blacking, *How Musical Is Man?*, 109.

6. See Dowling and Harwood, *Music Cognition*, 24.

7. An interval produced by the simultaneous sounding of two tones is called harmonic. An interval produced by two tones sounding successively is called a melodic interval. Intervals are labeled by the number of tones of the diatonic scale that are included in the distance between them. Thus the interval from C to the closest E is a third, because three tones of the diatonic scale fit into the distance between pitches: C, D, and E.

8. See Helson, *Adaptation-Level Theory*, 382–87. Helson attributes this theory to McClelland et al., *The Achievement Motive*.

9. Dowling and Harwood, *Music Cognition*, 87.

10. David Huron describes the opening of *The Rite of Spring* as shocking because of three departures from Western conventions for orchestral works: beginning with a solo, beginning with a solo by a bassoon, and putting the bassoon at the top of its range. See Huron, *Sweet Anticipation*, 270.

11. Lerdahl and Jackendoff, *A Generative Theory of Tonal Music*, 291.

12. *MLB*, 260.

13. For a discussion of the nonuniversality of scales, see Davies, *Musical Meaning and Expression*, 236.

14. A semitone is approximately the distance between two adjacent keys on the piano, for

example, C and C-sharp. I say "approximately" because the tuning of the piano is tempered tuning, not tuning in accordance with pure acoustics.

15. Ornaments, in this context, typically involve the addition of one or more additional notes (sometimes a standardized melodic figure) to a particular note.

16. Tran Van Khe, "Is the Pentatonic Universal?" Nevertheless, Tran concludes, "Don't you believe, as I do, after all of this, that the pentatonic phenomenon is truly universal?" (83).

17. Equal tempering evolved independently in China, and the baroque employment of equal tempering occurred after Europe learned in approximately 1630 of the discovery of a precise mathematics for this kind of tuning by Zhu Zaiyu (in approximately 1580). See Dowling and Harwood, *Music Cognition*, 94.

18. The equal temperament system as used in the West divides the octave into twelve steps that are logarithmically equal.

19. As we go around the circle of fifths, dissonance between the pure octave and the pure fifth becomes gradually greater. This results in intonation differences between instruments played in different keys.

20. For an interesting account of the way master musicians initially approach foreign music, see Hopkins, "Aural Thinking," 143–61. Hopkins observes that the musicians initially focused on the rhythmic pattern, attempting to relate it to rhythmic patterns with which they were familiar, and they demonstrated perplexity when they could not assimilate what they were hearing with categories to which they were accustomed.

21. *MLB*, 18.

22. Yuen Ren Chao, "The Non-Uniqueness of Phonemic Solutions of Phonetic Systems," 33n; reprinted in Joos, *Readings in Linguistics*, 1:51.

23. Davies, *Musical Meaning and Expression*, 245.

24. For an example, see Gettier, "Is Justified True Belief Knowledge?," 121–23.

25. Hood, "Universal Attributes of Music," 66.

26. See *MLB*, 11.

27. Ibid., 11.

28. Nattiez makes essentially this distinction, differentiating between "strategies of perception or esthetic strategies" and "strategies of production." See "Under What Conditions Can One Speak of the Universals of Music?," 102.

29. Dowling and Harwood, *Music Cognition*, 238–39.

30. Harwood, "Universals in Music," 524.

31. Ibid., 525. See also Herndon, "Analysis: The Herding of Sacred Cows?," 248.

32. Bregman, "Auditory Scene Analysis," 23.

33. See Blacking, "Extensions and Limits of Musical Transformations," paper presented at 1972 Society for Ethnomusicology conference, Toronto; cited in Feld, "Linguistic Models in Ethnomusicology," 207.

34. Walker, *Musical Beliefs*, 47.

35. See Harwood, "Universals in Music," 525.

36. Ibid., 525. For empirical support, see Bachem, "Time Factors in Relative and Absolute Pitch Determination"; and Deutsch, "Octave Generalization of Specific Interference Effects in Memory for Tonal Pitch."

37. See Dowling and Harwood, *Music Cognition*, 93, 113, and 238. Diana Deutsch and Richard C. Boulanger, however, point out in "Octave Equivalence and the Immediate Recall of Pitch Sequences" that perceptual recognition of octave equivalence can be enhanced or addled by contextual factors. Tonal music tends to reinforce octave equivalence by means of such techniques as frequent octave jumps and octave doubling, learned conventions, and the implication with regard to what the next tone in a series will be that either a tone or its octave double will be suitable. Steward Hulse and his colleagues also point out that when tones are not arranged into a musical structure, but are simply played in isolation, listeners do not reliably equate tones with their counterparts in other octaves, and that the ability to do so seems related to musical training. See Hulse, Takeuchi, and Braaten, "Perceptual Invariances in the Comparative Psychology of Music," 155–56.

38. Demany and Armand, "The Perceptual Reality of Tone Chroma in Early Infancy."

39. Dowling and Harwood note certain exceptions to this generalization. See *Music Cognition*, 93: "The only exceptions we have found are certain groups of Australian aborigines. In their cultures, melodic imitations at roughly octave intervals do not always use the same logarithmic scale intervals, and when men and women sing together, they do so in unison and not in octaves." In general, however, scales are developed on the basis of octave equivalence, with the size of differences in pitch being correlated with differences in frequency of vibrations. They consider the relationship between pitch differences and frequency ratios to be logarithmic (such that "equal differences in pitch correspond to equal ratios of frequency"), although they acknowledge that the notion of scales as logarithmic is not universally accepted (see 238). See, for example, Catherine J. Ellis's "Pre-Instrumental Scales," in which she argues that the scales for some of the Central Australian Aboriginals she studied appear to be arithmetical rather than logarithmic, as do some of the scales that others have studied.

40. See Ward, "Subjective Musical Pitch"; Hood, "Slendro and Pelog Redefined"; and Burns, "Octave Adjustment by Non-Western Musicians." Burns and Ward indicate that octave stretching seems to be fairly universal. See Burns and Ward, "Intervals, Scales, and Tuning," 263. See also Harwood, "Universals in Music," 526, and Dowling and Harwood, *Music Cognition*, 101–2 and 238.

41. See Dowling, "Scale and Contour"; Idson and Massaro, "A Bidimensional Model of Pitch in the Recognition of Melodies"; Kallman and Massaro, "Tone Chroma Is Functional in Melody Recognition"; Dowling and Harwood, *Music Cognition*, 23; and *MLB*, 23–24. Studies have shown, however, that contour becomes a less important processing factor as the length of melodies increases. See Edworthy, "Interval and Contour in Melody Processing"; and Dowling and Bartlett, "The Importance of Interval Information in Long-Term Memory for Melodies." Harwood cites a number of studies that have focused on the cross-cultural importance of contour. See Harwood, "Universals in Music," 527; Becker, *Traditional Music in Modern Java: Gamelan in a Changing Society*; Becker, "The Anatomy of a Mode"; Williamson, "Aspects of Traditional Style Maintained in Burma's First 13 Kyo Songs"; Kolinsky, "'Barbara Allen': Tonal versus Melodic Structure, Part I"; Kolinsky, "'Barbara Allen': Tonal versus Melodic Structure, Part II"; Seeger, "Versions and Variants of the Tunes of 'Barbara Allen.'" See also Carterette and Kendall, "On the Tuning and Stretched Octave of Javanese Gamelans"; Carterette, "Timbre, Tuning and Stretched Octave of Javanese Gamelans"; Carterette and Kendall,

"Comparative Music Perception and Cognition"; and Burns, "Octave Adjustment by Non-Western Musicians."

42. Harwood, "Universals in Music," 527. See also Dowling and Harwood, *Music Cognition*, 238. They point out that although piano tuning stretches octaves, the octaves on pianos are stretched by only half the amount that listeners subjectively stretch the octave, so that high frequency partials of piano strings are mutually consistent with each other. The fact that the stretched octave in piano tuning does not supplant subjective stretching is evidence "for the inherent nature of the stretched octave for successive tones" (103). The tuning of non-Western instruments provides further evidence, as does a study of non-Western listeners, in Burns, "Octave Adjustment by Non-Western Musicians," S25.

43. Chang and Trehub, "Auditory Processing of Relational information by Young Infants." For a practical illustration of the importance of contour, see Agawu, "Music in the Funeral Traditions of the Akpafu," especially 89.

44. See Bregman, "Auditory Scene Analysis: Hearing in Complex Environments," 21. See also Bregman and Dannenbring, "The Effect of Continuity on Auditory Stream Segregation."

45. My thanks to Stephen Davies for suggesting this example.

46. See Dowling and Harwood, *Music Cognition*, 239; Sloboda, *The Musical Mind*, 23; and *MLB*, 24–26 and 201. Sloboda notes greater evidence of categorical pitch perception among musicians than among nonmusicians (25). For experimental evidence that categorical perception corresponds to the intervals of the scales used in one's culture, see Perlman and Krumhansl, "An Experimental Study of Internal Interval Standards in Javanese and Western Music."

47. I refer to these beats as *acoustical* in order to differentiate them from the rhythmic beats (the "strong" and "weak" beats) involved in meter.

48. Trehub, "Human Processing Predispositions and Musical Universals," 431. See also Sachs, *The Rise of Music in the Ancient World, East and West*; Meyer, *Emotion and Meaning in Music*, hereafter *EMM*; Trehub, Schellenberg, and Hill, "The Origins of Music Perception and Cognition"; and *MLB*, 21–22.

49. Trehub, "Human Processing Predispositions and Musical Universals," 431.

50. See Tramo et al., "Neurobiology of Harmony Perception," 132. See also Malmberg, "The Perception of Consonance and Dissonance"; Guernsey, "The Role of Consonance and Dissonance in Music"; Butler and Daston, "Musical Consonance as Musical Preference"; and Agawu, "Music in the Funeral Traditions of the Akpafu," 90. Agawu notes the prominence of the fourth in funeral dirges of the Akpafu people in Ghana.

51. Trehub, "Human Processing Predispositions and Musical Universals," 431.

52. Burns and Ward, in "Intervals, Scales, and Tuning," observe that scales of discrete pitches are "essentially universal," the only exceptions being a few styles that lack discrete pitch relationships (see 243). See also Dowling and Harwood, *Music Cognition*, 90–91, 98, and 238. They note that Debussy and others have experimented with whole-tone scales (scales in which the distance between adjacent tones is uniformly two semitones), but conclude, "the consensus among musicians is that it fails to offer enough intervallic variety to qualify as anything more than a novelty" (98). Dowling and Harwood note, however, that there are also exceptions to the alleged universality of scales with discrete pitches, noting that some societies utilize chants that involve only two notes. They cite as an example Hawaiian *oli* chant, which focuses on a

single note but also employs a considerably lower, secondary pitch, although its distance from the first tone may vary. Such two-pitch chants also occur in other parts of the world, and the interval between the two tones may widen, "perhaps in continuous fashion," as the excitement of the chant grows (90–91). See also Roberts, *Ancient Hawaiian Music*, 70; Burns and Ward, "Intervals, Scales, and Tuning," 243; Sachs, *The Wellsprings of Music*, 61; and Malm, *Music Cultures of the Pacific, the Near East, and Asia*, 13.

Nicholas Cook also denies that it is appropriate to define music in terms of scales of discrete notes, given that some cultures' music fluctuates around "the notional pitches in terms of which the music is organized." He mentions "Japanese *shakuhachi* music and the *sanjo* music of Korea," as well as music that does not feature discrete pitches, such as "African percussion music" (*Music, Imagination, and Culture*, 10). The Samaritans near Tel Aviv and Nablus, according to Bruno Nettl, have a form of group singing that "has indistinct pitches and only very vaguely defined relationships among the voices" ("An Ethnomusicologist Contemplates Musical Universals," 471). Stephen Davies also points out that in certain music of the Australian Aborigines "glissandos and portamentos are so prominent that it is misleading to regard the sound structure as involving discrete notes or intervals. Many works contain untuned musical sounds—body slaps, hand claps, clap-sticks, rattle, tambourines, castanets, cymbals, tam tam, drums, unbossed gongs, wind machines, or typewriters." Davies, *Musical Works and Performances*, 49.

53. Peretz, "Brain Specialization for Music," 201.

54. See *MLB*, 17.

55. See Dowling and Harwood, *Music Cognition*, 93 and 238.

56. See Miller, "The Magical Number Seven, Plus or Minus Two."

57. See Dowling and Harwood, *Music Cognition*, 91. Burns and Ward, "Intervals, Scales, and Tuning," 246. See also *MLB*, 19.

58. See Dowling and Harwood, *Music Cognition*, 238; Francès, *The Perception of Music*, 34–35.

59. In some cases, however, this hierarchical weighting is relative. Monique Brandily points out that in the Teda people of Chad, "the status of each degree within the hierarchy is not constant throughout each piece. . . . On the contrary, the status of a scale degree varies according to its position in one or another of the segments constituting the whole." Brandily, "Songs to Birds among the Teda of Chad," 383.

60. See *MLB*, 20.

61. Don Harrán notes that the long and short durations of neumes derived "from the longs and shorts of ancient metrical poetry." Harrán, *Word-Tone Relations in Musical Thought*, 1.

62. Monahan and Carterette, in "Pitch and Duration as Determinants of Musical Space," demonstrate that experimental subjects relied more on durations than on pitches to make judgments of similarity in musical pattern. Widely differing rhythm patterns accompanying the same pitch pattern also influenced subjects to judge the pitch patterns different even when they were identical. See also McAdams and Matzkin, "The Roots of Musical Variation in Perceptual Similarity and Invariance," 90–91.

63. See Lerdahl and Jackendoff, *A Generative Theory of Tonal Music*, 70. However, cultures do show some variance in beat perception, at least when comparing music from their

own culture to that of another. Drake and Ben El Heni showed that French subjects keeping time to music did so more slowly for French music than for Tunisian, and that Tunisian subjects did the reverse. See Drake and Ben El Heni, "Synchronizing with Music: Intercultural Differences."

64. See McAdams and Matzkin, "The Roots of Musical Variation in Perceptual Similarity and Invariance," 90.

65. Drake and Bertrand, "The Quest for Universals in Temporal Processing," 25–28. See also Dowling and Harwood, *Music Cognition*, 186–87 and 239; and Sloboda, *The Musical Mind*, 28–30.

66. Sloboda, *The Musical Mind*, 29–30.

67. See Epstein, "Tempo Relations in Music: A Universal?" Dowling and Harwood (*Music Cognition*, 181–82) point out that much evidence supports the idea of "a weakly felt natural pace" of 1.3–1.7 psychological events per second, or events paced about 0.6 to 0.75 seconds apart. See also Bowlby, *Attachment and Loss*, 1:393–94. Bowlby points out that infants are soothed by rocking at the right speed (approximately sixty cycles per minute). Dowling and Harwood note, however, that this natural pace varies with persons, contexts, and tasks. They also note that "rhythmic subdivisions can . . . be said to be encoded in rhythmic contours of relative, not absolute, temporal relationships" (187–88). They refer to Monahan, *Parallels between Pitch and Time: The Determinants of Musical Space*. See also Clynes, *Sentics*, 88–90; and Clynes, "When Time Is Music." Clynes points out that there is remarkable consistency of timing among musicians who interpret the same work.

68. Specifically, he studied samples from "the !ko and G/wi groups in the Kalahari desert of Africa, from a Tibetan monastery, from the Navari caste of Nepal, from the Yanomami Indians in the Orinoco River region of South America (Venezuela), from the Medlpa of the Papua coastal region of New Guinea, and from the Eipo of the mountainous central highlands of New Guinea" (100). Epstein contends that if proportional tempo keeping is so precise across the world, there must be a biological basis for it.

69. Epstein, "Tempo Relations in Music: A Universal?" See, in particular, 112.

70. Leibniz, *Letters, Leibnitii Epistolae ad diversos*, ep. 154, as translated by E. F. J. Payne, in Schopenhauer, *The World as Will and Representation*, 1:256n. See also Leibniz, "Principles of Nature and Grace," 17.

71. Dowling and Harwood, *Music Cognition*, 154. Lerdahl and Jackendoff also emphasize the relevance of Gestalt principles of musical organization to their ambitious generative theory of tonal music. See *A Generative Theory of Tonal Music*, 40–43 and 302–7.

72. Meyer, "A Pride of Prejudices; or, Delight in Diversity," 276.

73. Trehub also describes "the relevance of gestalt principles of grouping" as a music processing universal. See "Human Processing Predispositions and Musical Universals," 431 and 435. See also Sloboda, *The Musical Mind: The Cognitive Psychology of Music*. Lerdahl and Jackendoff's generative theory of tonal music is also premised on Gestalt theory.

74. Schellenberg, "Expectancy in Melody." Schellenberg found that the expectation of pitch reversal held for adults but not for infants, which suggests that this "universal" is not hardwired. He suggests that the exaggerated prosody with which caregivers often speak to infants may delay their acquisition of this expectation for song. A study by Paul von Hippel

and David Huron, "Why Do Skips Precede Reversals? The Effect of Tessitura on Melodic Structure," showed that composers only tend to reverse pitch when it is approaching the edge of tessitura (the predominantly used area within a particular vocal part), quite sensibly in that a singer cannot continue indefinitely in the same direction. Huron refers to this phenomenon as "melodic regression." Nevertheless, listeners *expect* large skips to be followed by steps in the opposite direction regardless of the relation of the skip to tessitura. Huron speculates that listeners overgeneralize from the cases in which skips occur near the median pitch of a vocal range. See Huron, *Sweet Anticipation*, 80–85.

75. Diana Deutsch has suggested that we tend to misremember random skips, which might again suggest that the widespread structural tendencies of music are a consequence of the constraining influence of the limitations of memory. See Deutsch, "Facilitation by Repetition in Recognition Memory for Tonal Pitch"; and Deutsch, "Delayed Pitch Comparisons and the Principle of Proximity."

76. For a discussion of this and other Gestalt principles in connection with music, see Lipscomb, "Cognitive Organization of Musical Sound," 145–50.

77. See *EMM*, 92. Both Meyer and Lerdahl and Jackendoff cite Koffka's original formulation of the Law of Prägnanz: "Psychological organization will always be as 'good' as the prevailing conditions allow. In this definition the term 'good' is undefined. It embraces such properties as regularity, similarity, simplicity, and others." Koffka, *Principles of Gestalt Psychology*, 110. See *EMM*, 86, and Lerdahl and Jackendoff, 304. Meyer includes this law among the principles that structure our musical expectations, although he grants that deviations occur. On his account, deviation from expectations occasion affect; so none of the principles that establish our expectations are satisfied in every case. Dowling and Harwood insist that good continuation can be overridden by other patterning principles, such as repeated notes, proximity, or similarity of timbre. Dowling and Harwood, *Music Cognition*, 158–59. For example, we tend to track the timbre of a violin and to hear the movement of this timbre to be part of the same voice in a texture, even if the violin does not continue to follow a pattern in a fashion that conforms to our expectations.

78. *MLB*, 170–73. Patel's coinvestigators were John R. Iversen and Kengo Ohgushi. The study, "Perception of Nonlinguistic Rhythmic Stimuli by American and Japanese listeners," appeared in the *Proceedings of the Eighth International Congress of Acoustics*, Kyoto, Japan, 2004. For a popular account of the study, John R. Iversen and Kengo Ohgushi, "How the Mother Tongue Influences the Musical Ear," see http://www.acoustics.org/press/152nd/iversen_patel_ohgushi.html.

79. Huron, *Sweet Anticipation*, 95.

80. See ibid., 99.

81. I am assuming here and in the remainder of my discussion that the music under discussion is human music. I suspect that we interpret animal music as the result of movement, too, but my focus here is our grounds for recognizing something familiar in music from foreign human cultures.

82. In other words, even when sequentially performed, tones that form dissonant intervals will be heard as being in a dissonant relation to each other and will therefore imply a degree of instability that we expect to be resolved by means of subsequent consonance.

83. See Francès, *The Perception of Music*, 78, and Dowling and Harwood, *Music Cognition*, 86.

84. *MLB*, 199 and 199n.

85. Interestingly, some societies reverse the direction of the correlation, among them the Greeks, the Jews, and the Arabs. See Sachs, *The Rise of Music in the Ancient World, East and West*, 69–70, and Francès, *The Perception of Music*, 279. Both Sachs and Francès speculate that these correlations may have stemmed from the observation that long strings, that is, strings that extended "higher," produced the tones that we would call "lower," or that the "higher" status accorded to men made their voices "higher" by association.

86. See Zuckerkandl, *Sound and Symbol*, 275–76.

87. Our perception of spatial distances is not as universal as it might seem; we learn how to use auditory cues to perceive distances by experience. Feld observes that the rainforest context of Kaluli life has an impact on the acoustic features of the environment.

> Lack of visual depth cues couple with the ambiguities of different vegetation densities and ever-present sounds (like water hiss) to make depth often sensed as height moving outward, dissipating as it moves. . . . Even though I was aware of psychological evidence that humans are better at horizontal than vertical sound localization, and often subjectively sense high tones to be higher in space than they in fact are . . . I was acoustically disoriented in the forest for months. Kaluli laughed hysterically the first times they saw me look up to hear a sound that was deep, whether high or low to the ground. (Feld, "Aesthetics as Iconicity of Style, or 'Lift-up-over Sounding,'" 88–89.)

88. Nussbaum, *The Musical Representation*, 21.

89. Sloboda, *The Musical Mind*, 259.

90. For a discussion of pitch hierarchies, which can be used to distinguish pitches that are structural from those that are ornamental, see *MLB*, 201–2.

91. See London, *Hearing in Time*, 4. London argues that musical meter, an anticipatory schema that we impose, is a specific case of entrainment behavior, an outgrowth of our practice in entraining from our early childhood (6 and 12).

92. Benzon notes that our nearest primate relatives seem not to be able to do this. See *Beethoven's Anvil*, 27–28. Benzon also notes the study by Néda et al., "The Sound of Many Hands Clapping," which demonstrates that applause recurrently attains synchronization, which breaks up and then is restored (except at high frequencies). The nonsynchronized hand clapping was louder and at approximately twice the frequency.

93. Nietzsche, *The Gay Science*, §84, 139.

94. "Polythetic" is a technical phenomenological term, which Schutz defines as "step by step." See Schutz, "Making Music Together," 114–15.

95. Ibid., 118.

96. Repp, "Diversity and Commonality in Music Performance"; see also Patel's discussion in *MLB*, 114–15. This may, however, be an overgeneralization from a single case.

97. *MLB*, 47.

98. Ibid., 141.

CHAPTER 4

1. The first two paragraphs of this chapter were also published in Higgins, "Musical Education for Peace," 389.

2. Weintraub, *Silent Night*, 26–27 and 30. My thanks to Marilyn Maxwell for drawing my attention to this book.

3. Ibid., 37.

4. Lerdahl and Jackendoff, *A Generative Theory of Tonal Music*, 293.

5. Nettl, "On the Question of Universals," 5.

6. Davies, *Musical Works and Performances*, 22n.

7. See Harwood, "Universals in Music," 526. Dowling and Harwood point out that this tendency reflects the Gestalt principle of proximity, and that in experiments "violations of the proximity rule . . . led to patterns that were difficult to follow" (*Music Cognition*, 155–57).

8. Meyer, "A Pride of Prejudices; or, Delight in Diversity," 284 and 284n.

9. See McAllester, "Some Thoughts on 'Universals' in World Music," 379; Nettl, "An Ethnomusicologist Contemplates Universals in Musical Sound and Musical Culture," 468; Benzon, *Beethoven's Anvil*, 140. Lerdahl and Jackendoff point out that systems with a tonic sometimes also employ "a secondary point of stability" (*A Generative Theory of Tonal Music*, 295). They cite Indian ragas and Torah chant as examples. See also Erickson, "A Perceptual Substrate for Tonal Centering?" Erickson suggests that the evidence of traditional "neighbor" ornaments that circle specific tones reflect a tendency toward centering. He also suggests that the phenomenon of melodic fission may result in a tendency toward centering, since recurrent skips often result in the impression of two melody lines instead of one.

10. Nattiez, however, finds this putative universal so vague as to be almost meaningless. See "Under What Conditions Can One Speak of the Universals of Music?," 98.

11. See Sloboda, *The Musical Mind*, 253; Lerdahl and Jackendoff, *A Generative Theory of Tonal Music*, 295; and Sloboda and Juslin, "Psychological Perspective on Music and Emotion," 92.

12. Nettl, "On the Question of Universals," 5.

13. Huron, *Sweet Anticipation*, 76–77.

14. McAllester, "Some Thoughts on 'Universals' in World Music"; Nettl, "On the Question of Universals," 5.

15. Brown, Merker, and Wallin, "An Introduction to Evolutionary Musicology," 14. See also Gabrielsson and Lindström, "The Influence of Musical Structure on Emotional Expression," 226. They note Imberty's study that suggests that "high formal complexity combined with high dynamism means formal disintegration and expression of anxiety and aggressiveness." They refer to Imberty, *Entendre la musique*.

16. Nettl, "On the Question of Universals," 5.

17. Sloboda, *The Musical Mind*, 258. See also Dowling and Harwood, *Music Cognition*, 239.

18. Brown, Merker, and Wallin, "An Introduction to Evolutionary Musicology," 14. See also Sloboda, *The Musical Mind*, 259. Lerdahl and Jackendoff (98) point out that Alice Singer's study of the complex rhythms of Macedonian and Bulgarian folk music, for example, analyzes

all of them in terms of units of twos and threes. See Singer, "The Metrical Structure of Macedonian Dance."

19. Chernoff, *African Rhythm and African Sensibility*, 47.

20. See *MLB*, 88. In Western music theory, the octave, the fifth, and the fourth are described as "perfect" intervals.

21. See Simonton, "Emotion and Composition in Classical Music: Historiometric Perspectives," 214.

22. My thanks to Ron Grant for encouraging me to speculate about the basis for this "law."

23. Harwood, "Universals in Music," 528.

24. Nettl, "An Ethnomusicologist Contemplates Musical Universals," 469.

25. Mâche, "The Necessity of and Problems with a Universal Musicology," 475. Mâche considers pentatonic polyphony on a drone to be one of the few structural characteristics of human music that one does not find in any animal sonic production.

26. Van Damme, "Universality and Cultural Particularity in Visual Aesthetics," 258.

27. Ibid., 274.

28. Ibid., 274n.

29. Malm, *Music Cultures of the Pacific, the Near East, and Asia*, 33.

30. See Dowling and Harwood, *Music Cognition*, 37.

31. My thanks to Stephen Davies and Susan Pratt Walton for their explanations of the desired vocal qualities in these two cultures. See also *MLB*, 90. Patel points out that Bulgarian music shows a preference for "rough-sounding intervals such as the second," which are featured in some of its polyphonic vocal music.

32. Walker, *Musical Beliefs*, 45.

33. Ibid., 45–46.

34. *Intituta Partum de Modo Psallendi Sive Cantandi*, in *Scriptores Ecclesiastici de Musica Sacra Potissimum*, I, 5a, as cited in Harrán, *Word-Tone Relations in Musical Thought*, 45–46.

35. Lomax, "Folk Song Style," 933 and 936.

36. See Lomax, *Cantometrics: An Approach to the Anthropology of Music*. Lomax considered more than 3,000 songs from 233 cultures. He coded the songs on the basis of thirty-seven features.

37. Lomax, "Song Structure and Social Structure," 228–29.

38. Lomax, "Folk Song Style," 950.

39. Lomax, "Song Structure and Social Structure," 241.

40. Ibid., 237 and 239–40.

41. Feld, "Sound Structure as Social Structure," 384.

42. Ibid., 385.

43. Dowling and Harwood, *Music Cognition*, 229. They point out that Lomax, with Norman Berkowitz, made new cantometric studies, concluding that many of the relationships did not seem to be as universal as the initial studies had suggested, but that the cohesion of social singing did remain correlated with general social cohesion as did constricted voice and sexual repressiveness. See Lomax and Berkowitz, "The Evolutionary Taxonomy of Culture." See also Erickson, "Tradition and Evolution in Song Style."

44. See Erickson, "Tradition and Evolution in Song Style."

45. Feld, "Sound Structure as Social Structure," 406.

46. Van Damme, "Universality and Cultural Particularity in Visual Aesthetics," 282. For an extended defense of this suggestion, see Van Damme, *Beauty in Context*.

47. Schopenhauer, *The World as Will and Representation*, 1:258–59.

48. Emotional response to the melody may also have figured in this selection. Huron analyzes the melody of the "Ode to Joy" as involving a temporal deviation from what is predictable when the fourth phrase begins prematurely, a quarter note before the downbeat, right after the downward leap that ends the third phrase. The most common response he has gotten in an informal poll in which he has asked people how they characterize this moment has been that it is thrilling. See Huron, *Sweet Anticipation*, 278–79.

49. Meyer sees musical divergence as inherent to the hierarchical character of music: "One of the consequences of the discontinuity of hierarchies is that universal, high-level principles are invariably realized through lower-level, *cultural* constraints" ("A Pride of Prejudices; or, Delight in Diversity," 277).

50. See, for example, Lomax, "Appeal for Cultural Equity," 125–39; and Feld, "From Schizophonia to Schismogenesis," especially 286–88.

51. An example of transplanted music that has taken on local values, at least in terms of the lyrics, is Tanzanian hip-hop. Alex Perullo indicates the many ways in which hip-hop in Dar es Salaam has taken on local characteristics, rejecting sexual or violent references, favoring more moralistic messages of concern in the society, such as warnings about AIDS and the harms of domestic violence. See "'Here's a Little Something Local,'" 257–58 and 264–67. Perullo concludes, "To say that the West homogenizes non-Western cultures with its dominance of cultural forms is to lack understanding of local-level mediation that occurs as part of daily confluences of global and local trends" (268).

52. See, for example, Marl Young, Joint Testimony of Buddy Collette and Marl Young to the Hearing on the Preservation of Jazz in California, sponsored by the Legislative Black Caucus of the California Legislature, October 11, 1991. http//www.csulb.edu/~caljazz/about/LBC_Hearing/lbch01.html.

53. Turino, *Music as Social Life*, 46. "Wide" tuning separates tones in a given interval at a greater distance than is acoustically standard.

54. Ibid., 78. See also 91.

55. See ibid., 188.

56. Ibid., 31.

57. Cook, *Music, Imagination, and Culture*, 1–9. Cook denies that we can "reasonably demand that music must, by definition, yield all its meaning in perception" (8). But he does emphasize the importance of perception. "Some degree of meaningful or gratifying perceptual engagement with it is a prerequisite if one is to approach it as music at all" (9).

58. Davies, *Musical Meaning and Expression*, 326–27.

59. Idiophones are instruments, such as rattles, cymbals, bells, and scrapers, that produce a sound just by vibrating their basic material (wood or metal, for example).

60. The mbira is constructed with metallic attachments to the keys, so that rattling, metallic sounds coincide with the tones that are played. My thanks to Stephen Davies for this example. Turino considers such effort to create buzzy sounds to be a manifestation of a preference for

dense textures, a characteristic of participatory musical throughout the world. See *Music as Social Life*, 46.

61. See Dowling and Harwood, *Music Cognition*, 124 and 221. See also *MLB*, 22; Bartlett, *Remembering*, 85, 199–201, 312–13; Neisser, *Cognition and Reality*; and Mandler, *Mind and Body*, 55–65. Mandler points out that schemata operate in interaction with input from the environment but also select the evidence.

62. Perlman and Krumhansl, "An Experimental Study of Internal Interval Standards in Javanese and Western Musicians."

63. Lynch and Eilers, "Children's Perception of Native and Nonnative Musical Scales," 122.

64. Ibid., 121–32. Meyer points out that inculcated templates play a role in our assessment of when tones are structural and when they are inflected for expressive purposes.

Once the tonal relationships of Western music have been learned as categories of perception, if the third step of the major scale is gradually lowered, what we perceive is an increasingly out-of-tune major third until, at some point, a categorical shift occurs and we perceive a minor third. Were it not for categorical perception, the "blue note" would long since have lost its color. ("A Pride of Prejudices; or, Delight in Diversity," 289)

65. Huron, *Sweet Anticipation*, 215.

66. I wish to thank Stephen Slawek for this example.

67. See Wade, *Music in India*, 119.

68. Huron, *Sweet Anticipation*, 213.

69. For an example, see Schneider, "Sound, Pitch, and Scale," 512–14. Schneider points out that not only pitch but also timbre is "a multi-dimensional attribute of complex sounds," with similar cognitive challenges.

70. See Trainor, McDonald, and Alain, "Automatic and Controlled Processing of Melodic Contour and Interval Information Measured by Electrical Brain Activity." See also *MLB*, 27.

71. Hopkins, "Aural Thinking," 154.

72. See Lomax, "Song Structure and Social Structure"; Feld, "Sound Structure as Social Structure"; and Keil, *Tiv Song*.

73. Forster, *A Passage to India*, 16.

74. To the extent that fiction writers can convincingly get inside the minds of foreign characters, imaginative world-traveling across cultures is evidently possible, though the test would be whether a member of that culture found the presentation convincing. For a discussion of imaginative "world-traveling," see Lugones, "Playfulness, 'World'-Traveling, and Loving Perception."

75. *MLB*, 302.

76. See Huron, *Sweet Anticipation*, 207. The study he refers to is David Perrot and Robert Gjerdingen, "Scanning the Dial: An Exploration of Factors in the Identification of Musical Style," a paper presented at the Society for Music Perception and Cognition Conference, Evanston, Illinois.

77. See Huron, *Sweet Anticipation*, 209.

78. Ibid., 213.

79. See ibid., 215.

80. Davies, *Musical Meaning and Expression*, 328.

81. Cf. Davies, *Musical Works and Performances*, 235.

82. The studies are Lynch and Eilers, "Children's Perception of Native and Nonnative Musical Scales"; and Lynch, Short, and Chua, "Contributions of Experience to the Development of Musical Processing in Infancy." Trainor and Trehub mounted several criticisms, including the argument that because they used melodies at the same absolute pitch, the experimenters were unable to tell whether the infants were attending to intervals or absolute pitch levels. See "A Comparison of Infants' and Adults' Sensitivity to Western Musical Structure," 396. See also *MLB*, 83.

83. *MLB*, 85.

84. Huron, *Sweet Anticipation*, 47–48 and 53–55.

85. Ibid., 55. Patel supports the idea that it is possible to gain some appreciation of music from another culture "very quickly." See *MLB*, 300.

86. Davies, *Musical Meaning and Expression*, 329. See also p. 238n, where Davies remarks that "differences in musical styles of cultures" as well as

> other relativities might . . . make the expressive character of music from an unfamiliar society opaque. For example, it may be that different cultures do not always associate the same emotions with the same degrees of tension, or it may be that expressions of emotion play roles, or occupy places, other than those with which we are familiar.

87. Nettl contends that every culture associates some music with words: "Nowhere do we find cultures whose singing is completely without words, without poetry" ("On the Question of Universals," 5).

88. Harwood, "Universals in Music," 529.

89. Rhoma Irama, "Sahabat," *Smithsonian Folkways CD Music of Indonesia 2: Indonesian Popular Music: Kroncong, Dangdut, and Langgam Jawa* (SF-40056). See the translated lyrics included with the compact disc.

CHAPTER 5

1. Hanslick, *On the Musically Beautiful*, 30.

2. Lévi-Strauss, *The Raw and the Cooked*, 18.

3. Wittgenstein, *Culture and Value*, 62e.

4. Adorno, "Music, Language, and Composition," 401–14.

5. For a thoughtful discussion of the various levels on which music can be meaningful, see Koopman and Davies, "Musical Meaning in a Broader Perspective," 261–74.

6. See Brust, "Music and the Neurologist," 183.

7. Peretz, "Brain Specialization for Music," 194. She refers to Peretz, "Auditory Agnosia"; and Polster and Rose, "Disorders of Auditory Processing."

8. Specifically, the superior temporal plane and the Heschl gyrus are activated by both, as well as many parts of the primary and secondary auditory areas. Brain lateralization for lan-

guage and music is no longer held to be more or less absolute, as it once was. Instead, musical processing is recognized to involve multiple components and to depend on both hemispheres. See Zatorre, "Neural Specializations for Tonal Processing," 237. See also Parsons, "Exploring the Functional Neuroanatomy of Music Performance Perception, and Comprehension"; Besson and Schön, "Comparison between Language and Music," 274; Sergent et al., "Distributed Neural Network Underlying Musical Sight-Reading and Keyboard Performance." Patel contends that the hemispheres cooperate, citing evidence of "strong functional coupling between left posterior hemisphere and right hemisphere regions during the perception of melody-like sequences" ("A New Approach to the Cognitive Neuroscience of Melody," 341).

Sergent et al., "Distributed Neural Network Underlying Musical Sight-Reading and Keyboard Performance."

9. See Pinker, *How the Mind Works*, 529; Gould and Lewontin, "The Spandrels of San Marco and the Panglossian Paradigm"; Miller, "Evolution of Human Music through Sexual Selection"; Falk, "Hominid Brain Evolution and the Origins of Music," 213; Fitch, "The Biology and Evolution of Music"; Cross, "Music and Cognitive Evolution"; *MLB*, 355–415; and Davies, "Music, Fire, and Evolution."

10. Wittgenstein, *Lectures and Conversations on Aesthetics, Psychology, and Religious Belief*, 19.

11. Strictly, *auf* and *zu* are separable prefixes in this context, but without the verbs of which they are a part. Standing alone, they sound like prepositions.

12. See Lidov, *Is Language a Music?*

13. Ibid., 14.

14. Sloboda, *The Musical Mind*, 17.

15. Jacques Derrida argues polemically in *Of Grammatology* that spoken language is not primary, but instead that written language is the original case. Iterability is the essence of language, he claims, which means that the potential for citation is part of its essence. This is uncontroversial if what is meant is that repeatable units are essential to language as we understand it. However, it is hardly necessary that one etch the repeatable units in order to have this potential, although as soon as one has such reiterable units, it does seem that one has therewith the possibility of associating them with specific written shapes. What Derrida actually demonstrates is a feature that language has in common with music as it is practiced throughout the world.

16. Swain, *Musical Languages*, 11. Cf. Bright, "Language and Music: Areas for Cooperation."

17. See *MLB*, 74–75. The study he cites is Best and Avery, "Left-Hemisphere Advantage for Click Consonants Is Determined by Linguistic Significance and Experience."

18. See Harris, "From Phoneme to Morpheme." After three-minute familiarization periods, the infant subjects in this study were able to differentiate between familiar and unfamiliar sequences of tones, as indicated by differences in listening time. This was judged on the basis of how long it took for the infant to look away from the speaker from which the "tone language" emerged. See also Saffran, Aslin, and Newport, "Statistical Learning by 8-Month-Old Infants"; and Saffran et al., "Statistical Learning of Tone Sequences by Human Infants and Adults."

19. Drake and Bertrand, "The Quest for Universals in Temporal Processing," 25–28.

20. See McAdams and Matzkin, "The Roots of Musical Variation in Perceptual Similarity and Invariance," 90.

21. Francisco de Salinas (1513–1590) already expressed the importance of melodic contour in speech as well as music. See Salinas, *De Musica, Libri Septem*.

22. Falk, "Hominid Brain Evolution and the Origins of Music," 204.

23. Juslin and Laukka, "Communication of Emotions in Vocal Expression and Music Performance," 796.

24. Frick (in "Communicating Emotion") refers to the importance of "prosodic contours." Juslin refers to them as "expressive contours" ("Communicating Emotion in Musical Performance," 317–20).

25. Brown, "The 'Musilanguage' Model of Music," 289. Lidov complains that linguistics shortchanges "the feeling tones and gestural character of speech," suggesting that the bias favors what is expressible in writing as the essence of language (*Is Language a Music?*, 3).

26. Juslin and Laukka, "Communication of Emotions in Vocal Expression and Music Performance," 789.

27. Peretz, "Listen to the Brain," 123.

28. *MLB*, 184.

29. See Nooteboom and Kruyt, "Accents, Focus Distribution, and Perceived Distribution of Given and New Information."

30. See *MLB*, 186.

31. See Ratner, "Durational Cues Which Mark Clause Boundaries in Mother-Child Speech"; Hirsh-Pasek et al., "Clauses Are Perceptual Units for Young Infants"; and Morgan, *From Simple Input to Complex Grammar*, 20 and 111–28.

32. See Sloboda, *The Musical Mind*, 24.

33. Ibid., 25.

34. See *MLB*, 148.

35. See Sloboda, *The Musical Mind*, 23.

36. See Goodman, *Languages of Art*, 132. Goodman refers to the necessity of "character-indifference among the instances of each character," which amounts to the demand that characters be perceived, or at least interpreted, as instances of a category. Lerdahl describes as a constraint on compositional grammars the principle that "the musical surface must be capable of being parsed into a sequence of discrete events." Without this, he suggests, listeners have difficulty inferring the structure of what they hear. Cf. Swain, *Musical Languages*, 25.

37. The experiment is described and analyzed in Warren and Warren, "Auditory Illusions and Confusions." See also Swain, *Musical Languages*, 13–14.

38. In this range, nerves appear to directly transmit frequencies of sound vibrations to the brain. From 200 to 20,000 Hz, the sine waves of various frequencies appear to excite different positions along the basilar membrane of the inner ear. Dowling and Harwood point out that this is the range in which human beings directly perceive periodicity. See *Music Cognition*, 29. They acknowledge, however, that the theory of different spectrums of place and periodicity mechanisms for pitch perception is not universally accepted. See p. 41.

39. Dowling and Harwood, *Music Cognition*, 28. See also Tramo et al., "Neurobiology of

Harmony Perception," 134; and Houtsma and Goldstein, "The Central Origin of the Pitch of Complex Tones."

40. In this and all cases of the missing fundamental, the harmonics heard must be fairly loud, and musical context can also make the impression of the fundamental more obvious. See Dowling and Harwood, *Music Cognition*, 38–39.

41. Chinese in all its dialects has a large number of homophones because the standard word is a single syllable, and the same sound is typically connected with multiple characters. Auditors usually disambiguate spoken words by means of context.

42. For a further introductory discussion of the system of tones in Mandarin Chinese, see Pickle, "Written and Spoken Chinese," 24–25.

43. Brown, "The 'Musilanguage' Model of Music Evolution," 281. See also *MLB*, 42.

44. Brown, "The 'Musilanguage' Model of Music Evolution," 282.

45. Ibid., 282; citing Thorsen, "Intonation Contours and Stress Group Patterns in Declarative Sentences of Varying Length in ASC Danish"; Thorsen, "Intonation Contours and Stress Group Patterns in Declarative Sentences of Varying Length: Supplementary Data"; Liberman and Pierrehumbert, "Intonational Invariance under Changes in Pitch Range and Length"; and Ladd and Terken, "Modeling Intra- and Inter-Speaker Pitch Range Variation."

46. Brown, "The 'Musilanguage' Model of Music Evolution," 282.

47. I wish to thank Eva Man (Man Kit-Wah) for the information she provided me about the Cantonese language.

48. Richman, "How Music Fixed 'Nonsense' into Significant Formulas," 304. Besson and Schön ("Comparison between Language and Music") point out that for both spoken language and music, "specific events are expected at specific times." They also note that brain imaging studies "indicate that qualitatively similar processes seem to be responsible for temporal processing in language and music" (285), and that "similar brain areas were activated by temporal violations in both language and music" (287).

49. Richman, "How Music Fixed 'Nonsense' into Significant Formulas," 303. He argues that phrasing that includes open-slot formulas was presupposed before language could evolve.

50. Huttenlocher and Burke, "Why Does Memory Span Increase with Age?"

51. Condon and Sander, "Synchrony Demonstrated between Movements of the Neonate and Adult Speech," 456. See also Turino, *Music as Social Life*, 41–42. Breakdowns in movement synchrony with one's own speech can be symptomatic of psychological disorders, including aphasia, autism, and schizophrenia. See Condon and Brosin, "Micro Linguistic-Kinesic Events in Schizophrenic Behavior." See also Condon, "Multiple Response to Sound in Dysfunctional Children"; and Condon, "Communication: Rhythm and Structure."

52. Gregory, "Sounds of Power and Deference." See also Richman, "How Music Fixed 'Nonsense' into Significant Formulas," 305; Condon and Sander, "Synchrony Demonstrated between Movements of the Neonate and Adult Speech"; Condon and Ogston, "Sound Film Analysis of Normal and Pathological Behavior Patterns"; and Condon and Brosin, "Micro Linguistic-Kinesic Events in Schizophrenic Behavior." Feld observes that rhythmic expectations for speech vary across cultures. The Kaluli, he points out, overlap each other's spoken statements, just as they do each other's musical phrases, and they teach their children to par-

ticipate in conversation by adhering to the same pattern. Feld, "Aesthetics as Iconicity of Style, or 'Lift-up-over Sounding,'" 78–83.

53. See Collins, "Emotion as Key to Reconstructing Social Theory." See also Collins, "Toward Neo-Meadian Sociology of Mind."

54. Condon and Sander, "Synchrony Demonstrated between Movements of the Neonate and Adult Speech," 459. They have also shown that such synchronization occurs also among newborns, and that this remained so when language varied (see 461). Interestingly, disconnected vowel sounds did not result in the same degree of correspondence between movement and sound as does "ordinary rhythmic speech."

55. Cf. Lerdahl, "The Sounds of Poetry Viewed as Music," 414.

56. Ibid., 416–17.

57. Brown, "The 'Musilanguage' Model of Music Evolution," 273. Swain points out that syntax is not only a means "of organizing musical information into hierarchical orders"; it is also used as "the control of tension and resolution, which shapes not only the essential musical dynamic, the metaphor of motion, but also the very character of every musical language" (*Musical Languages*, 172).

58. Swain, *Musical Languages*, 11.

59. Saffran, "Mechanisms of Musical Memory in Infancy," 32. See also Fernald, "Intonation and Communicative Intent in Mothers' Speech to Infants: Is the Melody the Message?"; and Mehler et al., "A Precursor of Language Acquisition in Young Infants."

60. Papousek, "Music in Infancy Research: Biological and Cultural Origins of Early Musicality," 43. Babies seem to mentally represent and recall music in very precise form, suggesting that flexibility in recognizing similarity in music arises only gradually. However, babies do recognize familiar melodies performed in a different key. See Saffran, "Mechanisms of Musical Memory in Infancy," 38. See also Trehub, "Human Processing Predispositions and Musical Universals," 431; Trehub and Trainor, "Listening Strategies in Infancy"; and Trehub, Thorpe, and Trainor, "Infants' Perception of Good and Bad Melodies."

61. Dowling and Harwood, *Music Cognition*, 146, referring to Chang and Trehub, "Auditory Processing of Relational Information by Young Infants," 324–31; replicated in a more sophisticated fashion in Trehub, Bull, and Thorpe, "Infants' Perception of Melodies: The Role of Melodic Contour."

62. "Motherese" appears to be a culturally widespread phenomenon. However, Elinor Ochs and Bambi B. Shieffelin ("Language Acquisition and Socialization") have argued that it is not truly universal, in that some cultures do not direct much speech to young infants.

63. Trehub, "Human Processing Predispositions and Musical Universals," 437. She cites Fernald, "Intonation and Communicative Intent in Mothers' Speech to Infants"; Papousek, Papousek, and Symmes, "The Meanings of Melodies in Motherese in Tone and Stress Languages."

64. Note the Teletubbies, the characters on the BBC's series *Teletubbies*, BBC/Ragdoll Limited. The Teletubbies have been criticized for not articulating clearly; but the emphasis on musical characteristics of speech to the expense of articulational clarity is in keeping with the features of infant-directed speech, or "motherese," which are ubiquitous among adults addressing babies.

65. See Fernald, "Intonation and Communicative Intent in Mothers' Speech to Infants," 1498–99.

66. I will discuss this idea in more detail in conjunction with Daniel Stern's notion of "vitality affects" in chapters 6 and 8.

67. Condon and Sander, "Synchrony Demonstrated between Movements of the Neonate and Adult Speech," 462.

68. Mehler et al., "A Precursor of Language Acquisition in Young Infants." One of the experiments ruled out that the infants were responding to the specific spectra of the sounds used in the languages to which they were exposed. Cf. Ramus et al., "Language Discrimination by Human Newborns and by Cotton-Top Tamarin Monkeys," which indicates that primates can distinguish between utterances in two different languages on the basis of rhythmic difference.

69. They cite DeCaspar and Spence, "Prenatal Maternal Speech Influences Newborns' Perception of Speech Sounds"; Querleu and Renard, "Les perceptions auditives du fetus humain"; and Vince et al., "The Sound Environment of Foetal Sheep." See also Abrams et al., "Fetal Music Perception"; and Abrams and Gerhardt, "Some Aspects of the Foetal Sound Environment."

70. Mehler et al., "A Precursor of Language Acquisition in Young Infants," 175.

71. Banse and Scherer, "Acoustic Profiles in Vocal Emotion Expression."

72. Fernald, "Intonation and Communicative Intent in Mothers' Speech to Infants."

73. The Neo-Futurists, *Too Much Light Makes the Baby Go Blind*, first performed on December 2, 1988. The play consists of thirty plays in sixty minutes. The segment I mention appeared on "20 Acts in 60 Minutes," *This American Life*, Serial 241, produced by Chicago Public Radio, distributed by Public Radio International, first broadcast on July 11, 2003. For more on the Neo-Futurists, see www.neofuturists.org.

74. See Bright, "Language and Music," 26–27. Bright draws his information on this effect in Navajo music from Herzog, "Speech Melody and Primitive Music."

75. Bright, "Language and Music," 27.

76. Koelsch et al., "Music, Language and Meaning."

77. Ibid., 302.

78. Ibid., 303.

79. *MLB*, 50–51.

80. See Albert, Sparks, and Helm, "Melodic Intonation Therapy for Aphasia"; Sacks, *Musicophilia*, 214 and 218–23; and Brust, "Music and the Neurologist," 183.

81. Falk, "Hominid Brain Evolution and the Origins of Music," 204; citing Albert, Sparks, and Helm, "Melodic Intonation Therapy for Aphasia," 130–31.

82. Seeger, "Reflections upon a Given Topic," 398.

83. Dahlhaus, *The Idea of Absolute Music*, 6. See also p. 106 for a discussion of the role of Wilhelm von Humboldt's account of language in fortifying the analogy.

84. See Austin, *How to Do Things with Words*.

85. Bernstein, *The Unanswered Question*. Indeed, Bernstein explicitly sets out to "investigate musical universality" (8). He takes there to be three grounds for claiming that music is universal: (1) the acoustic properties of sound that it utilizes, (2) what he sees as a universal

musical grammar, and (3) music's symbolization of affective existence, which he takes to be a universal human endowment.

86. See ibid., 55–56 and 67.

87. It may be worth noting that much of the terminology used to describe music is originally derived from grammar and rhetoric. See Harrán, *Word-Tone Relations in Musical Thought*, 2. See also 48–49, 226, and 285.

88. Lerdahl and Jackendoff, *A Generative Theory of Tonal Music*, 13. See also 281.

89. Lidov criticizes the emphasis on disjunctive segments in Lerdahl and Jackendoff's theory in his "Our Time with the Druids," 104–21. His use of the druid image in connection with the tree structures of that theory is borrowed from Peter Child. See Lidov, *Is Language a Music?*, 81.

90. For an analysis of the various types of semiotic theories of music, see Tarasti, *A Theory of Musical Semiotics*, 3–58.

91. See Barthes, *Image Music Text*; and Nattiez, *Music and Discourse*.

92. See Lakoff and Johnson, *Metaphors We Live By*.

93. London, "Musical and Linguistic Speech Acts." Lakoff and Johnson use the convention of capitalizing all letters in the words that label basic conceptual metaphors.

94. Pinker, *How the Mind Works*, 534. Pinker does not spell out the mechanisms of the way music "tickles" us, but he does mention its connection with (1) our faculty for language (with which music can combine); (2) our analysis of auditory scenes (which makes us associate strings of sounds with particular soundmakers); (3) emotional calls (which musical inflections resemble); (4) habitat selection (in that sound helps us determine which habitats are unsafe or changing); (5) motor control (given that music and our movement are both associated with rhythm); and (6) "something else," since the previous five do not add to up to an explanation of "how the whole is more than the sum of its parts." The vagueness of (6) reveals how little interested Pinker is in giving a thorough explanation of music's role in human experience.

95. Ibid., 528.

96. James, *The Principles of Psychology*, 2:627.

97. Santayana, *The Life of Reason, or the Phases of Human Progress*, 4:15.

98. See Darwin, *The Descent of Man*, 569. See also Granit, *The Purposive Brain*, 13.

99. See also Scruton, *The Aesthetics of Music*, 191.

100. See, for example, Davies, "Life Is a Passacaglia."

101. Carterette and Kendall see this as a reason for denying that speech is music. "Music is temporally organized sound and silence that is areferentially communicative within a context. In contrast, speech is not music because it points outside itself" ("Comparative Music Perception and Cognition," 726).

102. Henson, "The Language of Music," 238–39.

103. Raffman, *Language, Music, and Mind*, 41 and 53–55.

104. Molino, "Toward an Evolutionary Theory of Music and Language," 170.

105. Brown, "The 'Musilanguage' Model of Music Evolution," 284. Swain, *Musical Languages*, 173.

106. McFee, "Meaning and the Art-Status of 'Music Alone,'" 32.

107. Scruton, *The Aesthetics of Music*, 173–74.

108. See Hamilton, *Music, Madness, and the Unworking of Language*, 160. Hamilton cites Hoffmann, Kierkegaard, Novalis, Wackenroder, Tieck, Jean Paul, and others.

109. Hoffmann, "The Poet and the Composer," 48.

110. Felix Mendelssohn, Letter to Marc André Souchay; Berlin, October 5, 1842, cited by Cooke, *The Language of Music*, 12. Cf. Martha Nussbaum: "Even when the music is accompanied by a text or program," she asserts, "the music . . . may be more definite in certain ways than the text, making the emotional movement precise in a way that the text by itself does not" (Nussbaum, *Upheavals of Thought*, 277). Cook and Dibben point out that Mendelssohn's view was influenced by E. T. A. Hoffmann, who claims that music offered access to a transcendent realm in contrast to the circumstances of everyday modern life. Cook and Dibben, "Musicological Approaches to Emotion," 48: "Seen in this light . . . the very lack of specificity that formerly consigned [music] . . . to a subordinate role was now construed as an infinite suggestiveness." See also Langer, *Philosophy in a New Key*, 233.

111. For a discussion of the interpretation of both language and music as representational systems that articulate the objective order of reality, see Bowie, *Music Philosophy, and Modernity*, 51–54. Bowie observes, "For eighteenth-century representational theories there is always a verbal equivalent of what music says, the apparently non-representational aspect of music being catered for by an underlying representational or mimetic conception of language as that which can render explicit what is only implicit in the music."

112. Ibid., 53.

113. Hamilton, *Music, Madness, and the Unworking of Language*. The idea that language is deficient *because* it is systematically providing categories and concepts to use in ordering our experience strikes many critics as bizarre. Cf. Davies, *Musical Meaning and Expression*, 154–62. He remarks, "The oddity consists in finding fault in the fact that language does not do a job that it is not designed to (and should not) perform" (156). He approvingly cites William Kennick's objection: "Works of art may serve as vehicles of illumination and enlightenment, but they do not do so by saying the unsayable, communicating the incommunicable. In so far as they say anything at all . . . what works of art say can be said in words" (Kennick, "Art and the Ineffable," 320). Kennick's paradigm for "saying" is obviously speech (although it is unclear whether or not he takes prosody to add anything to linguistic meaning); thus it would seem virtually analytic that anything that can be "said" can be said in language. Malcolm Budd argues that even if music had unique power to communicate a larger number of nuances of emotion, this would not demonstrate that the details communicated are of particular value, a point with which Davies concurs. See Budd, "Music and the Communication of Emotion," 129–38; and Davies, *Musical Meaning and Expression*, 158 and 162.

I am inclined to think that much of this debate is itself an indication of the MUSIC AS LANGUAGE metaphor leading us astray; it provokes the expectation that music and language are communicative structures of the same sort and thus potentially in a kind of rivalry. Although the critics of the romantic view seem correct in thinking that the adequacy of language should be assessed on the basis of whether it does what it is designed to do, I think the Romantics are right to celebrate music's unique power to do something else, namely, to communicate nuances of feeling. The value of communicating such nuances is not the special importance of the "message" conveyed but the intimacy that is established by virtue of sharing feelings of such specificity.

114. Bernstein claims that both serialists and expressionists aimed at greater semantic richness than their predecessors. See Bernstein, *The Unanswered Question*, 270 and 149–53. He makes ingenious comparisons between musical figures and figures of speech.

115. Cf. Pound, "Vers libre and Arnold Dometsch," 437: "Poetry is a composition of words set to music. . . . The amount or quality of the music may, and does, vary; but poetry withers and 'dries out' when it leaves music, or at least an imagined music, too far behind it."

116. Raffman, *Language, Music, and Mind*.

117. The musical grammar she has in mind is that articulated by Lerdahl and Jackendoff in *A Generative Theory of Tonal Music*.

118. Swain points out that every individual has a unique accent and voiceprint, and suggests that this gives speech "acoustic equivalents of octaves and instrumental colors in music" (*Musical Languages*, 10).

119. Music conjoined with words can, of course, involve all the speech acts of which words are capable.

120. Austin, *How to Do Things with Words*, 151.

121. London, "Musical and Linguistic Speech Acts," 57.

122. Tolstoy, *War and Peace*, 222.

123. Searle, *Speech Acts*, 44.

124. London, "Musical and Linguistic Speech Acts," 56.

125. Ibid., 61.

126. *Casablanca*. Directed by Michael Curtiz. Warner Brothers, 1942.

127. Ernoff, "A Cajun Poetics of Loss and Longing," 287–88. The reference to Dennis McGee is from Savoy, *Cajun Music*, 56.

128. Ernoff, "A Cajun Poetics of Loss and Longing," 288.

129. Staal, "Mantras and Bird Songs," 550. The reference is to Lorenz, "Über die Enstehung auslösender 'Zeremonien,'" 9–13.

130. Staal, "Mantras and Bird Songs," 555.

131. Ibid., 556.

132. See Turino, *Music as Social Life*, 9 and 237.

133. See Blacking, *How Musical Is Man?*, 237; and Merriam, *The Anthropology of Music*, 221.

134. Cross, "Music, Cognition, Culture, and Evolution," 46.

135. Ibid., 51–52.

136. One situation in which such multiple meanings occur is that of music that carries disguised political messages. The music of the Aboriginal Australians is also polysemic, encoding knowledge appropriate for different levels of maturity in the same songs as well as providing maps. See Ellis, *Aboriginal Music*, 17, 89, and 129.

137. Swain, *Musical Languages*, 48 and 174.

138. Lidov, *Is Language a Music?*, 10.

139. Feld, "Communication, Music, and Speech about Music," 8.

140. Ibid., 8.

141. Cf. the reported case of Sydney Morgenbesser's refutation of a speaker who claimed that although double negatives made a positive, double affirmatives did not make a negative.

Morgenbesser's response was to say "Yah-yah" in a tone that conveyed complete dismissal. My thanks to Stephen Davies for reminding me of the relevance of this story to my point here.

CHAPTER 6

1. Proust, *Swann's Way*, in *Remembrance of Things Past*, 1:36.

2. "Idiopathic synesthesia" is not my coinage. The term is used widely.

3. See Wheeler and Cutsforth, "Synaesthesia and Meaning," 361–84.

4. Photisms can also appear that are not patches of color per se, but in this case the phenomenon would not be aptly called "colored hearing."

5. For an account of the variety of musical idiopathic synesthesia, see Sacks, *Musicophilia*, 165–83.

6. Marks, Hammeal, and Bornstein, *Perceiving Similarity and Comprehending Metaphor*, 73. The studies cited are Marks, *The Unity of the Senses*; and Uttal, *The Psychobiology of Sensory Coding*.

7. Davies, "Philosophical Perspectives on Music's Expressiveness," 30.

8. Kant and Louis-Bertrand Castle are among the later investigators who pursued Aristotle's suggestion that the mathematical principles of musical harmony might also be relevant to color harmony. See Gage, "Synaesthesia," 4:349.

9. Aristotle, *De Anima*, 582.

10. Merleau-Ponty, *Phenomenology of Perception*, 229–30.

11. Hartshorne, *The Philosophy and Psychology of Sensation*, 80. Along these same lines, Benzon contends that we feel the impact of a hammer on a nail head. See Benzon, *Beethoven's Anvil*, 155.

12. Critchley, "Ecstatic and Synaesthetic Experiences during Musical Perception," 222. See also 226.

13. Marks, *The Unity of the Senses*, 191.

14. They cite Gardner, "Metaphors and Modalities"; Winner, Rosentiel, and Gardner, "The Development of Metaphorical Understanding"; Vosniadou and Ortony, "The Emergence of the Literal-Metaphorical-Anomalous Distinction in Young Children"; and Silberstein et al., "Autumn Leaves and Old Photographs."

15. Marks, Hammeal, and Bornstein, *Perceiving Similarity and Comprehending Metaphor*, 84.

16. Marks, "On Colored-Hearing Synaesthesia," 326–27.

17. Cytowic, *Synesthesia*, 324.

18. Marks, Hammeal, and Bornstein, *Perceiving Similarity and Comprehending Metaphor*, 73–74. The study they cite is Lawson and Turkewitz, "Intersensory Function in Newborns: Effect of Sound on Visual Preferences."

19. Marks, Hammeal, and Bornstein, *Perceiving Similarity and Comprehending Metaphor*, 73–74.

20. Stern characterizes the vitality affects as "amodal," which may seem to run counter to my characterization of vitality affects as synesthetic. But his point is that vitality affects are not perceived by a *particular* sensory modality. Instead, infants perceive sensory qualities that are

conjoined into an impression of a distinct dynamic agency. In this respect, vitality affects are a paradigm case of the sort of everyday synesthesia we have been considering.

21. Stern, *The Interpersonal World of the Infant*, 57–58.

22. Merlin Donald makes a similar point about the multimodal character of rhythmic sensitivity: "once rhythm is established, it may be played out with any motor modality, including the hands, feet, head, mouth, or the whole body. . . . Rhythm is therefore evidence of a central mimetic controller that can track various movement modalities *simultaneously* and in parallel." See Donald, *Origins of the Modern Mind*, 186.

23. Hornbostel, "The Unity of the Senses," 83–89.

24. Wolf, "Emotional Dimensions of Ritual Music among the Kotas, a South Indian Tribe," 379–422. It is perhaps worth noting that olfactory experiences are described in musical terms in the perfume industry, which describes the three basic components of a scent as high, middle, and low "notes."

25. See Ellis, *Aboriginal Music*, 68. Ellis notes that the same word is used for "taste" and "melody" in Pitjantjatjara. See also Chatwin, *The Songlines*, 58.

26. See Feld, "Sound Structure as Social Structure," 390–92. The Kaluli say that a song "hardens" when "poetic and performative structures" coalesce (390). On the involvement of multiple senses in aesthetic experience, see also Van Damme, *Beauty in Context*, 54, and Steager, "Where Does Art Begin on Puluwat?" MacDonald Critchley points out that multimodal terms for sense experience occur in a number of languages. See Critchley, "Ecstatic and Synaesthetic Experiences during Musical Perception," 229.

27. Nietzsche, *Twilight of the Idols*, 10: §11, 520.

28. Cf. Davies, "Perceiving Music and Perceiving Musical Colors," 33–34.

29. See also Clifton, *Music as Heard*, 137 and 288.

30. See Cytowic, *Synesthesia*, 307–8.

31. Boernstein also considered this connection to be fundamental to the experience of emotion (a view that seems to be given implicit support by those who consider emotion a stage of preparedness for fight or flight). See Boernstein, "Über die physiologischen Grundlagen des Wahrnehmens"; and Boernstein, "Perceiving and Thinking: Their Interrelationship and Organismic Organization." According to Boernstein, thinking developed as a means for human beings to engage in "internalized movement; i.e., a movement is first anticipated, and then carried out" (in Cytowic, *Synesthesia*, 306–7). Synesthesia, accordingly, was an essential component in the development of the capacity to think. R. H. Wheeler goes further, arguing that all striving is based upon kinesthetic sensations and that kinesthesis is the core of what we call meaning. See "The Synaesthesia of a Blind Subject," 360. Wheeler and his colleague T. S. Cutsworth also claimed that "synaesthesia *is* the act of perceiving, itself" ("Synaesthesia and Meaning," 370). See also Dann, *Bright Colors Falsely Seen*, 84.

32. Cytowic, *The Man Who Tasted Shapes*, 161.

33. Cf. Seashore, *Psychology of Music*, 26.

34. Diana Raffman makes a case that is formally similar when she argues that the similarities between the structural features of music and language trick the mind into expecting semantics in music, just as it finds semantics in language. See Raffman, *Language, Music, and Mind*.

35. My thanks to Jeffrey Malpas for this point. Malpas suggested this idea in response to P. F. Strawson's proposal in *Individuals* that we consider the nature of a world consisting only of sound. See Strawson, *Individuals: An Essay in Descriptive Metaphysics*, 56–80. Strawson, who grants that this is an example that does not correlate with our actual experience, raises the question of whether a sound and its repetition could be individuated in such a world. Malpas questions whether this thought experiment is even coherent, given the mutual reliance of the senses on each other (personal communication).

36. We should note, however, that Stern thinks musical experience returns most listeners to the psychological condition of the infant attending to vitality affects, as we shall consider further in chapter 8.

37. Clynes, *Sentics*, 18.

38. Lidov observes that Clynes's findings have not been duplicated "by independent, professional researchers." However, he reports that he acquired the equipment and did his own lab work, which more or less confirmed Clynes's results. See Lidov, *Is Language a Music?*, 131.

39. Cf. Walker, *Musical Beliefs*, 100. For a discussion of individual variations in meanings ascribed to music, see Higgins, "Musical Idiosyncrasy and Perspectival Listening."

40. See Sachs, *Wellsprings of Music*, 49–50. He cites a number of Western works that are mournful but written in major keys, as well as the many cultures in which the very notion of major or minor thirds (the intervals that differentiate major and minor chords) are inapplicable. Cf. Wittgenstein's comment, "In Schubert the major often sounds sadder than the minor." Wittgenstein, *Culture and Value*, 84e.

41. Becker's definition of trance is "a bodily event characterized by strong emotion, intense focus, the loss of the strong sense of self, usually enveloped by amnesia and a cessation of the inner language," adding that it is "felt to be ineffable, not easily described or spoken of." Becker, *Deep Listeners*, 43.

42. Becker points out that the peak of this phenomenon occurred from the fifteenth to the seventeenth centuries. See ibid., 34.

43. Ibid., 113.

44. Ibid., 114–15.

45. That these associations are entrenched but learned is confirmed by considerable empirical work. See, for example, Gregory, Worral, and Sarge, "The Development of Emotional Responses to Music in Young Children." Gregory and his colleagues point out that their seven- and eight-year-old subjects significantly correlated music in major keys with being happy and music in minor keys with being sad, while their three- and four-year-old subjects did not. This supports the idea that the association is learned and not innate. See also Clark and Teasdale, "Constraints on the Effects of Mood on Memory"; Kenealy, "Validation of a Music Mood Induction Procedure"; Kenealy, "Mood-State-Dependent Retrieval"; Martin and Metha, "Recall of Early Childhood Memories through Musical Mood Induction"; Parrott, "Mood Induction and Instructions to Sustain Moods"; Parrott and Sabini, "Mood and Memory under Natural Conditions"; Thompson, Schellenberg, and Husain, "Arousal, Mood, and the Mozart Effect"; Dalla Bella et al., "A Developmental Study of the Affective Value of Tempo and Mode in Music"; and Gerardi and Gerken, "The Development of Affective Response to Modality and Melodic Contour."

46. Portions of the following paragraph have appeared previously in Higgins, "Musical Idiosyncrasy and Perspectival Listening," 96.

47. Feld's idea of "interpretive moves" is discussed toward the end of chapter 5.

48. For further discussion of musically sensitive idiosyncratic responses to music, see Higgins, "Musical Idiosyncrasy and Perspectival Listening."

49. Koopman and Davies, "Musical Meaning in Broader Perspective."

CHAPTER 7

1. See Cooke, *The Language of Music*, 33, where the passage from Beethoven is cited.

2. Ibid., 210.

3. Pratt, *Music as the Language of Emotion*, 26. See also 19.

4. The *Shih Jing* contains poems written 1000–600 BCE. See Schirokauer, *A Brief History of Chinese Civilization*, 21.

5. Legge, *The She King, or the Book of Poetry*, 4:34.

6. See Miller, *Music and Song in Persia*, 74. Safvat Drayush points out, however, that the manner of playing has more to do with the emotions expressed by a particular work than the generic mood associated with its *dastgāh*. See Miller, *Music and Song in Persia*, 22–23. See also During, "The System of Persian Music," 77.

7. The ragas are scales, but more than scales. Harold S. Powers and Richard Widdess define a raga as "a continuum with scale and tune as its extremes," and Lewis Rowell comments that it is "something more specific than an array of pitches, but more variable than a composed melody." See Powers and Widdess, "India," 9:98; and Rowell, *Music and Musical Thought in Early India*, 167. A raga is also the germ of melody on which improvisation is based.

8. That is, both the classical music of northern India and that of southern India.

9. Rowell, *Music and Musical Thought in Early India*, 179.

10. Roseman, *Healing Sounds from the Malaysian Rainforest*, 157–58 and 169.

11. Feld, *Sound and Sentiment*, 221

12. See, for example, Rice, *May It Fill Your Soul*, 124; Agawu, "Music in the Funeral Traditions of the Akpafu," 75–105; Guilbault, "Fitness and Flexibility," 273–99. It should be noted, however, that some societies proscribe music during periods of mourning. See Waley, *The Analects of Confucius*, 7/9, 124, and 17/21, 214–15. See also Cadar, "The Role of Kulintang Music in Maranao Society," 241.

13. Al-Ghazali, "The Book of the Right Usages of Music and Trance," 195–252 and 705–48; cited in Rouget, *Music and Trance*, 257–58.

14. Rouget, *Music and Trance*, 282. He reports that the word was used in this way even as early as the seventh century. Judith Becker defines the primary meaning of the term *tarab* as "to be moved, agitated, while listening to music (to the extent that one may cry, faint or tear one's clothes)." Becker, *Deep Listeners*, 2.

15. For a thorough account of these views, see Davies, *Musical Meaning and Expression*.

16. See Plato, *Republic* III,1. 398–401.

17. Cf. Freud, *Beyond the Pleasure Principle*, 8–10. See also Nietzsche, *The Gay Science*, §334, 262.

18. Artusi and Zarlino contended that Plato took the mode to be imitative, and Galilei and Monteverdi believed that he found imitation in the particular melody. See Walker, *Musical Beliefs*, 119–20.

19. See Lippman, *A History of Western Musical Aesthetics*, 83–94.

20. Smith, "Of the Nature of That Imitation Which Takes Place in What Are Called the Imitative Arts," 170–71.

21. Beattie, "On Poetry and Music as They Affect the Mind," 111, 122, and 127.

22. Hanslick, *On the Musically Beautiful*, 9.

23. Ibid., 10. Hanslick focuses in this discussion on absolute music, that is, music without words, since these cases reveal what music can represent through its own resources, without the cues provided by texts. Many commentators since Hanslick have followed this strategy as well. Recently, Aaron Ridley has objected to this approach, which he admits he once followed. See Ridley, *The Philosophy of Music*, 2–3 and 76–83.

24. Hanslick, *On the Musically Beautiful*, 29.

25. Ibid., 32.

26. Hevner's experiments in the 1930s suggested that certain features of music (e.g., pace, flowingness, mode, rhythm, complexity of harmony, etc.) tended to connote particular emotional characteristics in the music. See Hevner, "Expression in Music: A Discussion of Experimental Studies and Theories"; and Hevner, "Experimental Studies of the Elements of Expression in Music." For more recent relevant work, see Scherer and Oshinsky, "Cue Utilization in Emotion Attribution from Auditory Stimuli"; and Scherer and Zentner, "Emotional Effects of Music." Scherer and Zentner propose a model that acknowledges the interaction of the effects of different expressive cues, only some of which are structural.

27. The suggestion that specific structural and dynamic features of music were appropriate to different emotional content had been made long before in Western musical thought. Nicola Vincentino claimed in 1555 that quick movement and major consonances rendered music expressive of happiness and related emotions, while slow movement and minor consonances tended to make it expressive of sadness and similar emotions. See Vincentino, *L'Antica Musica Ridotte Alla Moderna Prattica*, fol. P ii. See also Harrán, *Word-Tone Relations in Musical Thought*, 176. Zarlino similarly associated harder, happier emotions with major thirds and sixths and faster movements, and sadder, sweeter emotions with minor thirds and sixths and to slower rhythms (*Intitutioni Harmoniche*, 181, and 192). See Harrán, *Word-Tone Relations in Musical Thought*, 191–92. Adam Smith also challenged the imitation theory in 1795. See "Of the Nature of That Imitation Which Takes Place in What Are Called the Imitative Arts," 161.

28. See, for example, Callen, "Transfiguring Emotions in Music," 81.

29. Langer is convinced that the emotion represented in music cannot be equated with our usual emotional language, and hence she is not concerned that listeners differ in their characterization of the emotions represented by music.

30. Langer, *Philosophy in a New Key*, 218.

31. Ibid., 227–28.

32. See Lippman, *A History of Western Musical Aesthetics*, 87–92. Lippman notes that the conflation of imitation and expression was common among eighteenth-century theorists.

33. See, for example, Reid, *Lectures on the Fine Arts*, 49; Walker, *Musical Beliefs*, 131–32;

Morley, *A Plain and Easy Introduction to Practical Music*, 290; Liszt, "Berlioz and His 'Harold' Symphony," 109; Wagner, *Opera and Drama*, 71 and 33.

34. See, for example, Best, *The Maori*, 2:135; Burrows, *Native Music of the Tuamotus*, 54 and 56; Burrows, *Ethology of Futuna*, 138; and Burrows, *Songs of Uvea and Futuna*, 79.

35. Clip on *CNN International*, September 26, 2004.

36. In a tonal language, such as Chinese, the contour of a melodic line can reinforce tonal inflection of a word. Music literally enhances the impact of speech.

37. Hsün Tzu (Xunzi), "A Discussion of Music," in *Basic Writings*, 112.

38. Stravinsky, *Igor Stravinsky: An Autobiography*, 51.

39. Hanslick, *On the Musically Beautiful*, 78.

40. DeWoskin compares him to Langer, for Ji Kang contends that music has power to articulate what words cannot, a view that Langer defends. Ji Kang, however, held that music arouses emotion, but believed that the emotions aroused varied with individual listeners.

41. DeWoskin, *A Song for One or Two*, 117.

42. See Kant, *Groundwork of the Metaphysic of Morals*, 121–23.

43. See Dahlhaus, *Esthetics of Music*, 20–23.

44. See Abhinavagupta, *Locana*; Goswamy, *Essence of Indian Art*; Bharata Muni (attrib.), *The Nātyaśāstra*; Gerow, "Abhinavagupta's Aesthetics as a Speculative Paradigm," 186–208.

45. See Cone, *The Composer's Voice*, 94; Levinson, "Music and Negative Emotions," 321–22; Levinson, "Hope in *The Hebrides*," 338–39; Karl and Robinson, "Shostakovich's Tenth Symphony"; Ridley, *Music, Value, and the Passions*, 181–91; Newcomb, "Sound and Feeling," 637; Maus, "Music as Drama"; and Newcomb, "Action and Agency in Mahler's Ninth Symphony, Second Movement."

46. Levinson, "Hope in *The Hebrides*," 338.

47. See ibid., 336–75. Cf. Levinson, "Musical Expressiveness as Hearability-as-Expression," 192–221. There Levinson describes the persona as "almost entirely indefinite, a sort of minimal person, characterized only by the emotion we hear it to be expressing and the musical gesture through which it does so" (193–94).

48. Both Davies and Kivy compare the expressiveness of music to the expressiveness of the faces of particular breeds of dogs (basset hounds and St. Bernards, respectively). This leads Jenefer Robinson to term their views "The Doggy Theory" of musical expressiveness (*Deeper Than Reason*, 300–307).

49. See Davies, "Artistic Expression and the Hard Case of Pure Music." Davies terms the view that full understanding of a musical work requires imagining the work to present the narrative of a persona "hypothetical emotionalism."

50. Kivy, *Introduction to a Philosophy of Music*, 116.

51. Cf. Pratt, *Music as the Language of Emotion*, 20.

52. See Ridley, *Music, Value, and the Passions*, 183 and 181. Patel points out that some empirical evidence suggests that a persona figures in listeners' perceptions of leitmotifs. See *MLB*, 329.

53. Ridley, *Music, Value, and the Passions*, 191.

54. Ibid., 181.

Notes to Pages 126-128 219

55. The suggestion that a more detached analytic perspective and a more engaged empathetic one are both possible was defended by Leonard Meyer in 1956. We will consider his position directly.

56. Jerrold Levinson's "concatenationist" view—the position that "music essentially presents itself for understanding as a chain of overlapping and mutually involving parts of small extent, rather than either a seamless totality or an architectural arrangement"—would seem to lend support to this view (*Music in the Moment*, 13). Levinson claims, "The emotional content of music . . . is not primarily communicated to a listener by large-scale formal relations, consciously apprehended, but instead by suitably arranged parts small enough to fall within the scope of quasi-hearing" (27).

57. Merriam, *The Anthropology of Music*, 81. Merriam himself disagrees, for he thinks that cultural context may be essential for the musical arousal of emotion.

58. Burrows, *Native Music of the Tuamotus*, 54.

59. Seeger, *Why Suyá Sing*, 62.

60. *Emotional regulation* is the common term in psychology for efforts to manage a person's emotional state and expression. Often emotional regulation is self-directed.

61. Chou Tun-I (Zhou Dunyi), "Penetrating the Book of Changes" (*T'ung-Shu*), 473.

62. *Yo Kî* ("Record of Music"), XVII, II:9, 107-108. See also Hsün Tzu (Xunzi), "A Discussion of Music," in *Basic Writings*, 114-115.

63. According to the *Nātyaśāstra*, these include erotic love (*rati*), mirth (*hāsya*), sorrow (*śoka*), anger (*krodha*), energy (*utsāha*), fear (*bhaya*), disgust (*jugupsā*), and astonishment (*vismaya*).

64. These are the translations given in Manomohan Ghosh's translation of the *Nātyaśāstra*. See Bharata Muni (attrib.), *The Nātyaśāstra*, I, vol. 15, 102. See also Goswamy, *Essence of Indian Art*, 17-30. The *rasas* include the erotic (*śṛngāra*), the comic (*hāsya*), the pathetic (in the sense of sorrowful) (*kāuṇya*), the furious (*raudra*), the heroic (*vīra*), the terrible (*bhayānaka*), the odious (*bībhatsa*), and the marvelous (*adbhuta*).

65. See Schueller, *The Idea of Music*, 20, 26-27, 30-40, and 63.

66. See Shehadi, *Philosophies of Music in Medieval Islam*, 28.

67. The idea that the expressive character of music results in emotional arousal became the common view of many medieval Islamic thinkers. See ibid., 120.

68. Ibid., 62-64.

69. Ibid., 74-75. Although Ibn Sina does not consider expression to be the most important function of music, he believes that music is emotionally expressive, and that the distinctive function of music is the production of delight (see 72).

70. Ibid., 120-21.

71. See Butler, *The Principles of Music*, 1, 56-57; and Smith, "*Of the Nature of That Imitation Which Takes Place in What Are Called the Imitative Arts*," 160. For a discussion of the conflict between those who thought that music should reflect people's passions through a simple musical vocabulary and those who defended the complex music of opera, see Walker, *Musical Beliefs*, 122-34.

72. See Husain, Thompson, and Schellenberg, "Effects of Musical Tempo and Mode on Arousal, Mood, and Spatial Abilities," 156. The notion of demand characteristics is analyzed

in Orne, "On the Social Psychology of the Psychological Experiment with Particular Reference to Demand Characteristics and Their Implications."

73. See *EMM*, 8. See also Scherer and Zentner, "Emotional Effects of Music: Production Rules," 280.

74. Hindemith, *A Composer's World*, 38 and 45–46. One can raise the question here of whether one can have memories of feelings that are not themselves feelings; but apparently Hindemith thinks one can. Cf. Nussbaum, *Upheavals of Thought*, 266–67.

75. Pratt, *Music as the Language of Emotion*, 7–8. See also Pratt, *The Meaning of Music*.

76. Kivy grants that the beauty of music moves listeners, but he denies that everyday emotions are aroused. See Kivy, *Introduction to a Philosophy of Music*, 108–9.

77. See, for example, Pratt, *Music as the Language of Emotion*, 7–8.

78. *EMM*, 31.

79. Ibid., 32.

80. See Rowell, *Thinking about Music*, 197.

81. For an analysis of the relationship between valued experiences in life and the artistic form, which enables its audience to undergo an integral experience that runs its course to a culmination and aftermath, see Dewey, *Art as Experience*.

82. Juslin and Västfjäll, "Emotional Responses to Music," 559–75.

83. Ibid., 572–73. Alf Gabrielsson reports that 13 percent of the subjects in his study of strong emotions in connection with music reported some kind of mixed feelings. See Gabrielsson, "Strong Experiences with Music," 561.

84. See, for example, Juslin and Västfjäll, "Emotional Responses to Music," 560.

85. Sloboda and Juslin, "Psychological Perspectivers on Music and Emotions," 75. See also Davidson, "On Emotion, Mood, and Related Affective Constructs"; Frijda, "Varieties of Affect," 59–67; Goldsmith, "Parsing the Emotional Domain from a Developmental Perspective"; Kagan, "Distinctions among Emotions, Moods, and Temperamental Qualities"; Lazarus, "The Stable and the Unstable in Emotion"; Panksepp, "Basic Emotions Ramify Widely in the Brain, Yielding Many Concepts That Cannot Be Distinguished Unambiguously . . . Yet"; Watson and Clark, "Emotions, Moods, Traits, and Temperaments"; and Davidson and Ekman, "Afterword: How Are Emotions Distinguished from Moods, Temperament, and Other Related Affective Constructs?"

86. Robert Solomon makes this point regarding love. See *In Defense of Sentimentality*, 93. Peter Goldie also emphasizes the distinction between emotions and emotion-episodes in *The Emotions*, 12–14.

87. Ekman points out the cultural relativity even for display rules. See *Emotions Revealed*, 4.

88. See Ortony and Turner, "What's Basic about Basic Emotions?," 315–31.

89. Davidson, "On Emotion, Mood, and Related Affective Constructs," 54.

90. Nico H. Frijda has defended the view that emotions necessarily have action tendencies. See *The Emotions*, 69–73.

91. Ridley, *Music, Value and the Passions*, 33. Formal objects of emotions ascribe certain properties (e.g., being disgusting) to the target object.

92. Ibid., 161.

93. Ibid., 160. See also 169.

94. Solomon, "Emotions and Choice," 3–4.

95. Nussbaum, *Upheavals of Thought*, 276n.

96. Husain, Thompson, and Schellenberg, "Effects of Musical Tempo and Mode on Arousal, Mood, and Spatial Abilities."

97. Damasio, *The Feeling of What Happens*, 28.

98. Radford, "Emotions and Music," 75.

99. My thanks to Robert C. Solomon for this suggestion. This is effectively what Ridley argues when he claims that "many emotions have co-nominal feelings: depression may be either an emotion or a feeling; so may sadness, cheerfulness, happiness, irritation and joy, among others" (*Music, Value, and the Passions*, 33–34).

100. *Jaws* (1975), directed by Stephen Spielberg, Universal Studios. Video (1975), B0009 QN4EO.

101. *Titanic* (1997), directed by James Cameron, Paramount Pictures. Video (1997), 0792151712.

102. Unlike Kivy, Davies claims that listeners often "mirror" emotions expressed through emotion characteristics in appearance, that is, they experience the same emotion themselves (e.g., sadness in response to the "sadness" they hear in music). In this respect, he considers the response to musically expressed emotions different from the response to everyday expressive behavior, which often arouses different emotions from those that are communicated. See Davies, *Musical Meaning and Expression*, 178. Psychologists refer to the phenomenon of emotional contagion, the tendency to mimic the emotional responses of another person and to consequently share the emotional feeling of that person. See Hatfield, Cacioppo, and Rapson, *Emotional Contagion*.

103. Besides Davies, Levinson and Ridley also make this point. See Levinson, "Music and Negative Emotion," 320–21n; and Ridley, *Music, Value, and the Passions*, 13–14.

104. Berliner, "Give and Take," 25. For a discussion of performers' dynamic involvement in both action and perception, with the shifts of focus that this involves, see Clarke, *Ways of Listening*, 151–54.

105. Thom, *For an Audience*, 205.

106. Gabrielsson, "Emotions in Strong Experiences with Music," 441.

107. Frick, "Communicating Emotion"; and Juslin and Laukka, "Communication of Emotions in Vocal Expression and Music Performance."

108. Juslin and Laukka, "Communication of Emotions in Vocal Expression and Music Performance," 786.

109. Juslin, "Communicating Emotion in Music Performance," 322. Levinson, "Hope in *The Hebrides*."

110. Juslin, "Perceived Emotional Expression in Synthesized Performances of a Short Melody," 248. I have already cited a study by Sandra Trehub and her colleagues confirming the claim that adults can distinguish lullabies from nonlullabies in foreign music (Trehub, Unyk, and Trainor, "Adults Identify Infant-Directed Music across Cultures").

111. Balkwill and Thompson, "A Cross-Cultural Investigation of the Perception of Emotion in Music."

112. This is an interesting result in terms of *rasa* theory (Indian emotion theory, developed in connection with the performance arts), for while joy, sadness, and anger are universally acknowledged as being among the basic *rasas*, the inclusion of peacefulness is controversial. One might argue that the rationale that led to the inclusion of the specific eight rasas listed in the *Nātyaśāstra* is that they lend themselves to dramatic portrayal. The *Nātyaśāstra* is, after all, a compendium of knowledge about dramatic productions. Peacefulness, however, is not included in the original list from the *Nātyaśāstra*, nor does it lend itself easily to dramatic presentation.

113. See Thompson and Balkwill, "Cross-Cultural Similarities and Differences."

114. See Juslin, "Communicating Emotion in Music Performance"; Juslin and Laukka, "Communication of Emotions in Vocal Expression and Music Performance"; and Juslin and Timmers, "Expression and Communication of Emotion in Music Performance."

115. Benamou, "Comparing Musical Affect."

116. See Keil, "Motion and Feeling through Music"; Keil, "Participatory Discrepancies and the Power of Music"; Keil, "The Theory of Participatory Discrepancies"; and Progler, "Searching for Swing."

117. Hodeir, *Jazz*, 207. Hodeir proposes: "I would suggest that this drive is a manifestation of personal magnetism which is somehow expressed—I couldn't say exactly how—in the domain of rhythm."

118. Keil, "Motion and Feeling through Music," 345.

119. Ibid., 346. Keil is convinced that vital drive has widespread applicability to other forms of music as well, including much that is non-Western. See pp. 347–48.

120. Ibid., 275.

121. Patel implies that participatory discrepancies can contribute to vital drive. He observes that "a slight misalignment of grouping and beat can add rhythmic energy to a melody in the form of anacrusis or upbeat" (*MLB*, 203).

122. Becker, *Deep Listeners*, 52. She cites in connection with her first three examples Keil, *Polka Happiness*, 276; Katz, "Accepting 'Boiling Energy,'" 348; and Merriam, *The Anthropology of Music*, 82. See also the ancient Chinese *Yo Kī* ("Record of Music"), XVII, III:27, 127. DeWoskin observes, however, that the "Record of Music" treats the relationship between music and emotional states as more a matter of sympathetic resonance than causation (*A Song for One or Two*, 97). DeWoskin also notes that in the late Han there was a shift from describing music as influencing sentiments to expressing grave sentiments, in particular, on the qin (110).

123. Juslin et al., "A Questionnaire Study of Emotion Reactions to Music in Everyday Life." In answer to the question "How common is it that you feel the following emotions in connection with music?" the following numerical equivalents were used:

4 = always
3 = often
2 = seldom
1 = never.

In preliminary results, happiness received the highest score (3.06), followed by "pleasurable" feeling (2.97). See also Juslin and Laukka, "Expression, Perception, and Induction of Musical Emotions"; and Juslin et al., "An Experience Sampling Study of Emotional Reactions to Music."

124. See Solomon, "Against Valence ('Positive' and 'Negative' Emotions)."

125. According to a study by Husain and colleagues, "participants enjoyed the piece more when it was played quickly in major mode or slowly in minor mode, compared with when it was played quickly in minor mode or slowly in major mode." Husain, Thompson, and Schellenberg, "Effects of Musical Tempo and Mode on Arousal, Mood, and Spatial Abilities," 164. See also Trainor and Schmidt, "Processing Emotions Induced by Music," 316.

126. Husain, Thompson, and Schellenberg, "Effects of Musical Tempo and Mode on Arousal, Mood, and Spatial Abilities," 166. They refer to Ashby, Isen, and Turken, "A Neuropsychological Theory of Positive Affect and Its Influence on Cognition."

127. Blood and Zatorre, "Intensely Pleasurable Responses to Music Correlate with Activity in Brain Regions Implicated in Reward and Emotion," 11822.

128. Ibid., 11823.

129. Hanslick is a striking case in point. As a philosopher of music, he denied that music could represent emotion; but his writing was replete with emotional terminology when he played his more usual role of music critic, as Kivy points out. See Kivy, "Something I've Always Wanted to Know about Hanslick," 417.

130. Pater, *The Renaissance*, 238.

CHAPTER 8

1. Laing, *The Divided Self*, 39.

2. Ibid., 137–38.

3. Ibid., 50 and 92.

4. Bregman, "Auditory Scene Analysis," 17 and 28.

5. See ibid., 18–19 and 27–28.

6. This was established by A. James Hudspeth. See "Channel Protein Converts Vibrations to Electrical Signal," Howard Hughes Medical Institute, October 13, 2004. See also Corey et al., "TRPA1 Is a Candidate for the Mechano-Sensitive Transduction Channel of Vertebrate Hair Cells," 723–30.

7. Becker, *Deep Listeners*, 127.

8. Stern's "vitality affects" have struck a number of psychologists of music as particularly useful for making sense of the emotional character of music. See, for example, Sloboda and Juslin, "Psychological Perspectives on Music and Emotion," 81; and Bunt and Pavlicevic, "Music and Emotion," 194.

9. Cf. Dissanayake, *Art and Intimacy*; and Dissanayake "Antecedents of the Temporal Arts in Early Mother-Infant Interaction." See also Trevarthen, "Communication and Cooperation in Early Infancy"; and Trevarthen, "Emotions in Infancy."

10. Stern, *The Interpersonal World of the Infant*, 56.

11. Ibid., 54.

12. Ibid., 156.

13. Ibid., 157.

14. Ibid., 55–56.

15. Ibid., 57. Cf. Bunt and Pavlicevic, "Music and Emotion," 194.

16. See Levinson, "Music and Negative Emotion," 306–35; and Davies, *Musical Meaning and Expression*, 307–19.

17. Meyer notes a similar phenomenon in the case of certain other animals that abhor uncertainty, for example, baboons. See "Music and Emotions: Distinctions and Uncertainties," 352 and 352n. Levinson also claims that a sense of mastering negative emotions is one of the rewards of enjoying them in the context of music. See Levinson, "Music and Negative Emotion," 328.

18. Aaron Ridley similarly contends that a prior sense of safety is often necessary to enjoy the so-called negative emotions in music. See *Music, Value, and the Passions*, 151–54. Levinson also emphasizes that these emotions experienced in the context of music "typically *have no life-implications*," unlike emotion in everyday life ("Music and Negative Emotion," 324). I do not wish to rule out other reasons why we enjoy the musical arousal of emotions that we would not enjoy in everyday life. Levinson, for example, cites a number of rewards besides mastery that we gain in experiencing "negative" emotions in connection with music, including: catharsis, an enhanced grasp of the expressiveness of the musical work, the savor of feeling divorced from life-consequences, greater insight into our affective life, a gain in a sense of our own dignity owing to our capacity to feel deeply and our impression of the richness of our inner life, the opportunity to "tone up" our feelings in preparation for dealing with life situations, and perhaps the sense of "intimate contact with the mind and soul of another," that is, the composer. See pp. 322–29. Davies, although he takes issue with some of Levinson's suggestions, sees enjoyment of "negative" emotions as of a piece with the human willingness to face risks and confront pain and suffering in the course of life (see *Musical Meaning and Expression*, 319).

19. See Rouget, *Music and Trance*, xviii, 72, and 183.

20. See Becker, *Deep Listeners*, 29 and 131.

21. Becker, "Anthropological Perspectives on Music and Emotion," 144.

22. Henderson, "Emotion and Devotion," 440.

23. Ibid., 459–60.

24. This Hindu conception of the universal Self (*atman*) within everyone contrasts directly with the Buddhist doctrine that there is no self (*anatman*). Both views, however, postulate the same ontological status for every person.

25. Panzarella, "The Phenomenology of Aesthetic Peak Experiences," 69–85; citation from 73.

26. Herndon and McLeod, *Music as Culture*, 124. Cf. Sloboda and Juslin, "Psychological Perspectives on Music and Emotion," 87.

27. Herndon and McLeod, *Music as Culture*, 93–95.

28. Hāl is also the term for the ecstatic states that Sufi singers intermittently achieve. See Qureshi, *Sufi Music of India and Pakistan*, 80f. See also Becker, *Deep Listeners*, 8.

29. Safvate and Caron, *Iran: Les traditions musicales*, 232, cited and translated in Miller, *Music and Song in Persia*, 22.

30. Shankar, *My Music, My Life*, 57–58. Cf. Abhinavagupta, quoted in Gnoli, *The Aesthetic Experience According to Abhinavagupta*, 70.

31. Pope, "An Essay on Criticism," 1:318, 1008. Cf. Becker, *Deep Listeners*, 80, for a discussion of a similar complaint expressed in an eleventh-century Sufi text.

32. See Herndon and McLeod, *Music as Culture*, 112.

33. Turino, *Music as Social Life*, 48.

34. As was noted in chapter 4, Davies remarks on this tendency in *Musical Works and Performances*, 22n.

35. In rock music, according to Theodore Gracyk, "studio recordings have become the standard for judging live performances." Gracyk, *Rhythm and Noise*, 84.

36. Lomax, "Folk Song Style," *American Anthropologist* 61 (1959): 929.

37. Ibid., 930.

38. Dowling and Harwood, *Music Cognition*, 230–31. We should, however, note the transformations that the style might undergo as it encounters and is affected by other styles as a consequence of migration.

39. Turino, *Music as Social Life*, 48.

40. Meyer, "On Rehearing Music," 42–53.

41. See Meyer, "A Pride of Prejudices; or, Delight in Diversity," 275.

42. Serafine, *Music as Cognition*, 32; and Keil, "Participatory Discrepancies and the Power of Music."

43. Sloboda and Juslin, "Psychological Perspectives on Music and Emotion," 92.

44. Ibid., 92. See also Jackendoff, "Musical Processing and Musical Affect," 51–68. Gracyk suggests that a consequence of Raffman's view about nuance ineffability would seem to be that because we cannot store the nuances of a particular performance of music, a recording of that performance will, in effect, sound new every time. See Gracyk, *Rhythm and Noise*, 57–61, 236. Davies is skeptical about this conclusion. See *Musical Works and Performances*, 305.

45. Zajonc, "Exposure Effects, 194–203.

46. Ibid., 199–200. The study cited was Wilson, "Feeling More Than We Can Know."

47. Zajonc, "Exposure Effects," 202.

48. Portions of what follow appeared originally in Higgins, "Musical Idiosyncrasy and Perspectival Listening," 94.

49. Said, *Musical Elaborations*, 80.

50. Nietzsche, *The Gay Science*, §334, 262.

51. See Francès, *The Perception of Music*, 35. For a discussion of several such cases, see 34–38.

52. See *EMM*, 92.

53. Dowling and Harwood insist that good continuation can be overridden by other patterning principles, such as repeated notes or similarity of timbre. See *Music Cognition*, 158–59.

Earlier we noted that we track the timbre of a violin and hear the movement of this timbre as a continuation of the same voice in a texture, and do so even when the violin's melody goes on to deviate from what we were expecting. This observation does not, however, undercut my general point that hearing music involves a recognition of continuity. When we follow the timbre of the violin as it departs from a pattern, we are interpreting its distinctive voice as continuing. We do not experience new tones produced by the violin as unrelated to what has gone before.

54. Peirce, *Collected Papers*, 5:395.

55. Becker indicates how subdivision of cyclical time was crucial to the development and organization of music in Java in "Time and Tune in Java."

56. Zuckerkandl, *Sound and Symbol*, 118. Ethnomusicological accounts suggest that the tendency to attend to music's ongoing continuation in time is not restricted to Western listeners. The cyclical *talas*, the basic rhythmic patterns employed in classical Indian music, often become perceptually submerged in the complex texture of cross rhythms between instruments, often further subdivided. The practice of audience members maintaining the basic *tala* by means of hand gestures allows for a magic moment, when the *tala* again becomes pronounced, that appears exactly in accordance with the cycle maintained by the gestures. The gestures also make the continuation of the *tala* a pattern for ongoing physical activity. Listeners are, in effect, sustaining the continuation of the fundamental rhythm.

57. See Csikszentmihalyi, *Flow*.

58. Zuckerkandl, *Sound and Symbol*, 233.

59. Sacks, "The Man Who Mistook His Wife for a Hat," 17. See also his study, "The Lost Mariner," included in the same book.

60. Beardsley, "Understanding Music," 70–71.

61. See Herzog, "Music in the Thinking of the American Indian," 8–9.

62. See Schneider, "Primitive Music," 47–49. See also See Rowell, *Music in Ancient Indian Thought*, 185.

63. See Rowell, *Music and Musical Thought in Early India*, 185.

64. See Idel, "Conceptualizations of Music in Jewish Mysticism," 187–88. For a contemporary suggestion of this myth of music sustaining our world, consider Jefferson Airplane's version of Crosby, Stills, and Kanter's song "Wooden Ships," on *Volunteers*, Remastered RCA CD, 2004, B00028U6B8.

65. Dowling and Harwood, *Music Cognition*, 231.

66. Merriam, *The Anthropology of Music*, 225.

67. Hsün Tzu (Xunzi), "A Discussion of Music," in *Basic Writings*, 113.

68. The recording is Natalie Cole, with Nat King Cole, "Unforgettable," on *Unforgettable: With Love*, Elektra/Wea, 1991, B000002H8X.

CHAPTER 9

1. *Fahrenheit 9/11*, directed by Michael Moore, 2004. The soldier cites the Bloodhound Gang's "Fire, Water, Burn" (*One Fierce Beer Coaster*, Geffen Records, 1996, B0000000WJ) as the best song for the purpose.

2. The song was performed by a male choir in the 1966 Broadway musical from which the movie was derived. The music, including this song, was written by John Kander, and Fred Ebb wrote the lyrics.

3. Stokes, "Introduction: Ethnicity, Identity and Music," 6; citations from Barth, *Ethnic Groups and Boundaries*, and Chapman, Tonkin, and McDonald, *History and Ethnicity*.

4. Musical flash mobs of this sort are not the only kind. Flash mobs have sometimes featured dance, political demonstration, or simply bizarre activities. A dance flash mob famously performed at Oprah Winfrey's kickoff party for her twenty-fourth season. The hallmarks of sudden arrival at a public place and sudden dispersal seem, however, to be essential.

5. If a website of musical blunders published by the Cantus Quercus Press is to be believed, it has been used to sell quite a few other products as well. See http://www.cantusquercus.com/fauxmercial.htm.

6. See some of the comments from self-identified non-Christians cited in Steve Jalsevac, "Christmas Hallelujah Flash Mob Video Gets Huge Reaction," at www.lifesitenews.com/news/christmas-hallelujuh-flash-mob-video-gets-huge-reaction/.

7. See Freeman, *Societies of Brains*.

8. Ibid. See also http://www.ritholtz.com/blog/2010/12/christmas-food-court-flash-mob-hallelujah-chorus/.

9. Cf. Nietzsche, *The Birth of Tragedy* §8, 64, for a description of "Dionysian" music's power to break down social roles and achieve a religious transformation of consciousness.

10. Rorty, "Human Rights, Rationality, and Sentimentality," 122–23.

11. I emphasize narrow intraculturality here because in contemporary complex societies, one's own "culture" may include many musical subcultures, some of which may be alien to each other. In cases such as this, the relevant intraculturality may be that of a musical subculture.

12. See Turino, *Music as Social Life*, 210–24.

13. See Larkin, "Looking Back at Coltrane," 187. Larkin complains about Coltrane's "latter day religiosity, exemplified in turgid suites such as 'A Love Supreme' and 'Ascension' that set up pretension as a way of life; that wilful, hideous distortion of tone that offered squeals, squeaks, Bronx cheers and throttled slate-pencil noises for serious consideration."

14. For this reason we are more likely to find some perceptual affinity with music of another culture than with some atonal music that is deliberately contrived to thwart our musical expectations.

15. They are also the means through which we experience much music that is not foreign. Cf. Gracyk, *Rhythm and Noise: An Aesthetics of Rock*.

16. The personae I refer to here are the characters that singers personify while singing a particular song. They are not the same as the personae I discussed in chapter 7 in connection with instrumental music.

17. I suspect that the relative independence one often feels in music from the roles of daily life and their demands is the reason why some have termed music *solipsistic*. See Nussbaum, *The Musical Representation*, and Lidov, *Is Language a Music?*, 12. Lidov reveals the discrepancy between his use of "solipsism" and the standard philosophical sense when he remarks, "Insofar as we start out from representations of felt somatic states, we can note that music has a solipsistic bias, be it the solipsism of first person singular or plural. Music abounds in idealized

images of sociality (necessarily idealized because solipsistic)." In common philosophical usage, "solipsism" implies an isolation that is too complete to allow for a meaningful sense of first person plural. What Lidov calls solipsism I would be temped to call "identification."

18. Or on those occasions when we are particularly identified with a persona whose experience resembles our own or one who is pleading for a particular point of view (as in protest songs), we feel that the rest of the world *should* be singing with us.

19. Shakespeare, *Hamlet*, act 2, sc. 2, l. 303–8.

BIBLIOGRAPHY

Abhinavagupta. *Locana*. In *The Dhvanyāloka of Ānandavardhana, with the Locana of Abhinavagupta*, edited by Daniel H. H. Ingalls. Translated by Daniel H. H. Ingalls, Jeffrey Moussaieff Masson, and M. V. Patwardhan. Cambridge, MA: Harvard University Press, 1990.

Abrams, R. M., S. K. Griffiths, X. Huang, J. Sain, G. Langford, and K. J. Gerhardt. "Fetal Music Perception: The Role of Sound Transmission." *Music Perception* 15, no. 3 (1998): 307–17.

Abrams, Robert M., and Kenneth J. Gerhardt. "Some Aspects of the Foetal Sound Environment." In *Perception and Cognition of Music*, edited by Irène Deliège and John Sloboda, 83–101. Hove, UK: Psychology Press, 1997.

Adorno, Theodor W. "Music, Language, and Composition." Translated by Susan Gillespie. *Music Quarterly* 77, no. 3 (1993): 401–14.

Agawu, V. Kofi. "Music in the Funeral Traditions of the Akpafu." *Ethnomusicology* 32, no. 1 (1988): 75–105.

Albert, Martin L., Robert W. Sparks, and Nancy A. Helm. "Melodic Intonation Therapy for Aphasia." *Archives of Neurology* 29 (1973): 130–31.

Al-Ghazali. "The Book of the Right Usages of Music and Trance." In "Emotional Religion in Islam as Affected by Music and Singing. Being a Translation of a Book of the Iḥyā' Ulum al-Din of al-Ghazali with Analysis, Annotation, and Appendices," translated by Duncan B. MacDonald. *Journal of the Royal Asiatic Society of Great Britain and Ireland* (1901).

Allen, Warren Dwight. *Philosophies of Music History: A Study of General Histories of Music, 1600–1960*. New York: Dover, 1962.

Alperson, Philip, ed. *The Philosophy of the Visual Arts*. New York: Oxford University Press, 1992.

Aristotle. *De Anima*. In *The Basic Works of Aristotle*, edited by Richard McKeon, translated by J. A. Smith, 535–603. New York: Random House, 1941.

——. *Politics*. In *The Basic Works of Aristotle*, edited by Richard McKeon, translated by Benjamin Jowett, 1127–316. New York: Random House, 1941.

Armstrong, Louis. *New York Times*, July 7, 1971, 41.

Ashby, F. G., A. M. Isen, and A. U. Turken. "A Neuropsychological Theory of Positive Affect and Its Influence on Cognition." *Psychological Review* 106 (1999): 529–50.

Austin, J. L. *How to Do Things with Words*. Cambridge, MA: Harvard University Press, 1962.

Bachem, A. "Time Factors in Relative and Absolute Pitch Determination." *Journal of the Acoustical Society of America* 26 (1954): 751–53.

Balaban, Evan. "Bird Song Syntax: Learned Intraspecific Variation Is Meaningful." *Proceedings of the National Academy of Sciences, USA* 85 (1988): 3657–60.

Balkwill, Laura-Lee, and William Forde Thompson. "A Cross-Cultural Investigation of the Perception of Emotion in Music: Psychophysical and Cultural Cues." *Music Perception* 17, no. 1 (1999): 43–64.

Banse, Rainer, and Klaus R. Scherer. "Acoustic Profiles in Vocal Emotion Expression." *Journal of Personality and Social Psychology* 70 (1996): 614–35.

Barenboim, Daniel. "In the Beginning Was Sound." Reith Lectures, Lecture 1, delivered at Cadogan Hall, London, April 7, 2006. http://www.ellopos.net/music/library/barenboim.html and http://www.bbc.co.uk/radi04/reith2006/.

Barth, Fredrik, ed. *Ethnic Groups and Boundaries: The Social Organisation of Culture Difference*. London: Allen and Unwin, 1969.

Barthes, Roland. *Image Music Text*. Translated by Stephen Heath. New York: Hill and Wang, 1977.

Bartlett, Frederic C. *Remembering: A Study in Experimental and Social Psychology*. Cambridge: Cambridge University Press, 1932.

Batteux, Charles. *Les beaux arts reduits à un même principe*. Paris: Durand, 1747.

Beardsley, Monroe. "Understanding Music." In *On Criticizing Music: Five Philosophical Perspectives*, edited by Kingsley Price, 55–73. Baltimore: Johns Hopkins University Press, 1981.

Beattie, James. "On Poetry and Music as They Affect the Mind." In *Essays on the Nature and Immutability of Truth, in Opposition to Sophistry and Scepticism: On Poetry and Music, as They Affect the Mind, On Laughter, and Ludicrous Composition, and On the Utility of Classical Learning*. Dublin: Printed for C. Jenkin, 1778.

Becker, Judith. "The Anatomy of a Mode." *Ethnomusicology* 13, no. 2 (1969): 267–79.

——. "Anthropological Perspectives on Music and Emotion." In *Music and Emotion: Theory and Research*, edited by Patrik Juslin and John A. Sloboda, 135–60. Oxford: Oxford University Press, 2001.

——. *Deep Listeners: Music, Emotion, and Trancing*. Bloomington: Indiana University Press, 2004.

——. "Is Western Art Music Superior?" *Musical Quarterly* 72 (1986): 341–59.

——. "Time and Tune in Java." In *The Imagination of Reality: Essays in Southeast Asian Coherence Systems*, edited by A. L. Becker and Aram A. Yergoyan, 197–210. Norwood, NJ: Ablex, 1979.

———. *Traditional Music in Modern Java: Gamelan in a Changing Society*. Honolulu: University Press of Hawai'i, 1980.

Benamou, Marc. "Comparing Musical Affect: Java and the West." *The World of Music* 45 (2003): 57–76.

Benzon, William L. *Beethoven's Anvil: Music in Mind and Culture*. New York: Basic Books, 2001.

Berliner, Paul. "Give and Take: The Collective Conversation of Jazz Performance." In *Creativity in Performance*, edited by R. Keith Sawyer, 9–41. Greenwich, CT: Ablex, 1997.

Berman, Laurence. *The Musical Image: A Theory of Content*. Westport, CT: Greenwood Press, 1993.

Bernstein, Leonard. *The Unanswered Question: Six Talks at Harvard*. Charles Eliot Norton Lectures. Cambridge, MA: Harvard University Press, 1976.

Besson, M., F. Faita, I. Peretz, A.-M. Bonnel, and J. Requin. "Singing in the Brain: Independence of Lyrics and Tunes." *Psychological Science* 9, no. 6 (1998): 494–98.

Besson, Mireille, and Daniele Schön. "Comparison between Language and Music." In *The Cognitive Neuroscience of Music*, edited by Isabelle Peretz and Robert Zatorre, 269–93. Oxford: Oxford University Press, 2003.

Best, Catherine T., and Robert A. Avery. "Left-Hemisphere Advantage for Click Consonants Is Determined by Linguistic Significance and Experience." *Psychological Science* 10, no. 1 (1999): 65–70.

Best, Elsdon. *The Maori*. Wellington: Memoirs of the Polynesian Society, 1924.

Bharata Muni (attrib.). *The Nātyaśāstra*. Vol. I, chapters I–XXVII. 2nd ed., rev. Translated and edited by Manomohan Ghosh. Calcutta: Granthalaya, 1967.

Birdwhistell, Ray L. *Kinesics and Context: Essays on Body Motion Communication*. Philadelphia: University of Pennsylvania Press, 1970.

Blacking, John. "Can Musical Universals be Heard?" *The World of Music* 19, no. 1/2 (1977): 22.

———. *A Commonsense View of All Music*. Cambridge: Cambridge University Press, 1989.

———. "Extensions and Limits of Musical Transformations." Paper presented at the Society for Ethnomusicology conference, Toronto, 1972; cited in Feld, "Linguistic Models in Ethnomusicology," 207.

———. *How Musical Is Man?* Seattle: University of Washington Press, 1973.

———. "Music, Culture, and Experience." In *Music, Culture, and Experience*, 223–42. Chicago: University of Chicago Press, 1995.

———. *Music, Culture, and Experience*. Chicago: University of Chicago Press, 1995.

Blackwell, H. R., and H. Schlosberg. "Octave Generalization, Pitch Discrimination and Loudness Thresholds in the White Rat." *Journal of Experimental Psychology* 33 (1943): 407–19.

Blood, Anne J., and Robert J. Zatorre. "Intensely Pleasurable Responses to Music Correlate with Activity in Brain Regions Implicated in Reward and Emotion." *Proceedings of the National Academy of Science* 98 (2001): 11818–23.

Boernstein, W. S. "Perceiving and Thinking: Their Interrelationship and Organismic Organization." *Annals of the New York Academy of Sciences* 169 (1970): 673–82.

————. "Über die physiologischen Grundlagen des Wahrnehmens: Der Einfluss 'heller' und 'dunkler' Reize und den Melanophoren Zustand in Emphibien." *Archives Internationales de Pharmacodynamie et de Therapie* 61 (1939): 387–414.

Boesch, Cristophe. "Symbolic Communication in Wild Chimpanzees?" *Human Evolution* 6 (1991): 83.

Bowie, Andrew. *Music, Philosophy, and Modernity.* Cambridge: Cambridge University Press, 2007.

Bowlby, John. *Attachment.* Vol. 1 of *Attachment and Loss.* New York: Basic Books, 1969.

Brandily, Monique. "Songs to Birds among the Teda of Chad." *Ethnomusicology* 26, no. 3 (1982): 371–90.

Bregman, Albert S. "Auditory Scene Analysis: Hearing in Complex Environments." In *Thinking in Sound: The Cognitive Psychology of Human Audition,* edited by Stephen McAdams and Emmanuel Bigand, 10–36. Oxford: Clarendon Press, 1993.

Bregman, Albert S., and Garry L. Dannenbring. "The Effect of Continuity on Auditory Stream Segregation." *Perception and Psychophysics* 13 (1963): 308–12.

Bright, William. "Language and Music: Areas for Cooperation." *Ethnomusicology* 7, no. 1 (1963): 26–32.

Brown, Lee B. "Musical Works, Improvisation, and the Principle of Continuity." *Journal of Aesthetics and Art Criticism* 54, no. 4 (1996): 353–69.

Brown, Steven. "The 'Musilanguage' Model of Music Evolution." In *The Origins of Music,* edited by Nils L. Wallin, Björn Merker, and Steven Brown, 271–300. Cambridge, MA: MIT Press, 2000.

Brown, Steven, Björn Merker, and Nils L. Wallin. "An Introduction to Evolutionary Musicology." In *The Origins of Music,* edited by Nils L. Wallin, Björn Merker, and Steven Brown, 3–24. Cambridge, MA: MIT Press, 2000.

Brust, John C. M. "Music and the Neurologist: A Historical Perspective." In *The Cognitive Neuroscience of Music,* edited by Isabelle Peretz and Robert Zatorre, 181–91. Oxford: Oxford University Press, 2003.

Budd, Malcolm. "Music and the Communication of Emotion." *Journal of Aesthetics and Art Criticism* 47, no. 2 (1989): 129–38.

Bunt, Leslie, and Mercédès Pavlicevic. "Music and Emotion: Perspectives from Music Therapy." In *Music and Emotion: Theory and Research,* edited by Patrik Juslin and John A. Sloboda, 181–201. Oxford: Oxford University Press, 2001.

Burns, Edward M. "Octave Adjustment by Non-Western Musicians." *Journal of the Acoustical Society of America Supplement* 56 (1974): S25–26A.

Burns, Edward M., and W. Dixon Ward. "Categorical Perception of Musical Intervals." *Journal of the Acoustical Society of America* 55 (1974): 456(A).

————. "Categorical Perception—Phenomenon or Epiphenomenon: Evidence from Experiments in the Perception of Melodic Musical Intervals." *Journal of the Acoustical Society of America* 63 (1978): 456–68.

————. "Intervals, Scales, and Tuning." In *The Psychology of Music,* edited by Diana Deutsch, 241–69. New York: Academic Press, 1982.

Burrows, Edwin G. *Ethology of Futuna.* Honolulu: Bernice P. Bishop Museum Bulletin, 1936.

———. *Native Music of the Tuamotus*. Honolulu: Bernice P. Bishop Museum Bulletin 109, 1933.

———. *Songs of Uvea and Futuna*. Honolulu: Bernice P. Bishop Museum Bulletin 183, 1945.

Busoni, Ferruccio. *Sketch of a New Aesthetic of Music*. New York: Dover, 1962.

Butler, Charles. *The Principles of Music*. 1636. New York: Da Capo, 1970.

Butler, Gregory G. "Fugue and Rhetoric." *Journal of Music Theory* 21 (1977): 49–109.

Butler, Janet Wydom, and Paul G. Daston. "Musical Consonance as Musical Preference: A Cross Cultural Study." *Journal of General Psychology* 79 (1968): 129–42.

Cadar, Usopay H. "The Role of Kulintang Music in Maranao Society." *Ethnomusicology* 17, no. 2 (1973): 234–49.

Callen, Donald. "Transfiguring Emotions in Music." *Grazer Philosophische Studien* 19 (1983): 69–91.

Cantrick, Robert B. "If the Semantics of Music Theorizing Is Broke, Let's Fix It." *British Journal of Aesthetics* 35, no. 3 (1995): 239–53.

Carterette, Edward C. "Timbre, Tuning, and Stretched Octave of Javanese Gamelans." In *Proceedings of the Third International Conference on Music Perception and Cognition*, 103–4. Liège, Belgium: European Society for the Cognitive Sciences of Music, 1994.

Carterette, Edward C., and Roger A. Kendall. "Comparative Music Perception and Cognition." In *The Psychology of Music*, 2nd ed., edited by Diana Deutsch, 725–91. New York: Academic Press, 1999.

———. "On the Tuning and Stretched Octave of Javanese Gamelans." *Leonardo Music Journal* 4 (1994): 59–68.

Chan, Wing-Tsit, ed. *A Source Book in Chinese Philosophy*. Princeton, NJ: Princeton University Press, 1963.

Chang, Hsing Wu, and Sandra E. Trehub. "Auditory Processing of Relational Information by Young Infants." *Journal of Experimental Child Psychology* 24 (1977): 324–31.

Chapman, Malcolm, Elizabeth Tonkin, and Maryon McDonald. "Introduction." In *History and Ethnicity*, edited by Elizabeth Tonkin, Maryon McDonald, and Malcolm Chapman, 1–21. London: Routledge, 1989.

Charry, Eric. *Mande Music: Traditional and Modern Music of the Maninka and Mandinka of Western Africa*. Chicago: University of Chicago Press, 2000.

Chatwin, Bruce. *The Songlines*. New York: Penguin Books, 1987.

Chernoff, John Miller. *African Rhythm and African Sensibility: Aesthetics and Social Action in African Musical Idioms*. Chicago: University of Chicago Press, 1979.

Chou Tun-I (Zhou Dunyi). "Penetrating the Book of Changes (*T'ung-Shu*)." In *A Source Book in Chinese Philosophy*, edited by Wing-Tsit Chan, 465–80. Princeton, NJ: Princeton University Press, 1963.

Chuang Tzu. *The Complete Works of Chuang Tzu*. Translated by Burton Watson. New York: Columbia University Press, 1968.

Cirignola, Marcella. "WOMAD: A Celebration of Cultural Diversity." *Amazing Sounds*, 1997. Accessed April 26, 2011. http://www.amazings.com/articles/article0020.html.

Clapton, Eric P. *Official Tour Program 1998*. New York: Warner Brothers, 1998.

Clark, David M., and John D. Teasdale. "Constraints on the Effects of Mood on Memory." *Journal of Personality and Social Psychology* 48 (1985): 1595–608.

Clarke, Eric. *Ways of Listening: An Ecological Approach to the Perception of Musical Meaning.* Oxford: Oxford University Press, 2005.

Clement of Alexandria. "The Exhortation to the Greeks." In *Clement of Alexandria*, translated by G. W. Butterworth, 262–63. London: William Heinemann, 1919.

Clifton, Thomas. *Music as Heard: A Study in Applied Phenomenology.* New Haven, CT: Yale University Press, 1983.

Clynes, Manfred. *Sentics: The Touch of Emotion.* London: Souvenir Press, 1977.

———. "When Time Is Music." In *Rhythm in Psychological, Linguistic, and Musical Processes*, edited by James R. Evans and Manfred Clynes, 169–224. Springfield, IL: Charles C. Thomas, 1986.

Collette, Buddy, and Marl Young. "Joint Testimony to the Hearing on the Preservation of Jazz in California." Sponsored by the Legislative Black Caucus of the California Legislature, October 11, 1991. http//www.csulb.edu/~caljazz/about/LBC_Hearing/lbch01.html.

Collins, Randall. "Emotion as Key to Reconstructing Social Theory." Paper presented at the Emotion in Social Life and Social Theory conference, Canberra, Australia, July 9–11, 1997.

———. "Toward Neo-Meadian Sociology of Mind." *Symbolic Interaction* 12, no. 1 (1989): 1–32.

Condon, William S. "Communication: Rhythm and Structure." In *Rhythm in Psychological, Linguistic, and Musical Processes*, edited by James R. Evans and Manfred Clynes, 55–78. Springfield, IL: Charles C. Thomas, 1986.

———. "Multiple Response to Sound in Dysfunctional Children." *Journal of Autism and Childhood Schizophrenia* 5 (1975): 37–56.

Condon, William S., and Henry W. Brosin. "Micro Linguistic-Kinesic Events in Schizophrenic Behavior." In *Schizophrenia: Current Concepts and Research*, edited by D. V. Sankar, 812–37. Hicksville, NY: PJD Publications, 1969.

Condon, William S., and W. D. Ogston. "Sound Film Analysis of Normal and Pathological Behavior Patterns." *Journal of Nervous and Mental Disease* 143, no. 4 (1966): 338–47.

Condon, William S., and Louis W. Sander. "Synchrony Demonstrated between Movements of the Neonate and Adult Speech." *Child Development* 45 (1974): 456–62.

Cone, Edward T. *The Composer's Voice.* Ernest Bloch Lectures. Berkeley: University of California Press, 1974.

———. *Musical Form and Musical Performance.* New York: W. W. Norton, 1968.

Congreve, William. *The Mourning Bride* (1697). In *The Complete Works of William Congreve*, vol. 2, edited by Montague Summers, 173–271. New York: Russell and Russell, 1924.

Cook, Nicholas. *Music, Imagination, and Culture.* Oxford: Oxford University Press, 1990.

Cook, Nicholas, and Nicola Dibben. "Musicological Approaches to Emotion." In *Music and Emotion: Theory and Research*, edited by Patrik Juslin and John A. Sloboda, 45–70. Oxford: Oxford University Press, 2001.

Cooke, Deryck. *The Language of Music.* London: Oxford University Press, 1959.

Cooper, Robin Panneton, and Richard N. Salin. "Preference for Infant-Directed Speech in the First Month after Birth." *Child Development* 61 (1990): 1584–95.

Corey, David P., et al. "TRPA1 Is a Candidate for the Mechano-Sensitive Transduction Channel of Vertebrate Hair Cells." *Nature* 432 (December 9, 2004): 723–30.

Critchley, MacDonald. "Ecstatic and Synaesthetic Experiences during Musical Perception." In *Music and the Brain: Studies in the Neurology of Music,* edited by MacDonald Critchley and R. A. Henson, 217–32. London: William Heinemann Medical Books, 1977.

Cross, Ian. "Music and Cognitive Evolution." In *The Oxford Handbook of Evolutionary Psychology,* edited by Robin I. M. Dunbar and Louise Barrett, 649–67. Oxford: Oxford University Press, 2007.

———. "Music, Cognition, Culture, and Evolution." In *The Cognitive Neuroscience of Music,* edited by Isabelle Peretz and Robert Zatorre, 42–56. Oxford: Oxford University Press, 2003.

Csikszentmihalyi, Mihaly. *Flow: The Psychology of Optimal Experience.* New York: Harper and Row, 1990.

Cuddy, L. L. "The Color of Melody." *Music Perception* 2 (1985): 345–60.

Cutsforth, T. D. "The Role of Emotion in a Synaesthetic Subject." *American Journal of Psychology* 36 (1925): 527–43.

Cytowic, Richard E. *The Man Who Tasted Shapes: A Bizarre Medical Mystery Offers Revolutionary Insights into Emotions, Reasoning, and Consciousness.* New York: G. P. Putnam's Sons, 1993.

———. *Synesthesia: A Union of the Senses.* New York: Springer-Verlag, 1989. 2nd ed.: Cambridge, MA: MIT Press, 2002.

Dahlhaus, Carl. *Esthetics of Music.* Translated by William W. Austin. Cambridge: Cambridge University Press, 1982.

———. *The Idea of Absolute Music.* Translated by Roger Lustig. Chicago: University of Chicago Press, 1989.

Dalla Bella, Simone, Isabelle Peretz, Luc Rousseau, and Nathalie Gosselin. "A Developmental Study of the Affective Value of Tempo and Mode in Music." *Cognition* 80, no. 3 (2001): B1–B10.

Damasio, Antonio. *The Feeling of What Happens: Body and Emotion in the Making of Consciousness.* New York: Harcourt Brace, 1999.

Dann, Kevin T. *Bright Colors Falsely Seen: Synaesthesia and the Search for Transcendental Knowledge.* New Haven, CT: Yale University Press, 1998.

Dannenbring, Gary L., and Albert S. Bregman. "Stream Segregation and the Illusion of Overlap." *Journal of Experimental Psychology: Human Perception and Performance* 2 (1976): 544–55.

Danto, Arthur C. *The Transfiguration of the Commonplace.* Cambridge, MA: Harvard University Press, 1981.

Darwin, Charles. *The Descent of Man, and Selection in Relation to Sex, together with The Origin of Species by Means of Natural Selection.* Chicago: Encyclopædia Britannica, 1952.

Davidson, Richard J. "On Emotion, Mood, and Related Affective Constructs." In *The Nature of Emotion: Fundamental Questions,* edited by Paul Ekman and Richard J. Davidson, 51–55. New York: Oxford University Press, 1994.

Davidson, Richard J., and Paul Ekman. "Afterword: How Are Emotions Distinguished from

Moods, Temperament, and Other Related Affective Constructs?" In *The Nature of Emotion: Fundamental Questions*, edited by Paul Ekman and Richard J. Davidson, 94–96. New York: Oxford University Press, 1994.

Davies, Stephen. "Artistic Expression and the Hard Case of Pure Music." In *Contemporary Debates in Aesthetics and the Philosophy of Art*, edited by Matthew Kieran, 179–91. Malden, MA: Blackwell, 2006.

———. "The Expression of Emotion in Music." *Mind* 89, no. 1 (1980): 67–86.

———. "Life Is a Passacaglia." *Philosophy and Literature* 33 (2009): 315–28.

———. *Musical Meaning and Expression*. Ithaca, NY: Cornell University Press, 1994.

———. *Musical Works and Performances: A Philosophical Exploration*. New York: Oxford University Press, 2001.

———. "Music, Fire, and Evolution." *Politics and Culture* 1 (2010). http://www.politicsand culture.org/2010/04/29/music-fire-and-evolution/.

———. "Perceiving Melodies and Perceiving Musical Colors." *Review of Philosophical Psychology* 1 (2010): 19–39.

———. "Philosophical Perspectives on Music's Expressiveness." In *Music and Emotion: Theory and Research*, edited by Patrik Juslin and John A. Sloboda, 23–44. Oxford: Oxford University Press, 2001.

———. *Themes in the Philosophy of Music*. New York: Oxford University Press, 2003.

Davitz, Joel Robert, ed. *The Communication of Emotional Meaning*. New York: McGraw-Hill, 1964.

———. "Personality, Perceptual, and Cognitive Correlates of Emotional Sensitivity." In *The Communication of Emotional Meaning*, edited by Joel Robert Davitz, 57–68. New York: McGraw-Hill, 1964.

de Muris, Jean. *Summa Musicae*. In *Scriptores Ecclesiastici de Musica Sacra Potissimum*, edited by Martin Gerbert. St. Blaise: Typis San-Blasianis, 1784. Reprint: Hildesheim: Georg Olms, 1963.

DeCaspar, Anthony J., and Melanie J. Spence. "Prenatal Maternal Speech Influences Newborns' Perception of Speech Sounds." *Infant Behavior and Development* 9 (1986): 133–50.

Deliège, Irène, and John Sloboda, eds. *Musical Beginnings: Origins and Development of Musical Competence*. Oxford: Oxford University Press, 1996.

Demany, Laurent, and Françoise Armand. "The Perceptual Reality of Tone Chroma in Early Infancy." *Journal of the Acoustical Society of America* 76 (1984): 57–66.

Derrida, Jacques. *Of Grammatology*. Translated by Gayatri Chakravorty Spivak. Baltimore: Johns Hopkins University Press, 1976.

Deutsch, Diana. "Delayed Pitch Comparisons and the Principle of Proximity." *Perception and Psychophysics* 23 (1978): 227–30.

———. "Facilitation by Repetition in Recognition Memory for Tonal Pitch." *Memory and Cognition* 3 (1975): 263–66.

———. "Grouping Mechanisms in Music." In *The Psychology of Music*, edited by Diana Deutsch, 99–135. New York: Academic Press, 1982.

———. "Octave Generalization of Specific Interference Effects in Memory for Tonal Pitch." *Perception and Psychophysics* 13 (1973): 271–75.

Deutsch, Diana, ed. *The Psychology of Music*. New York: Academic Press, 1999.

Deutsch, Diana, and Richard C. Boulanger. "Octave Equivalence and the Immediate Recall of Pitch Sequences." *Music Perception* 2 (1984): 40–51.

Dewey, John. *Art as Experience*. New York: Perigee Books, 1934.

DeWoskin, Kenneth. *A Song for One or Two: Music and the Concept of Art in Early China*. Ann Arbor: Center for Chinese Studies, University of Michigan, 1982.

Dissanayake, Ellen. "Antecedents of the Temporal Arts in Early Mother-Infant Interaction." In *The Origins of Music*, edited by Nils L. Wallin, Björn Merker, and Steven Brown, 389–410. Cambridge, MA: MIT Press, 2000.

———. *Art and Intimacy: How the Arts Began*. Seattle: University of Washington Press, 2000.

Donald, Merlin. *Origins of the Modern Mind: Three Stages in the Evolution of Culture and Cognition*. Cambridge, MA: Harvard University Press, 1991.

Dowling, W. Jay. "Melodic Information Processing and Its Development." In *The Psychology of Music*, edited by Diana Deutsch, 413–29. New York: Academic Press, 1982.

———. "Musical Scales and Psychophysical Scales: Their Psychological Reality." In *Cross-Cultural Perspectives on Music*, edited by Robert Falck and Timothy Rice, 20–28. Toronto: University of Toronto Press, 1982.

———. "Scale and Contour: Two Components of a Theory of Memory for Melodies." *Psychological Review* 85 (1978): 342–54.

Dowling, W. Jay, and James C. Bartlett. "The Importance of Interval Information in Long-Term Memory for Melodies." *Psychomusicology* 1 (1981): 30–49.

Dowling, W. Jay, and Diana S. Fujitani. "Contour, Interval, and Pitch Recognition in Memory for Melodies." *Journal of the Acoustical Society of America* 49 (1971): 524–31.

Dowling, W. Jay, and Dane L. Harwood. *Music Cognition*. New York: Academic Press, 1986.

Drake, Carolyn, and Jamel Ben El Heni. "Synchronizing with Music: Intercultural Differences." *Annals of the New York Academy of Sciences* 999 (2003): 428–37.

Drake, Carolyn, and Daisy Bertrand. "The Quest for Universals in Temporal Processing in Music." In *The Cognitive Neuroscience of Music*, edited by Isabelle Peretz and Robert Zatorre, 21–31. Oxford: Oxford University Press, 2003.

Dryden, John. "A Song for St. Cecilia's Day" (1687). In *The Poems of John Dryden*, edited by John Sargeaunt, 196–97. London: Oxford University Press, 1925.

During, Jean. "The System of Persian Music." In *The Art of Persian Music: Lesson from Master Dariush Safvat*, edited by Jean During and Zia Mirabdolbaghi, 57–97. Washington, DC: Mage Publishers, 1991.

Edworthy, Judy. "Interval and Contour in Melody Processing." *Music Perception* 2 (1985): 375–88.

———. "Melodic Contour and Musical Structure." In *Musical Structure and Cognition*, edited by Peter Howell, Ian Cross, and Robert West, 169–88. London: Academic Press, 1985.

Ekman, Paul. "An Argument for Basic Emotions." *Cognition and Emotion* 6 (1992): 169–200.

———. *Emotions Revealed: Recognizing Faces and Feelings to Improve Communication and Emotional Life*. New York: Henry Holt, 2003.

Ekman, Paul, and Richard J. Davidson, eds. *The Nature of Emotion: Fundamental Questions.* New York: Oxford University Press, 1994.

Ellis, Catherine J. *Aboriginal Music, Education for Living: Cross-Cultural Experiences from South Australia.* St. Lucia: University of Queensland Press, 1985.

———. "Pre-Instrumental Scales." *Ethnomusicology* 9, no. 2 (1965): 126–37.

Epstein, David. *Shaping Time: Music, the Brain, and Performance.* New York: Schirmer Books, 1995.

———. "Tempo Relations in Music: A Universal?" In *Beauty and the Brain: Biological Aspects of Aesthetics*, edited by Ingo Rentschler, Barbara Herzberger, and David Epstein, 91–116. Basel: Birkhäuser, 1988.

Erickson, Edwin E. "Tradition and Evolution in Song Style: A Reanalysis of Cantometric Data." *Behavioral Science and Research* 11 (1976): 277–308.

Erickson, Robert. "A Perceptual Substrate for Tonal Centering?" *Music Perception* 2 (1984): 1–5.

Erlmann, Veit. "Trance and Music in the Hausa Boorii Spirit Possession Cult in Niger." *Ethnomusicology* 26, no. 1 (1982): 49–58.

Ernoff, Ron. "A Cajun Poetics of Loss and Longing." *Ethnomusicology* 42, no. 2 (1998): 283–301.

Falck, Robert, and Timothy Rice. *Cross-Cultural Perspectives on Music.* Toronto: University of Toronto Press, 1982.

Falk, Dean. "Hominid Brain Evolution and the Origins of Music." In *The Origins of Music*, edited by Nils L. Wallin, Björn Merker, and Steven Brown, 197–216. Cambridge, MA: MIT Press, 2000.

Feld, Steven. "Aesthetics as Iconicity of Style, or 'Lift-up-over Sounding': Getting into the Kaluli Groove." *Yearbook for Traditional Music* 20 (1988): 74–113.

———. "Communication, Music, and Speech about Music." *Yearbook for Traditional Music* 16 (1984): 1–18.

———. "From Schizophonia to Schismogenesis." In *Music Grooves*, edited by Charles Keil and Steven Feld, 257–90. Chicago: University of Chicago Press, 1994.

———. "Linguistic Models in Ethnomusicology." *Ethnomusicology* 18, no. 2 (1974): 197–217.

———. "Notes on 'World Beat.'" In *Music Grooves*, edited by Charles Keil and Steven Feld, 238–46. Chicago: University of Chicago Press, 1994.

———. *Sound and Sentiment: Birds, Weeping, Poetics, and Song in Kaluli Expression.* Philadelphia: University of Pennsylvania Press, 1982.

———. "Sound Structure as Social Structure." *Ethnomusicology* 28, no. 3 (1984): 383–409.

———. "Waterfalls of Song: An Acoustemology of Place Resounding in Bosavi, Papua New Guinea." In *Senses of Place*, edited by Steven Feld and Keith H. Basso, 91–135. School of American Research Advanced Seminar Series. Santa Fe: School of American Research Press, 1996.

Feld, Steven, and Keith H. Basso, eds. *Senses of Place.* School of American Research Advanced Seminar Series. Santa Fe: School of American Research Press, 1996.

Fernald, Anne. "Intonation and Communicative Intent in Mothers' Speech to Infants: Is the Melody the Message?" *Child Development* 60 (1989): 1497–510.

Fisher, John A. "The New Guinea Drone Beetle vs. the Teutonic Symphony Orchestra: Beholding Music Cross-Culturally." Paper presented at the American Society for Aesthetics Pacific Division Meeting, Asilomar, California, April 1994.

Fishman, Yonatan I., Igor O. Volkov, M. Daniel Noh, P. Charles Garell, Hans Bakken, Joseph C. Arezzo, Matthew A. Howard, and Mitchell Steinschneider. "Consonance and Dissonance of Musical Chords: Neural Correlates in Auditory Cortex of Monkeys and Humans." *Journal of Neurophysiology* 86 (2001): 2761–88.

Fitch, W. Tecumseh. "The Biology and Evolution of Music: A Comparative Perspective." *Cognition* 100 (2006): 173–215.

Forsburgh, L. "World's Oldest Song Reported Deciphered: Near-East Origin." *New York Times*, March 6, 1974, 1 and 18.

Forster, E. M. *A Passage to India*. San Diego: Harcourt, Brace, Jovanovich, 1952.

Francès, Robert. *The Perception of Music*. Translated by W. Jay Dowling. Hillsdale, NJ: Lawrence Erlbaum Associates, 1988.

Freeman, Walter. "A Neurobiological Role of Music in Social Bonding." In *The Origins of Music*, edited by Nils L. Wallin, Björn Merker, and Steven Brown, 411–24. Cambridge, MA: MIT Press, 2000.

———. *Societies of Brains: A Study in the Neuroscience of Love and Hate*. Hillsdale, NJ: Lawrence Erlbaum, 1995.

Freud, Sigmund. *Beyond the Pleasure Principle*. Translated and edited by James Strachey. Introduction and notes by Gregory Zilboorg. New York: W. W. Norton, 1961.

Frick, Robert W. "Communicating Emotion: The Role of Prosodic Features." *Psychological Bulletin* 97 (1985): 412–29.

Frijda, Nico H. *The Emotions*. Studies in Emotion and Social Interaction. Cambridge: Cambridge University Press, 1986.

———. "Varieties of Affect: Emotions and Episodes, Moods, and Sentiments." In *The Nature of Emotion: Fundamental Questions*, edited by Paul Ekman and Richard J. Davidson, 59–67. New York: Oxford University Press, 1994.

Frith, Simon. *Music and Society: The Politics of Composition, Performance, and Reception*. Cambridge: Cambridge University Press, 1987.

Gabrielsson, Alf. "Emotions in Strong Experiences with Music." In *Music and Emotion: Theory and Research*, edited by Patrik Juslin and John A. Sloboda, 431–49. Oxford: Oxford University Press, 2001.

———. "Strong Experiences with Music." In *Handbook of Music and Emotion*, edited by Patrik Juslin and John A. Sloboda, 547–74. Oxford: Oxford University Press, 2010.

Gabrielsson, Alf, and Erik Lindström. "The Influence of Musical Structure on Emotional Expression." In *Music and Emotion: Theory and Research*, edited by Patrik Juslin and John A. Sloboda, 223–48. Oxford: Oxford University Press, 2001.

Gage, John. "Synaesthesia." In *Encyclopedia of Aesthetics*, vol. 4, edited by Michael Kelly, 348–51. New York: Oxford University Press, 1998.

Gardner, Howard. "Metaphors and Modalities: How Children Project Polar Adjectives onto Diverse Domains." *Child Development* 45 (1977): 84–91.

Geissmann, Thomas. "Gibbon Songs and Human Music from an Evolutionary Perspective." In *The Origins of Music*, edited by Nils L. Wallin, Björn Merker, and Steven Brown, 103–23. Cambridge, MA: MIT Press, 2000.

Gerardi, Gina M., and Louann Gerken. "The Development of Affective Response to Modality and Melodic Contour." *Music Perception* 12 (1995): 279–90.

Gerbert, Martin. *Scriptores Ecclesiastici, de Musica Sacra Potissimum*. St. Blaise: Typis San-Blasianis, 1784. Reprint: Hildesheim: Georg Olms, 1963.

Gerow, Edwin. "Abhinavagupta's Aesthetics as a Speculative Paradigm." *Journal of the American Oriental Society* 114, no. 2 (1994): 186–208.

Gettier, Edmund. "Is Justified True Belief Knowledge?" *Analysis* 23, no. 6 (1966): 121–23.

Glausiusz, Josie. "The Genetic Mystery of Music." *Discover* 22, no. 8 (2001): 70–75.

Gnoli, Raniero. *The Aesthetic Experience According to Abhinavagupta*. Rome: Instituto Italiano per il Medio ed Estremo Orient, 1956.

Goehr, Lydia. *The Imaginary Museum of Musical Works*. Oxford: Clarendon Press, 1992.

———. *The Quest for Voice: On Music, Politics, and the Limits of Philosophy*. The Ernest Bloch Lectures. Berkeley: University of California Press, 1998.

Goethe, Johann Wolfgang von. *Goethe's Faust: Part One and Sections from Part Two*. Translated by Walter Kaufmann. Garden City, NY: Doubleday, 1961.

Goldie, Peter. *The Emotions: A Philosophical Exploration*. Oxford: Clarendon Press, 2000.

Goldsmith, H. Hill. "Parsing the Emotional Domain from a Developmental Perspective." In *The Nature of Emotion: Fundamental Questions*, edited by Paul Ekman and Richard J. Davidson, 68–73. New York: Oxford University Press, 1994.

Goodall, Jane. *The Chimpanzees of Gombe: Patterns of Behavior*. Cambridge, MA: Belknap Press of Harvard University Press, 1986.

Goodman, Nelson. *Languages of Art*. 2nd ed. Indianapolis: Hackett Publishing, 1976.

Goswamy, B. N. *Essence of Indian Art*. San Francisco: Asian Art Museum of San Francisco, 1986.

Gould, Stephen J., and R. C. Lewontin. "The Spandrels of San Marco and the Panglossian Paradigm: A Critique of the Adaptationist Programme." *Proceedings of the Royal Society of London*, Series B, Biological Sciences 205: 1161 (September 21, 1979): 581–98.

Gracyk, Theodore. *I Wanna Be Me: Rock Music and the Politics of Identity*. Philadelphia: Temple University Press, 2001.

———. *Rhythm and Noise: An Aesthetics of Rock*. Durham, NC: Duke University Press, 1996.

———. "Valuing and Evaluating Popular Music." *Journal of Aesthetics and Art Criticism* 57, no. 2 (1999): 205–20.

Graham, Gordon. "The Value of Music." *Journal of Aesthetics and Art Criticism* 53, no. 2 (1995): 139–53.

Granit, Ragnar. *The Purposive Brain*. Cambridge, MA: MIT Press, 1977.

Gregory, Andrew, Lisa Worral, and Ann Sarge. "The Development of Emotional Responses to Music in Young Children." *Motivation and Emotion* 20 (1996): 341–49.

Gregory, Stanford W., Jr. "Sounds of Power and Deference: Acoustic Analysis of Macro Social Constraints on Micro Interaction." *Sociological Perspectives* 37, no. 4 (1994): 497–526.

Guernsey, Martha. "The Role of Consonance and Dissonance in Music." *American Journal of Psychology* 40 (1928): 173–204.

Guilbault, Jocelyne. "Fitness and Flexibility: Funeral Wakes in St. Lucia, West Indies." *Ethnomusicology* 31, no. 3 (1987): 273–99.

Hamilton, James R. "Musical Noise." *British Journal of Aesthetics* 39, no. 4 (1999): 350–63.

Hamilton, John T. *Music, Madness, and the Unworking of Language*. New York: Columbia University Press, 2008.

Hamm, Charles. "Graceland Revisited." *Popular Music* 8 (1989): 299–304.

Hanslick, Eduard. *Music Criticisms, 1846–99*. Edited and translated by Henry Pleasants. New York: Dover, 1988.

———. *On the Musically Beautiful*. Translated by Geoffrey Payzant. Indianapolis: Hackett Publishing, 1986.

Harrán, Don. *Word-Tone Relations in Musical Thought, from Antiquity to the Seventeenth Century*. American Institute of Musicology. Neuhausen-Stuttgart: Hänssler-Verlag, 1986.

Harris, Zellig S. "From Phoneme to Morpheme." *Language* 31 (1955): 190–222.

Harrison, Frank. "Universals in Music: Towards a Methodology of Comparative Research." *World of Music* 19, no. 1/2 (1977): 35–36.

Hartshorne, Charles. "Metaphysics Contributes to Ornithology." *Theoria to Theory* 13 (1979): 127–40.

———. *The Philosophy and Psychology of Sensation*. Chicago: University of Chicago Press, 1934.

Harwood, Dane L. "Universals in Music: A Perspective from Cognitive Psychology." *Ethnomusicology* 20, no. 3 (1976): 521–33.

Hatfield, Elaine, John T. Cacioppo, and Richard L. Rapson. *Emotional Contagion*. New York: Cambridge University Press, 1994.

Hawkins, Sir John. *A General History of the Science and Practice of Music*. London: Novello, 1875.

Hegel, G. W. F. *Aesthetics: Lectures on Fine Art*. Edited by F. Bassenge (1842). Translated by T. M. Knox. Oxford: Clarendon Press, 1975.

Helson, Harry. *Adaptation-Level Theory: An Experimental and Systematic Approach to Behavior*. New York: Harper and Row, 1964.

Henderson, David. "Emotion and Devotion, Lingering and Longing in Some Nepali Songs." *Ethnomusicology* 40, no. 3, Special Issue: Music and Religion (1996): 440–68.

Henson, R. A. "The Language of Music." In *Music and the Brain: Studies in the Neurology of Music*, edited by MacDonald Critchley and R. A. Henson, 233–54. London: William Heinemann Medical Books, 1977.

Herndon, Marcia. "Analysis: The Herding of Sacred Cows?" *Ethnomusicology* 18, no. 2 (1974): 248.

Herndon, Marcia, and Norma McLeod. *Music as Culture*. Darby, PA: Norwood Editions, 1980.

Herzog, George. "Music in the Thinking of the American Indian." *Peabody Bulletin* (May 1983): 8–12.

———. "Speech Melody and Primitive Music." *Musical Quarterly* 20 (1934): 425–66.

Hevner, Kate. "The Affective Character of the Major and Minor Mode in Music." *American Journal of Psychology* 47 (1935): 103–18.

———. "The Affective Value of Pitch and Tempo in Music." *American Journal of Psychology* 49 (1937): 621–30.

———. "Experimental Studies of the Elements of Expression in Music." *American Journal of Psychology* 48 (1936): 248–68.

———. "Expression in Music: A Discussion of Experimental Studies and Theories." *Psychological Review* 42 (1935): 186–204.

Higgins, Kathleen Marie. *The Music of Our Lives*. Philadelphia: Temple University Press, 1991. Reissued: Lanham, MD: Lexington Books, 2011.

———. "Musical Idiosyncrasy and Perspectival Listening." In *Music and Meaning*, edited by Jenefer Robinson, 83–102. Ithaca, NY: Cornell University Press, 1997.

Hindemith, Paul. *A Composer's World: Horizons and Limitations*. The Norton Lectures. Gloucester, MA: Peter Smith, 1952.

Hirsh-Pasek, Kathy, Deborah G. Kelmer Nelson, Peter W. Jusczyk, Kimberly Wright Cassidy, Benjamin Druss, and Lori Kennedy. "Clauses Are Perceptual Units for Young Infants." *Cognition* 26 (1987): 269–86.

Hodeir, André. *Jazz: Its Evolution and Essence*. Translated by David Noakes. New York: Grove Press, 1956.

Hodges, Donald A. "Human Musicality." In *Handbook of Music Psychology*, 2nd ed., edited by Donald A. Hodges, 29–68. San Antonio: IMR Press, 1996.

———. "Neuromusical Research: A Review of the Literature." In *Handbook of Music Psychology*, 2nd ed., edited by Donald A. Hodges, 197–284. San Antonio: IMR Press, 1996.

———. "Psycho-Physiological Measures." In *Handbook of Music and Emotions: Theory, Research, Applications*, edited by Patrik N. Juslin and John A. Sloboda, 279–311. Oxford: Oxford University Press, 2010.

Hodges, Donald A., ed. *Handbook of Music Psychology*. 2nd ed. San Antonio: IMR Press, 1996.

Hoffmann, E. T. A. "The Poet and the Composer" (1816). Abridged. In *The Romantic Era*. Vol. 5 of *Source Readings in Music History*, edited by Oliver Strunk, 42–57. New York: W. W. Norton, 1965.

Hood, Mantel. "Slendro and Pelog Redefined." In *Selected Reports in Ethnomusicology* 1, 36–48. Institute of Ethnomusicology, University of California at Los Angeles, 1966.

———. "Universal Attributes of Music." *World of Music* 19, no. 1/2 (1977): 79.

Hopkins, Pandora. "Aural Thinking." In *Cross-Cultural Perspectives on Music*, edited by Robert Falck and Timothy Rice, 143–61. Toronto: University of Toronto Press, 1982.

Hornbostel, E. M. von. "The Unity of the Senses." *Psyche* 7 (1926): 83–89.

Houtsma, A. J. M., and J. L. Goldstein. "The Central Origin of the Pitch of Complex Tones: Evidence from Musical Interval Recognition." *Journal of the Acoustical Society of America* 51 (1971): 520–29.

Howard Hughes Medical Institute. "Channel Protein Converts Vibrations to Electrical Signal." October 13, 2004.

Hsün Tzu (Xunzi). *Basic Writings*. Translated by Burton Watson. New York: Columbia University Press, 1963.

Hubbard, Timothy L. "Synesthesia-Like Mappings of Lightness, Pitch, and Melodic Interval." *American Journal of Psychology* 109, no. 2 (1996): 219–39.

Hullah, John Pyke. *History of Modern Music.* Lectures delivered at the Institute of Great Britain. London: Parker, Son, and Bourn, 1862.

Hulse, Steward H., Annie H. Takeuchi, and Richard F. Braaten. "Perceptual Invariances in the Comparative Psychology of Music." *Music Perception* 10 (1992): 151–84.

Hunt, Gavin R., and Russell D. Gray. "Diversification and Cumulative Evolution in New Caledonian Crow Tool Manufacture." *Proceedings of the Royal Society of London B* 270 (2003): 867–74.

Huron, David. *Sweet Anticipation: Music and the Psychology of Expectation.* Cambridge, MA: MIT Press, 2006.

Husain, Gabriela, William Forde Thompson, and E. Glenn Schellenberg. "Effects of Musical Tempo and Mode on Arousal, Mood, and Spatial Abilities." *Music Perception* 20, no. 2 (2002): 151–71.

Huttenlocher, Janellen, and Deborah Burke. "Why Does Memory Span Increase with Age?" *Cognitive Psychology* 8 (1976): 1–31.

Idel, Moseh. "Conceptualizations of Music in Jewish Mysticism." In *Enchanting Powers: Music in the World's Religions*, edited by Lawrence Sullivan, 159–88. Cambridge, MA: Harvard University Press, 1997.

Idson, Wendy L., and Dominic W. Massaro. "A Bidimensional Model of Pitch in the Recognition of Melodies." *Perception and Psychophysics* 24 (1978): 551–65.

Imberty, Michel. *Entendre la musique.* Paris: Dunot, 1979.

———. "The Question of Innate Competencies in Musical Communication." In *The Origins of Music*, edited by Nils L. Wallin, Björn Merker, and Steven Brown, 449–62. Cambridge, MA: MIT Press, 2000.

Iversen, John R., Aniruddh Patel, and Kengo Ohgushi. "Perception of Nonlinguistic Rhythmic Stimuli by American and Japanese Listeners." Proceedings of the Eighth International Congress of Acoustics, Kyoto, Japan, 2004. Presented in popular form in John R. Iversen and Kengo Ohgushi. "How the Mother Tongue Influences the Musical Ear." http://www.acoustics.org/press/152nd/iversen_patel_ohgushi.html.

Iyer, Vijay. "Embodied Mind, Situated Cognition, and Expressive Microtiming in African-American Music." *Music Perception* 19, no. 3 (2002): 387–414.

Jackendoff, Ray. "Musical Processing and Musical Affect." In *Cognitive Bases of Musical Communication*, edited by Mari Riess Jones and Susan Holleran, 51–68. Washington, DC: American Psychological Association, 1992.

Jackson, J. H. "Singing by Speechless (Aphasic) Children." *Lancet* 2 (1871): 430–31.

James, William. *The Principles of Psychology.* New York: Dover, 1950.

Johnstone, Tom, and Klaus R. Scherer. "Vocal Communication of Emotion." In *Handbook of Emotions*, 2nd ed., edited by Michael Lewis and Jeanette M. Haviland, 220–35. New York: Guildford Press, 2000.

Jourdain, Robert. *Music, the Brain, and Ecstasy: How Music Captures Our Imagination.* New York: Avon Books, 1997.

Jürgens, Uwe. "Vocalization as an Emotion Indicator: A Neuroethological Study in the Squirrel Monkey." *Behaviour* 69 (1979): 88–117.

Juslin, Patrik N. "Communicating Emotion in Music Performance." In *Music and Emotions: Theory and Research*, edited by Patrik N. Juslin and John A. Sloboda, 309–37. Oxford: Oxford University Press, 2001.

———. "Emotional Communication in Music Performance: A Functionalist Perspective and Some Data." *Music Perception* 14 (1997): 383–418.

———. "How Does Music Arouse Emotions in Listeners? The AMUSE Project." Paper presented at the general meeting of the International Society for Research on the Emotions, University of Bari, Italy, July 13, 2005.

———. "Perceived Emotional Expression in Synthesized Performances of a Short Melody: Capturing the Listener's Judgment Policy." *Musicae Scientiae* 1 (1997): 225–56.

Juslin, Patrik N., and Petri Laukka. "Communication of Emotions in Vocal Expression and Music Performance: Different Channels, Same Code?" *Psychological Bulletin* 129, no. 5 (2003): 770–814.

———. "Expression, Perception, and Induction of Musical Emotions: A Review and a Questionnaire Study of Everyday Listening." *Journal of New Music Research* 33, no. 3 (2004): 217–38.

Juslin, Patrik N., Petri Laukka, Daniel Västfjäll, and O. L. Lundqvist. "A Questionnaire Study of Emotion Reactions to Music in Everyday Life." A paper presented at the general meeting of the International Society for Research on the Emotions, University of Bari, July 12, 2005.

Juslin, Patrik N., Simon Liljeström, Daniel Västfjäll, Gonçalo Barradas, and Ana Silva. "An Experience Sampling Study of Emotional Reactions to Music: Listener, Music, and Situation." *Emotion* 8 (2008): 668–83.

Juslin, Patrik N., and John A. Sloboda, eds. *Handbook of Music and Emotions: Theory, Research, Applications*. Oxford: Oxford University Press, 2010.

———. *Music and Emotion: Theory and Research*. Oxford: Oxford University Press, 2001.

Juslin, Patrik N., and Renee Timmers. "Expression and Communication of Emotion in Music Performance." In *Handbook of Music and Emotion: Theory, Research, Applications*, edited by Patrik N. Juslin and John A. Sloboda, 453–89. Oxford: Oxford University Press, 2010.

Juslin, Patrik N., and Daniel Västfjäll. "Emotional Responses to Music: The Need to Consider Underlying Mechanisms." *Behavioral and Brain Sciences* 31 (2008): 559–75.

Kagan, Jerome. "Distinctions among Emotions, Moods, and Temperamental Qualities." In *The Nature of Emotion: Fundamental Questions*, edited by Paul Ekman and Richard J. Davidson, 74–78. New York: Oxford University Press, 1994.

Kallman, Howard J., and Dominic W. Massaro. "Tone Chroma Is Functional in Melody Recognition." *Perception and Psychophysics* 26 (1979): 32–36.

Kant, Immanuel. *Critique of Judgment*. Translated by Werner S. Pluhar. Indianapolis: Hackett Publishing, 1987.

———. *Groundwork of the Metaphysic of Morals*. 3rd ed. Translated by H. J. Paton. New York: Harper and Row, 1964.

Karl, Gregory, and Jenefer Robinson. "Shostakovich's Tenth Symphony." In *Music and Meaning*, edited by Jenefer Robinson, 154–78. Ithaca, NY: Cornell University Press, 1997.

Katz, Richard. "Accepting 'Boiling Energy': The Experience of !Kia Healing among the !Kung." *Ethos: Journal of the Society for Psychological Anthropology* 19 (1982): 344–68.

Katz, Ruth. *A Language of Its Own: Sense and Meaning in the Making of Western Art Music.* Chicago: University of Chicago Press, 2009.

Keil, Charles. "Motion and Feeling through Music." *Journal of Aesthetics and Art Criticism* 24, no. 3 (1966): 337–50.

———. "Participatory Discrepancies and the Power of Music." *Cultural Anthropology* 2, no. 3 (1987): 275–83.

———. *Polka Happiness.* Philadelphia: Temple University Press, 1987.

———. "The Theory of Participatory Discrepancies: A Progress Report." *Ethnomusicology* 39, Special Issue: Participatory Discrepancies (1995): 1–19.

———. *Tiv Song: The Sociology of Art in a Classless Society.* Chicago: University of Chicago Press, 1979.

Kenealy, Pamela M. "Mood-State-Dependent Retrieval: The Effects of Induced Mood on Memory Reconsidered." *Quarterly Journal of Experimental Psychology: Human Experimental Psychology* 50A (1997): 290–317.

———. "Validation of a Music Mood Induction Procedure: Some Preliminary Findings." *Cognition and Emotion* 2 (1988): 41–48.

Kennick, William E. "Art and the Ineffable." *Journal of Philosophy* 58 (1961): 309–20.

Kieran, Matthew, ed. *Contemporary Debates in Aesthetics and the Philosophy of Art.* Malden, MA: Blackwell, 2006.

Kilmer, Anne Draffkorn, Richard L. Crocker, and Robert R. Brown. *Sounds from Silence: Recent Discoveries in Ancient Near Eastern Music.* Berkeley: Bit Enki Publications, 1976.

Kivy, Peter. "Feeling the Musical Emotions." *British Journal of Aesthetics* 39, no. 1 (1999): 1–13.

———. *Introduction to a Philosophy of Music.* Oxford: Oxford University Press, 2002.

———. "Platonism in Music: A Kind of Defense." *Grazer Philosophische Studien* 19 (1983): 123–28.

———. "Something I've Always Wanted to Know about Hanslick." *Journal of Aesthetics and Art Criticism* 46, no. 4 (1988): 413–17.

———. *Sound and Semblance: Reflections on Musical Representation.* Princeton, NJ: Princeton University Press, 1984.

———. *Sound Sentiment: An Essay on the Musical Emotions, Including the Complete Text of The Corded Shell.* Philadelphia: Temple University Press, 1989.

Koelsch, Stefan, Elisabeth Kasper, Daniela Sammler, Katrin Schulze, Thomas Gunter, and Angela D. Friederici. "Music, Language, and Meaning: Brain Signatures of Semantic Processing." *Nature Neuroscience* 7, no. 3 (2004): 302–7.

Koffka, Kurt. *Principles of Gestalt Psychology.* New York: Harcourt, Brace, and World, 1935.

Kolinsky, Mieczyslaw. "'Barbara Allen': Tonal versus Melodic Structure, Part I." *Ethnomusicology* 12, no. 4 (1968): 208–18.

———. "'Barbara Allen': Tonal versus Melodic Structure, Part II." *Ethnomusicology* 13, no. 1 (1969): 1–73.

Koopman, Constantijn, and Stephen Davies. "Musical Meaning in a Broader Perspective." *Journal of Aesthetics and Art Criticism* 59, no. 3 (2001): 261–74.

Kramer, Hilton, and Roger Kimball, eds. *The Future of the European Past*. Chicago: Ivan R. Dee, 1997.

Krumhansl, Carol L. "An Exploratory Study of Musical Emotion and Psychophysiology." *Canadian Journal of Experimental Psychology* 51 (1997): 336–52.

Krumhansl, Carol L., and Petri Toivianinen. "Tonal Cognition." In *The Cognitive Neuroscience of Music*, edited by Isabelle Peretz and Robert Zatorre, 95–108. Oxford: Oxford University Press, 2003.

Ladd, D. R., and J. Terken. "Modeling Intra- and Inter-Speaker Pitch Range Variation." *International Congress of Phonetic Sciences* 13 (Stockholm 2) (1995): 386–89.

Laing, R. D. *The Divided Self: An Existential Study in Sanity and Madness*. Harmondsworth: Penguin, 1960.

Lakoff, George, and Mark Johnson. *Metaphors We Live By*. Chicago: University of Chicago Press, 2003.

Langeheinecke, E. J., H.-U. Schnitzler, M. Hischer-Burhmeister, and K.-E. Behne. "Emotions in Singing Voice: Acoustic Cues for Joy, Fear, Anger, and Sadness." Poster presented at the Joint Meeting of the Acoustical Society of America and the Acoustical Society of Germany, Berlin, March 1999.

Langer, Susanne K. *Feeling and Form: A Theory of Art*. New York: Scribner, 1953.

———. *Philosophy in a New Key: A Study in the Symbolism of Reason, Rite, and Art*. Cambridge, MA: Harvard University Press, 1957.

Larkin, Philip. "Looking Back at Coltrane" (August 1967). In *All What Jazz: A Record Diary, 1961–1971*, rev. ed., 186–88. New York: Farrar, Straus, Giroux, 1985.

Lawson, Katharine Rieke, and Gerald Turkewitz. "Intersensory Function in Newborns: Effect of Sound of Visual Preferences." *Child Development* 51 (1980): 1295–98.

Lazarus, Richard. "The Stable and the Unstable in Emotion." In *The Nature of Emotion: Fundamental Questions*, edited by Paul Ekman and Richard J. Davidson, 79–85. New York: Oxford University Press, 1994.

Legge, James, ed. and trans. *The She King, or the Book of Poetry*. In vol. 4 of *The Chinese Classics*, edited by James Legge. Hong Kong: Hong Kong University Press, 1960.

Legge, James, trans. *Yo Kī* ("Record of Music"). In *The Sacred Books of China, Part 4: The Li Ki*, XI–XLVI. Delhi: Motilal Banarsidass, 1968.

Lerdahl, Fred. "The Sounds of Poetry Viewed as Music." In *The Cognitive Neuroscience of Music*, edited by Isabelle Peretz and Robert Zatorre, 413–29. Oxford: Oxford University Press, 2003.

———. "Cognitive Constraints on Compositional Systems." In *Generative Processes in Music: The Psychology of Performance, Improvisation, and Composition*, edited by John A. Sloboda, 231–59. Oxford: Clarendon Press, 1988.

Lerdahl, Fred, and Ray Jackendoff. *A Generative Theory of Tonal Music*. Cambridge, MA: MIT Press, 1983.

Levinson, Jerrold. "The Concept of Music." In *Music, Art, and Metaphysics: Essays in Philosophical Aesthetics*, 267–78. Ithaca, NY: Cornell University Press, 1990.

———. "Hope in *The Hebrides*." In *Music, Art, and Metaphysics: Essays in Philosophical Aesthetics*, 336–75. Ithaca, NY: Cornell University Press, 1990.

———. "Music and Negative Emotion." In *Music, Art, and Metaphysics: Essays in Philosophical Aesthetics*, 306–35. Ithaca, NY: Cornell University Press, 1990.

———. *Music, Art, and Metaphysics: Essays in Philosophical Aesthetics*. Ithaca, NY: Cornell University Press, 1990.

———. *Music in the Moment*. Ithaca, NY: Cornell University Press, 1997.

———. "Musical Expressiveness as Hearability-as-Expression." In *Contemporary Debates in Aesthetics and the Philosophy of Art*, edited by Matthew Kieran, 192–221. Malden, MA: Blackwell, 2006.

———. *The Pleasures of Aesthetics: Philosophical Essays*. Ithaca, NY: Cornell University Press, 1996.

Lévi-Strauss, Claude. *The Raw and the Cooked: Introduction to a Science of Mythology*. Translated by John and Doreen Weightman. New York: Harper and Row, 1969.

Levitin, Daniel J. *The World in Six Songs: How the Musical Brain Created Human Nature*. New York: Penguin, 2008.

———. *This Is Your Brain on Music: The Science of a Human Obsession*. New York: Penguin, 2006.

Lewis, Michael, and Jeannette M. Haviland, eds. *Handbook of Emotions*. New York: Guilford, 1993.

Liberman, Mark, and Janet Pierrehumbert. "Intonational Invariance under Changes in Pitch Range and Length." In *Language Sound Structure: Studies in Phonology*, edited by Mark Aronoff and Richard Oerhle, 157–233. Cambridge, MA: MIT Press, 1984.

Lidov, David. *Is Language a Music?: Writings on Musical Form and Signification*. Bloomington: Indiana University Press, 2005.

Liégeois-Chauvel, Catherine, Kimberly Giraud, Jean-Michel Badier, Patrick Marquis, and Patrick Chauvel. "Intracerebral Evoked Potentials in Pitch Perception Reveal a Functional Asymmetry of Human Auditory Cortex." In *The Cognitive Neuroscience of Music*, edited by Isabelle Peretz and Robert Zatorre, 152–67. Oxford: Oxford University Press, 2003.

Lippman, Edward. *A History of Western Musical Aesthetics*. Lincoln: University of Nebraska Press, 1992.

———. *A Humanistic Philosophy of Music*. New York: New York University Press, 1977.

———. "Symbolism in Music." *Musical Quarterly* 39 (1953): 554–75.

Lippman, Edward, ed. *Musical Aesthetics: A Historical Reader*. Vol. 1, *From Antiquity to the Eighteenth Century*. Aesthetics in Music 4. New York: Pendragon Press, 1986.

Lipscomb, Scott D. "Cognitive Organization of Musical Sound." In *Handbook of Music Psychology*, 2nd ed., edited by Donald A. Hodges, 154–61. San Antonio: IMR Press, 1996.

Liszt, Franz. "Berlioz and His 'Harold' Symphony" (abridged). In *Source Readings in Music History: The Romantic Era*, edited by Oliver Strunk, 107–33. New York: W. W. Norton, 1965.

Locke, Simeon, and Lucia Kellar. "Categorical Perception in a Non-Linguistic Mode." *Cortex* 9 (1973): 355–68.

Lockspeiser, Edward. *Debussy: His Life and Mind.* Vol. 1. London: Cassell, 1962.

Lomax, Alan. "Appeal for Cultural Equity." *Journal of Communication* 27 (1977): 125–39.

——. *Cantometrics: An Approach to the Anthropology of Music.* Berkeley: University of California Extension Media Center, 1976.

——. "Folk Song Style." In *The Garland Library of Readings in Ethnomusicology,* vol. 3, edited by Kay Kaufmann Shelemay, 59–68. New York: Garland Publishing, 1990. Originally published in *American Anthropologist* 61 (1959): 927–54.

——. "Song Structure and Social Structure." In *Readings in Ethnomusicology,* edited by David P. McAllester, 227–52. New York: Johnson Reprint, 1971. Originally published in *Ethnology* 1 (1962): 425–51.

Lomax, Alan, and Norman Berkowitz. "The Evolutionary Taxonomy of Culture." *Science* 177 (1972): 228–39.

London, Justin. *Hearing in Time: Psychological Aspects of Musical Meter.* New York: Oxford University Press, 2004.

——. "Musical and Linguistic Speech Acts." *Journal of Aesthetics and Art Criticism* 54, no. 1 (1996): 49–64.

Longfellow, Henry Wadsworth. "Ancient Spanish Ballads." In *Outre-Mer, A Pilgrimage beyond the Sea.* 3rd ed. Boston: William D. Ticknor, 1846/1848.

Lorenz, Konrad. "Über die Enstehung auslösender 'Zeremonien.'" *Die Vogelwarte* 16 (1951): 9–13.

Lucretius. *On the Nature of Things (De Rerum Natura).* Translated by Martin Ferguson Smith. Revised translation. Indianapolis: Hackett Publishing, 2001.

Lugones, María. "Playfulness, 'World'-Traveling, and Loving Perception." *Hypatia* 2 (1987): 3–19.

Lynch, Michael P., and Rebecca E. Eilers. "Children's Perception of Native and Nonnative Musical Scales." *Music Perception* 9, no. 1 (1991): 121–32.

Lynch, Michael P., Lori B. Short, and Rosario Chua. "Contributions of Experience to the Development of Musical Processing in Infancy." *Developmental Psychobiology* 28 (1995): 377–98.

Mâche, François-Bernard. "The Necessity of and Problems with a Universal Musicology." In *The Origins of Music,* edited by Nils L. Wallin, Björn Merker, and Steven Brown, 473–79. Cambridge, MA: MIT Press, 2000.

Maconie, Robin. *The Second Sense: Language, Music, and Hearing.* Lanham, MD: Scarecrow Press, 2002.

Maess, Burkhard, Stefan Koelsch, Thomas C. Gunter, and Angela D. Friederici. "Broca's Area: An MEG Study." *Nature Neuroscience* 4, no. 5 (2001): 540–43.

Malm, W. P. *Music Cultures of the Pacific, the Near East, and Asia.* Englewood Cliffs, NJ: Prentice-Hall, 1967.

Malmberg, Constantine Frithiof. "The Perception of Consonance and Dissonance." *Psychological Monographs* 25 (1918): 93–133.

Mandler, George. *Mind and Body: Psychology of Emotion and Stress.* New York: Norton, 1984.

Manstead, Antony S. R., Nico Frijda, and Agneta Fischer. *Feelings and Emotions: The Amsterdam Symposium*. Cambridge: Cambridge University Press, 2004.

Marin, Oscar S. M., and David W. Perry. "Neurological Aspects of Music Perception and Performance." In *The Psychology of Music*, edited by Diana Deutsch, 653–724. San Diego: Academic Press, 1999.

Marks, Lawrence E. "On Colored-Hearing Synaesthesia: Cross-Modal Translations of Sensory Dimensions." *Psychological Bulletin* 82, no. 3 (1975): 303–31.

———. *The Unity of the Senses: Interrelations among the Modalities*. New York: Academic Press, 1978.

Marks, Lawrence E., Robin J. Hammeal, and Marc H. Bornstein. *Perceiving Similarity and Comprehending Metaphor*. Commentary by Linda B. Smith. Monographs of the Society for Research in Child Development, serial no. 215, 52, no. 1 (1987).

Marler, Peter. "Origins of Music and Speech: Insights from Animals." In *The Origins of Music*, edited by Nils L. Wallin, Björn Merker, and Steven Brown, 31–48. Cambridge, MA: MIT Press, 2000.

Marler, Peter, and Christopher S. Evans. "Bird Calls: Just Emotional Displays or Something More?" *Ibis* 138 (1996): 26–331.

Marler, Peter, C. S. Evans, and Marc D. Hauser. "Animal Signals: Reference, Motivation, or Both?" In *Nonverbal Vocal Communication: Comparative and Developmental Approaches*, edited by Hanus Papousek, Uwe Jürgens, and Mechthild Papousek, 66–86. Cambridge: Cambridge University Press, 1992.

Martin, Martha Ann, and Arlene Metha. "Recall of Early Childhood Memories through Musical Mood Induction." *Arts in Psychotherapy* 24 (1997): 447–54.

Matravers, Derek. "Once More with Feeling: A Reply to Ridley." *British Journal of Aesthetics* 34, no. 2 (1994): 174–76.

Maus, Fred Everett. "Music as Drama." In *Music and Meaning*, edited by Jenefer Robinson, 105–30. Ithaca, NY: Cornell University Press, 1999.

———. "Narrative, Drama, and Emotion in Instrumental Music." *Journal of Aesthetics and Art Criticism* 55, no. 3 (1997): 293–303.

McAdams, Stephen, and Emmanuel Bigand, eds. *Thinking in Sound: The Cognitive Psychology of Human Audition*. New York: Oxford University Press, 1993.

McAdams, Stephen, and Daniel Matzkin. "The Roots of Musical Variation in Perceptual Similarity and Invariance." In *The Cognitive Neuroscience of Music*, edited by Isabelle Peretz and Robert Zatorre, 79–94. Oxford: Oxford University Press, 2003.

McAllester, David. *Enemy Way Music: A Study of Social and Esthetic Values as Seen in Navaho Music*. Papers of the Peabody Museum of American Archaeology and Ethnology, Harvard University, XLI, no. 3. Cambridge, MA: The Peabody Museum, 1954.

———. "Some Thoughts on 'Universals' in World Music." *Ethnomusicology* 15, no. 3 (1971): 379–80.

McAllester, David, ed. *Readings in Ethnomusicology*. New York: Johnson Reprint, 1971.

McClelland, David C., et al. *The Achievement Motive*. New York: Appleton-Century-Crofts, 1953.

McFee, Graham. "Meaning and the Art-Status of 'Music Alone.'" *British Journal of Aesthetics* 37, no. 1 (1997): 31–46.

Mehler, Jacques, Peter Jusczyk, Ghislaine Lambertz, Nilofar Halsted, Josiane Bertoncini, and Claudine Amiel-Tison. "A Precursor of Language Acquisition in Young Infants." *Cognition* 29 (1988): 144–78.

Mélen, Marc, and Julie Wachsmann. "Categorization of Musical Motifs in Infancy." *Music Perception* 18, no. 3 (2001): 325–46.

Merker, Björn. "Synchronous Chorusing and Human Origins." In *The Origins of Music*, edited by Nils L. Wallin, Björn Merker, and Steven Brown, 315–27. Cambridge, MA: MIT Press, 2000.

Merleau-Ponty, Maurice. *The Primacy of Perception*. Edited by James M. Edie. Translated by William Cobb et al. Evanston, IL: Northwestern University Press, 1964.

Merriam. Alan P. *The Anthropology of Music*. Evanston, IL: Northwestern University Press, 1964.

Meyer, Leonard B. *Emotion and Meaning in Music*. Chicago: University of Chicago Press, 1956.

———. "Music and Emotions: Distinctions and Uncertainties." In *Music and Emotion: Theory and Research*, edited by Patrik Juslin and John A. Sloboda, 341–60. Oxford: Oxford University Press, 2001.

———. "A Pride of Prejudices; or, Delight in Diversity." In *Spheres of Music: A Gathering of Essays*. Chicago: University of Chicago Press, 2000.

———. "On Rehearing Music." In *Music, the Arts, and Ideas: Patterns and Predictions in 20th-Century Culture*, 42–53. Chicago: University of Chicago Press, 1967. Originally published in *Journal of the American Musicological Society* 14, no. 2 (1961): 257–67.

———. "Some Remarks on Value and Greatness in Music." In *Music, the Arts, and Ideas: Patterns and Predictions in 20th-Century Culture*, 22–41. Chicago: University of Chicago Press, 1967.

———. *The Spheres of Music: A Gathering of Essays*. Chicago: University of Chicago Press, 2000.

———. *Style and Music: Theory, History, and Ideology*. Philadelphia: University of Pennsylvania Press, 1989.

———. "Universalism and Relativism in the Study of Ethnic Music." *Ethnomusicology* 4, no. 1 (1960): 49–54.

———. "A Universe of Universals." In *The Spheres of Music: A Gathering of Essays*, 281–303. Chicago: University of Chicago Press, 2000.

Miller, Geoffrey. "Evolution of Human Music through Sexual Selection." In *The Origins of Music*, edited by Nils L. Wallin, Björn Merker, and Steven Brown, 329–60. Cambridge, MA: MIT Press, 2000.

Miller, George A. "The Magical Number Seven, Plus or Minus Two: Some Limitations on Our Capacity for Processing Information." *Psychological Review* 63 (1956): 81–97.

Miller, Lloyd Clifton. *Music and Song in Persia: The Art of Āvāz*. Richmond: Surrey Curzon, 1999.

Mithen, Steven. *The Singing Neanderthal: The Origins of Music, Language, Mind, and Body*. London: Orion Publishing, 2005.

Molino, Jean. "Toward an Evolutionary Theory of Music and Language." In *The Origins of*

Music, edited by Nils L. Wallin, Björn Merker, and Steven Brown, 165–76. Cambridge, MA: MIT Press, 2000.

Monahan, Caroline B. "Parallels between Pitch and Time: The Determinants of Musical Space." PhD diss., University of California, Los Angeles, 1984.

Monahan, Caroline B., and Edward C. Carterette. "Pitch and Duration as Determinants of Musical Space." *Music Perception* 3 (1985): 1–32.

Morgan, James L. *From Simple Input to Complex Grammar*. Cambridge, MA: MIT Press, 1986.

Morley, Thomas. *A Plain and Easy Introduction to Practical Music*. Edited by R. Alec Harman. 1597. New York: Norton, 1952.

Morrongello, Barabara A. "Auditory Temporal Pattern Perception in 6- and 12-Month Old Infants." *Developmental Psychology* 20 (1984): 441–48.

Morton, Eugene S. "On the Occurrence and Significance of Motivation-Structural Rules in Some Birds and Mammal Sounds." *American Naturalist* 111 (1977): 855–69.

Nasr, Seyyed Hossein. "Islam and Music: The Legal and the Spiritual Dimensions." In *Enchanting Powers: Music in the World's Religions*, edited by Lawrence Sullivan, 219–35. Cambridge, MA: Harvard University Press, 1997.

National Aeronautics and Space Administration website. http://voyager.jpl.nasa.gov/spacecraft/languages/background.html.

Nattiez, Jean-Jacques. *Music and Discourse: Toward a Semiology of Music*. Translated by Carolyn Abbate. Princeton, NJ: Princeton University Press, 1990.

———. "Under What Conditions Can One Speak of the Universals of Music?" *The World of Music* 19, no. 1/2 (1977): 92–105.

Néda, Z., E. Ravasz, Y. Brechet, T. Vicsek, and A.-L. Barabási. "The Sound of Many Hands Clapping." *Nature* 403 (2000): 849–50.

Neisser, Uric. *Cognition and Reality*. San Francisco: Freeman, 1976.

Neo-Futurists. *Too Much Light Makes the Baby Go Blind*. First performed December 2, 1988.

Nettl, Bruno. "An Ethnomusicologist Contemplates Universals in Musical Sound and Musical Culture." In *The Origins of Music*, edited by Nils L. Wallin, Björn Merker, and Steven Brown, 463–72. Cambridge, MA: MIT Press, 2000.

———. "On the Question of Universals." *The World of Music* 19, no. 1/2 (1977): 2–7.

Newcomb, Anthony. "Action and Agency in Mahler's Ninth Symphony, Second Movement." In *Music and Meaning*, edited by Jenefer Robinson, 131–53. Ithaca, NY: Cornell University Press, 1997.

———. "Once More 'Between Absolute and Program Music': Schumann's Second Symphony." *19th-Century Music* 7 (1984): 233–50.

———. "Sound and Feeling." *Critical Inquiry* 10 (1984): 623–41.

Nielzén, Sören, and Zvonimir Cesarec. "On the Perception of Emotional Meaning in Music." *Psychology of Music* 9 (1981): 17–31.

Nietzsche, Friedrich. *Beyond Good and Evil: Prelude to the Philosophy of the Future*. Translated by Walter Kaufmann. New York: Random House, 1966.

———. *The Birth of Tragedy, together with The Case of Wagner*. Translated by Walter Kaufmann. New York: Random House, 1967.

————. *The Gay Science, with a Prelude in Rhymes and an Appendix of Songs.* Translated by Walter Kaufmann. New York: Random House, 1974.

————. *Twilight of the Idols.* Translated by Walter Kaufmann. In *The Portable Nietzsche*, edited by Walter Kaufmann. New York: Viking, 1954.

Nooteboom, S. G., and J. G. Kruyt. "Accents, Focus Distribution, and Perceived Distribution of Given and New Information: An Experiment." *Journal of the Acoustical Society of America* 82 (1987): 1512–24.

Nordau, Max. *Degeneration.* Translated from the 2nd German ed. Introduction by George L. Moss. 1892. New York: Howard Fertig, 1968.

Nussbaum, Charles O. *The Musical Representation: Meaning, Ontology, and Emotion.* Cambridge, MA: MIT Press, 2007.

Nussbaum, Martha C. *Upheavals of Thought: The Intelligence of Emotions.* Cambridge: Cambridge University Press, 2001.

Ochs, Elinor, and Bambi B. Shieffelin. "Language Acquisition and Socialization." In *Culture Theory: Essays on Mind, Self, and Emotion*, edited by Richard A. Shweder and Robert A. LeVine, 276–320. New York: Cambridge University Press, 1984.

Ohala, John J. "Cross-Language Use of Pitch: An Ethological View." *Phonetica* 40 (1983): 1–18.

Orne, M. T. "On the Social Psychology of the Psychological Experiment with Particular Reference to Demand Characteristics and Their Implications." *American Psychologist* 17 (1962): 776–83.

Ortony, Andrew, and Terence J. Turner. "What's Basic about Basic Emotions?" *Psychological Review* 97 (1990): 315–31.

Osborne, Harold. "Expressiveness: Where Is the Feeling Found?" *British Journal of Aesthetics* 23, no. 2 (1983): 112–23.

Owen, Richard. *On the Anatomy of Vertebrates.* 3 vols. London: Longmans, Green, 1866–68.

Panksepp, Jaak. "Basic Emotions Ramify Widely in the Brain, Yielding Many Concepts That Cannot Be Distinguished Unambiguously . . . Yet." In *The Nature of Emotion: Fundamental Question*, edited by Paul Ekman and Richard J. Davidson, 86–88. New York: Oxford University Press, 1994.

Pantev, C., A. Engelien, V. Candia, and T. Elbert. "Representational Cortex in Musicians." In *The Cognitive Neuroscience of Music*, edited by Isabelle Peretz and Robert Zatorre, 382–95. Oxford: Oxford University Press, 2003.

Panzarella, Robert. "The Phenomenology of Aesthetic Peak Experiences." *Journal of Humanistic Psychology* 20 (1980): 69–85.

Papousek, Hanus. "Music in Infancy Research: Biological and Cultural Origins of Early Musicality." In *Musical Beginnings: Origins and Development of Musical Competence*, edited by Irène Deliège and John Sloboda, 37–55. Oxford: Oxford University Press, 1996.

Papousek, Hanus, Uwe Jürgens, and Mechthild Papousek, eds. *Nonverbal Vocal Communication: Comparative and Developmental Approaches.* Cambridge: Cambridge University Press, 1992.

Papousek, Hanus, Mechthild Papousek, and D. Symmes. "The Meanings of Melodies in

Motherese in Tone and Stress Languages." *Infant Behavior and Development* 14 (1991): 415–40.

Parret, Herman. "Kant on Music and the Hierarchy of the Arts." *Journal of Aesthetics and Art Criticism* 56, no. 3 (1998): 251–64.

Parrott, W. Gerrod. "Mood Induction and Instructions to Sustain Moods: A Test of the Subject Compliance Hypothesis of Mood Congruent Memory." *Cognition and Emotion* 5, no. 1 (1991): 41–52.

Parrott, W. Gerrod, and John Sabini. "Mood and Memory under Natural Conditions: Evidence for Mood Incongruent Recall." *Journal of Personality and Social Psychology* 59 (1990): 321–36.

Parsons, Lawrence M. "Exploring the Functional Neuroanatomy of Music Performance, Perception, and Comprehension." In *The Cognitive Neuroscience of Music*, edited by Isabelle Peretz and Robert Zatorre, 247–68. Oxford: Oxford University Press, 2003.

Patel, Aniruddh D. *Music, Language, and the Brain*. New York: Oxford University Press, 2008.

———. "A New Approach to the Cognitive Neuroscience of Melody." In *The Cognitive Neuroscience of Music*, edited by Isabelle Peretz and Robert Zatorre, 325–45. Oxford: Oxford University Press, 2003.

Pater, Walter. *The Renaissance*. Chicago: Pandora Books, 1977.

Payne, Katharine. "The Progressively Changing Songs of Humpback Whales: A Window on the Creative Process in a Wild Animal." In *The Origins of Music*, edited by Nils L. Wallin, Björn Merker, and Steven Brown, 135–50. Cambridge, MA: MIT Press, 2000.

Peirce, Charles Sanders. *Collected Papers*. Cambridge, MA: Harvard University Press, 1965.

Peretz, Isabelle. "Auditory Agnosia: A Functional Analysis." In *Thinking in Sound: The Cognitive Psychology of Human Audition*, edited by Stephen McAdams and Emmanuel Bigand, 199–230. New York: Oxford University Press, 1993.

———. "Brain Specialization for Music: New Evidence from Congenital Amusia." In *The Cognitive Neuroscience of Music*, edited by Isabelle Peretz and Robert Zatorre, 192–203. Oxford: Oxford University Press, 2003.

———. "Music Perception and Recognition." In *The Handbook of Cognitive Neuropsychology: What Deficits Reveal about the Human Mind*, edited by Brenda Rapp, 521–40. Hove, UK: Psychology Press, 2001.

Peretz, Isabelle, and L. Gagnon. "Dissociation between Recognition and Emotional Judgments for Melodies." *Neurocase* 5 (1999): 21–30.

Peretz, Isabelle, and José Morais. "Music and Modularity." *Contemporary Music Review* 4 (1989): 277–93.

Peretz, Isabelle, and Robert Zatorre, eds. *The Cognitive Neuroscience of Music*. Oxford: Oxford University Press, 2003.

Perlman, Marc, and Carol L. Krumhansl. "An Experimental Study of Internal Interval Standards in Javanese and Western Music." *Music Perception* 14, no. 2 (1996): 95–116.

Perullo, Alex. "'Here's a Little Something Local': An Early History of Hip-Hop in Dar es Salaam, Tanzania, 1984–1997." In *Dar es Salaam: The History of an Emerging East African*

Metropolis, edited by Andrew Burton, James Brennan, and Yusuf Lawi, 250–72. London: British Institute and Mkuki na Nyota.

Pickle, Linda S. "Written and Spoken Chinese." In *An Introduction to Chinese Culture through the Family*, edited by Howard Giskin and Bettye S. Walsh, 9–39. Albany: State University of New York Press, 2001.

Pinker, Steven. *How the Mind Works*. New York: W. W. Norton, 1997.

Plato. *Ion*. Translated by Paul Woodruff. In *Plato: Complete Works*, edited by John M. Cooper, associate editor D. S. Hutchinson, 937–49. Indianapolis: Hackett Publishing, 1997.

———. *Republic*. Translated by Paul Shorey. In *The Collected Dialogues of Plato*, edited by Edith Hamilton and Huntington Cairns. Bollingen Series LXXXI. Princeton, NJ: Princeton University Press, 1961.

Polster, Michael R., and Sally B. Rose. "Disorders of Auditory Processing: Evidence for Modularity in Audition." *Cortex* 34 (1998): 47–65.

Pope, Alexander. "An Essay on Criticism" (1711). In *The Norton Anthology of English Literature*, revised, edited by M. H. Abrams et al., 1001–14. New York: W. W. Norton, 1968.

Pound, Ezra. "Vers libre and Arnold Dometsch." In *Literary Essays of Ezra Pound*, edited by T. S. Eliot, 437–40. New York: New Directions, 1935.

Powers, Harold S., and Richard Widdess. "India, Sub-Continent of, III.2 Raga." In *The New Grove Dictionary of Music*, edited by S. Sadie. London: Macmillan, 2001.

Pratt, Carroll C. *The Meaning of Music: A Study in Psychological Aesthetics*. New York: McGraw-Hill, 1931.

———. *Music as the Language of Emotion*. Washington, DC: Library of Congress, 1952.

Progler, J. A. "Searching for Swing: Participatory Discrepancies in the Jazz Rhythm Section." *Ethnomusicology* 39, Special Issue: Participatory Discrepancies (1995): 21–54.

Proust, Marcel. *Contre Saint-Beuve*. Paris: Gallimard, 1971.

———. *Remembrance of Things Past*. Vol. 1, *Swann's Way*. Translated by C. K. Scott Moncrief. New York: Random House, 1932.

Putnam, Daniel A. "Why Instrumental Music Has No Shame." *British Journal of Aesthetics* 27 (1987): 55–61.

Querleu, D., and K. Renard. "Les perceptions auditives du fetus humain." *Medicine et Higiene* 39 (1981): 2102–10.

Qureshi, Regula Burckhardt. *Sufi Music of India and Pakistan: Sound, Context, and Meaning in Qawwali*. Chicago: University of Chicago Press, 1995.

Radford, Colin. "Emotions and Music: A Reply to the Cognitivists." *Journal of Aesthetics and Art Criticism* 47, no. 1 (1989): 69–76.

Raffman, Diana. *Language, Music, and Mind*. Cambridge, MA: MIT Press, 1993.

Ramus, Franck, Marc D. Hauser, Cory T. Miller, Dylan Morris, and Jacques Mehler. "Language Discrimination by Human Newborns and by Cotton-Top Tamarin Monkeys." *Science* 288, no. 249 (2000): 349–51.

Ratner, Nan Bernstein. "Durational Cues Which Mark Clause Boundaries in Mother-Child Speech." *Journal of Phonetics* 14 (1986): 303–9.

Rauschecker, Josef P. "Functional Organization and Plasticity of Auditory Cortex." In *The*

Cognitive Neuroscience of Music, edited by Isabelle Peretz and Robert Zatorre, 357–65. Oxford: Oxford University Press, 2003.

Reid, Thomas. *Lectures on the Fine Arts*. Edited by Peter Kivy. The Hague: Martinus Nijhoff, 1973.

Rentschler, Ingo, Barbara Herzberger, and David Epstein, eds. *Beauty and the Brain: Biological Aspects of Aesthetics*. Basel: Birkhäuser, 1988.

Repp, Bruno H. "Diversity and Commonality in Music Performance: An Analysis of Timing Microstructure in Schumann's 'Träumerei.'" *Journal of the Acoustical Society of America* 92 (1992): 2546–68.

Rice, Timothy. *May It Fill Your Soul: Experiencing Bulgarian Music*. Chicago: University of Chicago Press, 1994.

Richman, Bruce. "How Music Fixed 'Nonsense' into Significant Formulas: On Rhythm, Repetition, and Meaning." In *The Origins of Music*, edited by Nils L. Wallin, Björn Merker, and Steven Brown, 301–14. Cambridge, MA: MIT Press, 2000.

Ridley, Aaron. *Music, Value, and the Passions*. Ithaca, NY: Cornell University Press, 1995.

———. "Musical Sympathies: The Experience of Expressive Music." *Journal of Aesthetics and Art Criticism* 53, no. 1 (1995): 49–57.

———. *The Philosophy of Music: Theme and Variation*. Edinburgh: Edinburgh University Press, 2004.

Roberts, Helen Heffron. *Ancient Hawaiian Music*. Bernice P. Bishop Museum Bulletin 29. Honolulu: Bernice P. Bishop Museum, 1926. Reissued: New York: Dover, 1967.

Robinson, Jenefer. *Deeper Than Reason: Emotion and Its Role in Literature, Music, and Art*. New York: Oxford University Press, 2005.

Robinson, Jenefer, ed. *Music and Meaning*. Ithaca, NY: Cornell University Press, 1997.

Roerderer, Juan G. "The Search for a Survival Value of Music." *Music Perception* 13 (1982): 350–56.

Rorty, Richard. "Human Rights, Rationality, and Sentimentality." In *On Human Rights, the Oxford Amnesty Lectures*, edited by S. Shute and S. Hurley, 112–34. New York: Basic Books.

Roseman, Marina. *Healing Sounds from the Malaysian Rainforest: Temiar Music and Medicine*. Berkeley: University of California Press, 1991.

Rosen, Charles. "Classical Music in Twilight." *Harper's*, March 1998, 52–58.

Rosenblatt, Jay S., Colin Beer, Marie-Claire Busnel, and Peter J. B. Slater. *Advances in the Study of Behavior*. Vol. 15. New York: Academic Press, 1985.

Rothstein, Edward. *Emblems of Mind: The Inner Life of Music and Mathematics*. New York: Avon Books, 1996.

Rouget, Gilbert. *Music and Trance: A Theory of the Relations between Music and Possession*. Translated by the author, revised by Brunhilde Biebuyck in collaboration with the author. Chicago: University of Chicago Press, 1985.

Roughley, Neil, ed. *Being Humans: Anthropological Universality and Particularity in Transdisciplinary Perspectives*. Berlin: Walter de Gruyter, 2000.

Rowell, Lewis. *Music and Musical Thought in Early India*. Chicago: University of Chicago Press, 1992.

———. *Thinking about Music: An Introduction to the Philosophy of Music*. Amherst: University of Massachusetts Press, 1983.

Rudinow, Joel. *Soul Music: Tracking the Spiritual Roots of Pop from Plato to Motown*. Ann Arbor: University of Michigan Press, 2010.

Sachs, Curt. *The Rise of Music in the Ancient World, East and West*. New York: W. W. Norton, 1943.

———. *The Wellsprings of Music*. The Hague: Martinus Nijhoff, 1962.

Sacks, Oliver. "The Lost Mariner." In *The Man Who Mistook His Wife for a Hat and Other Clinical Tales*, 23–42. New York: Harper and Row, 1985.

———. "The Man Who Mistook His Wife for a Hat." In *The Man Who Mistook His Wife for a Hat and Other Clinical Tales*, 8–22. New York: Harper and Row, 1985.

———. *The Man Who Mistook His Wife for a Hat and Other Clinical Tales*. New York: Harper and Row, 1985.

———. *Musicophilia: Tales of Music and the Brain*. New York: Alfred A. Knopf, 2007.

Saffran, Jenny R. "Mechanisms of Musical Memory in Infancy." In *The Cognitive Neuroscience of Music*, edited by Isabelle Peretz and Robert Zatorre, 32–41. Oxford: Oxford University Press, 2003.

Saffran, Jenny R., Richard N. Aslin, and Elissa L. Newport. "Statistical Learning by 8-Month-Old Infants." *Science* 274 (1996): 1926–28.

Saffran, Jenny R., Elizabeth K. Johnson, Richard N. Aslin, and Elissa Newport. "Statistical Learning of Tone Sequences by Human Infants and Adults." *Cognition* 70, no. 27 (1999): 27–52.

Safvate, Dariouche, and Nelly Caron. *Iran: Les traditions musicales*. Paris: Buchet-Chastel, 1966.

Said, Edward W. *Musical Elaborations*. The Welleck Library Lectures at the University of California, Irvine. New York: Columbia University Press, 1991.

Salinas, Francisco de. *De Musica, Libri Septem*. Salamanticae: Excudebat Mathias Gastius, 1577. Facsimile: Kassel: Bärenreiter, 1958.

Santayana, George. *The Life of Reason, or the Phases of Human Progress*. Revised by the author in collaboration with Daniel Cory. 1905. New York: Charles Scribner's Sons, 1953.

Savoy, Ann A. *Cajun Music: A Reflection of the People*. Vol. 1. Eunice, LA: Bluebird Press, 1984.

Sawyer, R. Keith, ed. *Creativity in Performance*. Greenwich, CT: Ablex, 1997.

Schaller, George B. *The Mountain Gorilla: Ecology and Behavior*. Chicago: University of Chicago Press, 1963.

Schellenberg, E. Glenn. "Expectancy in Melody: Tests of the Implication-Realization Model." *Cognition* 58 (1996): 75–125.

Scherer, Klaus R. "Vocal Affect Expression: A Review and a Model for Future Research." *Psychological Bulletin* 99 (1986): 143–65.

———. "Vocal Affect Signaling: A Comparative Approach." In *Advances in the Study of Behavior*, vol. 15, edited by Jay S. Rosenblatt, Colin Beer, Marie-Claire Busnel, and Peter J. B. Slater, 189–244. New York: Academic Press, 1985.

———. "Which Emotions Can Be Induced by Music? What Are the Underlying Mechanisms? And How Can We Measure Them?" *Journal of New Music Research* 33 (2004): 239–51.

Scherer, Klaus R., and James S. Oshinsky. "Cue Utilization in Emotion Attribution from Auditory Stimuli." *Motivation and Emotion* 1 (1977): 331–46.

Scherer, Klaus R., and Marcel R. Zentner. "Emotional Effects of Music: Production Rules." In *Music and Emotion: Theory and Research*, edited by Patrik Juslin and John A. Sloboda, 361–92. Oxford: Oxford University Press, 2001.

Schirokauer, Conrad. *A Brief History of Chinese Civilization*. San Diego: Harcourt, Brace, Jovanovich, 1991.

Schneider, Albrecht. "Sound, Pitch, and Scale." *Ethnomusicology* 45, no. 4 (2001): 489–519.

Schneider, Marius. "Primitive Music." In *Ancient and Oriental Music*, edited by Egon Wellesz, 1–82. London: Oxford University Press, 1957.

Schonberg, H. C. "World's Oldest Song Reported Deciphered: Out of Prehistory." *New York Times*, March 6, 1974, 1, 18.

Schopenhauer, Arthur. *The World as Will and Representation*. Translated by E. F. J. Payne. New York: Dover, 1958, vol. 1; 1969, vol. 2.

Schueller, Herbert M. *The Idea of Music: An Introduction to Musical Aesthetics in Antiquity and the Middle Ages*. Early Drama, Art, and Music Monograph Series 9. Kalamazoo, MI: Medieval Institute Publications, 1988.

Schutz, Alfred. "Making Music Together: A Study in Social Relationship." In *Symbolic Anthropology: A Reader in the Study of Symbols and Meanings*, edited by Janet L. Dolgin, David S. Kemnitzer, and David M. Schneider. New York: Columbia University Press, 1977. Originally published in *Social Research* 18, no. 2 (1951): 76–97.

Scruton, Roger. *The Aesthetics of Music*. Oxford: Oxford University Press, 1997.

———. "The Eclipse of Listening." In *The Future of the European Past*, edited by Hilton Kramer and Roger Kimball, 51–68. Chicago: Ivan R. Dee, 1997.

———. "Musical Understanding and Musical Culture." In *What Is Music? An Introduction to the Philosophy of Music*, edited by Philip Alperson, 349–58. New York: Haven, 1987.

Searle, John R. *Speech Acts: An Essay in the Philosophy of Language*. London: Cambridge University Press, 1969.

Seashore, Carl E. *Psychology of Music*. New York: Dover, 1967.

Seeger, Anthony. "What Can We Learn When They Sing? Vocal Genres of the Suyá Indians of Central Brazil." *Ethnomusicology* 23, no. 3 (1979): 373–94.

———. *Why Suyá Sing: A Musical Anthropology of an Amazonian People*. Cambridge: Cambridge University Press, 1987.

Seeger, Charles. "Reflections upon a Given Topic: Music in Universal Perspective." *Ethnomusicology* 15, no. 3 (1971): 385–98.

———. "Versions and Variants of the Tunes of 'Barbara Allen.'" *Selected Reports of the University of California Institute for Ethnomusicology* 1, no. 1 (1966): 120–67.

Serafine, Mary Louise. *Music as Cognition: The Development of Thought in Sound*. New York: Columbia University Press, 1988.

Sergent, Justine, Eric Zuck, Sean Terriah, and Brennan MacDonald. "Distributed Neural

Network Underlying Musical Sight-Reading and Keyboard Performance." *Science* 257 (1992): 106–9.

Shakespeare, William. *As You Like It*. In *The Complete Works of Shakespeare*, edited by David Bevington, 292–325. New York: Longman, 1997.

Shankar, Ravi. *My Music, My Life*. London: Jonathan Cape, 1969.

Shaw, Gordon L. *Keeping Mozart in Mind*. San Diego: Academic Press, 2000.

Shehadi, Fadlou. *Philosophies of Music in Medieval Islam*. Leiden: Brill, 1995.

Shelemay, Kay Kaufmann, ed. *The Garland Library of Readings in Ethnomusicology*. New York: Garland Publishing, 1990.

Shweder, Richard A., and Robert A. LeVine, eds. *Culture Theory: Essays on Mind, Self, and Emotion*. New York: Cambridge University Press, 1984.

Siddiqui, Mahmud Husain. *The Memoirs of Sufis Written in India*. Baroda, India: Maharaja Sayajirao University Press, 1979.

Siegel, Jane A., and William Siegel. "Categorical Perception of Tonal Intervals: Musicians Can't Tell Sharp from Flat." *Perception and Psychophysics* 22 (1977): 399–407.

Silberstein, Lisa, Howard Gardner, Erin Phelps, and Ellen Winner. "Autumn Leaves and Old Photographs: The Development of Metaphor Preferences." *Journal of Experimental Child Psychology* 34 (1982): 135–50.

Simonton, Dean Keith. "Emotion and Composition in Classical Music: Historiometric Perspectives." In *Music and Emotion: Theory and Research*, edited by Patrik Juslin and John A. Sloboda, 205–22. Oxford: Oxford University Press, 2001.

Singer, Alice. "The Metrical Structure of Macedonian Dance." *Ethnomusicology* 18, no. 3 (1974): 379–404.

Slater, Peter J. B. "Birdsong Repertoires: Their Origins and Uses." In *The Origins of Music*, edited by Nils L. Wallin, Björn Merker, and Steven Brown, 49–63. Cambridge, MA: MIT Press, 2000.

Slobin, Mark. *Fiddler on the Move: Exploring the Klezmer World*. New York: Oxford University Press, 2000.

Slobin, Mark, ed. *Global Soundtracks: Worlds of Film Music*. Middletown, CT: Wesleyan University Press, 2008.

Sloboda, John A. "Music Structure and Emotional Response: Some Empirical Findings." *Psychology of Music* 19 (1991): 110–20.

———. *The Musical Mind: The Cognitive Psychology of Music*. Oxford: Clarendon Press, 1985.

———. "Musical Performance and Emotion: Issues and Developments." In *Music, Mind, and Science*, edited by S. W. Yi. Seoul, Korea: Western Music Research Institute, 2000.

Sloboda, John A., ed. *Generative Processes in Music: The Psychology of Performance, Improvisation, and Composition*. Oxford: Clarendon Press, 1988.

Sloboda, John A., and Patrik N. Juslin. "Music and Emotions: Commentary." In *Music and Emotions: Theory and Research*, edited by Patrik N. Juslin and John A. Sloboda, 453–62. Oxford: Oxford University Press, 2001.

———. "Psychological Perspectives on Music and Emotions." In *Music and Emotions: Theory and Research*, edited by Patrik N. Juslin and John A. Sloboda, 71–104. Oxford: Oxford University Press, 2001.

Sloboda, John A., and Susan A. O'Neill. "Emotions in Everyday Listening to Music." In *Music and Emotion: Theory and Research*, edited by Patrik N. Juslin and John A. Sloboda, 415–29. Oxford: Oxford University Press, 2001.

Small, Christopher. *Musicking: The Meanings of Performing and Listening*. Hanover, NH: Wesleyan University Press/University Press of New England, 1998.

———. *Music, Society, Education*. Hanover, NH: Wesleyan University Press, 1980.

Smith, Adam. "Of the Nature of That Imitation Which Takes Place in What Are Called the Imitative Arts" (1795). In *The Early Writings of Adam Smith*, edited by J. Ralph Lindgren, 135–74. New York: Augustus M. Kelley, 1967.

Snowden, Charles T. "Expression of Emotion in Nonhuman Animals." In *Handbook of Affective Sciences*, edited by Robert J. Davidson, Klaus R. Scherer, and H. Hill Goldsmith, 457–80. New York: Oxford University Press, 2003.

Solomon, Robert C. "Against Valence ('Positive' and 'Negative' Emotions)." In *Not Passion's Slave: Emotions and Choice*, 162–77. New York: Oxford University Press, 2003.

———. "Emotions and Choice." In *Not Passion's Slave: Emotions and Choice*, 1–24. New York: Oxford University Press, 2003.

———. *In Defense of Sentimentality*. New York: Oxford University Press, 2004.

———. *The Joy of Philosophy: Thinking Thin versus the Passionate Life*. New York: Oxford University Press, 1999.

Sorrell, Neil. *A Guide to the Gamelan*. London: Faber and Faber, 1990.

Staal, Frits. "Mantras and Bird Songs." *Journal of the American Oriental Society* 105, no. 2 (1985): 549–58.

Steager, Peter W. "Where Does Art Begin on Puluwat?" In *Exploring the Visual Art of Oceania*, edited by Sidney Moko Mead, 342–53. Honolulu: University of Hawai'i Press, 1971.

Stern, Daniel. *The Interpersonal World of the Infant*. London: Academic Press, 1985.

Stockmann, Doris. "Some Aspects of Musical Perception." *Yearbook of the International Folk Music Council* 9 (1977): 67–79.

Stokes, Martin, ed. *Ethnicity, Identity, and Music: The Musical Construction of Place*. Oxford: Berg, 1994.

———. "Introduction: Ethnicity, Identity, and Music." In *Ethnicity, Identity, and Music: The Musical Construction of Place*, edited by Martin Stokes, 1–27. Oxford: Berg, 1994.

Stoquerus, Gaspar. *De Musica Verbali, Libri Duo*. Manuscript. Madrid: Biblioteca Nacional, 6486. Followed by De Vera Solfizationis. *Quam Vocant Docendae Ratione*. Folios 41–49, ca. 1570.

Stravinsky, Igor. *Igor Stravinsky: An Autobiography*. London: Calder and Boyars, 1975.

Strawson, P. F. *Individuals: An Essay in Descriptive Metaphysics*. London: Methuen, 1959.

Strunk, Oliver, ed. *Source Readings in Music History*. New York: W. W. Norton, 1965.

Sullivan, Lawrence E., ed. *Enchanting Powers: Music in the World's Religions*. Cambridge, MA: Harvard University Press, 1997.

Sundberg, Johan. *The Science of the Singing Voice*. DeKalb: Northern Illinois University Press, 1987.

Swain, Joseph P. *Musical Languages*. New York: W. W. Norton, 1997.

———. "The Range of Musical Semantics." *Journal of Aesthetics and Art Criticism* 54, no. 2 (1996): 135–52.

Tarasti, Eero. *A Theory of Musical Semiotics.* Bloomington: Indiana University Press, 1994.

Terhardt, Ernst. "The Concept of Musical Consonance: A Link between Music and Psychoacoustics." *Music Perception* 1 (1984): 276–95.

Thom, Paul. *For an Audience: A Philosophy of the Performing Arts.* Philadelphia: Temple University Press, 1993.

Thompson, W. F., and L.-L. Balkwill. "Cross-Cultural Similarities and Differences." In *Handbook of Music and Emotion: Theory, Research, Applications,* edited by Patrik N. Juslin and John A. Sloboda, 755–88. Oxford: Oxford University Press, 2010.

Thompson, William Forde, E. Glenn Schellenberg, and Gabriela Husain. "Arousal, Mood, and the Mozart Effect." *Psychological Science* 12, no. 3 (2001): 248–51.

Thorsen, N. "Intonation Contours and Stress Group Patterns in Declarative Sentences of Varying Length: Supplementary Data." *Annual Report of the Institute of Phonetics, University of Copenhagen* 15 (1981): 13–47.

———. "Intonation Contours and Stress Group Patterns in Declarative Sentences of Varying Length in ASC Danish." *Annual Report of the Institute of Phonetics, University of Copenhagen* 14 (1980): 1–29.

Thurlow, Willard R., and William P. Erchul. "Judged Similarity in Pitch of Octave Multiples." *Perception and Psychophysics* 22 (1977): 177–82.

Titon, Jeff Todd, ed. *Worlds of Music: An Introduction to the Music of the World's Peoples.* 2nd ed. New York: Macmillan, 1992.

Tolstoy, Leo. *War and Peace.* Translated by Ann Dunnigan. New York: New American Library, 1968.

Tonkin, Elizabeth, Maryon McDonald, and Malcolm Chapman, eds. *History and Ethnicity.* London: Routledge, 1989.

Trainor, Laurel J., Kelly L. McDonald, and Claude Alain. "Automatic and Controlled Processing of Melodic Contour and Interval Information Measured by Electrical Brain Activity." *Journal of Cognitive Neuroscience* 14 (2002): 430–42.

Trainor, Laurel J., and L. A. Schmidt. "Processing Emotions Induced by Music." In *The Cognitive Neuroscience of Music,* edited by Isabelle Peretz and Robert Zatorre, 310–24. Oxford: Oxford University Press, 2003.

Trainor, Laurel J., and Sandra E. Trehub, "A Comparison of Infants' and Adults' Sensitivity to Western Musical Structure." *Journal of Experimental Psychology: Human Perception and Performance* 18 (1992): 394–402.

Tramo, Mark Jude, Peter A. Cariani, Bertrund Delgutte, and Louis D. Braida. "Neurobiology of Harmony Perception." In *The Cognitive Neuroscience of Music,* edited by Isabelle Peretz and Robert Zatorre, 127–51. Oxford: Oxford University Press, 2003.

Tran Van Khe. "Is the Pentatonic Universal? A Few Reflections on Pentatonism." *The World of Music* 19, no. 1/2 (1997): 76–84.

Trehub, Sandra E. "The Developmental Origins of Musicality." *Nature Neuroscience* 6 (2003): 669–73.

———. "Human Processing Predispositions and Musical Universals." In *The Origins of Mu-*

sic, edited by Nils L. Wallin, Björn Merker, and Steven Brown, 427–48. Cambridge, MA: MIT Press, 2000.

——. "Musical Predispositions in Infancy: An Update." In *The Cognitive Neuroscience of Music*, edited by Isabelle Peretz and Robert Zatorre, 3–20. Oxford: Oxford University Press, 2003.

Trehub, Sandra E., Dale Bull, and Leigh A. Thorpe. "Infants' Perception of Melodies: The Role of Melodic Contour." *Child Development* 55 (1984): 821–30.

Trehub, Sandra E., E. Glenn Schellenberg, and David S. Hill. "The Origins of Music Perception and Cognition: A Developmental Perspective." In *Perception and Cognition of Music*, edited by Irène Deliège and John Sloboda, 103–28. Hove, UK: Psychology Press, 1997.

Trehub, Sandra E., Leigh A. Thorpe, and Laurel J. Trainor. "Infants' Perception of Good and Bad Melodies." *Psychomusicology* 9 (1990): 905–15.

Trehub, Sandra E., and Laurel J. Trainor. "Listening Strategies in Infancy: The Roots of Music and Language Development." In *Thinking in Sound: The Cognitive Psychology of Human Audition*, edited by Stephen McAdams and Emmanuel Bigand, 278–327. London: Oxford University Press, 1993.

Trehub, Sandra, Anna M. Unyk, and Laurel J. Trainor. "Adults Identify Infant-Directed Music across Cultures." *Infant Behavioral Development* 16 (1993): 193–211.

——. "Maternal Singing in Cross-Cultural Perspective." *Infant Behavior and Development* 16 (1993): 285–95.

Trevarthen, Colwyn. "Communication and Cooperation in Early Infancy: A Description of Primary Intersubjectivity." In *Before Speech: The Beginning of Human Communication*, edited by Margaret Bullowa, 321–47. Cambridge: Cambridge University Press, 1979.

——. "Emotions in Infancy: Regulators of Contact and Relationship with Persons." In *Approaches to Emotion*, edited by Klaus Scherer and Paul Ekman, 129–57. Hillsdale, NJ: Erlbaum, 1984.

Turino, Thomas. *Music as Social Life: The Politics of Participation*. Chicago: Chicago University Press, 2008.

Unyk, Anna M., Sandra E. Trehub, Laurel J. Trainor, and E. Glenn Schellenberg. "Lullabies and Simplicity: A Cross-Cultural Perspective." *Psychology of Music* 20 (1992): 15–28.

Uttal, William R. *The Psychobiology of Sensory Coding*. New York: Harper and Row, 1973.

Van Damme, Wilfried. *Beauty in Context: Towards an Anthropological Approach to Aesthetics*. Leiden: Brill, 1996.

——. "Universality and Cultural Particularity in Visual Aesthetics." In *Being Humans: Anthropological Universality and Particularity in Transdisciplinary Perspectives*, edited by Neil Roughley, 258–83. Berlin: Walter de Gruyter, 2000.

Vince, Margaret A., Sally E. Armitage, B. A. Baldwin, J. Toner, and R. C. J. Moore. "The Sound Environment of Foetal Sheep." *Behaviour* 81 (1981): 296–315.

Vincentino, Nicola. *L'Antica Musica Ridotta Alla Moderna Prattica*. Facsimile. Rome: Antonio Barre, 1555. Edited by Kassel Bärenreiter. Folio, 1959.

Visalberghi, Elisabetta, and William C. McGrew. "*Cebus* Meets *Pan*." *International Journal of Primatology* 18, no. 5 (1997): 677–81.

von Hippel, Paul, and David Huron. "Why Do Skips Precede Reversals? The Effect of Tessitura on Melodic Structure." *Music Perception* 18 (2000): 59–85.

Vosniadou, Stella, and Andrew Ortony. "The Emergence of the Literal-Metaphorical-Anomalous Distinction in Young Children." *Child Development* 54 (1983): 154–61.

Wade, Bonnie C. *Music in India: The Classical Tradition.* Englewood Cliffs, NJ: Prentice-Hall, 1979.

Wagner, Richard. *Opera and Drama.* Translated by William Ashton Ellis. Lincoln: University of Nebraska Press, 1995.

Waley, Arthur, ed. and trans. *The Analects of Confucius.* New York: Random House, 1989.

Walker, Robert. *Musical Beliefs: Psychoacoustics, Mythical, and Educational Perspectives.* New York: Teachers College Press, 1990.

Wallin, Nils L., Björn Merker, and Steven Brown, eds. *The Origins of Music.* Cambridge, MA: MIT Press, 2000.

Ward, W. Dixon. "Subjective Musical Pitch." *Journal of the Acoustical Society of America* 26 (1954): 369–80.

Warren, Richard M., and Roslyn P. Warren. "Auditory Illusions and Confusions." *Scientific American* 223, no. 6 (1970): 30–36.

Watson, David, and Lee Anna Clark. "Emotions, Moods, Traits, and Temperaments: Conceptual Distinctions and Empirical Findings." In *The Nature of Emotion: Fundamental Questions,* edited by Paul Ekman and Richard J. Davidson, 89–93. New York: Oxford University Press, 1994.

Weintraub, Stanley. *Silent Night: The Story of the World War I Christmas Truce.* New York: Free Press, 2001.

Weir, Alex A. S., Jackie Chappell, and Alex Kacelnik. "Shaping of Hooks in New Caledonian Crows." *Science* 297 (August 9, 2002): 981.

Weitz, Morris. "The Role of Theory in Aesthetics." *Journal of Aesthetics and Art Criticism* 15, no. 1 (1956): 27–35.

Welsch, Wolfgang. "Animal Aesthetics." *Contemporary Aesthetics* 2 (2004). http://www.contempaesthetics.org/newvolume/pages/article.php?articleID=243.

Whaling, Carol. "What's behind a Song? The Neural Basis of Song Learning in Birds." In *The Origins of Music,* edited by Nils L. Wallin, Björn Merker, and Steven Brown, 65–76. Cambridge, MA: MIT Press, 2000.

Wheeler, R. H. "Synaesthesia in the Process of Reasoning." *American Journal of Psychology* 35 (1924): 88–97.

———. "The Synaesthesia of a Blind Subject." *University of Oregon Publications* 1 (1920): 3–61.

Wheeler, R. H., and T. D. Cutsforth. "Synaesthesia and Meaning." *American Journal of Psychology* 33 (1922): 361–84.

Williamson, Muriel C. "Aspects of Traditional Style Maintained in Burma's First 13 Kyo Songs." In *Selected Reports in Ethnomusicology* 2, 117–63. Institute of Ethnomusicology, University of California at Los Angeles, 1975.

Wilson, William Raft. "Feeling More Than We Can Know: Exposure Effects without Learning." *Journal of Personality and Social Psychology* 37, no. 6 (1979): 811–21.

Winner, E., A. K. Rosentiel, and Howard Gardner. "The Development of Metaphorical Understanding." *Developmental Psychology* 12 (1976): 289–97.

Wittgenstein, Ludwig. *Culture and Value*. Edited by G. H. Von Wright, in collaboration with Heikki Nyman. Translated by Peter Winch. Chicago: University of Chicago Press, 1980.

———. *Lectures and Conversations on Aesthetics, Psychology, and Religious Belief*. Compiled from notes taken by Yorick Smythies, Rush Rhees, and James Taylor. Edited by Cyril Barrett. Berkeley: University of California Press, 1966.

Wolf, Richard K. "Emotional Dimensions of Ritual Music among the Kotas, a South Indian Tribe." *Ethnomusicology* 45, no. 3 (2001): 379–422.

Wright, Anthony A., Jacquelyne J. Rivera, Stewart H. Hulse, Melissa Shyan, and Julie J. Neiworth. "Music Perception and Octave Generalization In Rhesus Monkeys." *Journal of Experimental Psychology: General* 129 (2000): 291–307.

Yi, S. W., ed. *Music, Mind, and Science*. Seoul, Korea: Western Music Research Institute, 2000.

Yuen Ren Chao. "The Non-Uniqueness of Phonemic Solutions of Phonetic Systems." *Bulletin of the Institute of History and Phonology, Academia Sinica* 4, no. 4 (1934): 363–97. Reprinted in *Readings in Linguistics*. Vol. 1, *The Development of Descriptive Linguistics in America, 1925–1956*, prepared for the Committee on Language Programs of the American Council of Learned Societies, edited by Martin Joos, 38–54. Chicago: University of Chicago Press, 1966.

Zajonc, Robert B. "Exposure Effects: An Unmediated Phenomenon." In *Feelings and Emotions: The Amsterdam Symposium*, edited by Antony S. R. Manstead, Nico Frijda, and Agneta Fischer, 194–203. Cambridge: Cambridge University Press, 2004.

Zarlino, Gioseffo. *Le Institutioni Harmoniche*. Venice, 1558. Facsimile. New York: Broude Brothers, 1965.

Zatorre, Robert J. "Neural Specializations for Tonal Processing." In *The Cognitive Neuroscience of Music*, edited by Isabelle Peretz and Robert Zatorre, 231–46. Oxford: Oxford University Press, 2003.

Zatorre, Robert J., and Andrea R. Halpern. "Mental Concerts: Musical Imagery and Auditory Cortex." *Neuron* 47 (2005): 9–12.

Zentner, Marcel, and Klaus R. Scherer. "Which Emotions Can Be Induced by Music?" Paper presented at the general meeting of the International Society for Research on the Emotions, Bari, Italy, July 13, 2005.

Zheng, Su. *Claiming Diaspora: Music, Transnationalism, and Cultural Politics in Asian/Chinese America*. New York: Oxford University Press, 2010.

Zuckerkandl, Victor. *Sound and Symbol: Music and the External World*. Translated by Willard R. Trask. Bollingen Series XLIV. Princeton, NJ: Princeton University Press, 1956.

RECORDINGS

Beatles, The. "Norwegian Wood." *Rubber Soul*. Capitol CD B000002UAO, 1990.

Bloodhound Gang. "Fire, Water, Burn." *One Fierce Beer Coaster*. Geffen Records B000000WJ, 1996.

Bush, Kate. "Moving." *The Kick Inside*. EMI SW-17003, CD Indent Series B000005JH5, 1996.

Cole, Natalie. *Unforgettable: With Love*. Elektra/Wea B000002H8X, 1991.

Dylan, Bob. "The Times, They Are A-Changin.'" *The Times, They Are A-Changin'*. Sony CD B0000024RZ.

Irama, Rhoma. "Sahabat" ("Friends"). *The Smithsonian Folkways CD Music of Indonesia 2: Indonesian Popular Music: Kroncong, Dangdut, and Langgam Jawa*, SF-40056.

Lansky, Paul. *Homebrew*. BCD 9035 Bridge B000003GIT, 1992.

Simon, Paul. *Graceland*. Warner Bros/Wea CD B00000E907, 1990.

Simon, Paul, and Art Garfunkel. "El Condor Pasa." *Bridge over Troubled Waters*. Sony CD B00005NKKZ, 2001.

FILMS

2001: A Space Odyssey. Directed by Stanley Kubrick. Warner Studios, 1968. Videocassette.

Band of Brothers. HBO Home Video, 2001. Videocassette.

Cabaret. Directed by Bob Fosse. Warner Brothers, 1972. Videocassette.

Casablanca. Directed by Michael Curtiz. Warner Brothers, 1942. Videocassette.

Fahrenheit 9/11. Directed by Michael Moore. Columbia/Tristar Studios, 2004. Videocassette.

Fantasia. Directed by T. Hee and Norman Ferguson. Disney Studios, 1942. Videocassette.

Gandhi. Directed by Richard Attenborough. Columbia/Tristar Studios, 1982. Videocassette.

Invasion of the Body Snatchers. Directed by Don Siegel. Republic Studios, 1956. Videocassette.

Jaws. Directed by Stephen Spielberg. Universal Studios, 1975. Videocassette.

Titanic. Directed by James Cameron. Paramount Pictures, 1997. Videocassette.

INDEX